Christof Ebert • Reiner Dumke
Manfred Bundschuh • Andreas Schmietendorf

Best Practices in Software Measurement

How to use metrics to improve project and process performance

With 107 Figures and 37 Tables

Springer

Christof Ebert
Alcatel
54 rue la Boetie
75008 Paris, France
e-mail: christofebert@ieee.org

Reiner Dumke
Otto-von-Guericke-Universität Magdeburg
Postfach 4120
39016 Magdeburg, Germany
e-mail: dumke@ivs.cs.uni-magdeburg.de

Manfred Bundschuh
Fachbereich Informatik
Fachhochschule Köln
Am Sandberg 1
51643 Gummersbach, Germany
e-mail:
manfred.bundschuh@freenet.de

Andreas Schmietendorf
T-Systems Nova
Postfach 652
13509 Berlin, Germany
e-mail:
andreas.schmietendorf@t-systems.com

Library of Congress Control Number: 2004110442

ACM Computing Classification (1998): D.2.8, D.2.9, K.6.3, C.4, K.6.1, K.1

ISBN 3-540-20867-4 Springer Berlin Heidelberg New York

Springer is a part of Springer Science+Business Media

springeronline.com

Printed in Germany

Cover design: KünkelLopka, Heidelberg
Production: LE-TeX Jelonek, Schmidt & Vöckler GbR, Leipzig
Typesetting: by the authors
Printed on acid-free paper 45/3142/YL - 5 4 3 2 1 0

Preface

Not everything that counts can be counted.
Not everything that is counted counts.
—Albert Einstein

This is a book about software measurement from the practitioner's point of view and it is a book for practitioners. Software measurement needs a lot of practical guidance to build upon experiences and to avoid repeating errors. This book targets exactly this need, namely to share experiences in a constructive way that can be followed. It tries to summarize experiences and knowledge about software measurement so that it is applicable and repeatable. It extracts experiences and lessons learned from the narrow context of the specific industrial situation, thus facilitating transfer to other contexts.

Software measurement is not at a standstill. With the speed software engineering is evolving, software measurement has to keep pace. While the underlying theory and basic principles remain invariant in the true sense (after all, they are not specific to software engineering), the application of measurement to specific contexts and situations is continuously extended. The book thus serves as a reference on these invariant principles as well as a practical guidance on how to make software measurement a success.

New fields have emerged in the recent years. We therefore show how software measurement applies to current application development, telecommunications, mobile computing, Web design or embedded systems. Standards have emerged which we use and explain in their practical usage. We look specifically to the general measurement standard of ISO 15939 serving as a framework for the underlying measurement processes, the extended version of the product quality standards ISO 9126 and 14598, the CMM – and recently appearing CMMI – as very successful de-facto industry standards for process improvement, or the new approach on the area of functional size measurement ISO 19761 (COSMIC Full Function Points standard).

Underlying methodologies and theory have consolidated. It will not be repeated here, as it can easily be found in reference books, such as [Endr03], [Fent97], [McGa02], [Wohl00], and [Zuse97].

The book summarizes the experience of the authors in some industrial projects relating with companies such as Alcatel, Deutsche Telekom, Siemens, Bosch, and AXA Insurance Company. Some work published in this book has been supported by the German communities of the Interest Group on Software Measurement in the German Informatics Society (GI), the "Deutschsprachige Anwendergruppe für

Software-Metrik und Aufwandschätzung" (DASMA), the Canadian community of Interest Group in Software Metrics (CIM) and the international communities of the Common Software Measurement International Consortium (COSMIC) and the European Metrics Association's International Network (MAIN).

We would like to thank the members of various measurement communities for their cooperation during our projects and investigations like Grant Brighten, Dan Campo, Helge Dahl, Jozef De Man, Bryan Douglas, Casimiro Hernandez Parro, Jack Hofmann, Eric Praats, Manuel Ramos Gullon, Siegfried Raschke, Tian Lixin, Wu Zhen (Alcatel); Alain Abran, Pierre Bourque, Francois Coallier and Jean-Marc Desharnais (CIM); Roberto Meli, Pam Morris and Charles Symons (COSMIC); Günter Büren and Helmut Wolfseher (DASMA); Evgeni Dimitrov, Jens Lezius and Michael Wipprecht (Deutsche Telekom); Thomas Fetcke, Claus Lewerentz, Dieter Rombach, Eberhard Rudolph, Harry Sneed and Horst Zuse (GI); Luigi Buglione, Thomas Fehlman, Peter Hill (ISBSG); David A. Gustafson (Kansas State University); Geert Poels and Rini van Solingen (MAIN); Annie Combelles (Q-Labs); Niklas Fehrling, Ingo Hofmann and Willy Reiss (Robert Bosch GmbH); Ulrich Schweikl and Stefan Weber (Siemens AG); Mathias Lother, Cornelius Wille and Daniel Reitz (SML@b).

Special thanks go Springer and our editor, Ralf Gerstner, for their helpful cooperation during the preparation of this book.

All four authors are available via e-mail to address specific questions that readers might have when working with this book. We welcome such feedback for two reasons. First, it helps to speed up the sharing of software engineering knowledge and thus enriches the common body of knowledge. Second, since we anticipate a next edition, such feedback ensures further improvements.

Many helpful links and continuously updated information is provided at the Web site of this book at http://metrics.cs.uni-magdeburg.de.

We wish all our readers of this book good success in measuring and improving with the figures. We are sure you will distinguish what counts from what can be counted.

Paris, Magdeburg, Cologne, and Berlin
January 2004

Christof Ebert
Reiner Dumke
Manfred Bundschuh
Andreas Schmietendorf

Contents

1 Introduction

Count what is countable. Measure what is measurable.
And what is not measurable, make measurable.
—Galileo Galilei

The Purpose of the Book

Human performance improvement is essentially unlimited. The fastest time for the mile was 4.5 minutes in 1865, 4 minutes in 1954, and today it is around 3.6 minutes (depending on when you read this introduction). One might expect a 3-minute mile during this century. Can you imagine how little runners might have improved if there were no stopwatch or measured track? Unmeasured and unchallenged performance does not improve! And it will not improve if not fostered by – best practices – in the discipline.

Software development clearly is a human activity and as such is prone to continuous performance improvements. Software measurement is the approach to control and manage the software process and to track and improve its performance.

This book shows how to best use measurement for understanding, evaluating, controlling and forecasting. It takes a look at how to improve with the numbers. To measure is simple. To give meaning to numbers and take the right decisions is the stuff this book is made of. We coined it around what the four authors perceive as best practices in their respective domains.

Practices need time to mature towards what we perceive as best practices, and they are continuously challenged by new theories and practices. Are such best practices timeless? Certainly not in this fast-changing engineering discipline, however given the long time of maturing and the well-established foundation of software measurement since the early work during the 1970s, they face a life time, which exceeds that of the availability of such a book. They certainly are mostly invariant against changes of software engineering methods, paradigms, and tools.

Software metrics must provide answers first and foremost. They help in understanding how a project is performing compared to the targets. They indicate whether an organization is doing better or worse compared to a previous period. However, the needs of practitioners, managers and scientists are not the numbers but what is behind the numbers.

Software metrics are used in the following ways:

1. to understand more about software work products or underlying processes and to evaluate a special situation or (statistical) characteristic of software artifacts for making *ad hoc decisions* leading to special experiences (e.g., project tracking, rules of thumb, assessments and descriptions of situations)
2. to track, evaluate, analyze, and control the software project, product or process attributes for supporting a *continued decision making* leading to evaluations (e.g., project management, process improvement)
3. to estimate, predict or forecast software characteristics in order to keep a *knowledge-based management process* leading to general experiences (e.g., estimation formulas, development rules and general characteristics)
4. to evaluate work products or processes against established standards and to define and measure specific characteristics during the software life-cycle for support of the *controlled management process* leading to software metrics (standardized size and complexity measures)

We must not think of researchers who create a metric and users who only apply it. Metrics are mostly defined and used by exactly the same party. Therefore, the metrics users must have basic knowledge about the software measurement process itself. They must know how to build measurements or metrics, how to use the appropriate statistics and how to proof the validity of the measures or metrics.

A very helpful standard was developed in the recent years for implementing the software measurement process: the *ISO/IEC 15939 standard* [ISO02, McGa01]. Following this standard we can plan and implement a measurement process based upon best practices (Fig. 1.1). We initiated a lifecycle for a step-by-step optimization of the used resources, the software development process and the product itself that we also describe in this book.

Different persons will take different messages from using this book. The following examples show what that can mean in practice:

- The supplier learns to implement a software measurement process to address specific project or organizational requirements. He will focus on realistic targets and how to track and achieve them. He will improve performance based on quantitative targets to stay competitive.
- The acquirer learns to implement a software measurement process to address specific technical and project management information requirements. He contracts quantitative performance targets (e.g., service level agreements, quality levels, deadlines) and periodically monitors the supplier's conformance versus these agreements.
- The contract between an acquirer and a supplier specifies quantitative performance targets and defines to the necessary degree the software process and product measurement information to be exchanged.

Fig. 1.1 shows the scope of ISO 15939 with the feedback and integration aspects of the software measurement application.

The layout of this standard was used to structure this book for the presentation of our practical experiences and approaches in introducing the software measurement process in industrial areas. So, we will start with establishing and sustaining a measurement commitment as basic precondition for a successful software measurement process implementation in the information technology area.

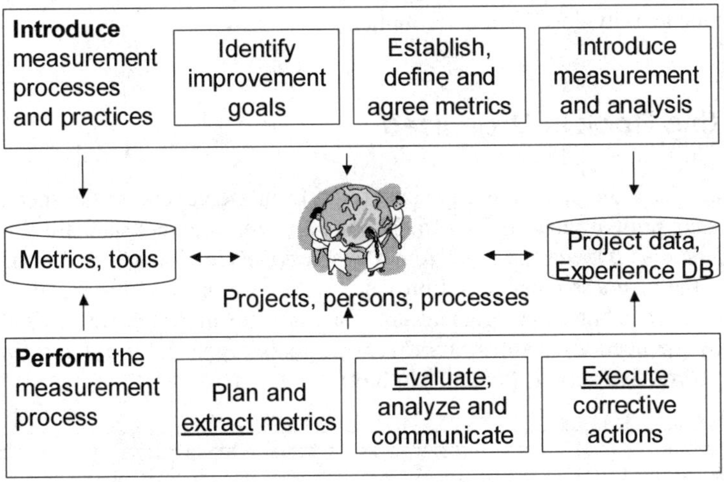

Fig. 1.1. Implementing a best practices measurement process based on ISO 15939

Many measurement programs fail. Metrics are collected but not used and lots of data is available but without any meaning behind it. This book tries to pinpoint common pitfalls and how to avoid them. We target the following measurement-related risks:

- Collecting metrics without a meaning. Measurement must be goal-driven, therefore we measure to improve. People realize quickly whether their managers and environment understand what they are doing or not, and they behave accordingly. Therefore each single metric must have a clear practical application or it not only is a waste of effort to collect but may also reduce morale.
- Not analyzing metrics. Measuring is easy, but working with the numbers is a real effort. Often the analysis effort is neglected. Numbers are put into charts and reports and distributed. This is insufficient, as numbers need profound analysis. They need to relate to objectives and performance. Metrics must be actionable or they distort rather than clarify matters.
- Setting unrealistic targets. Many managers, like those portrayed in the popular Dilbert cartoons become so fascinated by measurement – and the perceived accuracy and preciseness – that they pose targets that are entirely driven by the numbers. Sometimes they are not based on history and experience at all, or they drive an organization or team to their limits continuously. Dysfunctional performance and burned-out people result, just like what was seen during the dot-com bubble with the abuse of business metrics to make balance sheets and income statements shine.

- Paralysis by analysis. Metrics are used independent of underlying life cycle and development processes. Often too much information is collected, and organizations waste time on formalisms and bureaucracy. It is important to understand that measuring is a key part of engineering and project management – but not a separate activity done by the accountants.

How this Book Is Organized

The chapters of this book are organized to go from the general to the specific. All chapters are built around the ISO 15939 software measurement standard (Fig. 1.2).

We first discuss measurement from a business perspective. Chap. 2 brings metrics into the business context and provides some examples on the practical usage of metrics for change management and for portfolio management. This is comprised by the need to establish improvement goals (upper left box) and finally to execute corrective actions (lower right box).

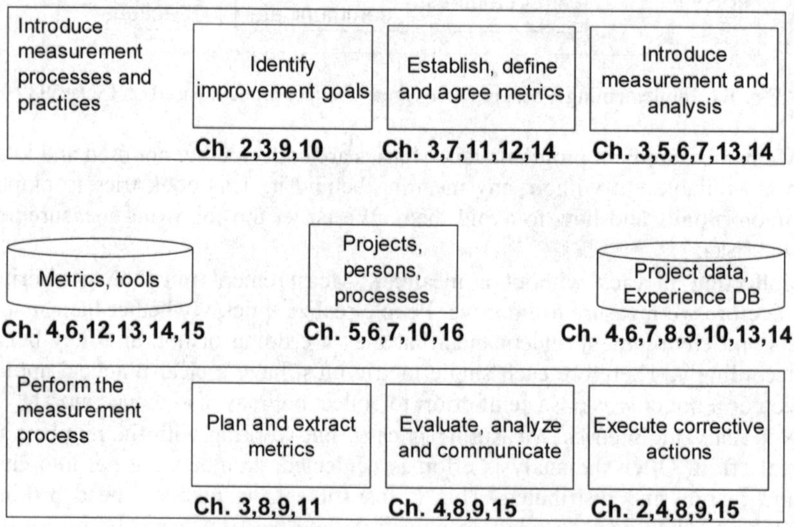

Fig. 1.2. The measurement process and the book's structure

Chaps. 3 and 4 elaborate how the measurement process and its infrastructure are introduced. Starting a measurement program is very difficult, as it implies culture change towards visibility and accountability for results. Often measurement programs fail because middle and senior management is not capable dealing with the visibility gained and trust needed to make metrics successful. We show in Chap. 5 how to best manage the cultural changes related to measurement. Anybody dealing with software measurement must consider the effects of metrics on the people and the effects of the people on the metrics. Often people are afraid of "being measured". Mostly this refusal has to do with a lack of knowledge about how to measure and what is in it when the numbers are used correctly. If metrics are used to threaten and punish before building a climate where targets are set realistically and are made achievable, trust will disappear and numbers will be faked. This explains the cynical behaviors we find in software management cartoons.

Measurement needs the right tools. Though the tools are not heavy or expensive, counting, presenting and analyzing manually is still common practice. We show in Chap. 6 what tooling should be used for different questions related to measurement.

Estimation is still one area in software measurement where many users struggle mightily – right from the start. It's introduced in Chap. 7. We also come back to the people dimension of metrics in this chapter. Project management, and specifically project control is at the core of Chap. 8. This chapter underlines the relationship between project success and "having the right numbers". Chap. 9 deals with quality control and defect detection. It contains lots of practical experience and rules of thumb on defects, estimation and prediction, all with the objective of obtaining the right quality and of reducing the cost of non-quality. It is a chapter that introduces empirical software engineering through the back door. While this easily could have been a chapter in its own, we thought it being better to understand if applied directly to the context of quality improvement.

Chap. 10 generalizes these aspects towards the broad field of process improvement. There has been a lot of misunderstanding about using metrics for process improvement. The Capability Maturity Model (CMM) has contributed in clarifying quantitative management within software engineering. While many people thought that metrics for most of us are only about tracking performance, the CMM underlines the benefits of managing organizational, project and process performance simultaneously. We try to clarify and explain how to set improvement objectives and how to reach them. Analogously to e-business, we coin the terminology of e-R&D to underline what measurement, methodologies and management are really about.

Information technology asks for measurement on performance and service availability. With Chaps. 11 and 12 we take a practical look into how to set up and ensure service level agreements and different scenarios. We cover different technologies, such as integrating applications with Enterprise Application Integration (EAI) or implementing Web services.

The next three chapters are shaped as case studies. They go back to some important measurement themes and show in very specific situations what was done in industry practice. Chapter 13 shows how to build a measurement infrastructure on an intranet and is directly linked with Chap. 6. Chapter 14 relates to Chaps. 7 and 8 in showing how function points are introduced into the full life-cycle of a software product. Chapter 15 takes a look into metrics for maintenance. Often we tend to neglect the fact that a vast majority of our effort in software engineering goes into enhancing legacy systems. This chapter looks into quality measurement especially in such situations and thus relates to Chap. 9.

Finally, Chap. 16 summarizes the major software measurement communities and organizations. URLs are provided for the Internet sites of these organizations.

A glossary and index wrap up the book. The glossary should serve as a baseline reference for the many terms we use throughout this book. It draws the fine line between metrics and measurements and has other frequently used terms for consistency reasons.

To ensure enduring value of this book, we keep the information updated at this book's Web site at http://metrics.cs.uni-magdeburg.de.

Who Should Read this Book?

If you develop software for a living and if you are interested in the practical aspects of measurement, this book will show how you can better understand and control what you are doing. The book will help you in understanding what measurement means in practical terms. It will also help in selecting what counts from the perspective of understanding, evaluating, tracking, controlling and forecasting. We further recommend [Fent97] as a practical introduction providing the mathematical and statistical background of software measurement.

If you manage software projects or organizations, this book will show you what measurement techniques to select in front of various needs from estimating size and effort to project and portfolio management. It will also describe the softer parts of measurement, such as introducing a measurement program or coping with resistance. [McCo98] is the classic text on how to make your software projects a success. We highly recommend it. We also recommend [Grad92] as a comprehensive summary what HP did in terms of practical software measurement with focus on managing projects.

If you are responsible for improving quality, performance, or processes in an organization, this book will show how to set targets and how to reach them. It introduces the recent tools and environments of making measurement more efficient. We recommend in this domain [Hump89] as the baseline for what process improvement really means. [ISO00] is the appropriate standard for software measurement and should not be missing on any standards bookshelf in our domain. [McGa01] explains the usage of this ISO standard. [Jone96], though a little bit dated, provides a huge set of experience data which you can relate to your own measurements to have some initial benchmarking.

If you are engaged in software engineering research, the book will show what's ongoing out there, what's working and what not, and how it relates to specific needs the practitioners still expect to be answered by an improved body of knowledge. [VanS00] and [Zuse97] are good introductory textbooks on the scientific background of software measurement. We recommend them for those who want to engage into empirical research.

For all of you the book provides lots of practical hints and concrete examples. Any single entry to this book comes from practical work in industry and has been validated in front of real-world requirements.

Authors

Christof Ebert (christofebert@ieee.org) is Director, Software Coordination and Process Improvement of Alcatel in Paris, France. He drives R&D innovation and improvement programs within Alcatel. His current responsibilities include establishing shared software platforms and leading Alcatel's global CMM/CMMI programs (which means a great deal of measurement). A senior member of the IEEE, Dr. Ebert lectures at the University of Stuttgart and serves as a keynote speaker and on program committees of various software engineering conferences. Since the end of 1980s, he has been an educator, researcher and consultant in software measurement. He is a member of the editorial board of the *Journal of Systems and Software* and is *IEEE Software* associate editor-in-chief. He serves on the board of the German Interest Group on software metrics within the German Informatics Society (GI). For this book he worked especially on Chaps. 2, 5, 8, 9 and 10.

Reiner Dumke (dumke@ivs.cs.uni-magdeburg.de) has studied mathematics and worked as a programmer and systems analyst. He holds a PhD on the operational efficiency of large-scale database systems. Since 1994, he has been a full professor in software engineering at the University of Magdeburg. His research interest is in software measurement, CAME tools, agent-based development methods, e-measurement and distributed complex systems. He is the leader of the German Interest Group on software metrics within the German Informatics Society (GI) and he works as a member of the COSMIC, DASMA, MAIN, IEEE and ACM communities. He founded the Software Measurement Laboratory (SML@b) at the University of Magdeburg. He is coeditor of the *Metrics News Journal* and the publisher and editor of more than 30 books about programming techniques, software metrics, metrics tools, software engineering foundations, component-based software development and web engineering. More information about the projects and teaching is found at http://ivs.cs.uni-magdeburg.de/~dumke. Prof. Dumke provided Chaps. 3, 4, 7 and 13.

Manfred Bundschuh (manfred.bundschuh@freenet.de) has worked as banker, teacher and IT consultant in Hamburg; he has been the quality manager in AXA Service AG in Cologne for over 20 years. In 1983 he was appointed professor for software engineering and project management at the University of Applied Sciences (http://www.gm.fh-koeln.de/~bundschu) in Cologne and supervised more than 220 students. M. Bundschuh lectures for various organizations and has published more than 40 papers (some in books) and 9 books (3 as copublisher). He is president of the *Deutschsprachige Anwendergruppe für Softwaremetrik und Aufwandschätzung* (DASMA). His hobbies are traveling, reading and astronomy, archeology and philosophy. He worked on Chaps. 5, 7, 14 and 16.

Andreas Schmietendorf (andreas.schmietendorf@t-systems.com) holds academic degrees in technical computer science, telecommunications and general informatics from the TFH Berlin, FHTW Berlin and HTW Dresden (Universities of

Applied Science). He holds MS and PhD degrees in computer science from the University of Magdeburg. Since 1993 he has worked as a consultant for system and software development in the information technology department of Deutsche Telekom AG. Currently he is the leader of a group for integration solutions and chief architect for the development center in Berlin. His main research interest is in software performance engineering, component software development and software measurement. He is an active member in the German society of computer science (GI), the Central Europe Computer Measurement Group (CECMG) and the German interest group on software metrics and effort estimation (DASMA). He lectures at the University of Magdeburg and FHTW Berlin (University of Applied Science). Dr. Schmietendorf's attention was directed to Chaps. 6, 11, 12 and 15.

2 Making Metrics a Success – The Business Perspective

When the smoke clears,
the thing that really matters to senior management is the numbers.
—Donald J. Reifer

2.1 The Business Need for Measurement

It is eight o'clock in the morning. You are responsible for software engineering. On your way to the company building you run into your CEO. He inquires on the status of your current development projects. No small talk. He wants to find out which projects are running, about their trade-offs, the risks, and whether you have sufficient resources to implement your strategy. He is interested whether you can deliver what he promises to the customers and shareholders – or whether you need his help. That's your chance! Five minutes for your career and success!

Sounds familiar? Maybe it is not the CEO but a key customer for a self-employed software engineer. Or perhaps you are a project manager and one of the key stakeholders wants to see how you are doing. The questions are the same as is the reaction if you have not answered precisely and concisely.

Is there sufficient insight into the development projects? If you are like a majority of those in IT and software companies, you only know the financial figures. Too many projects run in parallel, without concrete and quantitative objectives and without tracking where they are with respect to expectations. Project proposals are evaluated in isolation from ongoing activities. Projects are started or stopped based on local criteria, not by considering the global trade-offs across all projects and opportunities. Only one third of all software engineering companies systematically utilize techniques to measure and control their product releases and development projects [Meta02, CIO03, IQPC03] (for project control see also Chap. 8).

No matter what business you are in, you are also in the software business. Computer-based, software-driven systems are pervasive in today's society. Increasingly, the entire system functionality is implemented in software. Where we used to split hardware from software, we see flexible boundaries entirely driven by business cases to determine what we best package at which level in which component, be it software or silicon.

The software business has manifold challenges, which range from the creation process and its inherent risks to direct balance sheet impacts. For example, the Standish Group's Chaos Report annually surveys commercial and government information technology (IT) projects. They found that only 26% of the projects finished on time and within budget, a staggering 28% were cancelled before delivery, and of the remaining projects, which finished late and/or over budget, they only delivered a fraction of the planned functionality [Stan02].

Software metrics ensure that the business is successful. They help to see what is going on, and how one is doing with respect to forecasts and plans. And they ultimatively guide decisions on how to do better.

Success within a software business is determined and measured by the degree the software projects and the entire product portfolio contribute to the top line (e.g., revenues) and to the bottom line (e.g., profit and loss). Late introduction of a product to market causes a loss of market share; cancellation of a product before it ever reaches the market causes an even greater loss. Not only is software increasing in size, complexity and percentage of functionality, it is increasing in contribution to balance sheet and P&L statements.

Software metrics do not distinguish first-hand between IT projects, development projects or maintenance projects. The approach is the same. Most techniques described in this book can be applied to different types of software engineering, software management and IT management activities.

We portray the measurement process as an inherent part of almost any business process (Fig. 2.1). It consists of the three steps that were already introduced in Fig. 1.1:

- extract information (metrics) for a specific need
- evaluate this information in view of a specific background of actual status and goals
- execute a decision to reduce the differences between actual status and goals

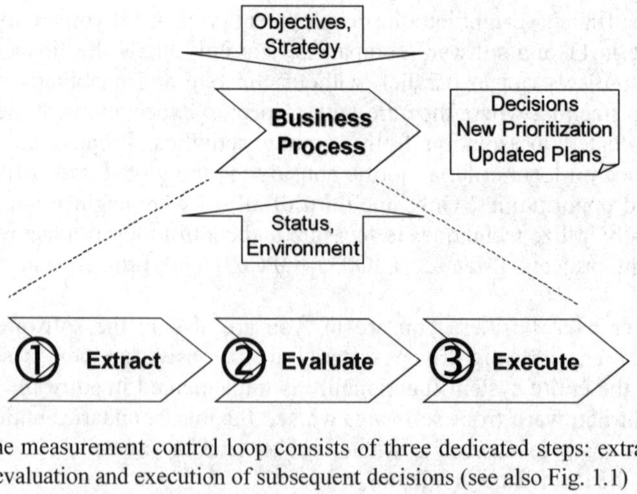

Fig. 2.1. The measurement control loop consists of three dedicated steps: extraction of information, evaluation and execution of subsequent decisions (see also Fig. 1.1)

This process is a closed control loop, and we insist that it must be closed by means of the third step, that is, execute decisions based on the information collected. There is no use in extracting information and only recording it for potential further usage. If metrics are not used on the spot, if they are not analyzed and evaluated, chances are high that the underlying data is invalid. Without the pressure to have accurate metrics available, collection is done without much care. Where there is no direct use for information, the information is useless and so is the effort behind the collection.

If done properly, there are many benefits to metrics, such as

- visibility of project and process performance
- improved predictability
- accountability for results due to verifiable commitments
- maximized value generation of the engineering investments
- transparent, fair and repeatable decisions on funding of projects
- optimized balance of content, technology, risk and funding
- improved interfaces and communication between engineering and business/sales/marketing management
- harmonized decision-making of product technology and content with business needs
- efficient and effective resource allocation
- fewer redundant projects and fewer overlaps
- outsourcing and supplier monitoring
- simplified and transparent cancellation of projects.

On the cost side we found that a metrics program – similar to other controlling activities – costs some 0.3–1% of related engineering (or IT) effort. If the size of the organizational unit where metrics are introduced is 100 persons, one should budget approximately a half person-year for metrics collection and analysis. During the introduction phase the effort needed may almost double, due to training and communication needs and due to introducing templates, collection mechanisms or tools. Where there are intranet portals, access to metrics and project information can be provided with low effort, which will over time further reduce the running cost of metrics collection. The effort for evaluation and execution naturally will not decrease, as this is a management responsibility, starting from the level of an individual engineer who, for instance, wants to improve their own performance and thus looks into her productivity or the quality of her deliverables.

Metrics must be goal-oriented. Since metrics drive management decisions on various levels, they are directly linked to respective targets. Fig. 2.2 shows this relationship with different stakeholder needs and which benefits they achieve by using metrics. Each group naturally has their own objectives, which are not necessarily aligned with each other, and they need visibility how they are doing with respect to their own goals. On the senior management level, certainly metrics relate to business performance. A project manager needs timely and accurate information on a project's parameters. An engineer wants to ensure she delivers good quality and concentrates on the team's objectives (see also Chap. 3).

There is some additional literature around taking a business perspective on software. Most looks into examples and case studies to generalize principles [Deva02, Benk03, Reme00]. Some look into dedicated tools and techniques and their application, such as project control and management [Royc98, McGa01] (see also Chap. 8), management of global development projects [Eber01] or knowledge management in R&D projects [Auru03]. A good introduction to the topic of business cases for software projects is provided by Reifer [Reif02]. A special issue of *IEEE Software* summarizes the state of the practice of "software as a business" [Mill02].

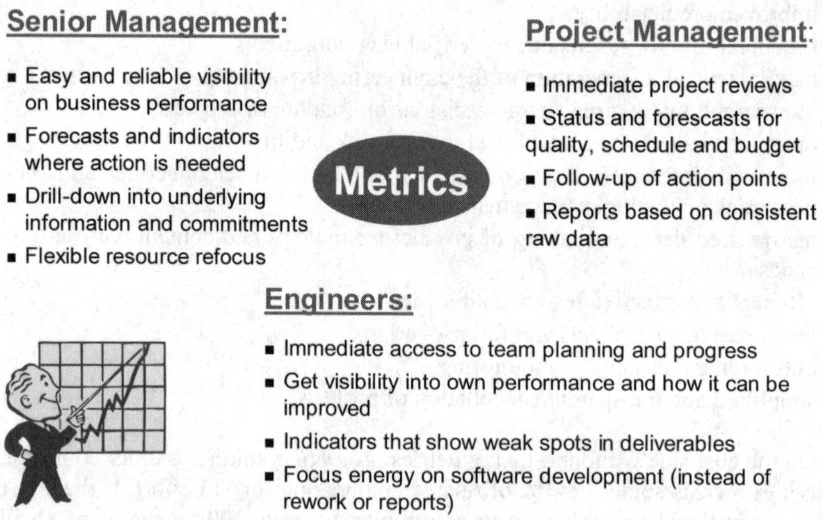

Fig. 2.2. Metrics depend on stakeholder needs. Their goals of what to control or improve drive the selection and effective usage of metrics

This chapter introduces the business perspective of software measurement. It looks into IT control, project control, and portfolio management techniques. Section 2 proceeds with a global introduction on managing by the numbers. We structure the entire measurement and management process into three parts, namely extraction of information, evaluation and execution. We will not discuss here *how* metrics are selected, as this is specific to the objectives and goals of a specific process or an application area. We will come back to this question during the other chapters of this book.

Section 3 provides some concrete application areas on how management decisions are guided by software metrics. We have selected areas with very different underlying management objectives to underline the broad scope where metrics are used. In this section we introduce to portfolio management, which is a methodology of increasing relevance to simultaneously manage a set of different products or projects. We will look into managing technology change and disruptive technology introduction. We also show how product and release planning are guided by metrics. These few examples should indicate the necessity of good metrics to manage the software business. Finally, Sect. 4 summarizes how to make metrics a success and how to be successful with metrics.

2.2 Managing by the Numbers

2.2.1 Extraction

The first step of any measurement process is to collect the right information. Measurement is not so much about collection of numbers but rather about understanding what information is necessary to drive actions and to achieve dedicated goals. Extraction therefore means to derive measurement needs from the objectives of the respective entity, to specify how the metrics are collected and then to extract this information from operational activities. This includes available and needed resources, skills, technologies, reusable platforms, effort, objectives, assumptions, expected benefits and market share or market growth. A consistent set of indicators must be agreed upon, especially to capture software project status information.

Metrics selection is goal-oriented (see also Chap. 3). An initial set of internal project indicators can be derived from the Software Engineering Institute's (SEI) core metrics [Carl92]. They simplify the selection by reducing the focus on project tracking and oversight from a contractor and program management perspective. Obviously additional indicators must be agreed to evaluate external constraints and integrate with market data.

Often the collected metrics and resulting reports are useless and only create additional overhead. In the worst case they hide useful and necessary information. We have seen reports on software programs with over 50 pages full of graphs, tables and numbers. When asked about topics such as cost to complete, expected cost of non-quality after handover, or time to profit they did not show a single number. Sometimes they are even created to hide reality and attract attention to what is looking good. **Be aware that metrics are sometimes abused to obscure and confuse reality!**

A good starting point is to identify how the projects and activities are viewed from the outside. Ask questions that impact the organization's and thus your own future. What is hurting most in the current business climate? Are deadlines exceeded or changed on short notice? Is the quality level so poor that customers may move to another supplier? Are projects continuously over budget? Is the amount devoted to the creation of new and innovative technology shrinking due to cost of poor quality, rework, testing and maintenance? Who feels this pain first in the company? Which direction should the product portfolio take? What exactly is a project, a product or a portfolio? Is this what sales and marketing communicate? Where does management get information from? Is it reliable and timely? What targets and quarterly objectives drive R&D?

To make metrics a success, more is needed than just facts. It's necessary to look at opportunistic and subjective aspects. What role and impact do you have inside the enterprise? Who benefits most from the projects, and who creates the most difficulties for the projects? Why is that? What could you do to help this person or group or customer?

Fig. 2.3 shows this goal-driven relationship between business goals, concrete annual targets or objectives on an operational level to dedicated indicators or metrics. Goals cannot be reached if they are not quantified and measured. Or as the saying goes, managers without clear goals will not achieve their goals clearly. We show in Fig. 2.3 concrete instances of objectives and metrics. Naturally, they should be selected based on the market situation, the maturity and certainly the priorities in the projects.

To make the right assessments and decisions, the necessary information must be collected up-front. Which factors (or targets, expectations, boundary effects) impact the investment? How did the original assumptions and performance indicators evolve in the project? Is the business case still valid? Which assets or improvements have been implemented? Which changes in constraints, requirements or boundary conditions will impact the projects and results? Are there timing constraints, such as delays until the results are available, or timeline correlations?

Often indicators are available but are not aggregated and integrated. For instance, a quality improvement program measures only defects and root causes, but fails to look into productivity or shortened cycle times. Or in a newly created sales portal only access and performance information is known, while sales figures or new marketing mechanisms are left out of the picture. Fig. 2.4 shows how this aggregation is implemented in the various levels of an organization

Goal	Concrete objectives	Metrics
Increase productivity	Reduce cost of engineering over Sales by x% within 3 years	Effort spent, project size Productivity
Reduce development elapse time and improve schedule adherance	x months for generic platform y months for application project z weeks for new service < x% delay on schedule	Elapse time Delivery accuracy/predictability Feature completeness Budget adherance
Improve quality	Improve field failure rate by x% Reduce cost of non-quality by y%	Number of failures Cost of non-quality Efficiency during validations
Processes, technology and people	New technology: tbd Innovation: tbd People: tbd	Usage of new technology Average age of products Patents and license income

Fig. 2.3. Metrics are derived from business goals

Projects aggregate information on a dashboard level, for instance, showing performance of milestones versus the planned dates, or showing the earned value at a given moment (for dashboards, see also Chaps. 4 and 8). This helps to examine those projects that underperform or that are exposed to increased risk. Project managers would look more closely and examine how they could resolve such deviation in real time within the constraints of the project. All projects must share the same set of consistent metrics presented in a unique dashboard. Lots of time is actually wasted by reinventing spreadsheets and reporting formats, where the project team should rather focus on creating value.

Fortunately, such a dashboard need not be time-consuming or complex. Metrics such as schedule and budget adherence, earned value, or quality level are typical performance indicators that serve as "traffic lights" on the status of the individual project. Only those (amber and red) projects that run out of agreed variance (which, of course, depends on the maturity of the organization) would be investigated and further drilled down in the same dashboard to identify root causes. When all projects follow a defined process and utilize the same type of reporting and performance tracking, it is fairly easy to determine status, identify risks and resolve issues, without getting buried in the details of micromanaging the project.

A standardized project dashboard is easy to set up and will not incur much operational cost. It builds on few standard metrics that are aggregated and represented typically in an intranet accessible format to facilitate drill-down. It leverages on existing project management and collaboration tools from which it draws its raw data (e.g., schedule information, milestones, effort spent, defects detected, etc.). It is self-contained and easy to learn. Key information is collected in a single repository with access control to protect especially the consolidated information. Having such a dashboard in place will ensure that project issues remain on the radar screen of the stakeholders at their convenience. By fostering early risk management, it will once and for all take away the "I didn't see that coming" response.

Performance monitoring is key. Standard metrics must be collected from each project and then consolidated for all the projects to evaluate the portfolio's alignment with business objectives and performance requirements (Fig. 2.4). For the senior management levels the same information is further condensed into a scorecard that relates different businesses to the annual objectives. Scorecards should be balanced [Kapl93] to avoid local optimization of only one target.

Combining and aggregating the raw data creates useful management information. For instance, a product with a new technology should be looked at from different angles. By using Linux instead of a proprietary operating system one might not only look into skills and introduction cost, but also into financial health of the packaging company or liability aspects in the medium-term. It is necessary to extract indicators from all operational areas and assess them in combination [Kapl93, Hitt95].

As an example, let us look at different ways to measure success or returns from software engineering activities. Obviously there are operational figures that point to benefit calculation, such as phase durations in the product life cycle, time to profit, time to market, cycle time for single processes, maintenance cost, cost of non-quality, cycle time for defect corrections, reuse rate, or license cost and revenues. Another dimension that is often neglected is improvements in productivity or people, such as cost per engineer, learning curves, cost per employee (in different countries), cost evolution, output rates per engineer or capital expenses per seat.

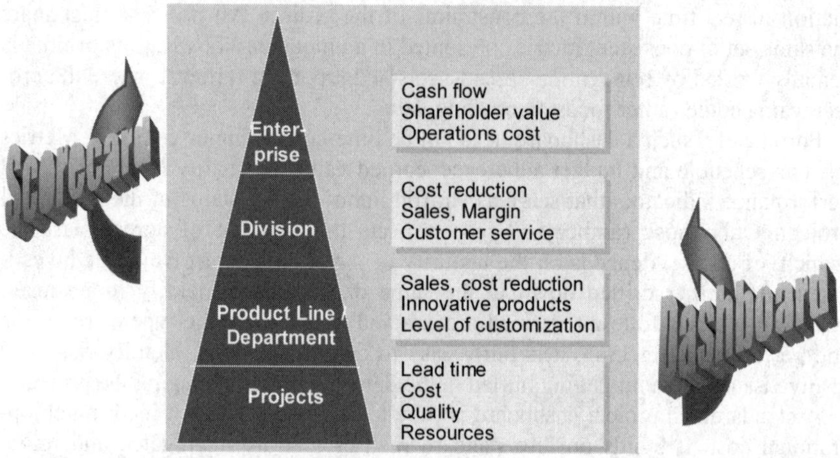

Fig. 2.4. Metrics are aggregated following the organizational needs. On project level focus is on dashboards, while on division or enterprise level it is on scorecards

From these indicators one can select the few that reflect the assumptions of the original business case for the underlying products. They will help to further trace and predict costs and benefits. Indicators should be translated into the "language" of the projects or stakeholders to allow seamless extraction from regular project reviews without much overhead. Fig. 2.5 provides an example of how the same overarching dimensions of quality, productivity, deadlines, and employees are translated into different metrics depending on the perspective taken. An internal process view necessarily looks more into how processes can be improved, while the external perspective takes more a service- or product-related perspective. Often this is underlined by the type of agreements or contracts in the different client schemes of business processes.

Often, forward-looking figures need some education, to be consistent in estimating cost at completion of a project or following up earned value. Such a "dashboard" or status report compiles exactly those figures one need when comparing all projects. Try to automate the reporting, because for the project manager it is a useless – because overly aggregated – report. He should not be charged with such an effort.

Once the necessary indicators are aggregated and available in one central repository or from a single portal, it is easy to generate reports covering the entire set of activities, projects, products or departments. Frequently asked queries are accessible online to save time and effort. Such reports, for instance, provide a list of product releases sorted to their availability. They can show average delays or budget overheads. One can single out projects with above-average cost and compare with their earned value, or one can portray products according to revenues, market shares and life cycle positioning. This reduces the effort to identify outliers, which need special treatment.

Let us look at the scenario of deciding whether a project should be stopped before its planned end. This is typically a difficult situation, not only for the project manager and the people working on the project, but because many organizations consider a stopped project a failure. Well, it might be from a financial perspective, but it will be an even bigger failure if it is not finished. Only few deal with such "failure" constructively, learn their lessons, and work on the next project. We will look at the decision from a higher-level perspective. There are costs after the decision to stop, such as ongoing infrastructure write-offs, leasing contracts and relocation costs. Often these cost are close to the cost of bringing the project to the intended end, which implies a delivery. On the other hand, opportunistic factors should be considered, because the engineers could work on other projects that generate more sales.

	Quality	Productivity	Deadlines	Employees
Internal process view	Fault rate Fault density Cost per fault Root causes	FP / Person year FP / Calendar month Tool usage	Percentage of work products within the 10% time frame	Skills Willingness Overtime Absence
External customer view	Customer satisfaction Delivered product quality Functionality	Cost per feature	Delivery accuracy of final product to contracted date	Satisfaction with contact persons (sales, after sales, engineers)

Fig. 2.5. Different stakeholder viewpoints determine how goals are translated internally and externally

2.2.2 Evaluation

After indicators and relevant project and marketing tracking information have been agreed upon and are available, evaluation of this information starts. This includes cost versus benefits, business case evaluation, usefulness of the results from projects, market readiness – all as future scenarios in terms of opportunities and risks. Such evaluation happens continuously and for the totality of projects. Even if product lines are not related technically or perhaps they even address fully different markets, it makes sense to evaluate mutual dependencies or synergies, such as resource consumption or asset generation.

Certainly a monthly exercise for products or a yearly exercise for portfolios as was done historically in many companies is far too coarse and falls behind the facts. Even the monthly or quarterly exercises preceding budget cycles and agreements turn out to be illustrative rather than guiding. On the project-level a weekly reassessment of assumptions should be a best balance of effort and benefits. On the level of products and portfolios, a monthly reassessment still allows one to actively steer the evolution reflecting market changes. If projects change or deviate from the agreed objectives or if the risk level gets higher and the chances that the project manager can recuperate within the project get smaller, it is time to reevaluate and realign the project and portfolio with reality.

It is crucial to simultaneously evaluate *cost and benefits* or *trade-offs* between objectives. Regarding cost, the following questions could be addressed: Where are the individual elements of the portfolio (i.e. the products, product releases or projects) with respect to cost and cost structure? Is cost evolution following the approved plans and expectations? Is cost structure competitive (e.g., the share of test effort of the total development cost)? How is the evolution of the entire cost structure (e.g., is the trend going in a direction that allows sustainable growth)? Are the different elements of engineering cost under your control or are they determined from outside? Are all operational cost elements appropriately budgeted (e.g., covering maintenance, service, product evolution, corrections)?

We do the same for the benefits. Do the components of the portfolio follow the original assumptions? Is one investment better than others? Why is this the case? Which factors impact benefits? Which revenue growth relates to certain decisions or changes that have been implemented? What are the stakeholders' benefits from the IT or the R&D, both financially (e.g., return on assets (ROA), return on capital employed (ROCE)) as well as operationally (e.g., value generation for customers' businesses, market expectations, competitive situation)? What are the major impacts on performance and capacity to grow? How do internal processes and interfaces influence innovativeness, capability to learn or improvements?

Today "time to profit" is more relevant than "time to market" when evaluating benefits from different software projects. A delayed market entry in the world of Internet applications as well as other software solutions immediately reduces ROI dramatically. Entry levels for newcomers are so low and the global workforce is growing so fast that the market position is never stable. Even giants like Microsoft feel this in times of open source and an overwhelming number of companies who all want to have their own piece of the pie. As a rule of thumb one can consider that in a fast-changing market – as is the case for many software applications and services – a delay of only three months impacts revenues by 20% because of being late and the related opportunistic effects such as delays of subsequent releases.

We will look at an example with only five software projects in the portfolio that can be influenced (Fig. 2.6). We will first use the classic picture of a portfolio [Benk03], which is very easy to utilize for software engineering projects. Obviously we need to consider market information to avoid the case in which engineering projects are judged by an engineering perspective only. The matrix shows the projects in three dimensions, namely the market share, the market growth and the internal – still expected – net present value of the investment (the size of the bubbles). The idiomatic denominations of "stars" or "cash cows" is the standard vocabulary and relates to the perceived potential of a certain matrix element.

Fig. 2.6 suggests that projects 4 and 5 need more support while project 1 should be stopped. It is also evident that this portfolio is not healthy: it is not sustainable because in no area there is a benefit from high market share and high market growth. In the case of smaller companies who do not know their exact market position, other indicators could be used to indicate their position. Market growth should be used in any case, as it provides an external view on the business evolution.

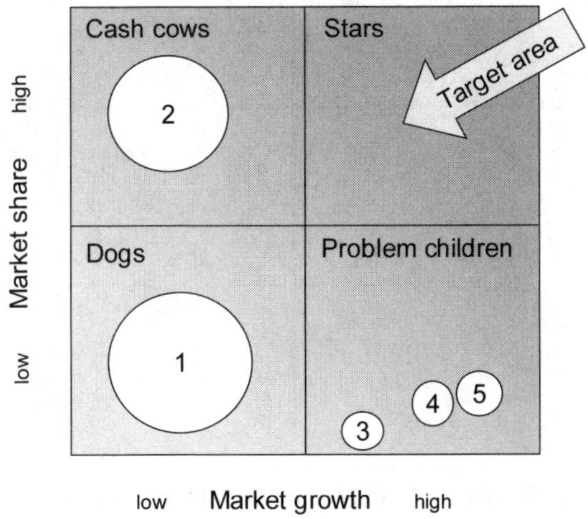

Fig. 2.6. A simple set-up of a portfolio layout for different software products

Often it is necessary to derive from several of the above-mentioned analysis techniques and the resulting timelines even-more-distant representations of the portfolio matrix just to play with the impact of different alternatives. This holds not only when deciding on technology frameworks or product-line content but also if the company serves and depends on a few customers (or suppliers) whose future one might want to assess in order to make more informed project and portfolio analyses for the company's future.

Evaluating software engineering projects is only valid if all projects and possible decisions around those projects are portrayed in the same larger picture. The prominent review approach is still that project reviews are done in isolation for each project. This is necessary to judge whether the project will deliver versus the agreed assumptions at project start. But they must be accompanied by a look to the totality of the projects. Often there are ripple effects caused by shared resources, suppliers, technology or platforms. A good way to relate such dependent management decisions in multiproject constraints is to hierarchically cluster the projects based on mutual dependencies or synergies. Such cluster analysis takes away the risk of overly fast aggregation and the comparison of apples to pears.

We will look at another example to see how software engineering decisions depend on market evolution (Fig. 2.7). We portray five different product lines or clusters of related products and product releases. The matrix in Fig. 2.7 shows all five product-lines in three dimensions, namely revenue growth, market growth, and net present value of investments (size of circles). The picture shows that product line 1 should be cashed in with a reduced budget, product line 2 needs to be reduced, product line 3 needs increased investments, product line 4 can stay as it is, and product line 5 should be sold or killed.

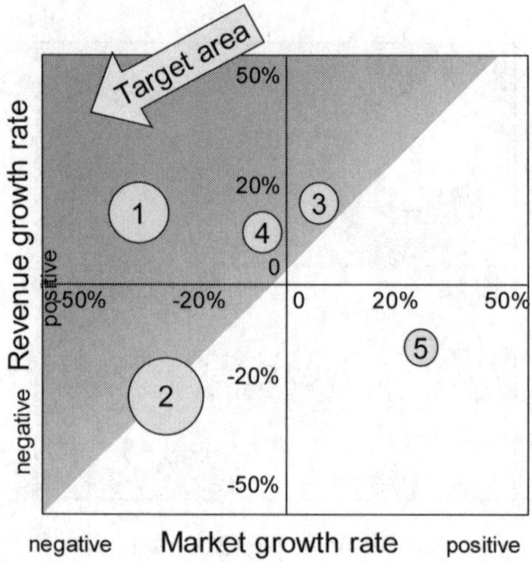

Fig. 2.7. A portfolio map to help in deciding to which software engineering projects to allocate scarce resources

2.2.3 Execution

After having extracted the necessary information and having evaluated the projects comprehensively, it is time to decide and to execute the decisions. Management means to actively take decisions and implement changes. The implications on different managerial levels are comparable. Whether it is on the project or the portfolio level, decisions need to suit the proposed scenarios. For instance, if risks grow beyond what the project can handle, it is time to reconsider features and project scope. Maybe incremental deliveries can help with coping too big a scope and not manageable size or duration.

If the value and benefits from a product release turn out to be below the standard expected return on the investments (e.g., current interest rates for this risk level), they should be cancelled. Only those projects and products should remain in the portfolio that represent the biggest value and shortest time to returns. A certain percentage of the software budget should always be reserved for new projects and new technology to avoid being consumed by the legacy projects and products and becoming incumbent.

Different alternatives for decisions result from the previous two steps (extraction and evaluation). You decide only on this basis, as you otherwise invalidate your carefully built tools. Decisions should be transparent to influence behaviors and maintain trust and accountability. Particularly if projects are going to be cancelled it is important to follow an obvious rule set so that future projects can learn from it. For instance, if there is insufficient budget, a project is immediately stopped or changed instead of dragging on while everybody knows that sooner or later it will fail. Basic decision alternatives include doing nothing, canceling the project or changing the project or the scope of the project.

Don't neglect or rule out any of these three basic options too early. Different options should be further broken down in order to separate decisions, which have nothing to do with each other. For instance, whether and which new technology is used in a project should not depend on the supplier. Each decision brings along new risks and assumptions that one need to factor into the next iteration of the evaluations. If one of the key assumptions turns out to be wrong or a major risk materializes, it is the time to implement the respective alternative scenario.

To ensure effective execution on project and product level, software measurement should be closely linked and integrated in the company's product life-cycle management (PLM). Typical software life cycles might follow IEEE 1074 or IEEE 12207 [ISO97a, ISO97b]. They have in common a gating process between major phases based on defined criteria. These gates enforce evaluating the overall status (both commercial and technical) and deciding on whether and how to proceed with the project [Wall02]. PLM is the overall process that governs a product or service from its inception to the end of its life in order to achieve the best possible value for the business of the enterprise and its customers and partners.

We will illustrate the dependencies with an example. Fig. 2.8 shows a simplified product life cycle in the upper part. It consists of mentioned decision gates and between them, four individual phases. For each of the four phases the lower part of the picture shows some indicators that are relevant in order to derive the subsequent go/no-go decisions.

Especially for software engineering projects, it is important to consider mutual dependencies (Fig. 2.4). At the top is the enterprise portfolio, which depicts all products within the company and their markets and respective investments. Further down one details a product-line or product cluster view, which is aligned with platform roadmaps and technology evolution or skill building of engineers. For each product there should be a feature catalogue across the next several releases covering the vision, market, architecture and technology. From such product roadmap a technology roadmap is derived, which allows one for instance to select suppliers or build partnerships. It also drives the individual roadmaps of releases and projects, which typically have a horizon of a few months up to a maximum one year. On the project level, these decisions are implemented and followed through to success.

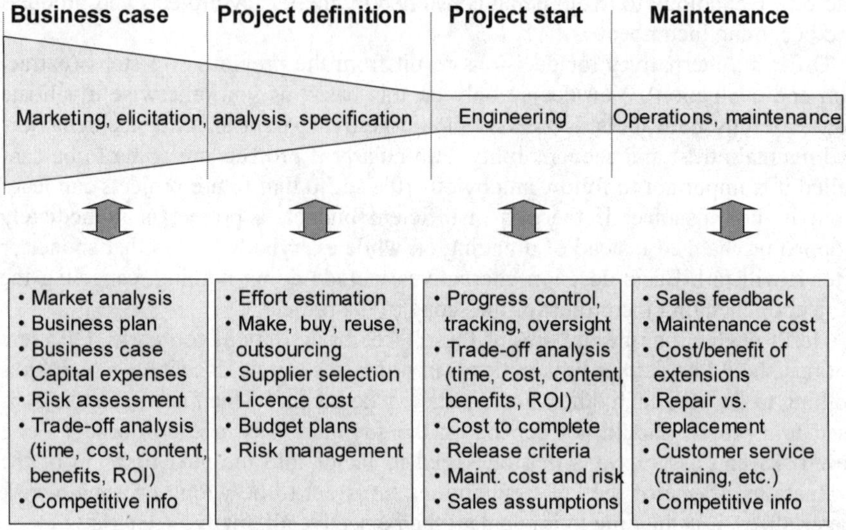

Fig. 2.8. During each phase of the product life cycle dedicated indicators are used. Product development can be stopped at each of the gates

2.3 Metrics for Management Guidance

2.3.1 Portfolio Management

Portfolio management is the collection and evaluation of product and project information and the decision based on the totality of all projects in order to maximize their value for the enterprise. This includes the following aspects (Fig. 2.9):

- building an inventory of the overall software engineering assets in terms of products, reusable software, ongoing projects and their opportunities, employees, etc.
- continuous evaluation of new opportunities in comparison with ongoing activities
- combined evaluation of static and dynamic assets (e.g., platforms, tools versus skills and customers)
- deciding which resources will be allocated in the (near) future to which assets and opportunities

Portfolio management in software projects means assessing all projects continuously and in totality. It is not a project review and should, in fact, not be mixed with regular tracking and oversight. It means that costs and benefits, contents and roadmaps, threats, risks and opportunities are evaluated comprehensively in order to implement a coherent strategy. It is independent of the size of the enterprise. To simplify the definition: Portfolio management is the project management of the totality of all projects, services or product releases.

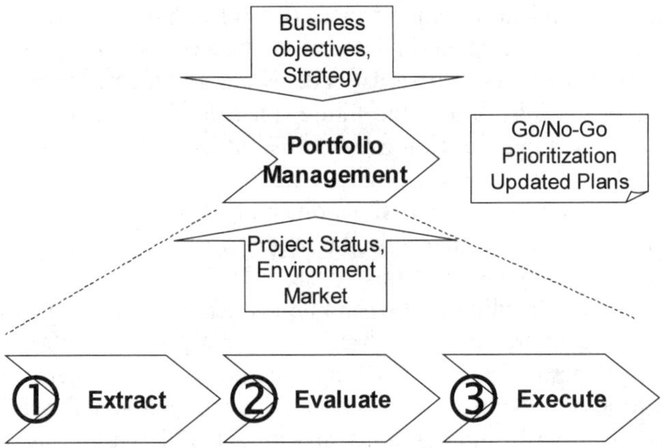

Fig. 2.9. Three steps towards portfolio management following the measurement control loop in Fig. 2.1

Good portfolio management will help to allocate resources in the best possible way, to reduce the number of projects to what is effective and to improve the communication between projects, departments, and functional areas in the company. It also allows management to pull the emergency brake earlier, if necessary. It will normally save around 5—10% of the software engineering budget as the people work on the projects that provide the biggest yield [Meta02, CIO03].

What is the difference between portfolio management and project management? Project management means doing the project the right way. Portfolio management means doing the right projects.

The major bridge from portfolio management to projects and vice versa is the business case. It summarizes – before the launch of the project – the technical, marketing and commercial inputs to make a decision on a business proposal and to later follow up against key assumptions. A business case combines three elements, a business vision or concept of a solution, a concrete and quantitative value proposition and a commercial or marketing positioning.

Is there a difference between managing an IT portfolio (e.g., internal applications and business processes) from managing the portfolio of software engineering projects and products? The questions one asks and the applied techniques are definitely the same. Are scarce resources allocated to the right activities? Are the short- and medium-term targets well balanced? Do they line up with the strategy and with the way the enterprise now earns and will make money in the future? What could engineering or IT do to make the enterprise more profitable? These questions apply across the entire scope of software engineering activities.

What is different is the ways one can interfere and impact decisions. The interfaces are certainly different as is the proximity to the customers and markets. If one is engaged in the engineering of products (e.g., embedded systems, applications, solutions, etc.), one will influence the product strategy, the feature roadmap, the technology mix, the software processes and their interfaces to business processes. For internal applications and services (i.e., IT activities) you influence business processes and their automation, integration, cost or service levels.

Portfolio management looks on today's decisions and their impact on the evolution and value of the portfolio in the future. Previous investment is only considered to learn from results, not to judge because of the amount of money that has been invested. Many errors in making assumptions and decisions can be avoided when looking into previous similar situations and scenarios. However, the investment decisions of today consider only the required further investment and effects in future. What is already paid is "sunk" cost.

If challenged with deciding to discontinue a software engineering project, look into what is still required for completion and compare this with the returns from sales once the project is finished. Compare this project with other projects in the software portfolio and evaluate their individual costs and benefits as of today to see which is underperforming. Future investment and returns are always discounted into "present value" to allow for comparison from today's perspective.

2.3.2 Technology Management

How can software measurements be effectively used for technology management? We will apply the above-mentioned steps of extraction, evaluation and execution to the decision-making process of introducing new or even disruptive technologies.

First, you need to extract data that describes what the technology means for you and your business. Running with each new technology because of its hype is certainly not the answer. And it is expensive too. The major question to ask in this first step is, what are the new or disruptive technologies. Many enterprises or R&D departments have only vague answers. A good indicator to identify such "hot" technologies is to simply check what provides the most confrontations and disputes inside the company. Do the software people dispute on a technology with marketing? Do customers challenge the sales or technology people with proposals that were not yet included in the roadmap?

The second step naturally is the evaluation. What are the impacts of this specific technology? Are there alternative technologies to which it should be compared?

Similar to the case with the product portfolio, you also need to picture the products and markets that are addressed in a spectrum of different technologies. Questions are rarely as simple as asking whether one would introduce Java or a specific framework or tool, and they should not be asked in such isolated mode. It is better to identify what the technologies mean in a specific environment and in the context of other technologies. At what speed do they evolve? How much energy do other companies or leading players put into it?

For instance, open source development and especially Linux or Eclipse became a major effort with companies like Sun and IBM engaging hundreds of people in it, and educating their sales forces what that means for the future of software engineering. For what will these technologies substitute? Are there examples from one's own past or that are externally available that indicate how a similar technology change came up and evolved?

Finally, the third step is to decide on the technologies. What will be the answer to this new technology? One possible answer, which might be the safe side regarding risk and cost, is to decide firmly to wait for one period or one year. This is legitimate to avoid being consumed by continuous fads. Or one might decide for a very small and limited pilot project to see how a dedicated service might relate to the application development.

Take as an example Web services, which initially were exaggerated. However, after a two-year period with shaping of major standardization bodies and industrial groups, it re-emerged as a more solid technology, with early applications being available for trial and for linking to one's own infrastructure. Which market or customer or user needs the technology first? How much would they be willing to pay for it? How is a new feature positioned? Which investments are devoted to it? Which type of pilots or experiments? When do you expect what concrete results or further decision points?

We have summarized in Fig. 2.10 how different points within the life-cycle trajectory of a technology would yield different evaluations and decisions. We distinguish the typical four distinct phases that characterize the technology life cycle [Bowe95]. For each of these phases we apply a different strategy.

Starting from the experimental or "hype" phase (point 1), the technology can evolve on different tracks. If it appears with many open questions or unresolved constraints (e.g., Web services; points 1 and 2), one should take enough time to not bet on the wrong horse. This is at times difficult, because the engineers might be very excited. However, one can spend the engineering money only once, and do not want to engage into the war of the big companies who only drive their proprietary formats. If the technology change and its impact are very fast and determined (e.g. embedded mobile applications), one should find the own position before the market and the customers conclude that the company is not in this field (points 2 and 3).

Often such legacy behavior happens to leaders in a technology because all their focus is on improving the existing technology and fine-tuning its application, rather than on questioning it in favor of newer technology. Finally, each technology will reach the point where retreat is in order (point 4). To miss this exit point is also expensive because one must provide skills and resources for maintenance, thereby taking them from innovations. Product lines that are in such situation have too many old products and lots of branches in their roadmaps. That is how the different techniques of portfolio management will help. An evaluation of where you are with respect to market position, market growth, revenues or age of products gives a good indicator of how much priority to give for a new technology.

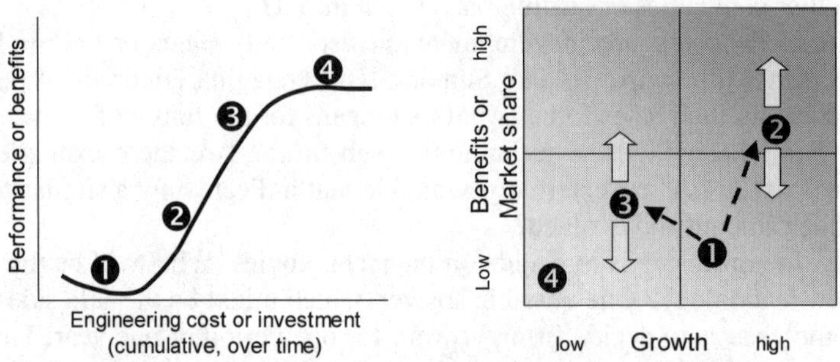

1. experimentation (learning curve, investment, low pay-off => decide next steps)
2. growth (benefits grow fast, market positioning happens => invest if in favor)
3. saturation (technology applied by many players, efficiency improvements => reduce investments depending on market position, get out returns)
4. end of life (technology becomes a legacy => manage maintenance, phase-out)

Fig. 2.10. Portfolio management and technology management

2.3.3 Product and Release Planning

Projects do not run independently; they influence each other in various dimensions. For instance, they share skills from the same resource pool and they compete for the best skills with all other projects. They might build on each other, especially in product-line architectures or in multirelease contracts. They might reuse common components or frameworks, or they simply address the same customers, both internally and externally.

In particular, product lines and multirelease dependencies ask for transparent and consistent roadmap management of the overarching evolution of all products and projects in the enterprise. We can consider this yet another interface between project and business management. We already explained the hierarchical dependencies between portfolio, product line, product release and individual project. A dependable release roadmap and excellent project management are critical success factors for good portfolio management.

Dependable means that agreed-upon milestones, contents or quality targets are maintained as committed. For instance, within a product-line architecture the underlying generic product, platform or components, upon which many customization products build, must be on time and provide the agreed contents. Otherwise there will be numerous ripple effects. Naturally, project management techniques differ between a generic and an application product. While the platform has to build in resource buffers, the application product can easily work with feature prioritization and time boxing.

Organizations on the capability maturity model's (CMM) initial level 1 have rarely a chance to be successful in portfolio management (see also Chap. 10). Most of their projects run in firefighting mode, and predictability is not known. With each project being managed ad-hoc and without learning effects, scalability between projects does not exist. What exists are dependencies of the form that resources are taken away from a project to satisfy more urgent needs in another projects. This, however, is done in a rather chaotic way. Such organizations first need to improve their project management.

The following steps during setting up a release roadmap will help to improve its predictability [Eber03a]:

- Identify similarities and dependencies across markets and technologies.
- Evaluate existing functionality depending on customer value, cost structure (e.g., capital investments, operational cost, recent changes in cost structure, new revenue sources, opportunistic factors), complexity in development and maintenance, extendibility or internal life-cycle cost.
- Describe and maintain a functional (based on contents) roadmap for each of the product lines that is also mapped to the major customers or markets. A commercial off-the-shelf (COTS) requirements management tool will help to maintain different views on the same underlying evolution paths and feature catalogues.
- Describe and follow the own technology roadmap. It should describe within defined and agreed steps what functions should arrive and what their dependencies are. Identify clear evolution tracks within specification, architecture and roadmap documents. Determine dependencies, cost/investment, priorities and major milestones. Try to have a modular architecture, which for allows splitting of features or merging related customer needs.
- Decide on and make explicit within the entire company which products, platforms, features or even markets are active, which are on their phase-out and for which you have effectively stopped support. Agree on communication strategies with marketing and sales so that engineers in a customer meeting would confuse the picture with their own opinions. Implement migration roadmaps that allow the customers to move from one release to the next.
- Introduce a full incremental or iterative approach spanning the product definition and engineering processes. To achieve time-to-profit targets it is key to stay predic**table** and conform to project plans.

2.3.4 Making the Business Case

A business case presents a business idea or proposal to a decision maker. It should essentially prove that the proposal is sufficiently solid and that it fits economically and technically to the company's strategy. It is part of a more general business plan and emphasizes on costs and benefits, financing the endeavor, technical needs, feasibility, market situation and environment and the competition. It is created early in the product life cycle and serves as the major input *before* a decision for investment is taken.

Many projects and products fail simply because the business case was never done or it was not done correctly. The key to a successful business case is that it connects well the value proposition with the technical and marketing concept and with the market evolution and the company's potential. Lacking on one of these four dimensions invalidates the entire business case.

The business case consists of the following elements:

1. summary
2. introduction (motivation of the business proposal, market value, relationship to existing products, solutions or services, own capabilities and capacity)
3. market analysis (market assumptions, industry trends, target market and customers, volume of the target market, competitors, own positioning, evaluation of these assumptions by strengths, weaknesses, opportunities and threats)
4. marketing plan (marketing contents, sales strategies)
5. business calculation (sales forecasts, profit/loss calculation, cash flow, financing the expenses, business risk management, securities, present value of investments, evaluation of assumptions)
6. operations plan (customer interfaces, production planning, supply chain, suppliers, make versus reuse versus buy, platforms and components to be used, service needs, management control, quality objectives and quality management)
7. project and release plan (resources, skills, milestones, dependencies, risk management)
8. organization (type of organization, management structure, reporting lines, communication)
9. attachments with details to above chapters.

A business case has to prove that the proposed concept fits both technically and commercially to the enterprise. It is part of the business plan and is created before the launch of a product development. **Preparing the software business case consists of several steps**:

1. Coin a vision and focus. What is the message you want to get across? What will be different with the proposed product or solution? Use language that is understood by decision-makers and stakeholders, which means being concise and talking about financial and marketing aspects more than technology. Focus on what you are really able to do.
2. Analyze the market environment and commercial situation. How will you sell? How much? To whom? With what effect? For improvement projects identify the symptoms of poor practice and what they mean for your company (e.g., cost of non-quality, productivity, cycle time, predictability). Quantify the costs and benefits, the threats and opportunities. For IT projects you should consider that the IT direct cost is only the tip of the iceberg. The true value proposition is in the operational business processes.
3. Plan the proposed project. Show how it will be operationally conducted, with what resources, organization, skills and budgets. What are the risks and their

mitigation? What suppliers? Perform a reality check on your project. Does the combined information make sense? Can you deliver the value proposed in step 1? How will you track the earned value? What metrics and dashboard will be utilized?

How does the business case relates to software measurement and metrics? The business case is quantitative by nature. It builds upon assumptions and propositions, which must be evaluated from different perspectives on the validity, consistency and completeness. This is where software metrics come into the picture. They provide for instance the guidance for performing a feasibility study. They relate expected volume or size of the project to effort and schedule needs and thus indicate whether the proposed plan and delivery dates are viable. Fig. 2.11 shows an example for such a feasibility study. Different project scenarios are portrayed for a given size and productivity. The curves represent respective time and cost for a size and productivity following the Raleigh equation provided in the picture [Putn03]. The example indicates that for a given (estimated) size, the target cost and dates are not feasible. Setting up the project to reach either the schedule or budget limitations is presented by dots 2 and 3, respectively. It is impossible with the given productivity and constraints to achieve both schedule and budget targets. Obviously one solution would be to "improve productivity" (dot number 5). However, this is not something that can be done over night. It would only indicate poor management if such unrealistic assumptions are taken. Only by adjusting project contents, thus reducing size, allows to stay in the allowed targets, while having a feasible project (dot number 4).

Software metrics guide in the risk analysis and later in risk management. They indicate uncertainties and together with software engineering techniques guide the risk mitigation. For instance, knowing that requirements change with 2–3% per month is a starting point for planning releases and incremental deliveries.

2.4 Hints for the Practitioner

Your **indicators** should satisfy some simple criteria:

- **Sustainable**. The metrics must be valid and useful over some period of time. They should be portrayed and compared over time. Often markets show cyclic behaviors, which can only be assessed if the same indicators are followed up for several years.
- **Timely**. The indicators must be available literally on a push-button approach. They must be valid and consistent with each other. If market data is one month old and quality reports arrive only half-yearly, this makes no sense. If cost to complete is derived monthly and you have project reviews on weekly basis, decisions are not consistent.
- **Meaningful**. The indicators should provide exactly the information you ask for. They should be aggregated to the level useful to make decisions. To avoid overloading occasional readers there should be few numbers with concise ex-

planations. Further details should be drilled down from your portals and warehouses.
- **Goal-oriented**. Metrics must be oriented to address concrete objectives. They are only created and reported if there is a specific need and decision you want to take based on these metrics.
- **Balanced**. Look into all directions that are or will be relevant for your business. Most reporting has some blind spots. Often they appear at interfaces between processes, such as cost of an engineering activity or net present value of a platform with its evolution. Knowing about them is a first step to removing them. Starting from goals, it is easy to see why goals and metrics cannot and must not be separated.

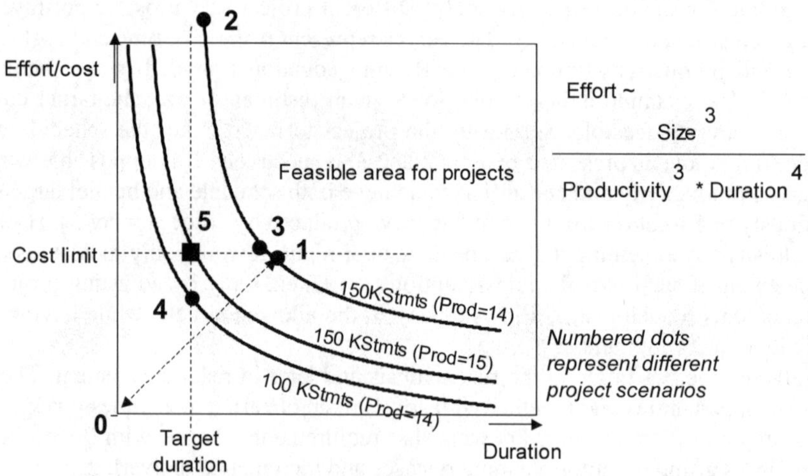

Fig. 2.11. Example for a project feasibility study with different scenarios related to allowed cost and time (duration) limits following the Raleigh relationship [based on Putn03]

Good objectives or goals should be "smart". Smart goals are (and the first letters obviously show why we call them "smart"):
- **s**pecific (or precise)
- **m**easurable (or tangible)
- **a**ccountable (or in line with individual responsibilities)
- **r**ealistic (or achievable)
- **t**imely (or suitable for the current needs)

Here are some practical reporting hints:
- First, summarize in your reports all your results from a business perspective (an "executive summary"). Keep it short and to the point. Indicate conclusions and actions to be taken. Do not talk in this summary about the technology, as everybody trusts your technology competence – and they will probe further anyway once they go to the details.

- Always distill the value proposition to monetary numbers. Your management normally does not like what is not tangible and not traceable. They want to see the impact of a decision in money values.
- Distinguish clearly between capital expenses (e.g., licenses, hardware within your products) and project cost (e.g., persons, infrastructure). Often these means come from different sources or budgets; sometimes they are taxed differently. Certainly they appear in different sections in your profit and loss statement (P&L) and balance sheet.
- Review figures carefully and repeatedly. Many good ideas were killed too early because their presentation was superficial and included obvious errors. A small error in calculating metrics or a wrong underlying assumption will make all your efforts invalid.
- The metrics and numbers will mean different things to different persons. If you provide numbers, ensure that they are accompanied with precise definitions. That is simple with today's online intranet technology, however, equally necessary for your presentations. Have a short definition in small letters on the same sheet, if the numbers are not well known in your company. Frequently presentations are distributed further or even beyond your reach. Often something is copied or sent out of context, and thus having the explanations on one sheet avoids unnecessary questions.
- Use industry standards as far as possible. Today many figures have standards and agreed-upon definitions that can easily be reused [McGa01, Reif02, Kapl93].

There are several techniques around for evaluating health of software engineering projects. We look at both **business analyses** as well as more technical assessments.

- **Break-even-analysis**. When will accumulated costs and benefits or returns match each other? From when onwards will there be positive cash flow?
- **Investment analysis**. Which investment will provide most returns in the short-term? Common techniques include ROI, ROA and ROCE.
- **Value analysis**. Which benefits will occur in the future and what is their net present value compared to outstanding investments? Which of several alternative decisions will generate the most value? This technique is often used to assess the risk level of technology decisions.
- **Sensitiveness**. What are the effects of project- and product-related parameters that are under your control (e.g., resource allocation to projects, technologies to be utilized, content of projects, make versus reuse versus buy decisions for components and platforms)?
- **Trend analysis**. What is the evolution of impacts over time? Are there cyclic effects that with some delay change the entire picture? Portraying current decisions and their future impacts over time is necessary prior to platform or product-line decisions.

2.5 Summary

Introducing a complete and hierarchically consistent measurement program is not easy and often takes several years. It asks for training, communication, shared beliefs and values, and accountable engineering processes. Though there is no immediate need of heavy tools and methods, the effort to continuously manage a complex portfolio requires the intensive and sustainable cooperation of the different stakeholders, such as engineering, product management and marketing.

It is unrealistic to assume that all these methods and approaches would be introduced to the company or department on a "push-button" approach. It is therefore better to introduce the three elements of portfolio management in steps. "First things first" means in this context that portfolio management should be applied first to the top 20% of the projects or products. A good question to ask is, which are the products or projects on which one would bet the future of the company?

Utilize the metrics and evaluation processes first "in vitro". That is, introduce necessary changes stepwise and don't confuse and overload the project managers with too much new reporting and assessments at one time. Many indicators might look interesting, however, maybe just a few standard tracking elements combined with market data will help to get transparency across the portfolio.

The three steps of the measurement process (extract, evaluate, execute) should be introduced in just that order. First, look into the available data and how to achieve or improve visibility. Set up an inventory of all the projects, assets and proposals for capital investment. Add to this list, and following the same structure break down all the current actuals per project or proposal and the respective targets in terms of quality, effort, total cost, deadlines, sales and profit expectations.

Link to the underlying business cases. Introduce simple yet effective project tracking metrics to have an aligned project follow-up. Stop ad hoc project reports where each one has a different layout. This is unnecessary cost to produce and to read.

Start with the major or critical projects to pilot such dashboards and track the metrics versus estimations, expectations and commitments. Better to have fewer metrics and thorough follow-up than huge telephone books without any insight where you are.

Take firm decisions and execute them in the weeks after. Do not delay the cancellation of a project, if there is no longer a belief in its success. Always execute what brings the company closer to its targets, such as maximizing the value of the assets, improving the ROI from all investments, reducing the age of products, decreasing maintenance efforts or improving quality and customer satisfaction. Hold the project managers accountable for achieving their commitments. Hold the product managers accountable to achieving the business case and underlying assumptions. Even if you are not successful in the first attempt, reassess the assumptions of the business case after the project is finished in order to learn from it.

Feedback is the key to benefiting from measurements. Metrics being only collected in so-called data cemeteries are of no use. They result in useless overheads.

If there is one single message from this chapter, than it is to actually **use** metrics. Using metrics means to analyze and evaluate them, to draw conclusions, to base decisions on facts and to communicate the metrics and the consequences resulting from metrics. Pro-active usage of course is better than analyzing after the facts. Good measurement programs result in good estimation and planning. They result in good predictions. And they drive sound decision-making – away from the chaotic fire-fighting behaviors of so many managers.

The described metrics-based management approach asks for a close link from engineering tasks and expenses to business objectives and the overall strategy of the company. Cost, benefits, technologies or capital investments are assessed and decided in combination. The R&D portfolio and investment is part of the overall portfolio and is thus subject to the same rules for evaluation. It is certainly helpful and ensures transparency if the portfolio information is closely linked with the product catalogues and product release information. Do not establish a full new reporting scheme and instead ensure that appropriate security mechanisms and access rights are established to control who gets visibility.

Fig. 2.12 shows in a simple yet effective intranet portal how a drill-down would start from the enterprise level to the individual portfolios (e.g., business areas, product lines) to the level of project management with specific progress tracking and details on content, responsibilities, plans and so on.

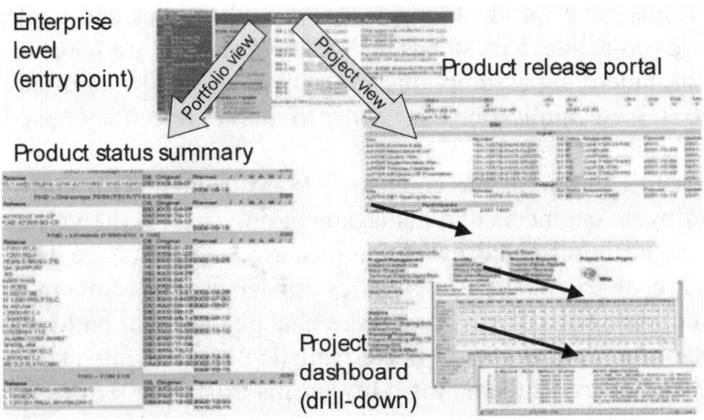

Fig. 2.12. Example of a portfolio portal, which allows zooming from a product summary into single engineering projects and their respective project status information

The numbers, which are utilized, will be questioned from all angles, because so much depends on them. Often (and unfortunately) software management will be reduced to the numbers alone. As this is normal given the relevance of well-founded decisions, this should be accepted and any figures that are provided must be provided with utmost care. **What is released is public.**

Someone who is able to generate numbers on the spot and off the top of his head might be a genius, but they are rare. Normally he has just invented them and has so far been lucky not to get burned. As a consumer do not accept such figures; ask for the context. Do not just quote them, as you will suddenly be the source.

Managing with metrics consists of three individual steps, namely to extract information, to evaluate this information and to execute decisions on the future of the projects. These three steps need to be done continuously. To facilitate smooth and continuous data collection and aggregation without generating huge overheads extraction should be highly automated and accessible from intranet portals (Fig. 2.12). If constraints or assumptions are changing, the evaluation must be changed.

Metrics properly applied first of all help to set objectives and to provide a mechanism to track progress towards these objectives. They will help the company or software department or business manager to obtain visibility and to improve, not only for the CEO or analyst or customer, but also for oneself.

Metrics have a positive business case. The introduction cost (for the first year) can account for 1—2% of the total R&D or IT effort. Later they will account for 0.25—1% of the effort. This effort is primarily due to evaluating the metrics. Collection should be automated. Due to better visibility and more accurate estimations and thus less delays, the immediate savings can be in the range of more than 5% of the R&D or IT spending. Some companies reported up to 10—20% savings due to introducing technical control and a software measurement program [Kütz03].

What value can one achieve for the customers? First, they are offered more choices and better-tailored solutions from the different product lines or business units. Having aligned product life-cycle processes and consistent visibility of status and results of all products inside the portfolio, sales and marketing initiatives are more pro-active. Milestones and gating decisions are feasible and visible. The effects of underlying assumptions are known and can be adjusted to changing business needs. New applications are faster to market once they have been developed before for another market.

What does this mean for the company? **Measurement is a cultural change**. Too often software engineers and management only realize the value of measurement when some unfortunate event has occurred. Projects are failing, product quality is below all expectations, deliveries are delayed, or teams realize that they will never meet the objectives. The culture change means to build upon visibility and accountability. People should make realistic commitments and are later held accountable for achieving them. Visibility means trust. The figures are not "made up" for reports, they are a normal (self-) management tool. Not providing visibility or not delivering committed results is the failure. Deviations that are out of a team's or a project's own control are flagged in due time to allow resolution on the next higher level. Accountability also means to set realistic and measurable objectives. Objectives like "reduce errors" or "improve quality by 50%" are pointless. The objective should be clear and tangible, such as "reduce the amount of late projects by 50% for this year compared to the previous year". These objectives must end up in a manager's key performance indicators. **Goals that are measured will be achieved!**

3 Planning the Measurement Process

In physical science a first essential step in the direction of learning any subject
is to find principles of numerical reckoning and methods for
practicably measuring some quality connected with it.
—Lord Kelvin

3.1 Software Measurement Needs Planning

Usually the software measurement process is embedded in software engineering processes and depends on the environmental characteristics such as

- the *estimation* of the next or future product components, process aspects and resource levels for keeping a successful continuous project in the software development ([Aher03], [Dumk02b] and [NASA95])
- the *analysis* of artifacts, technologies and methods in order to understand the appropriate resources for the software process ([Dumk99b], [Dumk02a] and [Wang00])
- the *structuring* of the software process for planning the next steps including the resource characteristics ([Dumk97], [Dumk03b] and [Kene99])
- the *improvement* of techniques and methodologies for software development as software process improvement ([Aher03], [Dumk01], [Eber03b], [Eman98], [Garm95], [Muta03] and [Warb94])
- the *control* of the software process, including the analysis of the product quality aspects and their relationships ([Dumk01], [Eber03b], [Eber97b], and [Kitc96])

As such software measurement needs planning like any other project activity. Otherwise the risk is high that resources are not available or skills and tools are insufficient.

This chapter considers the aspects if planning a software measurement process, including the different models, approaches and standards. The first part describes the usefulness of current measurement paradigms based on the literature in this area. The discussion of measurement planning is supported through an industrial example of the evaluation of customer satisfaction, which was investigated in a project at the Deutsche Telekom.

At first the analysis of a concrete project needed the identification of the measurement goals, from it derived the measurement aspects and finally the usable measures and evaluation methods. Interviews with project members assisted in that matter. To derive the specific benchmark goals we used *goal-oriented measurement approaches*, which are explained, in the next section.

3.2 Goal-Oriented Approaches

Goal-oriented approaches address special aspects, characteristics or intentions of the software process, product or resources. Typical examples in software engineering are *usability engineering, performance engineering* (Chap. 11) or *security engineering.* Other approaches choose a special aspect, like maintenance costs, developer productivity or error proneness. The general characteristics of these approaches are to define a strategy for achieving the considered goal(s). In following we describe a general methodology for goal-directed analysis and evaluation as a very practical method.

3.2.1 The GQM Methodology

Goal-Question-Metric (GQM) is a concept of how to proceed during measurement and was created by Basili and Weiss 1984. Measurement is necessary to control the software development process and the software product. The basic idea of GQM is to derive software measures from measurement questions and goals. The GQM method was originated by Basili and Weis as a result of both practical experience and academic research. By now, GQM has proven its quality in the problems of metrics selection and implementation (see especially [VanS00]). Measurement's main task is making understanding of the specific process or product easier for the user. Successful improvement of software development is impossible without knowing what your improvement goals are and how they relate to your business goals. The most difficult question is how to define particular improvement goals in terms of business goals or with respect to particular project needs. Measurement provides the means to identify improvement goals. By applying measurement to a specific part of the process, problems within the process can be identified for which improvement goals can be defined. Currently, software process improvement (SPI) is one of the most used goal. Several improvement models, methods and techniques are available, divided into two major classes.

- *Top-down approaches*, which are based on assessment and benchmarking. For example: the Capability Maturity Model (CMM), the CMM Integrated (CMMI), the Software Process Improvement and Capability detErmination (SPICE), BOOTSTRAP (see [Aher03], [Eman98], [Muta03] and the detailed descriptions in Chaps. 5, 9 and 10),
- *Bottom-up approaches*, mainly apply measurement as their basic guide for improvement; an example of this type of approach is GQM.

It is possible, and often very useful, to combine two approaches, for example, GQM with CMM or CMMI. For simplicity we will stick here to the term CMM (capability maturity model), though recognizing that integrated CMM, CMMI, will replace the CMM over the next years. In this context we will not see a difference. Generally speaking, the CMMI gives even more attention to measurement.

A capability maturity model (that is, CMM or CMMI) helps organizations to improve the maturity of their software process and in that way decrease the level of risk in performance. **Process maturity suggests that you can measure only what is visible.** Using both CMM and GQM thus gives a more comprehensive and complete picture of what measures will be the most useful. GQM answers why we measure an attribute, and CMM tells us if we are capable of measuring it in a meaningful way.

Goal-oriented measurement points out that the existence of explicitly stated goals is of the highest importance for improvement programs. GQM presents a systematic approach for integrating goals to models of the software processes, products and quality perspectives of interest, based upon the specific needs of the project and the organization. In order to improve a process you have to define measurement goals, which will be, after applying the GQM method, refined into questions and then into metrics that will supply all the necessary information for answering those questions. The GQM method provides a measurement plan that deals with the particular set of problems and the set of rules for interpretation of the obtained data. The interpretation answers whether the project goals were attained. The GQM approach provides a framework involving three steps [VanS00]:

1. Set concrete goals for your change, performance improvement, project behaviors, or visibility (e.g., to improve customer satisfaction or productivity).
2. Ask questions how goals would be achieved (e.g., specific changes), or what effect you would see when the goals are achieved (e.g., concrete operational results).
3. Determine metrics that show that goals are achieved (e.g., defects after handover, effort for a standardized maintenance requirement).

Fig. 3.1 shows the different aspects and intentions used in the application during the three steps of the GQM approach.

The GQM methodology contains four phases, which we explain in following:

- The *planning phase*, during which the project for measurement application is selected, defined, characterized and planned, resulting in a project plan.
- The *definition phase*, during which the measurement program is defined (goal, questions, metrics and hypotheses are defined) and documented.
- The *data collection phase*, during which the actual data collection takes place, resulting in collected data.
- The *interpretation phase*, during which the collected data is processed with respect to the defined metrics into measurement results, which provide answers to the defined questions, after which goal attainment can be evaluated.

Fig. 3.2 shows the topology of the GQM components considering the intentions of the ISO 15939 standard.

In Table 3.1 we show an example of a GQM hierarchy adapted from [Fent97] in his original self-documented manner. Another example is discussed in Chap. 2. Achieving higher granularity within the GQM approach is defined in the CAME approach discussed in the next section.

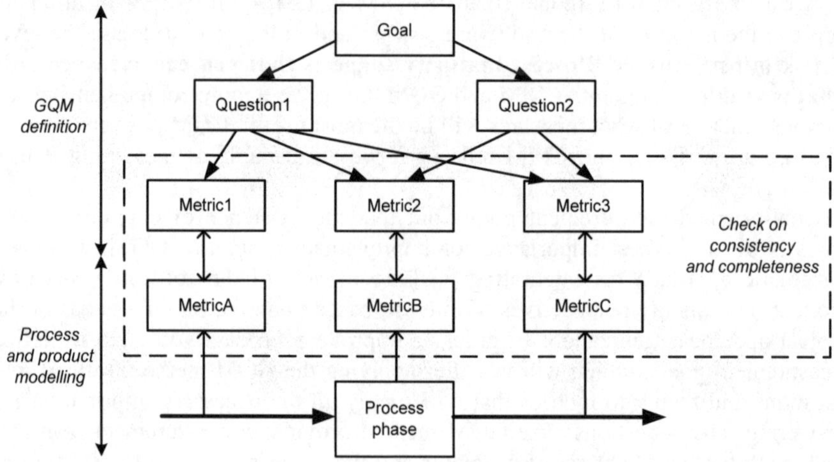

Fig. 3.1. The GQM approach

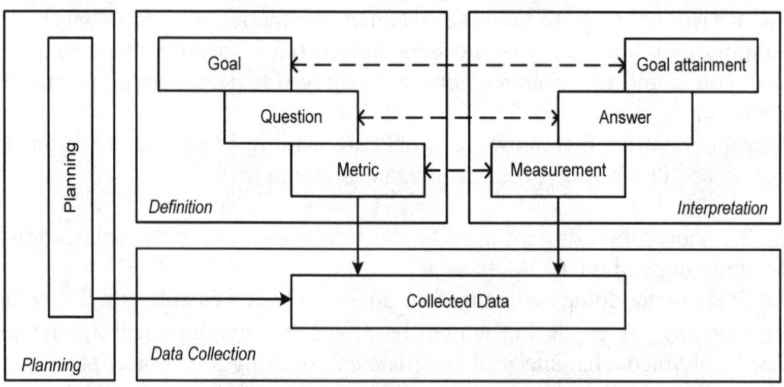

Fig. 3.2. The GQM methodology

3.2.2 The CAME Approach

The following approach was developed in an academic environment but was applied to different industrial measurement projects like software reuse (Deutsche

Telekom), object-oriented development (Alcatel), evaluations of customer satisfaction (Deutsche Telekom) and embedded system development (Siemens AG). We will discuss this approach to demonstrate the detailed aspects of the software measurement planning process. We assign the acronym CAME three meanings to meet the requirements of software measurement. The CAME aspects are defined in a layer model, which is described in Fig. 3.3

Table 3.1. GQM example

Goal	Questions	Metrics
Plan	How much does the inspection process cost?	Average effort per KLOC Percentage of the re-inspections
	How much calendar time does the inspection process take?	Average effort per KLOC Total KLOC inspected
Monitor and control	What is the quality of the inspected software?	Average faults detected per KLOC Average inspection rate Average preparation rate
	To what degree did the staff conform to the procedures?	Average inspection rate Average preparation rate
	What is the status of the inspection process?	Average lines of code inspected Total KLOC inspected
Improve	How effective is the inspection process?	Defect removal percentage Average faults detected per KLOC
	What is the productivity of the inspection process?	Average effort per fault detected Average inspection rate Average preparation rate Average lines of code inspected

The **CAME strategy** is addressed in the background of measurement intentions and stands for

- **Community.** the necessity of a group or a team that is tasked with and has the knowledge of software measurement to install software metrics. In general, the members of these groups are organized in metrics communities such as our German Interest Group on Software Metrics (Chap. 16).
- **Acceptance.** the agreement of the (top) management to install a metrics program in the (IT) business area. These aspects are strongly connected with the knowledge about required budgets and personnel resources (Chap. 5).
- **Motivation.** the production of measurement and evaluation results in a first metrics application that demonstrates the convincing benefits of the metrics application. This very important aspect can be achieved by the application of essential results in (world-wide) practice that are easy to understand and that should motivate the management. One of the problems of this aspect is the fact that the management wants to obtain one single (quality) number as a summary of all measured characteristics (Chap. 2).
- **Engagement.** the acceptance of spending effort to implement the software measurement as a permanent metrics system (with continued measurement, different statistical analysis, metrics set updates, etc.). This aspect also includes

the requirement to dedicate personnel resources such as measurement teams, etc.

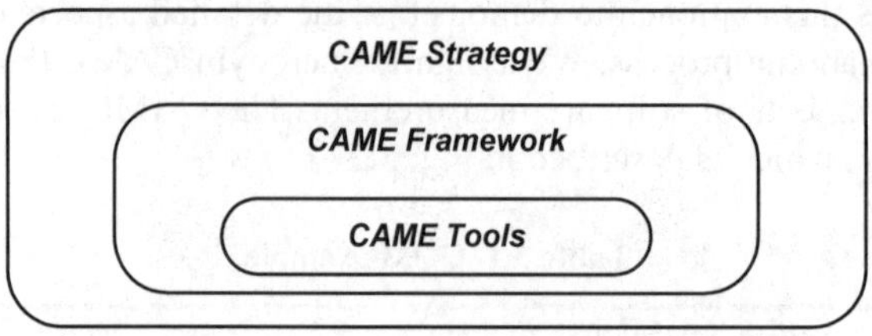

Fig. 3.3. The CAME approach

The **CAME framework** itself consists of the following four phases ([Fent97], [McGa01] and [Zuse97]):

- **Choice.** the selection of metrics based on a special or general measurement view on the kind of measurement and the related measurement goals (as a *set of metrics*) based on goal-directed approaches, which we discuss in Chap. 10,
- **Adjustment.** the measurement characteristics of the metrics for the specific application field (as *measurement characteristics of the metrics*) as we describe in Chaps. 5 and 9,
- **Migration.** the installation and integration of the measurement approach in the software development process (as *application of the metrics in a measurement and controlling process*), discussed by examples in Chaps. 8, 10 and 14,
- **Efficiency.** the automation level as construction of a tool-based measurement (as *implementation of the measurement process*) for which we provide examples in Chaps. 4, 6 and 13.

The phases of this framework are explained in the following sections, including the role of the CAME tools. As an example, we use the experiences in a project with Deutsche Telekom for the evaluation of customer satisfaction relating to Telekom software products and processes [Dumk00a].

3.3 Measurement Choice

Goal-oriented measurement starts with the question "What do we want to achieve?" However, practically building a measurement system involves the following two additional questions "What is necessary to measure?" and "What is feasible to measure?" Obviously, we only want to measure what is necessary. But, in most software engineering areas, this aspect is unknown (especially for modern software development paradigms or methodologies).

In order to stick to the traditional form of customer satisfaction evaluation, we implemented the following three methods:

- The *customer satisfaction index* (CSI) by Mellis (see in [Simo98]) as

$$CSI = \sum_{i=1}^{n} (W_i \times Z_i) ,$$

  with W_i as feature weight for feature *i,* and Z_i as satisfaction value for the feature *i*. The CSI considers the weights of the evaluation features. It can serve as a yardstick for the comparison of current with past test results for the same product/project or for the comparison of the examined product/project with others.
- The *weighted total satisfaction* [Scha98] considers likewise the satisfaction and the weights of the evaluation features:

$$Z_{ges} = \sum_{k=1}^{22} \Big(\sum_{i=1}^{n} (EZ_{ik} - (|EZ_{ik} - W_{ik}|/ 7)) / n \Big) / 22$$

  with EZ_{ik} as satisfaction of customer *i* with feature *k,* and W_{ik} as the weighting of feature *k* by the customer *i*.
- The *customer satisfaction index* by Simon [Simo98] is given as

$$CSI = 1/n \ \sum_{i=1}^{n} Z_i$$

  with Z_i as satisfaction value for feature *i*.

For the measurement of the customer satisfaction, we have chosen or defined as a first approximation *one metric* for *one empirical criterion.* Table 3.2 includes a general description of this kind of mapping.

The investigations of the mapping between satisfaction aspects and metrics are denoted by *adjustment* of the metrics values related to different ordinal values of the traditional customer satisfaction evaluation. Therefore, we have defined a set of aspects for the traditional empirical evaluation. These criteria and the optional software metrics for mapping are shown in Fig. 3.4 (based on [Dumk99a]).

On the other hand, it is necessary to map the possible metrics values to the ordinal scale of the empirical criterion. We have chosen a unified ordinal scale for the empirical criterion from *1 (worst)* to *5 (best)* of the customer satisfaction level (CS level). This aspect is at most indeterminate in our approach. Hence, its tool support requires high flexibility for the adjustment or tuning of the measurement process of the customer satisfaction determination. Based on this first step of mapping software metrics to the empirical aspects of customer satisfaction, we have defined a default mapping table in order to determine the customer satisfaction based on the different intervals of the metrics values.

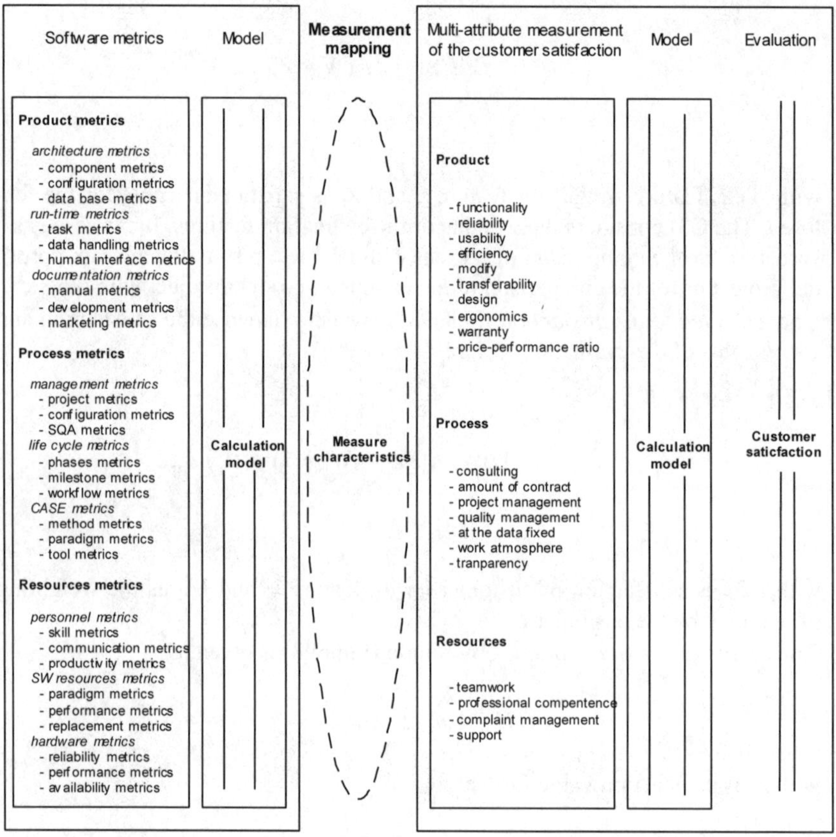

Fig. 3.4. The empirical criteria and the possible metrics for mapping

3.4 Measurement Adjustment

The adjustment is related to the experience (expressed in values) of the measured attributes for the evaluation. The adjustment includes the metrics validation and the determination of the metrics algorithm based on the *measurement theory* ([Fent97] and [Zuse97]).

The steps in the measurement adjustment are

- the determination of the *scale type* and (if possible) the *unit*
- the determination of the favorable values (as *thresholds*) for the evaluation of the measurement component, e.g., by discussion in the development or quality team, analyzing the examples in the literature, using of the thresholds of the metrics tools, considering the results of appropriate case studies

- the *tuning* of the thresholds (see [Endr03] and [Wohl00]) as approximation during the software development from other project components, the application of a metrics tool for a chosen software product that was classified as a good
- the *calibration* of the scale (as transformation of the numerical scale part to the empirical part) depends on the improvement of the knowledge in the problem domain. This step can require some kinds of experimentation (see [Erdo02], [Juri01a] and [Sing99]).

In our example of the evaluation of customer satisfaction we can establish the following scale types:

- **Nominal scale**. ISO 9000 certification
- **Ordinal scale**. CMMI evaluation, programmer experience, etc.
- **Ratio scale**. the mean time (*MT*) metrics above and some of the time related estimations.

The adjustment must be based on the experience in the given IT area and should improve during the evaluations of the customer satisfaction.

3.5 Measurement Migration

This step describes the installation of the mentioned measurement process. An example of this process integration is shown in Fig. 3.5. COSAM stands for *customer satisfaction measurement* and represents the distributed architecture for this approach. The main migration steps based on the COSAM approach are

- **Configuration**. The installation of the different components of the COSAM tool by choosing one the evaluation version shown in Fig. 3.5.
- **Adjustment**. The mapping of different metrics values to the appropriate level of customer satisfaction (CS) based on experiences and feedback received.
- **Experiences**. The given knowledge about the typical thresholds of the metrics values in the considered IT area.

The process of measurement and evaluation itself were supported by the following COSAM components or processes:

- **Customer survey.** The definition of the weights of every customer satisfaction criteria by the customer himself.
- **Evaluation**. The selection of the kind of execution the customer satisfaction through one of the given CS indexes.
- **Acquisition values of metrics.** In the case of metric-based CS evaluation, the project manager should record the given metrics values as shown in Fig. 3.5.

Table 3.2. Mapping of metrics to the empirical criteria

Empirical Criterion	Appropriate Software Metric or Measure	Examples of Adjustment
	Product-based evaluation	
Functionality	Traceability measure as relation between specified requirements and the given requirements in the problem definition	≤60%: 1; >60–70%:2; >70–80%: 3; >80–90%: 4; >90–100%: 5
Reliability	Mean Time To Failure (MMTF)	Unit: hours
Usability	Completeness of the documented product components	Percentage
Efficiency	Performance of response time of the considered systems	Unit: second
Modify	"Neighborliness" costs of maintenance	Unit: Euro
Transferability	Portability as relation between the effort of new development and the effort for transformation and adaptation	≤0.33: 1; >0.33–0.4: 2; >0.4–0.55: 3; >0.55–0.75: 4; >0.75: 5
Design	Topology equivalence of the designed screens	Percentage
Ergonomics	The level of the help support as number of online-documented system components	Percentage
Warranty	Guarantee of software components in years	≤0.5: 1; >0.5–1: 2; >1–2: 3; >2–4: 4; >4: 5
Price-performance	Price level of the software related to the current market level	Percentage
	Process-based evaluation	
Consulting	Mean Time To Repair (MTTR)	Unit: hours
Amount of the contract	ISO 9000 assessment/certification	No: 1, 2, 3; yes: 4 and 5
Project management	Capability maturity model evaluation	CMM level = CS level
Quality management	ISO 9000 assessment/certification	No: 1, 2, 3; yes: 4 and 5
Complaint management	Frequency of complaints per week	Unit: weeks
At the date fixed	Average deviation from milestone dates	Unit: days
Support	Availability of service in percent of the used cases	Percentage
Work atmosphere	Environmental factor as relation between working hours without any break to the total working hours on the day	0: 1; >0–0.25: 2; >0.25–0.5: 3; >0.5–0.75:4; >0.75–1: 5
	Resource-based evaluation	
Teamwork	Provision of time as relation between the spent time to the necessary time for communication of every team member	Percentage
Professional competence	Years of experience as level of developer skills	0: 1; >0–1: 2; >1–3: 3; >3–5: 4; >5: 5

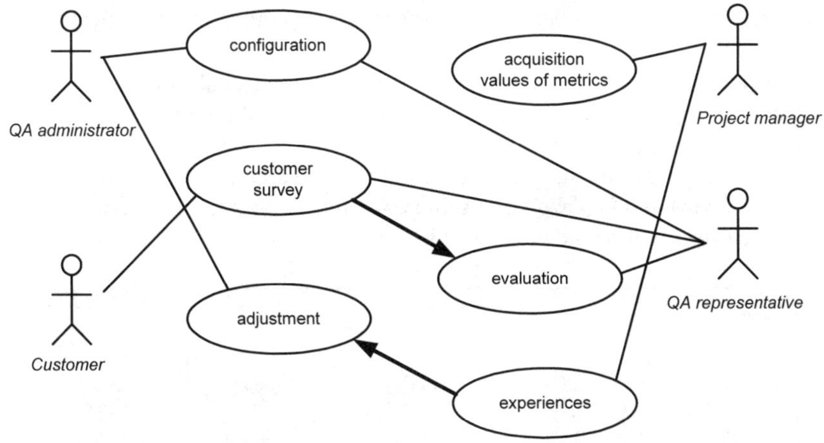

Fig. 3.5. The user profile of the COSAM tool

3.6 Measurement Efficiency

This step includes the *instrumentation* or the *automation* of the measurement process by tools. It requires analyzing the algorithmic character of the software metrics and the possibility of the integration of tool-based "control cycles" in the software development or maintenance process. In most cases, it is necessary to combine different metrics tools and techniques related to the measurement phases. The COSAM tool was implemented as a distributed system in order to perform a Web-based system application.

The COSAM tool enables variations in traditional customer satisfaction evaluation by choosing the empirical aspects and the evaluation method. It also allows a metrics-based evaluation. The measurements are manually collected (Fig. 3.6). Based on this record, we can carry out the customer satisfaction evaluation by using one of the three implemented evaluation methods. The COSAM tool is available for downloading at

http://ivs.cs.uni-magdeburg.de/sw-eng/agruppe/forschung/.

3.7 Hints for the Practitioner

Goal-directed measurement approaches should look to following practical experiences:

- Goal-oriented approaches address special aspects, characteristics or intentions to the software process, product or resources. Typical examples in software engineering are usability engineering, performance engineering or security engineering.

- GQM presents a systematic approach for integrating goals to models of the software processes, products and quality perspectives of interest based upon the specific needs of the project and the organization.
- Since process maturity suggests that you can measure only what is visible, using both CMM and GQM gives a more comprehensive and complete picture of what measures will be the most useful.

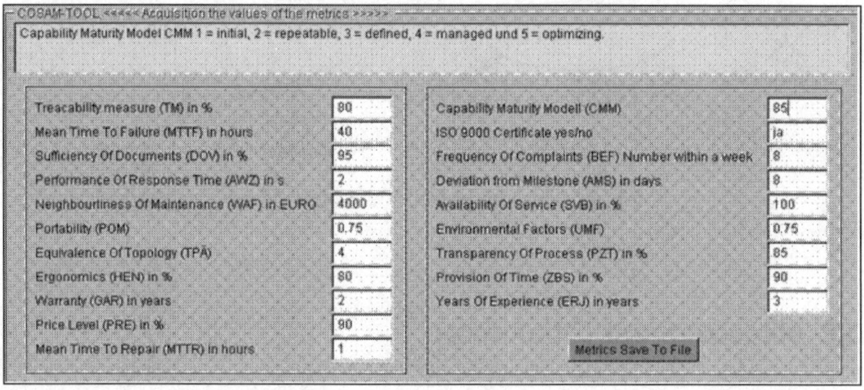

Fig. 3.6. The COSAM screen for metrics value recording

Furthermore, the CAME approach helps to determine your software measurement level itself. Based on the metrics list on the left side in Fig. 3.6, you can see what areas of the software product, process or resources are measured or evaluated by the chosen metrics. But, you can also see, which areas of your software development are *out of control*. On the other hand, you can consider the metrics (scale) level explicitly. The main intentions and experience of the CAME approach for the practitioners are:

- The CAME approach considers both sides **of** software measurement: the detailed measurement process (methods, metrics and scales) and the measurement process environment (strategy, motivation and installation).
- Considering also the both sides of software metrics application, that is, the numerical metrics side and the empirical goal side.
- Investigating the scale characteristics of the metrics or measures carefully in order to obtain the correct answers of the goal-based questions.
- Integrating the different kinds of measurement methods in the process that should be managed.
- Aggregating the different intentions and measurement tools in your measurement concept or approach.
- Constructing a profound architecture of metrics databases or measurement repositories.

3.8 Summary

Goal-oriented approaches are well-established methods of constructive and successful improvement in the IT area and address special aspects, characteristics or intentions of the software process, product or resources. They can be used in different granularities: as a small aspect of product or process improvement or as a complex set of criteria for managing and controlling some of the IT processes themselves.

The CAME framework description showed the step-by-step planning of the installation of a software measurement process in the chosen environment of customer relationships including a prototypical implementation of this approach. The structure of the metrics selection and analysis should be helpful for appropriate adaptation in chosen process areas.

In general, the CAME approach supports the characterization of the metrics or measurement level and helps to understand the necessary steps or activities for improving, managing or controlling the different IT processes. Some levels of the measurement characterization are the following:

- the measurement of only few product artifacts
- the consideration of basic product and process aspects
- the orientation of resource efficiency
- the dominance of the ordinal measurement as a simple kinds of ranking

Most of all, goal-oriented approaches are meaningful way in order to achieve measurable success and quality in the IT area.

4 Performing the Measurement Process

A science is as mature as its measurement tools.
—Louis Pasteur

4.1 Measurement Tools and Software e-Measurement

The efficiency of the software measurement process depends on the level of automation by tools. The importance of metrics tools is as obvious as the tool support in the different disciplines of software engineering. The purpose of determining the performance of the software process is to produce and collect the measurement data supported by so called *metrics tools*. Therefore, in this chapter we describe the current situation in the area of metrics tools and an outlook on future evolution. The first section includes an overview of some metrics tools and the current situation in the area of software e-measurement. Fig. 4.1 gives an overview of software tools, where CASE stands for computer-aided software engineering and CARE means computer-aided reengineering.

We choose the notion of computer assisted software measurement and evaluation (CAME) tools for identifying all the kinds of metrics tools in the software life cycle [Dumk97]. CAME tools are tools for modeling and determining the metrics of software development components referring to the process, the product and the resource. Presently, the CAME tool area also includes the tools for model-based software components analysis, metrics application, presentation of measurement results, statistical analysis and evaluation.

In general, we can establish CAME tools for classification, for component measurement, for process or product measurement and evaluation, as well as for training in software measurement. The application of CAME tools is based on the given measurement framework (see [Dumk96a], [Dumk96b], [Dumk96c], [Oman97], [Zuse97], Chaps. 3 and 6). The integration of CAME tools in the tool-based environments in the software engineering cycle is given in Fig. 4.1. On the other hand, CAME tools can be classified according to the degree of integration in software development environments such as integrated forms, external coupling forms and stand-alone metrics tools.

We will describe some classes of CAME tools based on the tool investigations in the Software Measurement Laboratory at the University of Magdeburg (SML@b) during the last ten years.

4.2 Applications and Strategies of Metrics Tools

CAME tools are useful in all areas of software engineering such as software product evaluation, process level determination and the measurement of the quality of the resources. We provide here a list of metrics tools for these different aspects in software development and maintenance (for the detailed description of these tools see [Dumk96a], [Smla03] and http://ivs.cs.uni-magdeburg.de/sw-eng/us/CAME/). Naturally such selection of tools is subjective and non-exhaustive.

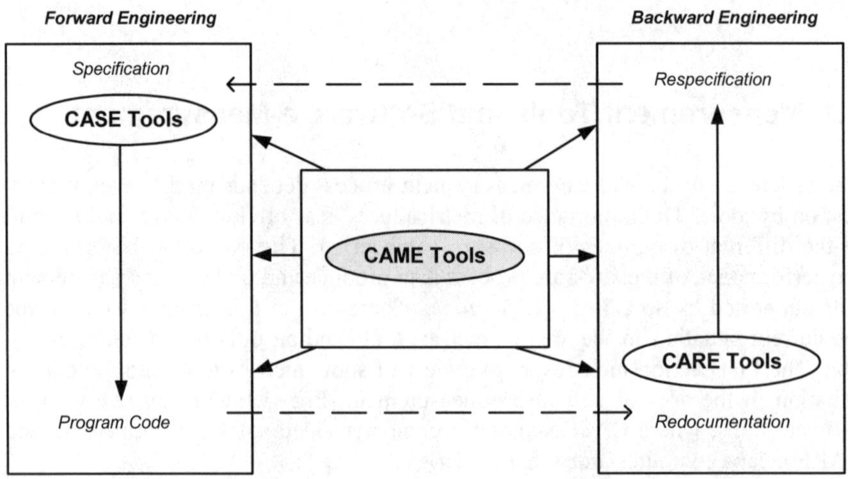

Fig. 4.1. Tool support during software development, maintenance and reengineering

4.2.1 Software process measurement and evaluation

The following CAME tools are used and tested in the SML@b [Smla03]. They are helpful for application during the measurement of the software process phases, components and activities.

- AMI Tool (France). The tool name means the Application of Metrics in Industry. The AMI tool is based on the GQM approach and gives an evaluation based on the "classical" CMM method. The tool is very helpful for generating a GQM-based measurement plan.
- CHECKPOINT (USA). This estimation/feasibility tool uses a lot of experience implicitly. One of the used size measure is function points. A lot of helpful project information is executed and printed based on many input parameters such as product, process and resource characteristics.
- COSTAR (USA). The COSTAR tool supports the software estimation based on the COCOMO II approach. The execution is based on different variants of components and size measures.

- SLIM Palm Tool (University of Magdeburg, Germany). This CAME tool implements the software lifecycle management (SLIM) formula for the Palm computer. It is an example of the appropriateness of handhelds for the application of useful CAME tools.
- SOFT-ORG (Germany). This tool helps to define a general enterprise-based measurement model as the essential basic for a successful metrics application.

Fig. 4.2 shows the layout of the *COSTAR tool,* which supported the cost estimation during the earlier phases of software development based on the COCOMO II approach. Other cost estimation tools are discussed in Chaps. 6, 7, 11, 13, and 14.

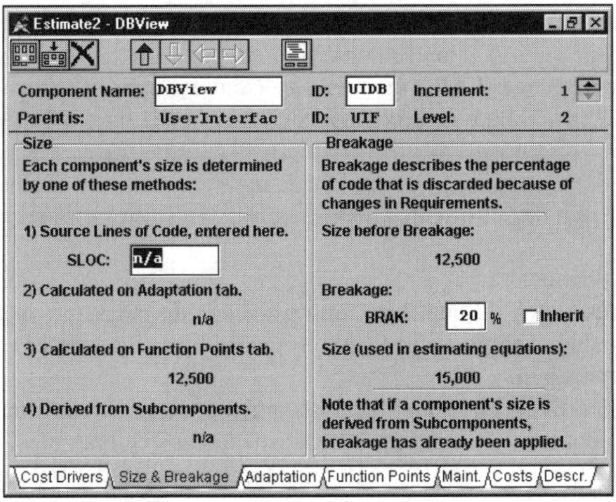

Fig. 4.2. Layout of COSTAR cost estimation based on COCOMO II

4.2.2 Software Product Measurement and Evaluation

In this section we consider the different phases during the software development relating to efficient CAME tool support. We will choose only a few examples to demonstrate the essential aspects.

Requirement analysis and specification:

- RMS (Germany). The reading measuring system (RMS) supports the analysis of the quality of documentation by using some of the text quality and readability metrics.
- Function Point Workbench (Australia). The FPW supports all the steps of the IFPUG 4.x evaluation and can be considered as the main used FP tool with a large background of measurement experience.

- SOFT-CALC (Germany). This CAME tool supports the cost estimation for different point-based approaches such as function points, data points and object points. The SOFT-CALC tool is compatible to SOFT-ORG.
- COSMOS (Netherlands). COSMOS stands for cost management with metrics of specification and realizes an evaluation of different programming and formal specification languages such as LOTOS, Z, etc. The tool has a good variance in metrics definition, adjustment and calibration.

Software design:

- MOOD (Portugal). The MOOD concept as metrics for object-oriented design implements an evaluation of object-oriented class libraries based on the well-established object-oriented software metrics.
- Metrics One (USA). This Rational tool supports the measurements of unified modeling language (UML) diagrams by counting a lot of aspects from and between the basic charts and components of an UML-based software specification.
- SmallCritic (Germany). This Smalltalk measurement and evaluation tool supports essential object-oriented metrics during the software development itself.

Program evaluation:

- CodeCheck (USA). CodeCheck implements code measurement based on language parsing. The price for this high flexibility is the greater effort for learning its application.
- QUALMS (UK). This quality analysis and measurement tool supports the code measurement including varieties of statistical data exploration.
- DATRIX (Canada). This CAME tool implements code measurement for C, C++, etc. and is based on a large experience in practice.
- LOGISCOPE (USA). LOGISCOPE supports code measurement including quality evaluation of large-scale software. Against to the static metrics-based evaluation, this tool supports the dynamic testing including the essential coverage metrics.
- PC-METRIC (USA). This small tool is very helpful for code measurement based on the Halstead and McCabe measures and has a high stability in the measurement results.
- PMT (University of Magdeburg, Germany). (This Prolog measurement tool supports the software measurement of Prolog programs by using new kinds of descriptive metrics.
- MJAVA (University of Magdeburg, Germany). This CAME tool implements the object-oriented measurement of Java-based metrics including Chidamber/Kemerer metrics.

Fig. 4.3 shows one of the methods of code evaluation by the *LOGISCOPE tool* using the Kiviat diagram. This tool includes variants of code visualization (flow graph, call graph, etc.), Further on LOGISCOPE evaluates software systems based on a complex quality model, which must be carefully considered in order to keep the correct or appropriate intentions of the tool customer.

Now, we continue the list of CAME tools that are available and useful in the different phases of the software development process (for more details see Chap. 6).

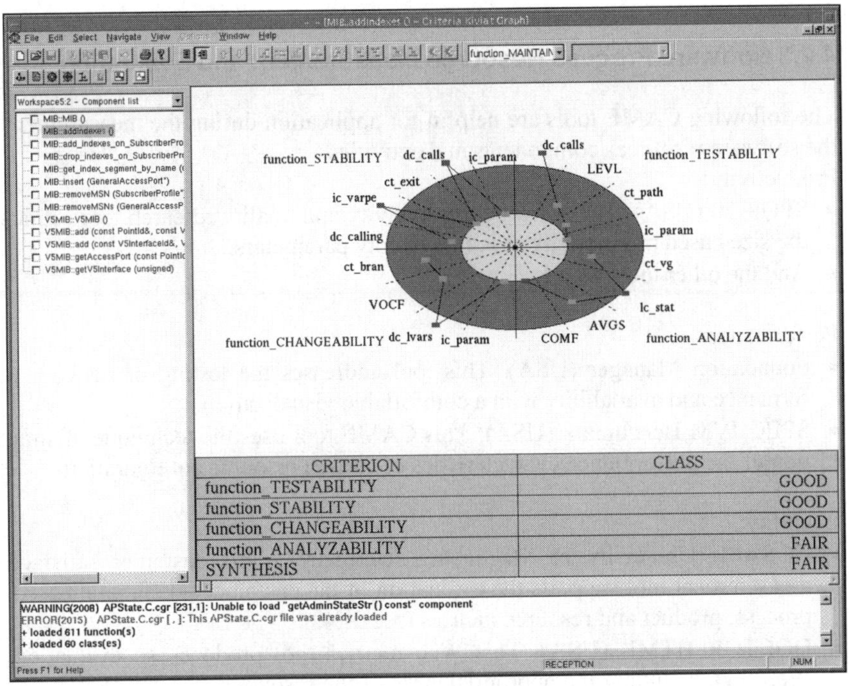

Fig. 4.3. Code evaluation by the LOGISCOPE metrics tool

Software testing:

- LDRA (UK). This testbed includes a complex test environment applicable for different programming languages and supports the user by flexible program visualization.
- STW-METRIC (USA). The software test workbench implements a concept of statistical analysis and test support and is a component of general software analyzing and evaluation system.

Software Maintenance:

- Smalltalk Measure (University of Magdeburg, Germany). This Smalltalk extension by code measurements executes the size and complexity metrics for every class, application or system level in the Smalltalk system itself.

- COMET (University of Magdeburg, Germany). The CORBA measurement tool supports the measurement of object-oriented Java applications including the CORBA components.
- Measurement Aglets (University of Magdeburg, Germany). This set of measurement agents supports the measurement of distributed Java code by Java agents themselves as aglets.

4.2.3 Software Process Resource Measurement and Evaluation

The following CAME tools are helpful for application during the measurement of the software resources components and activities.
Productivity:

- SPQR/20 (USA). The software productivity and quality research tool estimates the size based productivity based on twenty parameters.
- And the other tools above

Performance:

- Foundation Manager (USA). This tool addresses the testing of network performance and availability with a comfortable visualization.
- SPEC JVM Benchmark (USA). This CAME tool uses the technique of simulation of the performance characteristics of chosen resource configurations.

Usability:

- COSAM (University of Magdeburg, Germany). This customer satisfaction measurement tool supports the evaluation of the customer satisfaction based on process, product and resource metrics (see 3.3).
- DOCTOR HTML (USA). This Web metrics tool produces an evaluation of Web sites including the appropriateness of the resources like the Web browser acceptability.

4.2.4 Software Measurement Presentation and Statistical Analysis

In order to analyze and evaluate the software measurement results, the following CAME tools are helpful for application during these activities.

- Excel (USA) and other similar spreadsheet programs (e.g., from StarOffice or OpenOffice). This well-established spreadsheet tool can be used for data presentations and analysis. Other common office spreadsheet tools work equally well.
- SPSS (USA). This statistical package for the social science is a data exploration tool including the essential statistical methods and should be used for careful data analysis and explorations.

4.2.5 Software Measurement Training

The following CAME tools are helpful for learning und understanding the phases, components and activities of software measurement including their theoretical background.

- METKIT (UK). The metrics tool kit represents a European initiative for measurement education and training. The most components are tutorials for learning the software measurement theory and practice.
- ZD-MIS (Germany). This Zuse Drabe measurement information system is addressed to the metrics education based on the measurement theory including more the 1500 analyzed software metrics and references.

The following Fig. 4.4 shows the layout of the *Zuse Drabe MIS tool,* which is very helpful for learning the basic characteristics of metrics aspects, scales and metrics validity [Zuse97].

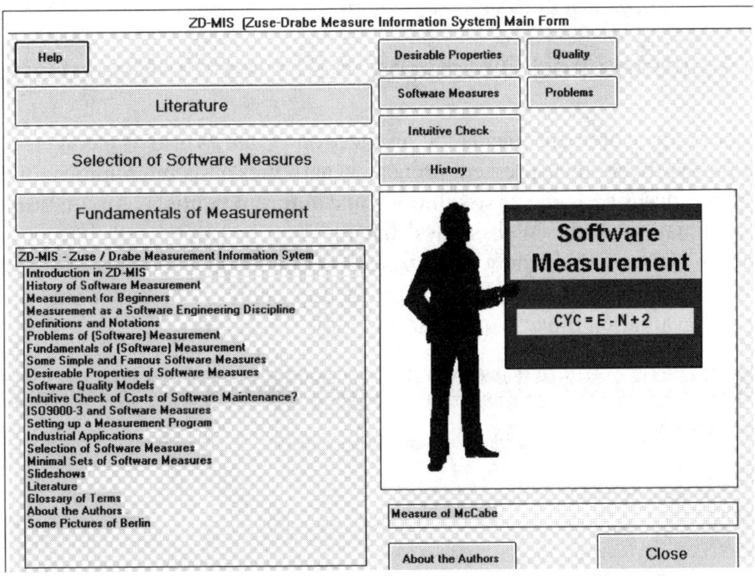

Fig. 4.4. Layout of the Zuse Drabe measurement information system

The tools of the University of Magdeburg can be downloaded at: http://ivs.cs.uni-magdeburg.de/sw-eng/agruppe/forschung/.

The CAME tools should be embedded in a software measurement framework that includes the software process characteristics and their assessment and control. In order to use CAME tools efficiently, some rules should be kept in mind that we define in the following manner. The present CAME tools are not a suitable means of complex software evaluation. They are mostly based on existing assessment methodologies such as the Function Point method. The applied metrics must be algorithmic. The selection of a software measurement tool should be influenced by the following considerations:

- The tool should be designed specifically for the respective software/hardware platform.
- The philosophy of the CAME tool should be applied carefully. The tool-specific conception of modeling, presentation and metrics evaluation should not be violated.
- Both hardware and software platforms are subject to a highly dynamic development process.

Specific parameters of the software development environment should be known to ensure correct and complete input information for the CAME tool. A profound analysis of the empirical aspects such as effort and costs is an imperative precondition for the proper use of any selected CAME tool (for the *right use* of the *right metrics tool*).

4.3 Solutions and Directions in Software e-Measurement

Software e-measurement means the application of the World Wide Web in order to support software measurement processes, activities and communities. In the following we describe some first solutions and future potentials. An analysis of the current situation in the Web shows that in some research areas like physics or chemistry we can find many Web-based measurement examples and activities. Fig. 4.5 includes such a service, where the user could participate at the measurement and evaluation process of e-learning tools [Emea03].

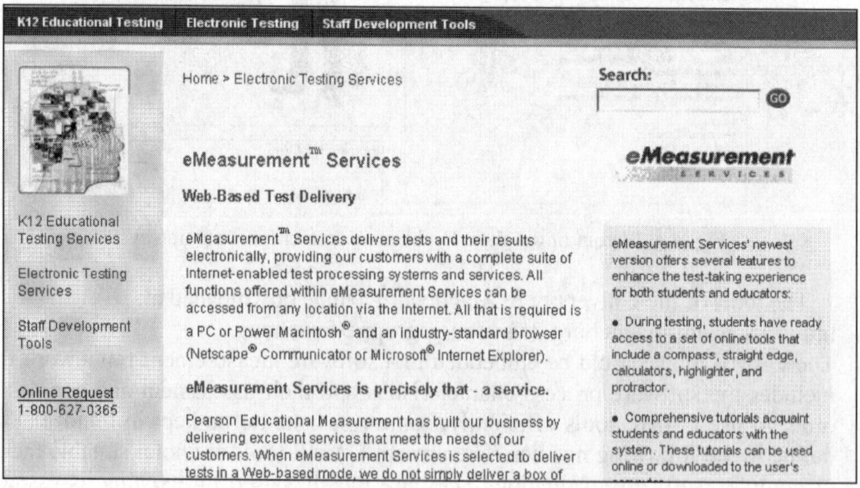

Fig. 4.5. Example of an e-measurement service

The current approaches in the area of the e-measurement could be classified in the following manner:

1. The use of the World Wide Web for the *presentation and exploration of any measurement data,* such as in biology, in physics, in chemistry, in finance, etc. ([NIST03])
2. The *measurement of the Web itself* considering the frequency of use, the usability, the web site quality and complexity of the Web application (e. g. for the notion "Web measurement" the Web search tools show more than two million links) ([Econ03], [Mend02], [Webm03b])
3. The application of the Web for every kind of intention and activity for the measurement and evaluation of software systems in the sense of *software e-measurement.*

In order to consider the third point we will describe the essential Web technologies. The kinds and different approaches of Web technologies are very broad and do not permit a summary. But, we will look to the appropriate technologies for software e-measurement (for details see [Dumk03a], [Muru01] or [Thur02]):

- The basic intention of the Web consists of referencing (multimedia) Web pages by the URI (Unified Resource Identifier) building a *Web content.* Current Web systems are mostly *document-oriented systems* like information systems and multimedia presentations, etc. So we can implement Web-based presentations as tutorials or information systems based on the Synchronized Multimedia Integration Language (*SMIL*).
- *Dynamic Web site generation* is a special technique of Web site presentation (using CGI, DOM, DHTML, JavaScript, PHP, etc.). This technology is helpful in order to implement ad hoc information services or different business processes. On the other hand, large *data and knowledge bases* are useful for information resources on different areas of education, business, administration and science (as technology see *JDBC, ADO, MySQL, XML* or *XSLT*).
- The *Semantic Web* combines the Web documents in a logical manner so that really knowledge management is possible (with the methodologies of data mining, text mining and *Web mining*). Key technologies in this area are *RDF, DAML, OIL* or *WebIN.*
- A special kind of Web applications is *Web services* supported by *ASP, JSP, JMS, WSDL, SOAP, UDDI, Sun ONE,* etc. Based on a simple unified implementation technology, Web services are very helpful for customers (see *BPEL* and *ebXML*). The information and the user context for these services are founded in existing Web portals in different networks, infrastructures and service providers.
- Further technologies support the *mobility,* like *WML, WIDL, MIDlets, GSM* and *UMTS.* Methodologies on this area are the general availability (as *ubiquitous computing*) or the more widespread distribution of software applications (as *pervasive computing*).
- The flexibility and the usability of Web systems were improved by the application of software agents and their technologies (see, for example, *Aglets, JATlite,*

Grasshopper, ACML, JavaSpace or *JDMK*). *Web agents* implement many operational features that run in the "background" of Web applications or that support Web analysis and controlling.
- Last but not least, currently *operational Web systems* are implemented more and more, including different functionalities for measurement, problem identification and controlling devices or machines. Technologies for implementing such operational features are *Jini, MUML,* etc.

The use of software measurement can range from a simple measurement of a situation to supporting the quality assurance to full process control and improvement. Fig. 4.6 shows some different dimensions for the levels of software e-measurement.

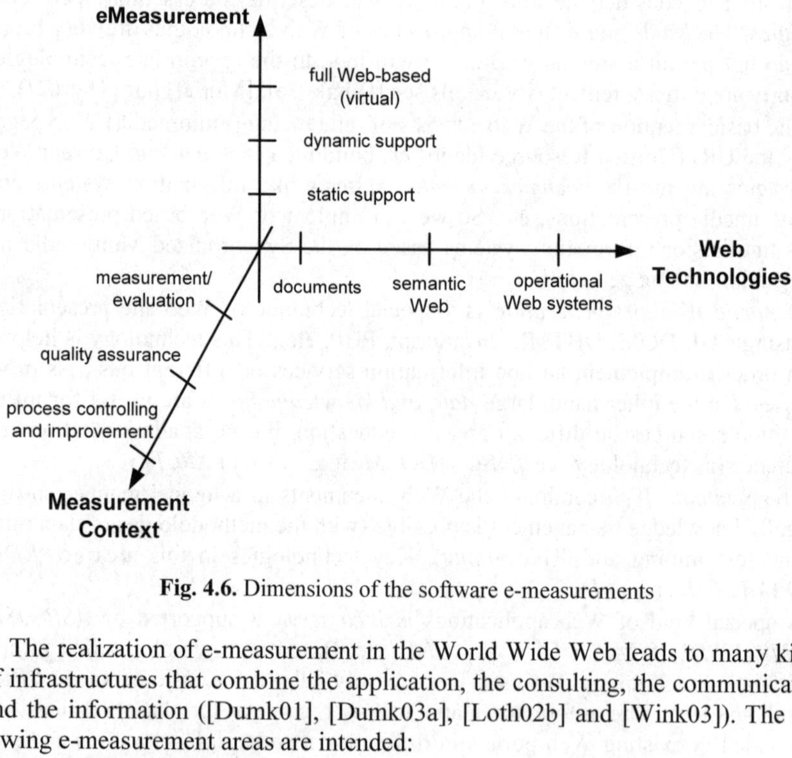

Fig. 4.6. Dimensions of the software e-measurements

The realization of e-measurement in the World Wide Web leads to many kinds of infrastructures that combine the application, the consulting, the communication and the information ([Dumk01], [Dumk03a], [Loth02b] and [Wink03]). The following e-measurement areas are intended:
- The application of software measurement in the IT area does not have an appropriate implementation in many companies. Therefore, the creation and the hosting of *e-measurement communities* should be helpful in order to improve this current situation.
- Services or measurement realization and the presentation of the measurement results are meaningful supports and could be provided by special companies on

the Web. Further, the collaboration on the Web between companies could produce some new kinds or levels of *e-measurement services*.

- Based on the incremental Web use and the technologies of mobility, software quality assurance can be supported by *e-quality services*. This means that the software quality process would be divided in subprocesses and subcomponents that are available in the Web.
- In order to support the implementation of measurement processes, *e-measurement consulting* could be helpful. These kinds of services include consulting during the measurement planning, the measurement performance and the measurement exploration processes.
- Especially, the comparison of measurement results between companies or the discussion about measurement results could be supported by some kinds of *e-experience* and/or *e-repositories* in the World Wide Web.
- Fundamental knowledge about software measurement is an essential part of a successful software measurement process. Hence, some kinds of *measurement e-learning* would be helpful managing these tasks.
- Finally, services for certifying the quality or performance of IT areas that is present in the Web leads to *e-certification* in the Web.

In the following, we will discuss some existing initiatives or services on the Web that considers the new kinds of e-measurement intentions.

e-Communities for software measurement. Let us briefly discuss some examples to show how communities are working. A more comprehensive summary of metrics communities is provided in Chap. 16. The ISERN (International software engineering research network) is an example of a measurement community [Endr03]. This research network includes some of the leading companies or research centers in the area of empirical software engineering. Many initiatives and experiments were realized in this community. The International Network of Metrics Associations (MAIN) is the European community for software metrics, and DASMA is the German partner in this area (see especially Chap. 16). The SML@b is one of the academic research centers [Smla03]. The information, conference planning and motivation are essential tasks realized in these communities.

e-Experience and e-repositories. These kinds of measurement services are based on realized measurements and help the user for decision making in their IT area. The SML@b includes a small set of general experiment descriptions that are helpful for analogous use in one's own IT environment. The service of the Software Engineering Institute *(SEI)* at Carnegie Mellon University is helpful for structuring the measurement approach and choosing the appropriate software metrics. Fig. 4.7 shows the Web sites of these experience resources.

Measurement e-learning. Another essential aspect concerns the support of e-learning in the area of software measurement. Most of these current solutions include support for the organization of courses (participation and examination). Only a few real e-learning solutions are known currently. So, the course in Software Engineering at the University of Magdeburg was supported, for example, by training implemented as Java applets (http://se.cs.uni-magdeburg.de/). Other examples are given in the virtual SML@b [Smla03]. Fig. 4.8 shows a tutorial for learning the GQM method (http://ivs.cs.uni-magdeburg.de/sw-eng/us/java/GQM/).

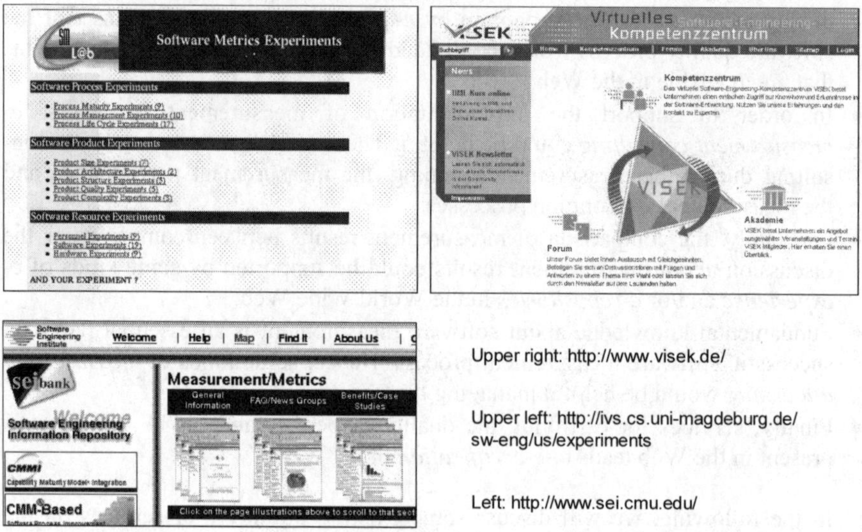

Fig. 4.7. Examples of e-experience and e-repository

Fig. 4.8. Example of measurement e-learning in the SML@b

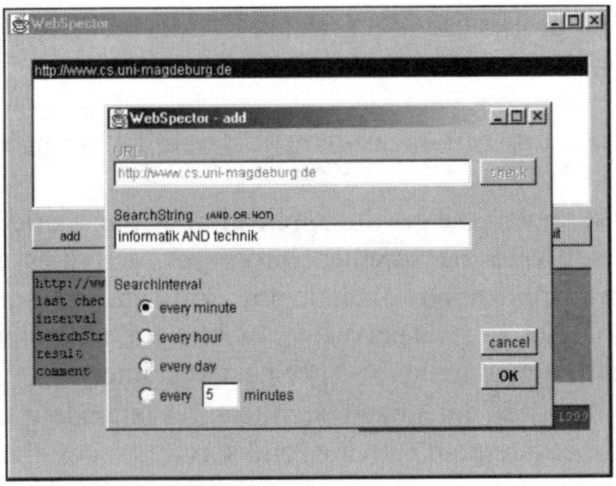

Fig. 4.9. Web site measurement by WebSpector

e-Measurement services. Finally, Web services themselves could be very helpful for supporting the software measurement areas and processes. Some of these current solutions are

- The service of downloadable metrics tools, e. g. at the NASA/Goddard Software Engineering Laboratory (SEL) in Maryland using WebME [Webm03a]
- The tool-based service of Web analysis and evaluation, e.g. with the WebSpector, which allows Web site analysis for chosen frequencies. Fig. 4.9 shows the layout of this metrics tool [Loth03b].

4.4 Hints for the Practitioner

Metrics tool application should be guided by the following reasoning and goals:

- The efficiency of the software measurement process depends on the level of automation of the tools. That means you should try to achieve a complete tool-basic solution for your measurement process. But, you must consider the different methodological and platform-related requirements of these CAME tools carefully.
- Metrics tools should cover the whole software measurement process, starting with establishing measurement, and continuing by planning, performing the measurement and exploring the results for process, product and resource evaluation. This aspects help you for embedding the measurement in the software development environments for assessing, improving and controlling the origin IT processes.
- The philosophy of the metrics or CAME tool should be applied in the proper order. The applied CAME tools should be embedded compatible in a software measurement framework
- Specific parameters of the software development environment should be known to ensure correct and complete input information for the CAME tool. A profound analysis of the empirical aspects such as effort and costs is an imperative

precondition for a proper use of a selected CAME tool *(for the right use of the right metric tool).*

The use of the features of e-measurement should be arranged in the following manner:

- Software e-measurement means the application of the World Wide Web in order to support software measurement processes, activities and communities. Therefore, future applications include the software measurement combined with new technologies such as pervasive, mobile and ubiquitous computing. Inform you about the actual trends and perspectives timely.
- e-Measurement leads to integrated architectures including e-learning, the e-community and measurement activities and services themselves. You should be oriented to other partners, companies and coworkers for the conception, installation and using these new kinds of measurement systems based on different roles in the Web.
- e-Measurement implies a great deal of potential for initiatives and successful cooperation in the area of software measurement. Are motivated and interested for participation at this future.

4.5 Summary

Performing the measurement process includes using effective measurement tools. The efficiency of the software measurement process depends on the level of automation by tools. This chapter has given a short description about these CAME tools.

We primarily addressed new technologies and concepts for measurement tools based on the World Wide Web. Our overview of e-measurement includes visions and existing solutions and should motivate further activities in this area.

5 Introducing a Measurement Program

The best engineers or scientists don't work for a company,
a university or a laboratory; they really work for themselves.
—Watts S. Humphrey

5.1 Making the Measurement Program Useful

Software metrics can perform four functions (see also Chap. 1). They can help us to understand more about software work products or underlying processes. They can be used to evaluate work products or processes against established standards. Metrics can provide the information necessary to control resources and processes to produce the software. And they can be used to predict attributes of software entities in the future.

To make your measurement program really useful, we need to talk not only about technical factors and processes, like most chapters of this book. It's important to realize that measurement success is also determined by soft factors. We will in this chapter look first into selecting and defining appropriate metrics. Section 3 describes the underlying roles and responsibilities in a measurement program. We will then investigate about positive and negative aspects of software measurement and provide some guidance for counteracting counterarguments during introduction of a measurement program. We conclude with practical guidance for a stepwise introduction of a measurement program, describing also the time horizons to consider.

5.2 Metrics Selection and Definition

The very first step of selecting and introducing appropriate measurements must start with a useful and accurate definition. A measurement is no end in itself, but a way to achieve and monitor achieving an objective. Any metrics definition must therefore explicitly state the objective, directly linked to external business objectives, and the attribute of the entity being measured. The problem with many software metrics is that they are typically not described in business terms and are not linked or aligned to the needs of the business. While traditional business indicators look on revenue, productivity or order cycle time, their counterparts in software development measure size, faults or effort. Clearly both sides must be aligned to identify those software product or process metrics that support business decisions.

One of the first steps towards relating the many dimensions of business indicators was the Balanced Scorecard concept (see Chap. 2) [Kapl92]. The link to software metrics is given by investigating the operational view and the improvement view of the balanced scorecard. Questioning how the operational business can stay competitive yields critical success factors (e.g., cost per new/changed functionality, field performance, maturity level).

Relating the current actual project situation (e.g., project duration, delivered quality or project cost for an average set of requirements) to the best-of-practice values in most cases motivates a process improvement program. Keeping these relationships from business objectives towards critical success factors to operational management and finally to software processes in mind ensures that customer-reported defects are not seen as yet another fault category and percentage to be found earlier, but within the broader scope of customer satisfaction and sustained growth.

A project-specific measurement plan links the generic metrics definition to concrete projects with their individual goals and responsibilities. Additional metrics to be used only in that project are referred to in the measurement plan. The measurement plan is linked to the quality plan to facilitate alignment of targets.

Often terminology must be reworked and agreed upon with different parties to ensure proper usage of terminology. The good news with metrics definitions is that they ask for precision. It is basically impossible to sustain a "fluffy definition", and many past improvement programs indicated that with the metrics program a lot of other terminology and process imprecision could be cleaned up [Hump89, Grad92].

Try to **use one consistent metrics template** that provides both definition and concrete usage in typical project situations (Table 5.1).

Each metric definition should ensure consistent interpretation and collection across the organization. Capturing precise metrics information not only helps with communicating the rationale behind the figures but also builds the requirements for automatic tools support and provides basic material for training course development.

Most tracking metrics cover work product completion, open corrective action requests, and they review coverage to identify and track the extent to which development and quality activities have been applied and completed on individual software deliverables (see Chap. 8, Fig. 8.3, Fig. 8.4, Fig. 8.5). These metrics provide visibility to buyers and vendors about the progress of software development and can indicate difficulties or problems that might hamper the accomplishment of quality targets.

Progress during design activities can be tracked based on effort spent for the respective processes on the one side and defects found on the other hand. Especially defect-based tracking is very helpful for reaching high-level management attention because this is the kind of decision driver that accompanies all major release decisions.

When effort is below plan, the project will typically be behind schedule because the work simply is not getting done. On the other hand, design might have progressed but without the level of detail necessary to move to the next development phase. Both metrics should be reported weekly and can easily be compared with a planning curve related to the overall estimated effort and defects for the two phases. Of course, any design deliverables might also be tracked (e.g. UML descriptions); however, these come often late in the design process and are thus not a good indicator for focusing management attention.

Table 5.1. Metrics template

Template entry	Explanation
Unique identifier	Name and identifier of the metric
Description	Brief description of the metric
Motivation and benefits	Relationships to goals or improvement targets, such as quality factors, business goals or tracking distinct improvement activities; every metric should be traced to business objectives at organizational level and to the goals and risks at program level
Definition	A concise and precise calculation and extraction algorithm
Measurement scale	The underlying scale (e.g., normal, ordinal, rank, interval, absolute)
Underlying raw data	Raw data and other metrics used to calculate this metric (e.g., metrics primitives used for calculating the metric or indirect metrics)
Tools support	Links and references to the supporting tools, such as databases, spreadsheets, etc.
Presentation and visualization	References to report templates; e.g., chart or table type, combination with other metrics, visualization of goals or planning curves
Reporting frequency	Describes how often the metric is extracted, evaluated or reported
Cost of the metric	Covering one-time introduction and continuous collection effort
Analysis methods	Proposed/allowed statistical tests and analyses (including a validation history if applicable)
Target, control limits and alarm levels for interpretation	Control limits for quantitative process management (e.g., release criteria, interpretation of trends)
Configuration control	Links to storage of (periodically collected) metrics
Distribution control	Determines visibility and how a valid report is accessible (e.g., availability date, audience, access control)
Training	In case that a dedicated training is available or necessary for using this metric
Example	A real project case showing how the metric and the presentation look in practice

5.3 Roles and Responsibilities in a Measurement Program

The introduction of software metrics to projects has to follow a stepwise approach that must be carefully coached. Each new metric that needs tools support must be piloted first in order to find out whether definitions and tools descriptions are sufficient for the collection. Then the institutionalization must be planned and coached in order to obtain valid data. Independent of the targets of a measurement program, it will only be taken seriously if the right people are given responsibility for it [McGa01, Fent97] (see Chap. 7 for roles in the estimation process). For that reason the following three roles are recommended (Fig. 5.1).

1. **Metrics responsibles** for the projects serve as a focal point for engineers and the project management of the project. They ensure that the metric program is uniformly implemented and understood. The role includes support for data collection across functions and analysis of the project metrics. The latter is most relevant for project managers because they must be well aware of progress, deviations and risks with respect to quality or delivery targets. By creating the role of a project's metric responsible we guaranteed that the responsibility was clearly assigned as of project start, while still allowing for distributed (functional) metrics collection.
2. **A small central metrics team** coordinates metrics and project control beyond locations. It ensures that rationalization and standardization of a common set of metrics and the related tools and charts is accelerated. A key role of such metric team is consistent education across the company. This includes training to project managers and project teams on effectively using metrics. Upon building a company-wide metrics program and aligning processes within the software process improvement activities, the creation of a history database for the entire organization is important to improve estimates. It also maintains metrics definitions and related tools.
3. Optionally **local metrics teams** are introduced in each location or division of a distributed organization. They serve as focal points for all metrics-related questions, to synchronize metrics activities, to emphasize commonality and to collect local requirements from the different projects. Besides being the focal point for the metrics program in a single location they provide training and coaching of management and practitioners on metrics, their use and application. In addition they ensure that heterogeneous tools are increasingly aligned or that tools and forms for data collection and analysis are made available to the projects and functional organization.

This structure guarantees that each single change or refinement of metrics and underlying tools as well as from projects can be easily communicated from a single project to the whole organization. Use of teams should, however, be done cautiously. While a team has the capability to take advantage of diverse backgrounds and expertise, the effort is most effective when there are not more than three people involved in a distinct task. Larger teams spend too much time backtracking on metrics choices. We also found that when potential users worked jointly to develop the metrics set with the metrics support staff, the program was more readily accepted.

The related measurement process is applicable in the day-to-day project environment (see Chap. 8, Fig. 8.2). It is based on a set of defined metrics and supports the setting up and tracking of project targets and improvement goals:

1. Based on a set of predefined corporate metrics, the first step is to select metrics suitable for the project.
2. The raw data is collected to calculate metrics. Be aware of the operational systems that people work with that need to supply data. If the data is not available easily chances are high that the metric is inaccurate and people tend to ignore further metrics requests. People might then comply with the letter of the definition but not with the spirit of the metric.
3. Metrics are analyzed and reported through the appropriate channels. Analysis includes two steps. First, data is validated to make sure it is complete, correct, and consistent with the goals it addresses. Do not assume that automatic metrics are always trustworthy; at least perform sample checks. The real challenge is the second step, which investigates what is behind the metrics. Some conclusions are straightforward, while others require an in-depth understanding of how the metrics relate with each other. Consolidating metrics and aggregating results must be done with great caution, even if apples and apples might fit neatly, so to speak. Results are useless unless reported back to the people who make improvements or decisions.
4. Finally, the necessary decisions and actions are made based on the results of the analysis. The same metrics might trigger different decisions based on the target audience. While senior management may just want to get an indication how well the improvement program is doing, a process improvement team will carefully study project and process metrics to eliminate deficiencies and counteract negative trends.

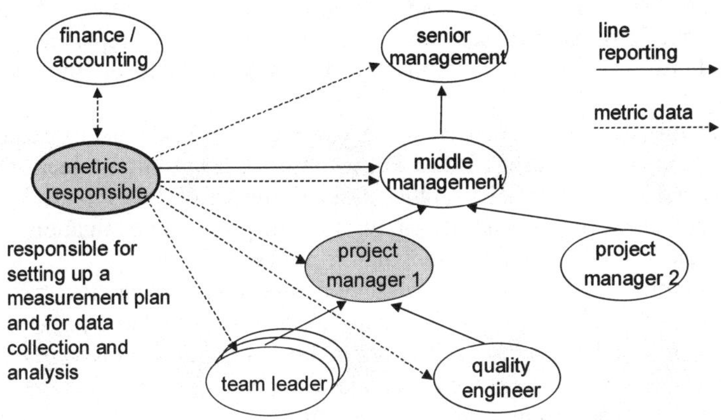

Fig. 5.1. Roles and responsibilities within a metrics program

5.4 Building History Data

Project management as well as tracking portfolio information or improvement projects needs a wealth of historic data. Only what has been collected in the past projects can be utilized to draw conclusions for the current and new projects. Having an accurate history database of past projects helps to identify risks during launch and along the project, thereby improving estimations, assessing feasibility of project proposals and identifying which processes are suboptimal.

Building history data is time consuming. It takes many projects to complete in order to have a sufficiently comprehensive set of key performance metrics from finished projects in order to make valid judgments on new projects. Different needs require different amounts of history data. Simple project tracking can actually be done without much own history data. It is just necessary to accurately track the progress versus commitments. Project tracking thus is the first step in building history data. Agree on standard metrics and set up a dashboard for the ongoing projects. After some ten finished projects you will obtain the first set of history data to use for the second step.

Estimating future work builds upon this initial history data. Naturally, the confidence and granularity of the estimates depends on the accuracy and details collected in the first step. If only project size and effort are collected, do not expect to estimate quality or cost. There are ways to predict quality based on incomplete raw data such as size information which we explain in Chap. 7.

A third step comprises managing projects and processes quantitatively. This includes activities such as statistical process control (SPC) as well as empowering every engineer towards resolving process issues on the spot. Measurement, like process maturity, grows first from chaotic ad hoc behaviors to organizational competence and further on back to projects and individuals.

Data quality is a major need while building the history database. It comprises dimensions such as accuracy (i.e., recorded values conform to actual values), completeness (i.e., information comprises all projects and sources), consistency (i.e., recorded information when compared does not show discrepancies or errors) and timeliness (i.e. metrics and history data are available on the spot when needed).

Data quality depends on the actual usage of the metrics and history information. What may be considered good data in one case for a specific project or process need may not be sufficient in another case. While an effort estimate in person-weeks is sufficient for a feasibility study of a new project or evaluation of a portfolio, it is clearly not enough for tracking the project internally.

Data quality comes at a cost. Usually the first need is to ensure that the same information is only collected once. For instance, precision can always be aligned to needs, but storing the precision of the original data certainly helps to reuse history data in the future when your needs may have evolved. While defect tracking in a CMM Level 1 organization might only look into avoiding critical defects after delivery to a customer, more mature organizations follow through the totality of defects created per phase or detected per verification and validation activity. Having gained such experiences these organizations start to address deviations from targets early in the development process thus effectively moving defect detection towards the phase that generated the defect. At the end of this growth is effective defect prevention.

Having more data recorded than presented helps in adjusting reports to the stakeholders' and users' specific needs. The project manager is interested to see all his milestones and how they are with respect to original commitments. A senior executive might be interested in seeing how much *anticipated* delays or budget overruns there are in her portfolio. A process manager might want to know how well estimates and predictions correlate with actually achieved reality.

To improve data quality and ensure that metrics usage is evolving, we recommend frequent reviews of the contents of the history database. This should be done before each major reporting cycle, as well as when a project is finished. The owner of the raw data per project should be the project manager. Her role comprises having accurate project information. She is in the best position to judge the quality of all reported information of her own project. The project manager can trigger dedicated corrective actions at any point during her project if some information is missing or invalid. This is hardly possible after the end of the project.

Too often, measurement is used to record the past, instead of anticipating the future. A history database is a means to stimulate forward looking. It is not supposed to be a metrics graveyard or repository for the sake of audits. One way to ensure forward-looking measurement is to make strategy reviews, performance indicators and annual objectives depend directly on actual metrics. This will stimulate the question: do we have metrics in place that will serve as early warning indicators of future problems? Metrics will be asked to indicate whether projects are doing well or not, or whether organizations are doing better or not. From a portfolio management perspective metrics will be asked that can signal future opportunities.

Once management perceives the dashboard and project metrics as reliable, there is a natural transition towards using measurements in the daily decision-making processes. We found in industrial settings that, depending on the education of management and maturity of the organization (if not management), it can take months until they would use the metrics. Basing key performance indicators on the metrics and setting up annual targets in line with business needs will accelerate usage. No reasonable manager will agree to objectives without a baseline. If it takes several months and still no progress is seen, the failure is either due to wrong attitude or incompetence, which must change from the top.

5.5 Positive and Negative Aspects of Software Measurement

Tracy Hall et al. [Hall01] show in an interesting empirical study of 13 groups of developers, 12 groups of project managers and 4 groups of senior managers in 11 associations, done between October 1999 and March 2000, positive and negative opinions of these interviewed relating to the use of IT metrics. Their joint result is that many of the positive aspects are more beneficial for the project mangers than for the developers, manifest in the declaration of a developer: “if any of us came up with a workable approach to metrics we’d become very rich.“

Table 5.2 shows that the overwhelmingly positive perception of measurement cited by developer groups was that measurement data allows progress to be tracked (69%) and that it improves planning and estimation (38%).

Table 5.2. Perceived general positive aspects of software measurement

Benefits of software measurement		Percentage of groups		
		Developers	Project managers	Senior managers
P1	Know whether the right things are being done	23	25	50
P2	Finding out what is good and what is bad	23	58	50
P3	Identify problems	8	42	25
P4	Support/improve planning and estimating	38	25	25
P7	Track progress	69	58	50
P8	Makes what you‘re saying more substantial	15	8	50
P9	Provides feedback to people	8	25	25

Project managers and senior manager have a more positive view of IT metrics (Table 5.3). Project managers favor the use of IT metrics for estimation purposes (P1, P2, P7) and for the identification of specific problems (P3).

Table 5.3. Favorite aspects of software measurement

Favorite aspects of software measurement		Percentage of groups		
		Developer	Project managers	Senior managers
B1	Can target effort into things (that are) not doing so well	8	8	25
B4	A check that what you are doing is right	15	17	50
B5	People can not argue	8	25	0
B6	The confidence they give	8	17	50

Three negative aspects of software measurement were mentioned from 38% of the developers:

- Developers are often not informed/do not know if and how the measured data are used.
- There is no feedback about the measured data
- Data collection is time consuming for the developers (which was also confirmed by 67% of the project managers). It is interesting that this insight did not lead to the requirement for automatic measurement.

Tables 6.3 and 6.4 demonstrate that 23% of the developers dislike the extra effort for data collection and the rather scarce presentation of the results. About 60%

of the project managers said that they had difficulties in identifying and collecting the data for the correct software measure. A quarter of them added that software measures do not always measure what you want them to measure. Senior mangers mostly found the following negative aspects (Table 5.4):

- Data collection detracts from the main engineering job.
- It is difficult to collect, analyze and use the right measures.
- Software measurement must be used for the right reason.

Table 5.4. Perceived general negative aspects of software measurement

General negative aspects of software measurement		Percentage of groups		
		Developers	Project managers	Senior managers
N3	Hard to measure what you want to measure	15	25	0
N6	Do not know how or if the data is being used	38	8	0
N7	No feedback from the data	38	8	0
N8	Detracts from the main engineering job	8	8	50
N10	Difficult to collect, analyze and use the right measures	23	58	50
N11	Time consuming to collect the data	38	67	25
N12	They must be used fort the right reason	15	33	50
N13	There must be integrity in the data	15	17	25
N17	They can be used against people	0	0	25

A quarter of them commented that measurement should not be used against people. It is interesting that none of the other two groups identified this issue. We can speculate on a variety of reasons for this. Maybe developers and project managers had not experienced measurement being abused and so it did not occur to them as a problem. Or – most often the case – senior managers have not been educated on practical measurement (i.e., not being exposed to this book) and fear the metrics as a pointer to previous decisions, thus creating an accountability that they don't like.

The least favorite rated aspects were (Table 6.5)

- Poorly presented data (50% of senior managers and 23% of developers)
- Difficult to compare data across systems or projects (25% of project leaders
- Poor quality data (25% of project leaders)
- Can be misunderstood (25 % of senior managers)
- Not used enough (25 % of senior managers)

All positive aspects fell into the following three categories:

- Assessment (P1, P2, P3)
- Planning (P4, P7)
- Decision support (P8)

All negative aspects fell into the following three categories:
- Implementation (N6, N7, N12, N13)
- Time and effort (N8, N11)
- Measurement immanent difficulties (N10)

This book practically explains how the mentioned disadvantages or risks perceived with the use of metrics can be best handled and mitigated in order **to make your measurement program a success.**

Table 5.5. Least favorite aspects of software measurement

Least favorite aspects of software measurement		Percentage of groups		
		Developers	Project managers	Senior managers
L1	Extra work	23	8	0
L3	Difficult to compare data across systems or projects	0	25	0
L4	Can be misunderstood	15	8	25
L5	Not used enough	8	17	25
L6	Poorly presented data	23	17	50
L7	Data too abstract to use easily	15	17	0
L8	Poor quality data	15	25	0

5.6 It is People not Numbers!

An effect often overlooked in establishing a measurement program is the impact on the people involved. Software is developed by engineers, and not by machines. Although introducing metrics means a cultural change to typically all involved parties, the focus is too often only on tools and definitions. If faults, efficiency or task completion are measured, it is not some abstract product that is involved, it is the practitioners who know that they will be compared. Staff at all levels are sufficiently experienced to know when the truth is being obscured.

Introducing measurement and analysis will change behavior – potentially in dysfunctional ways. Knowing the benefits of metrics for better project management or for steering the course of improvement initiatives does not at all imply that people will readily buy into the decision to be measured. To clearly explain the motivation from the beginning and to provide the whole picture is better than superficial statements about project benefits.

The result of lacking acceptance can lead to a general behavior of resistance in different forms, such as
- passive resistance
- work (only) on order
- active resistance

We thus recommend collecting several behavioral arguments – in addition to some slogans – that can readily help you to oppose resistance, as e.g., in Table 5.6.

It must be said explicitly that there is an immense interdependency between motivation and acceptance. Hence a major success factor for the implementation of measurement and estimation is the construction of a motivational system. It should have the goal to positively influence the staff for active cooperation and, last but not least, to identify the individual processes or techniques. The three most important pillars of such a motivational system are information, training and participation – the so-called king's road for introduction of innovations. This recommendation cannot be stressed enough.

Table 5.6. Fighting resistance

Resistance …	Fighting resistance:
is naturally and unavoidable!	expect resistance!
can often not be seen at a glance!	find resistance!
has many causes!	understand resistance!
discuss the hesitations, not the arguments!	confront resistance!
there is not only one way to fight resistance!	manage resistance!

Plan to position metrics from the beginning as a management tool for improvement and state that one of the targets is to improve efficiency in the competitive environment. Make explicit what the results will be used for. When used for competition and benchmarking, first stimulate that people work with their measurements and start improving. For instance if faults are counted for the first time over the life cycle, establish a task force with representatives from different levels to investigate results from the viewpoint of root cause analysis and criticality reduction. Educate your senior management. Uneducated managers tend to use metrics without reasoning about context. If there are many defects in a software component, they would conclude that the designer doesn't know his job. More often, however, the valid conclusion is that a specific piece of software is error-prone because of high complexity or many changes in the past.

Restricted visibility and access to the metrics helps in creating credibility among practitioners especially in the beginning. For instance, progress or defects for an individual engineer is not the type of information to be propagated across the enterprise. It is often helpful to change perspective towards the one providing raw data: is the activity adding value to her daily work? Statistical issues might not automatically align with emotional priorities. Remember especially with metrics that their perception is their reality.

Good communication is necessary in every business to be successful and to reduce friction, whether it is from engineer to manager, manager to engineer, or engineer to engineer. It is easy for software to be relegated to a low priority in a company focused on other technologies in its products. Software engineers need to speak out clearly and be heard and understood by management. Both sides need to learn how to address each other's real needs. Management does not care for techno-babble, while engineers are easily bored with capitalization or depreciation questions regarding their software.

5.7 Counter the Counterarguments

A typical killer argument is "lack of time" ("we have to do more important things" or "we must reach the deadline"). The answer to this is threefold [Bund00a].

1. In our experience, even for larger IT projects, an estimate can be done in a couple of days. Medium and smaller projects can normally be estimated within half a day or a day (with the aid of a competence center). This is a small effort compared to the whole project size. Only for large IT projects (more than 100 person years), might this effort be double or triple. Normally, an IT project should have the necessary and current information for measurement and estimation readily available. If this is not the case see point 3. In any case compared to the overall project effort the effort for the estimation is negligible.
2. If there is truly a lack of time, it has to be stated that there are (time) problems in a very early stage of that project. Thus the project leader should be asked if he should not stop the project before starting it, since experience shows that time will become scarcer during the project progress. It is a high risk to not quantify the project size.
3. The effort for the measurement and estimation increases significantly when the project team has to search for the necessary documentation or they cannot find it since it does not exist. The detection of such deficits allows management to bring the quality of projects to an acceptable level. This is much the same as the statement that the necessary documentation is not up to date or is not complete. This shows that measurement and estimation have a quality assurance function as a side effect. The effort for fixing such deficits is erroneously accounted as estimation effort. In reality it is a neglected documentation task. This again fosters the prejudice that estimation takes too much effort.

Further obstacles for the dissemination of software measurement and estimation are deficits in usability, relevance, end user efficiency and the poor presentation of software metrics. Other obstacles are lack of discipline and the chaotic nature of many IT organizations.

In many organizations the dissemination of estimation methods that are used in one department fails in other departments because of the "not invented here" syndrome. This syndrome exists internationally and leads to the habit that nobody is responsive, or that valuable ideas are ignored or repulsed in order to use politically correct but less valuable estimations.

On the other hand, the newest trends in software development are copied, and the newest propagated innovation is blindly adapted. The existence of a realistic and positive effect on the performance, however, is not evaluated. The demand to deliver software solutions faster and cheaper also leads to a tendency to start with a "quick and dirty" programming approach before the requirements of the end users are understood correctly. This again leads to lower product quality.

Acceptance problems can also be solved by experts in the domain who have done it before (i.e. *consultants*). At the beginning their assistance is a *conditio sine qua non* to start quickly and effectively with the right concept for estimation. On the other hand, problems will arise if their assistance is too great: the staff might feel that the management does not have enough confidence in their staff. The good thing is that management listens more readily to consultants (gurus) than to their own staff. There is the additional danger that too much knowledge will be lost to the organization if it is not transferred to the employees before the consultants leave. This is mostly neglected for time- and cost-saving reasons.

5.8 Information and Participation

Success with software measurement demands that project leaders and project team members get frequent and timely information about the goals and the effects of the implementation of measurement. For this reason a competence center can, e.g., publish its own newsletter, which regularly informs readers about the actual work of the competence center. It can also use the estimation training sessions to inform the participants about actual measures.

It is also important that experiences are exchanged with other organizations in order not to become mired in one's own problems. The participation in conferences like the annual SEPG conferences, local SPIN meetings, or those organized by DASMA or the MAIN Network – the joint European IT metrics organizations – offers the opportunity to learn from other organizations that face the same problems or that are a step ahead. This allows one to participate and benefit from other experiences, see positive examples or help to avoid errors reported from third parties. Often useful contacts can be made that might lead to an exchange of experiences with partners between such conferences.

The next logical step on the way to acceptance is participation. The goal of participation is the creation of widespread cooperation of all involved persons leading to active teamwork. Hence it is of immense importance to not blindly import existing processes. Instead, elaborate an adaptation according to the requirements of the own organization and in dialogue with the involved staff. This can typically be done with a neutral (external) consultant together with the staff in a pilot project. These staff members will be the promoters of the new methods in one's organizations. Fig. 5.2 presents some highlights of problems during the implementation of an estimation and measurement program.

Besides acceptance problems there are a number of other challenges associated with the implementation of estimation and measurement. The focus should be that processes are measured, not persons. If one does not follow this rule the motivation of the staff will be undermined and honesty of estimation cannot be fostered. Measurement and estimation should be integrated into the software lifecycle. Otherwise the necessary tasks will be regarded as overhead. The most important of all measures is support from management. Lack of support from managers will allow the project leaders to neglect the necessary tasks for measurement and estimation. It will thus help to delay the implementation process.

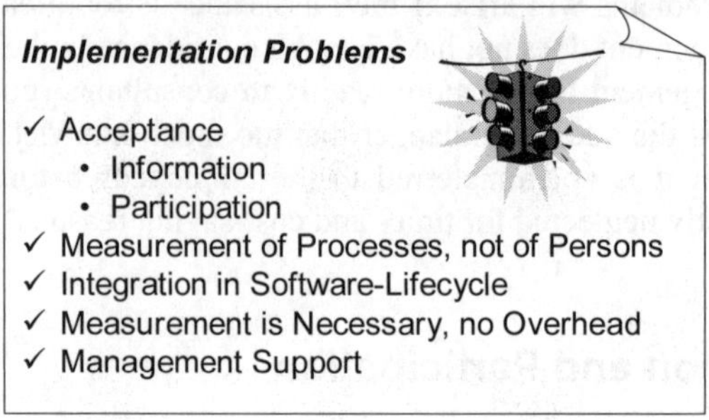

Fig. 5.2. Implementation problems

5.9 Hints for the Practitioner

Metrics are the vehicle to facilitate and reinforce visibility and accountability. The following key success factors could be identified during the introduction:

- **Metrics start with improvement goals**. Goals must be in line with each other and on various levels. The business strategy and the related business goals must be clear before discussing lower-level improvement targets. From the overall business strategy those strategies and goals must be extracted that depend on successful software development, use and support. Size or defect metrics alone do not give much information; they become meaningful only as an input to a decision process. This is where the balanced scorecard approach comes in and helps in relating the measurement program to specific corporate goals [Kapl93]. Business goals must be broken down to project goals and these must be aligned with department goals and contents of quality plans.
- **Motivate measurements and project control with concrete and achievable improvement goals**. Unless targets are achievable and are clearly communicated to middle management and practitioners, they will clearly feel metrics as yet another instrument of management control. Clearly communicated priorities might help with individual decisions.
- **Start small and immediately**. An initial timetable is provided in Table 5.7. This timetable indicates that setting up a measurement program consists of a lot of communication and training. Kick-off meetings with management, project teams or practitioners ensure that metrics are understood and used consistently. Especially senior management needs good training to avoid they abuse metrics for penalizing – before understanding what to effectively gain with this new visibility. It is definitely not enough only to select goals and metrics. Tools and reporting must be in line, and all of this takes its time. It must, however, be clearly determined what needs to be measured instead deciding based on what can be measured.

- **Actively use metrics for daily decision making (e.g., for project control).** Data collected at phase end or on monthly basis is too late for real-time control.
- **Avoid statistical traps.** Metrics have individual scales and distributions that determine their usage and usefulness. Avoid showing average values, which often compensate the good, the bad and the ugly. For instance, making an average across all delivery dates necessarily balances nicely the ugly delays with those that were severely overestimated. Both is bad from a performance management perspective. In such case showing quartiles makes much more sense. In other cases we advice showing not only a mean value but also the maximum and minimum values. Often a scatterplot already reveals the real message behind the numbers.

Table 5.7. Timetable for setting up a metrics program

Activity	Elapsed time	Duration
Initial targets set up	0	2 weeks
Creation and kick-off of metric team	2 weeks	1 day
Goal determination for projects and processes	3 weeks	2 weeks
Identifying impact factors	4 weeks	2 weeks
Selection of initial suite of metrics	5 weeks	1 week
Report definition	6 weeks	1 week
Kick-off with management	6 weeks	2 hours
Initial tool selection and tuning	6 weeks	3 weeks
Selection of projects/metric plan	6 weeks	1 week
Kick-off with project teams/managers	7 weeks	2 hours
Collection of metric baselines	7 weeks	2 weeks
Metric reports, tool application	8 weeks	Continuously
Review and tuning of reports	10 weeks	1 week
Monthly metric-based status reports within projects	12 weeks	Continuously
Application of metrics for project tracking and process improvement	16 weeks	Continuously
Control and feedback on metric program	24 weeks	Quarterly
Enhancements of metric program	1 year	Continuously

- **Determine the critical success factors** of the underlying improvement program. The targets of any improvement program must be clearly communicated and perceived by all levels as realistic enough to fight for. Each single process change must be accompanied with the respective goals and supportive metrics that are aligned. Those affected need to feel that they have some role in setting targets. Where goals are not shared and the climate is dominated by threats and frustration, the metrics program is more likely to fail.
- **Provide training both for practitioners**, who after all have to deliver the accurate raw data, **and for management** who will use the metrics. The cost and effort of training often stops its effective delivery. Any training takes time, money and personnel to prepare, update, deliver or receive it. Good training is worth the effort. If metrics are not used for decision-making or wrong decisions are taken, the cost is higher than that of training. Training can be class-room or

e-learning. In any case it should include lots of concrete project examples preferably from your own projects. Use external consultants where needed to get additional experience and authority.

- **Establish focal points** for metrics in each project and department. Individual roles and responsibilities must be made clear to ensure a sustainable metrics program. This is small effort but very helpful to achieve consistent use of metrics and related analysis.
- **Define and align the software processes to enable comparison of metrics.** While improving processes or setting up new processes, ensure that the related metrics are maintained at the same time. Once estimation moves from effort to size to functionality, clearly the related product metrics must follow.
- **Collect objective and reproducible data**. Ensure that the chosen metrics are relevant for the selected goals (e.g., tracking to reduce milestone delay) and acceptable for the target community (e.g., it is not wise to start with productivity metrics). If metrics are only considering what is measurable but do not stimulate improvements they will be used for hiding issues and creating fog.
- **Get support from management**. The enduring buy-in of management can only be achieved if the responsibility for improvements and the span of necessary control are aligned with realistic targets. Since in many cases metrics beyond test tracking and faults are new instruments for parts of management, they must be provided with the necessary training.
- **Avoid abuse of metrics by any means**. The objective is to get control on project performance, not to assign blame. Metrics must be "politically correct" in a sense that they should not immediately target persons or satisfy needs for personal blame. **Metrics might hurt but should not blame.**
- **Communicate success stories** where metrics enabled better monitoring or cost control. This includes identifying metrics advocates that help in selling the measurement program. Champions must be identified at all levels of management, especially at senior levels, that really use metrics and thus help to support the program. Metrics can even tie in an individual's work to the bigger picture if communicated adequately. When practitioners get feedback on the data they collect and see that it is analyzed for decision-making, it gives them a clear indication that the data is being used rather than going into a data cemetery.
- **Slowly enhance the metrics program**. This includes defining "success criteria" to be used to judge the results of the program. Since there is no perfect metrics program, it is necessary to determine something like an "80% available" acceptance limit that allows declaring success when those metrics are available.

Do not overemphasize the numbers. Having lots of numbers and no reasoning will not keep you in business; it's useless overhead. It is much more relevant what they bring to light, such as emerging trends or patterns. After all, the focus is on successful projects and efficiency improvement and not on metrics.

5.10 Summary

There are a number of positive and negative aspects associated with measurement and estimation. Regarding these can help to motivate the employees for better acceptance. Management support and clear guidelines are a prerequisite for a positive estimation culture and estimation honesty. A roadmap for successful implementation of measurement and estimation should start with building the foundations followed by strategic planning for implementation and establishment of the processes. The strategic plan should comprise frequently asked questions about the effort and the right moment for estimation as well as the pros and cons for centralized and decentralized measurement and estimation.

The implementation of measurement and estimation faces many acceptance problems. There are a lot of killer arguments to be countered, e.g., lack of time and too much effort for estimation. Additionally there are a lot of accompanying obstacles hindering the implementation process. The "not invented here" syndrome is a well known example. The advice from the experts is to solve all these problems using the king's road for introduction of innovations: overall information, sound training and participation of all involved persons. An alternative would be the counsel of experts.

Lacking acceptance fosters all kind of resistance damaging the process of implementation. This resistance has to be expected, found, understood, confronted and managed. Acceptance can be gained via correct information policy and exchange of experiences with metrics organizations or business partners. Participation creates cooperation and motivation. Many metrics organizations and experts offer trainings and certifications. Awareness has to be fostered for the insight that measurement and estimation are necessary and no overhead. Management assistance plays an important role for the success of the implementation process. There exist a lot of known positive and negative aspects of measurement that can be used for setting up measures to support the measurement and estimation program. Estimation conferences are not only beneficial for team-building but also give useful hints for risk-management. Estimation honesty can be fostered by motivation and stressing the benefits of measurement and estimation. Given all this positive prerequisites supported by clear goals an estimation culture can evolve. This is a time-consuming process.

The crucial part of a measurement and estimation program is the process of implementation. It starts with the definition of the goals and information. A standard process has to be defined and pilot projects have to be found. Training and motivation have to be organized, awareness and expertise to be created. Planning, budgeting, scheduling and resource coordination have to be performed and structures, processes, methods and tools have to be defined in order to establish precedence. Accompanying measures for support of the implementation process are the discussion of frequently asked questions, e.g., effort, cost and timing, centralized or decentralized measurement and estimation. The overall experience is that there are only a few technical challenges for successful implementation of measurement and estimation, but many psychological challenges.

6 Measurement Infrastructures

In God we trust.
All others bring data.
—W. Edwards Deming

6.1 Access to Measurement Results

The use of metrics in the development of industrial software is gaining importance. Metrics are particularly suited to qualitative and quantitative assessment of the software development process, of the resources used in development and of the software product itself. However, software metrics can only be used effectively if the requisite measurements are integrated into the software development process and if these measurement values are taken at regular intervals. An effective software measurement process produces an extensive series of measurements and thus the need for efficient measurement data management, which must include the contexts to enable discourse on the measurements that are taken as well as to provide extensive evaluation options.

It should also be possible to store the results of validation of a measurement as a new experience within the database. In this context it is possible to use a simple structure based on a file system, a standard portal solution, an explicit developed metrics database system or, finally, an experience factory. After a short introduction of the International Software Benchmarking Standards Group (ISBSG) approach we show possible sources of metrics, requirements of a metrics database and an implementation of a real system of a metrics database (called metricDB). The metricDB project focused on an application for metrics management in object-oriented software development.

6.2 Introduction and Requirements

6.2.1 Motivation: Using Measurements for Benchmarking

One important activity in context of software measurement access is benchmarking. Benchmarking is used internally to a company for comparing projects and externally for comparing best practices. There are several databases that allow open access to benchmarking data, such as the ISBSG International Repository (http://www.isbsg.org). The goal of the ISBSG is to provide a multi-organizational repository of software project data. The ISBSG grows, maintains and exploits two repositories of software project metrics:

1. Software Development and Enhancement
2. Software Maintenance and Support

The ISBSG approach considers different project data, such as the functional size of a specific software solution, information about the development project itself (elapsed time, team size, required resources) or information about the used technologies for implementation.

By mid-2003, this benchmarking repository contained more than 2000 projects. The repository can be used for a minimal fee and provides the following services:

- The repository itself can be used as an alternative to one's own metrics database.
- Contribution of one's own realized project benchmarks
- Comparison of submitted projects with others of the same class within the repository
- The Benchmark and other reports about the content of the repository

6.2.2 Source of Metrics

Metrics tools mostly address the original source of software metrics data. These tools support different kinds of software modeling, measurement and evaluation. We can establish the following storage techniques and structures for the metrics values:

- Some tools present the metrics value in a fleeting manner only in the evaluation moment.
- Most tools produce a metrics value file with some explanations or in a simple value-divided-by-delimiter form.
- The metrics values are stored for two evaluations for some tools to compare two variants (an old and a new/modified one).
- Some tools support a file hierarchy for the project-related storage of the code metrics data; an append technique helps to combine different measurements of different project parts to compare the different evaluated aspects.
- Some tools have a lot of facilities for the presentation and analysis of the metrics data, but the final values are hidden from the user.
- In some tool classes there exists a data-handling tool with the possibility of detailed analysis of the metrics data.

The examples above demonstrate some interesting aspects of software metrics data storage and handling but are mainly oriented to a special measurement area (process or code evaluation) or to a special environment (platform or language related). Fig. 6.1 shows the possible sources of software metrics according to [Evan94a].

6.2.3 Dimensions of a Metrics Database

Fig. 6.2 summarizes possible aspects for design and implementing a metrics database ([Folt98]). Industrial acceptable metrics databases are constructed based on some chosen aspects in every dimension of the above model.

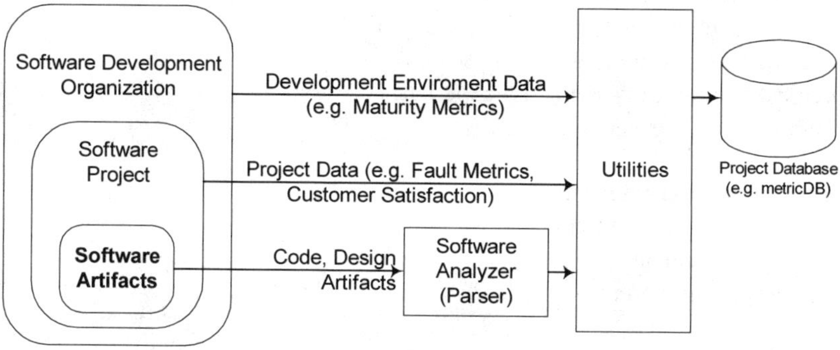

Fig. 6.1. Sources for a metrics database (adapted from [Evan94a])

Database characteristics:

- kind of used database model (relational, object-relational, hierarchical/XML-based and so on)
- architecture (layer, kind of possible access, components)
- user concept (query language, GUI, provided services)
- security and safety (access control, etc.)
- quality (consistency, redundancy, performance)

Data characteristics:

- kind of value (number, flag, text)
- metadata (precision, tolerance, accuracy, unit, domain)
- structure and type (aggregation level)
- source (measurement, statistical operation, default setting)

System characteristics:

- stand-alone (data analysis, decision support)
- embedded system (controlling, management)
- distributed systems (client/server, mobile)
- Web-based solution (portal, Web services)

Input types:

- measured value
- output from a specific tool
- prediction or estimation

Output types:
- kind of values
- input for specific tools
- statistical report

Metrics characteristics:
- single measured value (interval, ratio scaled)
- estimated value (nominal, ordinal scaled)
- predicted value (by formula, by experience)
- multi value (tuple, set, tree, tensor)

Measurement characteristics:
- model-based measurement
- direct measurement
- prediction/estimation

Application characteristics:
- part of management systems
- source of assessments
- part of control systems
- source of education

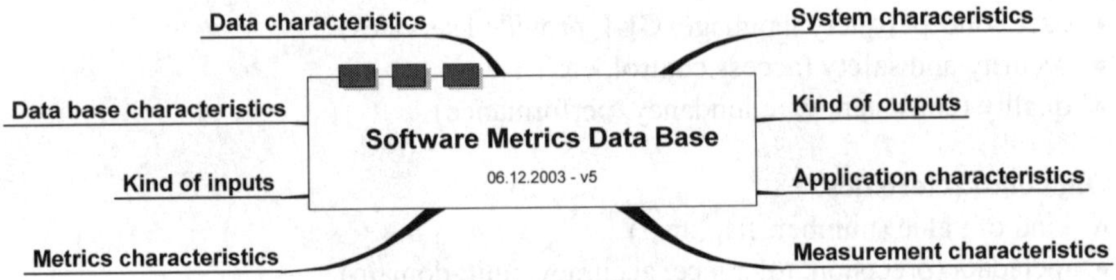

Fig. 6.2. Aspects of a metrics database

6.2.4 Requirements of a Metrics Database

All software development projects should always have the special requirements of future users of the information system as their starting point. Additional requirements relate to the adaptability of the application to new situations, the use of different procedural models for software development and possibly also the use of different metrics sources. The target of the metrics database is to cater to the needs of different users and, in particular, to make it easier to control the quality and cost of software projects (independently from the used procedure). In a workshop with potential customers (e.g., project managers) of the metrics database, requirements were identified and used as a starting point for data and function modeling. These requirements are summarized below (see also Chaps. 5, 8 and 9):

- The effort involved in using and maintaining/administration of a metrics database must be kept to a minimum, which results in the need for extensive automation.
- It must be possible to map the procedure (e.g., functional or object-oriented development) that is selected for a concrete software development project in the metrics database. It must also be possible to configure the created software artifacts (diagrams, documents, source texts) and to assign measurements that are taken of them.
- Different user types must be served with project-specific rights. Planning currently involves application administrators (creating new projects), the project manager/developer (use of prefabricated evaluations) or academic staff who can subject the metrics to statistical analysis using external tools such as SPSS.
- It should include automatic problem detection in software development on the basis of exceeded, configurable threshold values in addition to offers of solution alternatives. It should be possible to store different threshold values (external, company- and project-specific experiences) in the system.
- It should allow for presentation of metrics flow and comparison with other projects by means of graphs and control diagrams.
- It should include an "experience database" for project development and control, effort estimation, productivity/efficiency and (indirect) cost control.
- It should incorporate automation of part of effort estimation (as in the present version, e.g., the object point method according to Sneed) in order to estimate effort and perform historical costing at different phases of the project.
- It should allow users to check qualitative modeling or implementation criteria by using validated metrics, for example, maintainability, compliance with the object-oriented paradigm and stability of an object model in the face of change.
- The system must be able to incorporate new metrics and their interpretations into the database relatively easily. To this end, an internal adaptable metrics catalogue should be defined to which it must be possible to interactively map the results produced by measuring tools.
- It should allow for the possibility of integrating evaluations that are not implemented on the basis of the standard functions offered by the application, such as an Excel or SPSS analysis.
- It should also be possible for users to transfer analyses to their specific documents (e.g., OpenOffice) via file referencing or file embedding mechanisms (e.g., DotGNU, web services, clipboard).
- Easy access through intranet.

6.3 Case Study: Metrics Database for Object-Oriented Metrics

6.3.1 Prerequisites for the Effective Use of Metrics

The objective to develop a database management system for object-oriented metrics followed a whole range of preliminary activities. It was necessary to select metrics especially for object-oriented software development from the large number of metrics proposed in the academic discourse (see also Chaps. 3 and 5).

Attributes for measurement selection

Effectiveness answers the question as to the degree to which a selected metric can meet company objectives, such as reducing error rates. Here it may be suitable to apply the Goal-Question-Metric (GQM) Method according to Basili et al.

Feature coverage. It must be possible to apply the selected metrics to as many results and software artifacts that are produced during development as possible (e.g. models, program code, documentation) and to all phases of development.

Effort minimization. Executing continual measurements within the software life cycle requires the use of measurement tools that are able to make metrics largely automatically available from measured software artifacts.

Empirical evaluation. As there is often no experience to build upon when a software metric is first introduced, it is sensible to adopt the "initial settings" (i.e., threshold values), which are suggested in the measurement tools or in the relevant literature.

Data protection and security. Metrics must not be used to draw conclusions about person-related data.

Scale features (nominal, ordinal, interval, ratio) of the metrics in use define the information content of the data used and the statistical analysis methods and mathematical operations that can be executed on them.

For an iterative life cycle (e.g., Unified Process [OMG01]) this results in 4 measurement points per cycle/increment/iteration, whereby often 3–5 cycles are run so that a total of 12–20 measurement points should normally be available in a development project. Besides creating stable general conditions with a binding procedural model, further standardization such as defining standard development technologies and the introduction of programming standards was necessary to enable individual projects to be compared. When using metrics, it is also important to standardize the methods and tools that are to be used for software development. For example, it would not have been recommendable to introduce metrics tools for model and source code metrics before the tools used in development had been declared as standards that were binding throughout the company.

6.3.2 Architecture and Design of the Application

The main components of the application are the database server (MS SQL Server or MySQL), a Web server (e.g., Apache or Internet Information Server), a Windows-based administration client and a Web client based on a standard browser (e.g., Mozilla).

Fig. 6.3 shows the current software architecture of the metricDB application. The Web server contains the HTML files and the relevant Java applets from the application, which are downloaded to the Web client via HTTP. The database is accessed from the Java applet via the JDBC driver, which runs as middleware on the Web server. At the core of the application is the database, set up as a relational database management system.

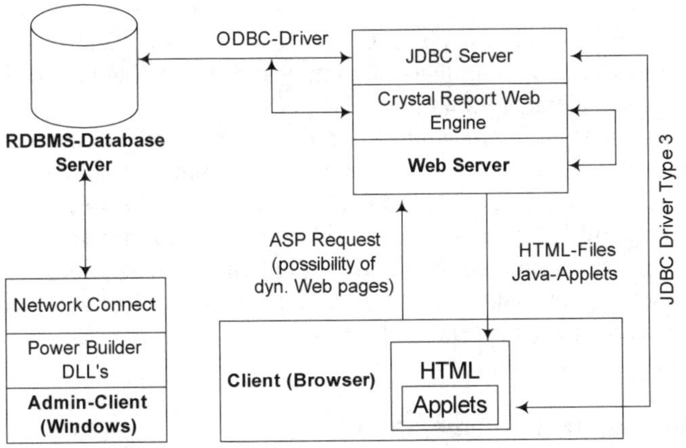

Fig. 6.3. Software architecture of the application

Despite the resulting paradigm inconsistency between the object-oriented application and database management based on the relational model, the following factors influenced the choice of the system:

- Proven database management technology with extensive tool support and offering standard interfaces such as Open Database Connectivity (ODBC) and Java Database Connectivity (JDBC).
- Possibility of using the database contents under standard tools such as Excel and SPSS for statistical data analysis via the ODBC interface.

- Infrastructure, for example, for software distribution or appropriate centralized backup procedures is available in the company.
- To a high degree the administration client under Windows and the Web clients both execute update-intensive operations, which make the use of Online Analytical Processing (OLAP) or data warehouse technologies doubtful.

Use of the type-3 JDBC driver permitted a three level client/server architecture to be implemented in the application on the Internet site. The administration client was linked directly to the database. Despite producing some disadvantages in terms of possible scalability, this is acceptable as it requires very few administrators in relation to Web-based users. The architecture we have implemented enables all application components to be executed on one system or, alternatively, the use of dedicated computer systems as database and Web servers. The number of administration and Web clients that can be used depends on the performance of the server systems and the load profiles caused by users.

The application, in particular the database component, was modeled using Rational Rose. Fig. 6.4 shows the packages that are currently used and that contain the actual classes or entities. As most packages were described and implemented through parameterizable classes, this resulted in a highly generic data model, permitting various adjustments to be made within the application. For example, metadata is used to describe the structural elements (software artifacts) of a project, the hierarchic levels (mapping of the concrete procedural model) with, for example, cycles, phases, segments, activities and the milestones in the temporal project flow (management view).

On the one hand, this procedure safeguards the option of adapting to various procedural models in software development, on the other, it allows us to consider various sources of metrics, related to the defined structural elements. Inherent in a generic concept of this type is the disadvantage of increased administration effort for application operations. For this reason, the template technology was used several times, storing basic administration work, such as mapping a procedural model for object-oriented development, in the system.

6.3.3 Details of the Implementation

The computation of aggregate metrics refers at present to effort estimation according to object point [Snee96]. The metrics that were imported via Computer Aided Measurement and Evaluation (CAME) tools and those that had to be input into the system manually (not measurable) were both used in computation. This is implemented technically via "store procedures", on the database server. Using these technologies offers performance advantages but has the disadvantage that it is dependent on the actual database system that is in use, here MS SQL Server.

Within the store procedures the computation formulae for determining object points are mapped using variables so that the application administrator can assign the concrete metrics that are to be used from the metrics catalogue stored in the system. This enables the computation rule to be adapted to whatever metrics the system offers, thereby achieving independence of the concrete measurement tool in use. For other aggregate metrics, it is possible to define new store procedures. Full disclosure of these program parts, which are written in Standard SQL92 (approximately 80 effective LOC), makes this task relatively easy without the need for changes to the application itself.

Templates in the application support the transfer of measurements performed using CAME tools. At present, the application offers templates for the data output formats of MetricsONE (see also [Numb97]) and RSM (see also Resource Standard Metrics [RSM98]). The functionality of the templates includes parsing the output file created by the CAME tools and writing the measurement values it reads to a temporary file. It is then possible to interactively assign (mapping) the imported measurement values to the metrics that were mapped to the database via the defined metrics catalogue. In this way, the basic output format of the CAME tools can be retained while new versions are adapted to the metrics database by the application administrator.

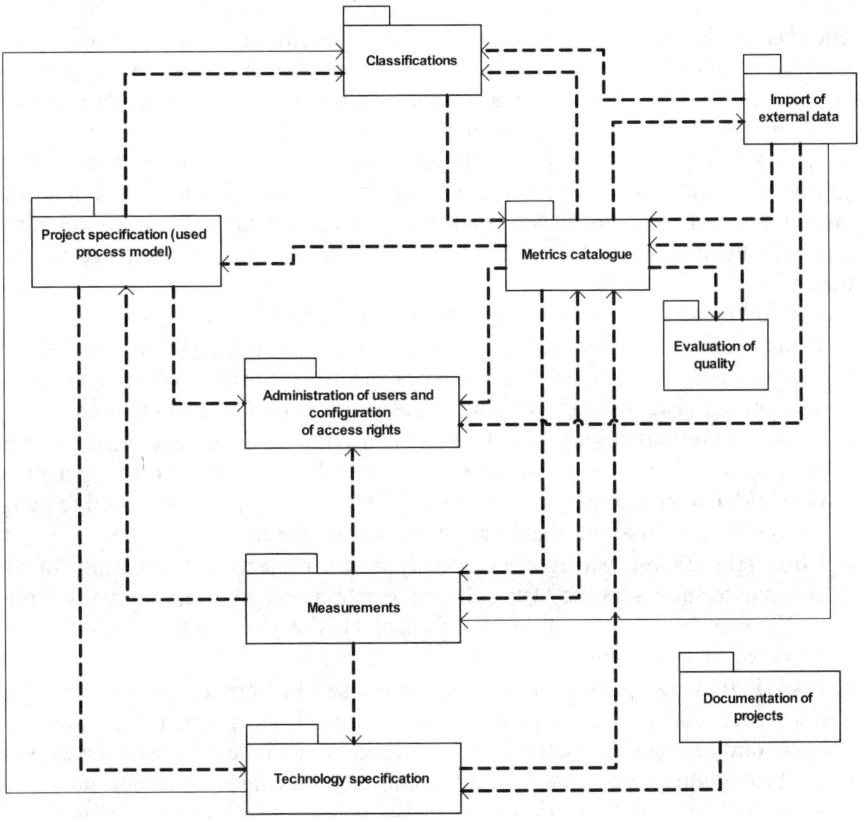

Fig. 6.4. Overview of the packages used in the metrics database

In the case of MetricsONE, a comma-separated output file is created. That's also a common default for spreadsheet export/import mechanisms. This consists of a specification of the type of element (package, class, operation, use case) that was measured, the name of the metric and the actual measurement value. The sequence of datasets may vary, depending on the measurement tool settings, as it is possible, for example, to not display certain metrics. This is taken into account by the parser. The parser works on the basis of the defined keywords.

It would only be possible to import data fully automatically if the definition of the elements administered in the metrics database were mapped to the output format of the metrics tool. The necessity of defining a standard interface for metrics tools became particularly apparent during processing. This standard should contain a generic metrics description, as well as define the grammar used inside the output file.

6.3.4 Functionality of the Metrics Database (Users' View)

The metrics database provides mainly an administration view and a project users view. Most of the functions described in this section are supported by templates in the metrics database, making administration easier. This means that, for example, once adjustment to a special procedural model has taken place, this template can be used for all projects that follow this procedure. Before the information system can be used for a concrete project, the application administrator must store the project structure in the database. In addition, the users who work with the application must be assigned rights for their specific projects; the templates also support this.

The following describes the main functions used to set up a project:

- **Project structure.** Here the software artifacts used in the project are defined; they can be, for example, diagram types according to the UML notation (e.g., packages, classes, use case) or simply the source code files that are used.
- **Types of methodologies.** This function is used to map the concrete product or development life cycle model used (e.g., with Unified Process it is inception, elaboration, construction and transition, [OMG01]). A template is used to transfer this to configurations that have already been executed.
- **Life cycle stages.** Management usually views projects independently of the concrete technology used. Typically, milestone plans are used, normally representing concrete tasks in sequential format. This function enables milestones to be stored in the system.
- **CAME tool integration.** This function is used to import measurements that have been taken to the database and has already been mentioned from the viewpoint of implementation. Here, a definition of where the measurement values belong must take place. Relevant information includes the project name, the stage and cycle reached, as well as phase, date of measurement, the measurement tool used and selection of a specific template to import it into the database.

- **Metrics catalogue.** Here, the metrics that are used are assigned to the administered project structure. New metrics can also be defined or aggregate metrics determined. The details that must be specified are the type of metric, the default tool that was used to import the metric and assignment to a structural element. Threshold values (the permitted boundaries of a metric) are also defined here. The metrics database currently contains three types of threshold values: a default limit, which can be taken from external publications; one that has been declared mandatory within the company; and one which can be adapted to meet the needs of specific projects. Any threshold values that are exceeded are clearly displayed at present on the Web client in red color.

The use of the metrics database (after a specific project instance is available) is provided by a Web client. The appearance of the application is shown in Fig. 6.5, the buttons on the left are used to select the requisite application function, which is then made available within a Java applet.

An exception is selection of the report functionality, which creates tabular and graphics output using Crystal Reports. For user orientation, the status displays the function that is currently selected (in Fig. 6.5, Measurements) and the project currently being viewed (Current Project). The prerequisite for executing individual application functions is that the user has been assigned the right to do so by the application administrator.

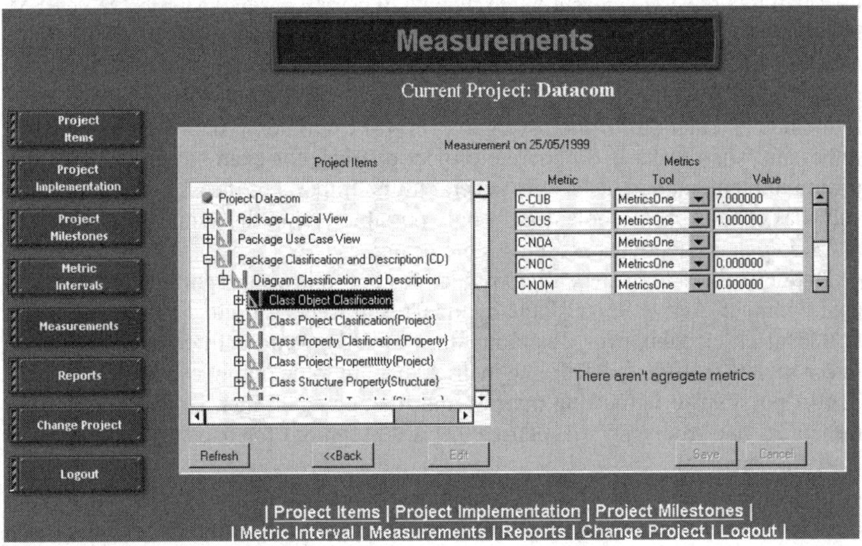

Fig. 6.5. User interface on the Web client

Project item. This function enables users to assign concrete entries to the project structures defined by the application administrator. This includes, for example, the project name, the names of the packages used, the files used and the concrete class names.

Project implementation. The product or development life cycle stages are preferably used as navigation structure, e.g., in the case of Unified Process (inception, elaboration, construction and transition), and the method related to the concrete technology used (phase, activity). The start and end of the stages can be entered here, as well as cycles within a stage. When a stage is running, it is assigned a green check mark. Definition of a cycle after selecting a stage (number of cycle, start and end of the cycle and a description) is possible.

Project milestones. These correspond to the project milestones that are defined in the administrator module. They are independent of a concrete technology and correspond to those, for example, used in MS Project (mapping currently not available). Current and planned milestones for the entire project can be assigned here.

Metric intervals. Outputs the metric intervals or threshold values used. The reports always use the "lowest level" of the defined intervals. If a project-specific threshold value has been defined, this is used; otherwise the one defined within the company or the one copied from external sources is used.

Measurements. The defined metrics catalogue is administered and the metrics are assigned to structural elements under the Admin module. Each measurement is allocated to a stage, a cycle and a phase. Thus there could be, for example, three measurements within one phase. The dialogue shows which metrics it is possible to assign to a concrete measurement, how they were recorded (MetricsONE, RSM, manually – none) or computation of the object points, whereby the previous results are deleted. The results of a calculation are also written to the database. At present, the OP computation is executed at project level, but it would make sense to include calculation for the package level, for example, in later versions. This is important when tasks in a concrete project overlap, for example, in order to distribute implementation tasks over several users. Imports of measurements from result files of the CAME tools used is only possible within the administration client, as Java applets cannot access the system resources.

Reports. Support is currently provided for the following reports, which are created within an Active Server Page by the Crystal Reports used. They can be represented in either tabular or diagrammatic form. By using a filter over the period under review (start/end dates), the metrics that are to be output can be restricted. It is also possible to output the metrics and the aggregate metrics that are actually measured, and to display all metrics that are measured for one structural element (software artifact).

- *Statistics on elements of a project.* These reports are used to output the metrics of a structural element over a defined period, in relation to global project stages, to the project cycles or to the project phases already run.
- *Summary of project.* This type of report displays metrics in aggregate over global stages, cycles and phases of the project, with the result that relationships to individual structural elements of the project are no longer shown. The report also displays the possible intervals of a metric. If a measured value exceeds

this, it is displayed in red, if it does not reach it, in blue, and in black if it is within the normal range.
- *Comparison of projects*. Because of consistency rules that have to be complied with, it is only possible to compare the metrics of two projects if they have the same stage or phase structural elements. In this way it is possible to display the temporal development of metrics, such as the number of attributes defined by "public" over the phases of the project that have already run.
- *Additional reports*. Additional reports can be used to watch the entire defined metrics catalogue (including defined threshold values), the status of the current project (phases and cycles of the project in relation to concrete timeframes) and the last measurement performed on a selected structural element.

6.4 Hints for the Practitioner

Before an organization starts with the implementation of a metric database it is necessary to improve the maturity of the corresponding development process. Otherwise it's difficult to associate metrics to life cycle iterations, project activities, etc. Therefore we recommend to start with simple solutions for the storage of metrics. The following ways are possible:
1. Individualized storage of software metrics by applying standard office/spreadsheet tools. Each user stores his respective metrics. This fragmented and ad-hoc approach is not recommended as huge overheads and inconsistencies are created.
2. Use of externally provided repositories, like the ISBSG approach. Storage of project data like functional size, work effort, error statistics, and so on.
3. Use of a simple storage structure based on a shared file system. We strongly recommend using a configuration management system on top of such file system.
4. Use of a Web-based portal (e.g., Microsoft Share Portal Services or Microsoft Share Point Team Services) and application of a simple visualization. This type of access is especially useful for distributed development organizations or in context of offshore activities. Typically the portal links into operational databases and aggregation mechanisms.
5. **Use of a dedicated centralized metrics database**, like the proposed solution within this chapter. The solution should be adaptable to different development methods, to different development tools and also usable for process, resource and product metrics. Measuring data should be adopted as automated as possible into the data base. Manual interfaces are to be avoided. The output forms should be simple evaluations (bar diagrams, value tables etc.) and are used as input for the statistical tools. The characteristics of the stored measurement data should be different in the scale type and of a different life cycle phase. The metrics database should be distributed and stand-alone, and should allow an interactive use. The platform should be server-based by the use of an application server and a relational database management system (e.g., Oracle or Microsoft

SQL-Server). Furthermore we recommend the use of Web-based technologies as user interface. The metrics database should keep the goals of the metrics tool and controlled experiment evaluation and should deliver experience in distributed application of metrics based process and product controlling. It should also be possible to store the results of validation of a measurement as a new experience within the database, this implies also the use of the metrics database system as discussion forum.

In principle, every type of a storage should offer the possibility to further use the measurement data with external tools like statistical analysis or reporting tools.

6.5 Summary

We have introduced to the needs for software measurement infrastructures. A common usage scheme for such infrastructures is benchmarking or portfolio management. We showed with a case study how T-Systems has built such metric database. The approach is visible and can be extended to your own environment. The current version of the metrics database primarily considers software artifacts. Planning foresees extending this in the future to include metrics of software development organization, e.g. importing metrics for maturity valuation in accordance with the CMM model (Chap. 10). To summarize the results of the current version, it is a highly adaptable information system that is able to take into consideration the continually changing conditions in software development, such as new procedural models, new metrics tools and a successive increase in experiences, and thus meets the needs of investment protection. The easy-to-use Web interface makes evaluations available to a wide range of users, helping them to gain experience in the use of metrics and, implicitly, in metric validation.

7 Size and Effort Estimation

What you see is what you see.
—Frank Stella

7.1 The Importance of Size and Cost Estimation

Estimating size and cost are one of the most important topics in the area of software project management. The dynamics of the software market lead to extended or new kinds of methods for the estimation of product size or development effort in the background of *cost estimation.* Some of these approaches are

- the *Constructive Cost Model* (COCOMO II:2000) based on the size estimation for the "future" source code with the interesting modifications as constructive phased schedule and effort model (COPSEMO), the cost estimation of rapid application development model (CORADMO), the cost estimation of COTS (COCOTS), the constructive quality estimation model (COQUALMO) [Boeh00]
- the Software Lifecycle Management (SLIM) method based on the estimation of the system effort in the entire life cycle [Putn03].

  These methods are also discussed in the Chaps. 7, 8 and 15.

In this chapter we will primarily consider the functional size measurement (FSM) methods, currently one of the major topics in the area of cost estimations. At the beginning we describe some of the well-established FSM methods with their benefits and weaknesses. Especially we discuss their experience background, their CAME tool support, and their current status of testing and confirmation.

This chapter is an overview to estimations. It covers both technical aspects (i.e., specific estimation methods and their use), as well as the estimation process and its introduction. The *COSMIC Full Function Points* (COSMIC FFP) standard ISO 19761 is described including the basic intentions and activities in order to use it in different kinds of software systems – especially for *embedded systems*. We will give a short overview about this approach and demonstrate the steps in order to consider the feasibility of the FFP application in an industrial environment. Soft factors are equally captures, since especially estimations are subject to lots of "political" influences, be it during bidding (i.e., the customer wants the project at lowest cost, while the supplier at a best match of effort and duration) or internally during the feasibility study and inception of a project.

7.2 A Short Overview of Functional Size Measurement Methods

Functional size measurement is of increasing importance for the area of software development, since it adds engineering methods and principles to it. Fig. 7.1 adapted from [COSM03] shows the general procedure for functional size measurement. As can be seen, there are basically two phases, a mapping phase, where concepts and definitions are applied to the representation of the software, and an evaluation phase, where the extracted elements are counted/measured according to specific rules and procedures. Further investigations that resulted in the proposal of a generalized structure of functional size measurement were done by Fetcke [Fetc99].

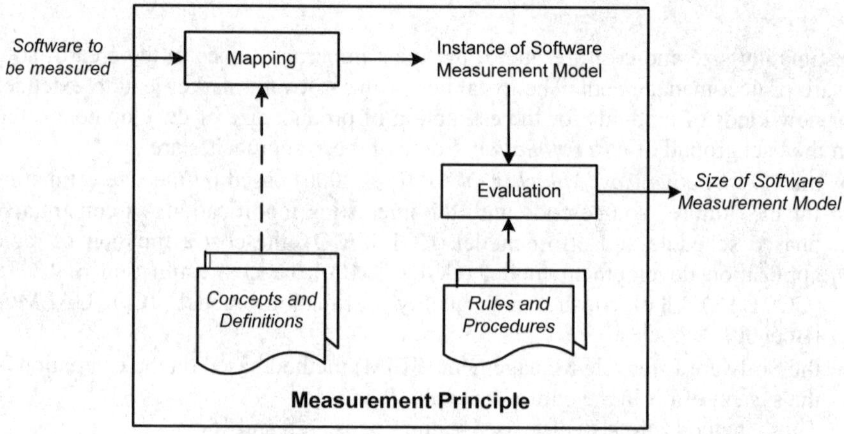

Fig. 7.1. Measurement principle of functional size measurement

Since the first worldwide publication of Function Points in 1979 a lot of changes, extensions and alternative approaches to the original version have been introduced. In Fig. 7.2 (adapted from [Loth01]) important steps of this evolution can be seen in a timeline, including those methods described in detail below. Arrows between the methods indicate influences and extensions. The latest method in the figure is the COSMIC Full Function Points approach. Some details of the history of the COSMIC consortium are mentioned in Chap. 16.

Now we will consider an evaluation of some characteristics of the functional size measurement methods according to

- their suitability for different functional domains
- the degree of penetration and the experience background
- the tool support
- the testing and confirmation
- the standardization status and
- the validation

As could be seen in the overview of functional size measurement methods in Fig. 7.2 these methods aim to certain *software/functional domains*. If there is the need to choose one of these methods, it is important to know if there is a method that fits the functional domains used. Table 7.1 shows the suitability of the different methods to the functional (software) domains according to Morris [Morr02].

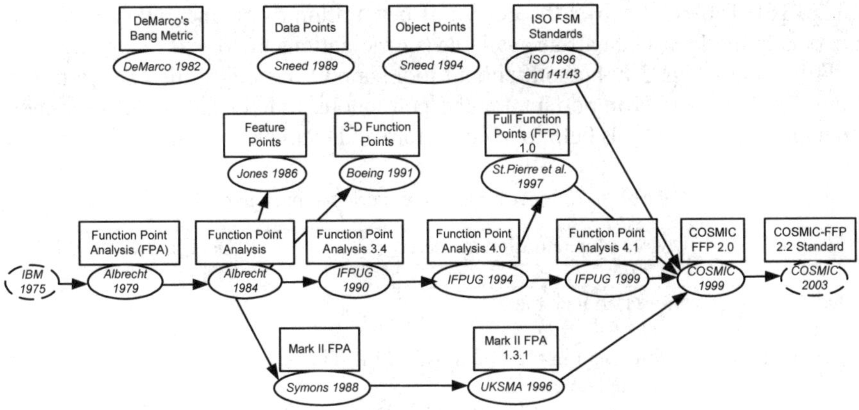

Fig. 7.2. Development of functional size methods

Table 7.1. Methods per functional domain (A/S, 'Algorithmic/Scientific', MIS, 'Management Information Systems', RT, 'Real-time embedded', CS, 'Control Systems')

Method	A/S	MIS	RT	CS
DeMarco's Bang		X		
Feature Points	X			
Boeing 3-D			X	
IFPUG		X		
Mark II FPA		X	Potentially	
FFPv1			X	X
FFPv2		X	X	X

Table 7.1 shows that data-strong and control-strong systems are covered by the existing methods. Because of the widespread use and the long-term experience with Function Points for MIS most tools and experiences are in this domain. Full Function Points version 1 is the most viable method for real-time embedded and control systems until the Full Function Points version 2 method is released [Morr02]. The problem of function-strong systems (scientific and algorithmic) is not yet solved. This is an area where further research is still required.

Another important criterion for the use of a method is *the number of users* of this method and *the existing experience background*. This is important due to the fact that only a community can establish a standard and thus enable comparability (also to software outside their own company) and repeatability.

Furthermore the probability for training opportunities, consulting and continuous improvement of the method itself increases, the larger the community is. An experience database is important to compare one's own measurement data with measurements of others. In the area of functional size measurement there is the *International Software Benchmarking Standards Group* (ISBSG) data base (see Chap. 16). Table 7.2 shows the degree of penetration of the methods and if there are data in the ISBSG database available (investigations by Morris [Morr02]).

Following Chap. 3 a method without tool support has only little chance to survive. *Tool support* is important for the continuous functional size measurement application because tools help to handle, store and evaluate the data.

Table 7.2. Penetration and experience background

Method	Degree of penetration in users	Data in the ISBSG database
DeMarco's Bang	No importance today	No
Feature Points	A few users in the US, mostly SPR clients, not supported anymore	No
Boeing 3-D	Very small, rarely used outside Boeing	No
IFPUG	Most widely used method	Yes, dominant
Mark II FPA	>50% in UK, only a few users outside UK	Yes, rare
FFPv1	Users in Australia, Canada, Europe, Japan and USA	Yes, very rare
FFPv2	Users in Australia, Canada, Finland, India, Japan, UK and USA	Yes, rare but increasing

Of course, fully automated functional size measurement is desired, but as far as we know, that problem is not solved yet. The reason for this problem is: Some items that have to be counted/measured cannot be counted/measured automatically, but there are some approaches to this topic (see also Chap. 3). Thus, tool support and automatic measurement have to be distinguished. Table 7.3 shows an overview of tools that can support the application of measurements as well as the analysis of results. It can be seen that there is tool support for the existing functional sizing methods.

More information about these tools can be found in Dumke [Dumk96a] and Bundschuh [Bund00a] (see also [Schw00] and [Symo01]). The FPC-Analyzer for Palm computers, developed at the University of Magdeburg by Reitz [Reit01], supports the Full Function Points version 1.

An important criterion for the maturity of the methods is if *they are tested and confirmed.* MacDonnell [Macd94] investigated if the complete model was tested using real world data (criteria tested) and if it was evaluated using systems other than those employed in testing the model (criteria confirmed). Table 7.4 shows that all the functional size methods considered so far have been tested with real-world data. Also, most of the methods have been confirmed and thus can be applied. This may be different for other sizing methods, e.g., the alternative approaches introduced below, which may still be under development and continuous change.

Table 7.3. Tool support for the methods

Method	Tool Support
Data Points	PCCALC, SoftCalc
Object Points	SoftCalc
Feature Points	Checkpoint/KnowledgePlan
IFPUG	Checkpoint/KnowledgePlan, PCCALC, ISBSG-Venturi, Function Points Workbench, COSTAR, FPLive
Mark II FPA	MK II Function Points Analyzer
FFPv1	HierarchyMaster FFP, FPC-Analyzer, Palm-FFP
FFPv2	COSMIC Xpert

Table 7.4. Status of testing and confirmation

Method	Tested	Evaluated
Bang Metric	Yes	No
Feature Points	Yes	-
Boeing 3-D	Yes	-
IFPUG	Yes	Yes
Mark II FPA	Yes	Yes
FFPv1	Yes	Yes
FFPv2	Yes	Yes

Another motivation for the selection of a certain sizing method is its *status of standardization*, that is, whether a method is accepted as a standard or not. Methods that are accepted as international standards will probably have higher maturity and a higher user acceptance. The following methods were developed through the ISO as international standards:

- Full Function Points version 2.1, ISO/IEC 19761
- IFPUG Function Points, ISO/IEC 20926
- Mark II Function Points, ISO/IEC 20968 and
- NESMA (the Netherlands adaptation of IFPUG Function Points, this method is not considered here), ISO/IEC 24570.

The *validation of functional size measurement methods* determines whether the methods measure what they are intended to measure and how well this is done. According to Kitchenham and Fenton [Kitc95], for the decision whether a measure is valid or not it is necessary to confirm the following aspects:

- attribute validity (e.g., if the entity is representing the attribute of interest)

- unit validity (e.g., appropriateness of the used measurement unit)
- instrument validity (e.g., valid underlying model)
- protocol validity (e.g., acceptable measurement protocol)

Kitchenham and Fenton found some definition problems with Albrecht Function Points, for example, that ordinal scale measures are added, which violates basic scale type constraints. For Mark II function points they state that the measure can be valid only if Mark II function points are considered as an effort model rather than as a sizing model. Other interesting work in this area was done by Fetcke [Fetc00] who investigated IFPUG Function Points, Mark II Function Points and Full Function Points with respect to the mathematical properties of dominance and monotony. He found significant differences in the empirical assumptions made by these functional size measurement methods. Among other things, Fetcke's results are [Fetc00]:

- While Mark II Function Points and Full Function Points assume the axiom of dominance, IFPUG Function Points do not.
- The axiom of monotony is assumed by Full Function Points version 2, and by Mark II Function Points partially. Full Function Points version 1 and IFPUG Function Points violate this axiom.

As can be seen in this section the area of validation is very important but also very complex, thus a more detailed discussion is given in [Fetc99] and [Loth02a].

7.3 The COSMIC Full Function Point Method

The COSMIC full function point measurement method (COSMIC-FFP) is a standardized measure of software functional size as *ISO/IEC 19761*. The COSMIC-FFP measurement method involves the application of models, rules and procedures to a given piece of software as it is perceived from the perspective of *Functional user requirements* (see [Abra01a], [Abra01b] and [COSM03]). The result of the application of these models, rules and procedures is a numerical "value of a quantity" representing the functional size of the software, as measured from its Functional user requirements.

The COSMIC-FFP measurement method is designed to be independent of the implementation decisions embedded in the operational artifacts of the software to be measured. To achieve this characteristic, measurement is applied to the FUR of the software to be measured expressed in the form of the COSMIC-FFP *generic software model*. This form of the FUR is obtained by a mapping process from the FUR as supplied in or implied in the actual artifacts of the software (Fig. 7.3).

Software is bounded by hardware. In the so-called "front-end" direction, software used by a human user is bounded by I/O hardware or by engineered devices such as sensors or relays. In the so-called "back-end" direction, software is bounded by persistent storage hardware.

Four distinct types of movement can characterize the functional flow of data attributes. In the front-end direction, two types of movement (ENTRIES and EXITS) allow the exchange of data with the users across a *boundary*. In the back-end direction, two types of movement (READS and WRITES) allow the exchange of data attributes with the persistent storage hardware Fig. 7.4.

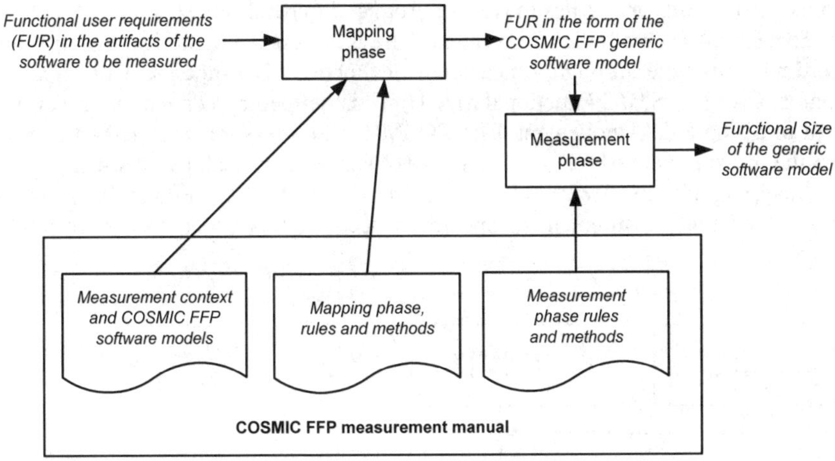

Fig. 7.3. COSMIC-FFP measurement process model

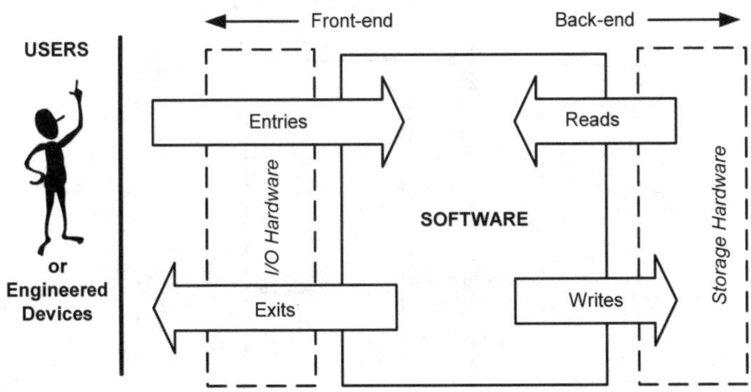

Fig. 7.4. Generic data flow through software from a functional perspective

Different abstractions are typically used for different measurement purposes. For business application software, the abstraction commonly assumes that the users are one or more humans who interact directly with the business application software across the boundary; the I/O hardware is ignored. In contrast for real-time software, the users are typically the engineered devices that interact directly with the software, that is, the users *are* the I/O hardware.

The architectural reasoning of boundaries is given through the *software layers* such as tiers, service structures or component deployments. The functional size of software is directly proportional to the number of its *data transactions.* All data movement subprocesses move data contained in exactly one data group. Entries move data from the users across the boundary to the inside of the functional process; exits move data from the inside of the functional process across the boundary to the users; reads and writes move data from and to persistent storage.

To each instance of a data movement there is assigned a numerical quantity, according to its type, through a measurement function. The measurement standard, that is, C_{FSU} (COSMIC Functional Size Unit), is defined by convention as equivalent to a single data movement. The COSMIC-FFP measurement method considers the measurement of the functional size of software through two distinct phases: the mapping of the software to be measured to the COSMIC-FFP generic software model and the measurement of specific aspects of this generic software model (Fig. 7.5).

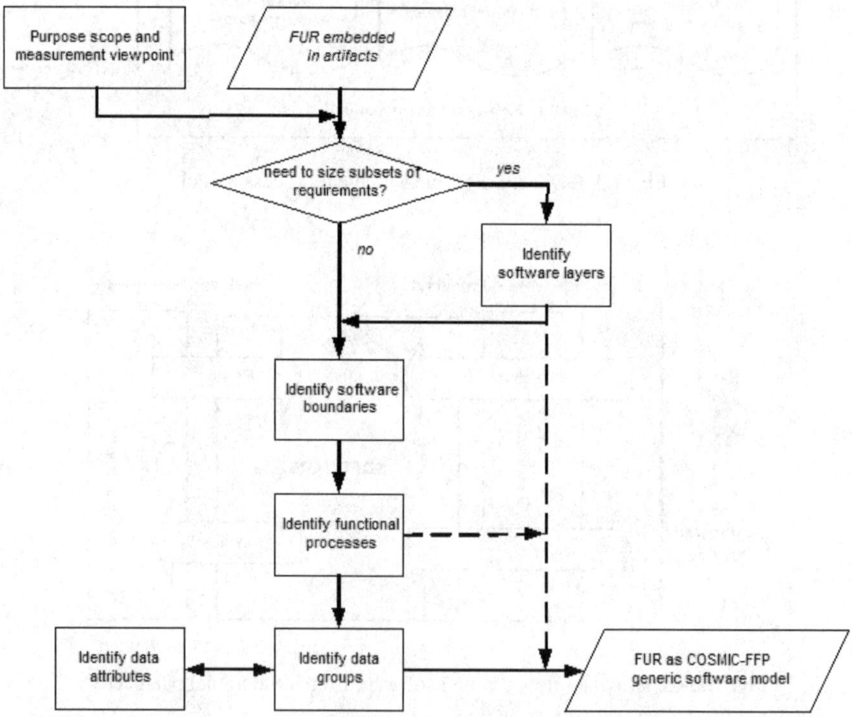

Fig. 7.5. The general method of the COSMIC-FFP mapping process

The increasing number of COSMIC-FFP method applications show the usability of this approach for size measurement in several functional domains and thus as one of the basics for effort and cost estimation [Abra01a], [Büre99], [Dumk01], [Dumk03b], [Loth03a].

7.4 Case Study: Using the COSMIC Full Function Point Method

In the following we describe a *feasibility study* in order to evaluate the appropriateness of the COSMIC-FFP method in an industrial environment at Bosch [Loth03a]. The project results described in a feasibility study arose from the ambition to continually improve the software development processes (in efforts towards a CMM Integration (CMMI) level-3/CMMI level-4 certification), adding new ideas, measurements and thus new value to the processes. In order to obtain business data, e.g., effort estimation, critical computer resources, market value and productivity measurements, the need for a software size measure was recognized. Lines of code (LOC) have been proven to be insufficient for several reasons, e.g., because of the late point of LOC measurements and because they are counterproductive (especially when software has to be very efficient in order to fit into the electronic control unit memory). For that reason, another applicable software size measurement approach to replace LOC had to be identified and tested. The main project goal was the determination of a functional size measure as a basis for the improvement of existing effort estimation techniques, for the determination of the software market value as well as for other business considerations.

The selection of a FSM method is affected by several influencing factors such as the software's functional domain and the particularities of the software development process. The typical automotive software as considered here can be characterized as real-time, embedded control software. A high ratio of the developed software results from a so-called variant development (where existing software is modified/extended or the development is continued in different ways/branches at a certain point of time) and has specifically a high algorithmic complexity. The measurement/counting automation, the general tool support and the convertibility between different sizing methods have not been subject of these selection considerations. The question of objectivity/repeatability of the measurements in the homogeneous target environment is assumed.

Now, we present the main results of the feasibility study (see [Loth03a] for more details). We consider that the measurement is divided into a mapping phase and a measurement phase.

Mapping Phase – Layer (proof of the appropriateness of the (functional) domain). Since the analyzed piece of software is not characterized by a client/server structure and no different levels of abstraction can be identified, the layer concept cannot be applied. Because of the manner of the software, for single software components layers are not expected at all within the given application area. Only if a whole system with several components (client/server) is under investigation, can layers possibly play a role.

Mapping Phase – Boundary (evidence of suitable structuredness). For single software components the boundary can be identified very easily, because the software under investigation is a self-contained control process. The boundary is right around the software component. Three areas for data exchange have been identified: input signals from the CAN bus, output signals to the CAN bus and influencing parameters from the ROM. Since the value of the parameters directly influences the functionality of the software under investigation, this part was explicitly integrated in the measurements. Fig. 7.6 shows the typical boundary model for the measured software components in the application area.

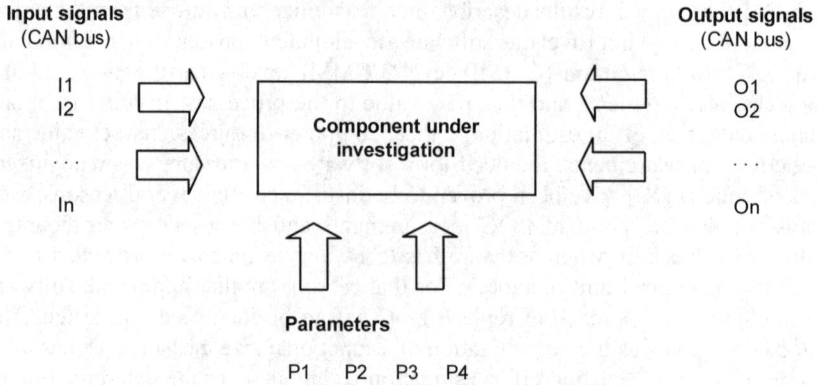

Fig. 7.6. Typical boundary model

Mapping Phase – Functional Processes/Trigger/Data Groups (examination of the necessary scalability). The software component under investigation has only one functional process that is triggered when the CAN bus contains the appropriate message. This behavior is symptomatic for nearly all components in the application area, and so most of the components contain only one functional process. The grouping of data attributes to data groups will be shown in the measurement phase (Fig. 7.7).

Measurement Phase – Subprocess Identification and Counting (proof of efficient (tool-based) countability). The available functional description mainly consists of a hierarchical ordered set of block diagrams. Because of the representation style of the information in the beginning it is difficult to extract the needed information for the subprocess identification. With a bit of experience the information can be transferred to the following schematic diagram (Fig. 7.8).

Measurement Phase – Measurement Summary (evidence of empirical-based explorability). One functional process has been identified within the component under investigation; the final COSMIC FFP size is 19 C_{FSU}.

Summary: All of the considered components under investigation could be transferred to such a schematic diagram easily. Because of the described properties and the similarities of the components under investigation, a procedure has been identified that easily allows the application of the FFP measurement for the given specifications. According to widely accepted statements, for a successful FSM certain conditions must be met, thus knowledge of the functional domain and the measurement domain is required as well as an adequate source of information.

Now, we will share our effort data. In the beginning of the project we had good knowledge about the FFP, but were not very experienced in counting FFP in a real environment. For that reason expertise was built up with help of an FFP expert. In the area of embedded systems we had no experience. Thus, the notation of the functional description (mostly as block diagrams) was particularly difficult to understand.

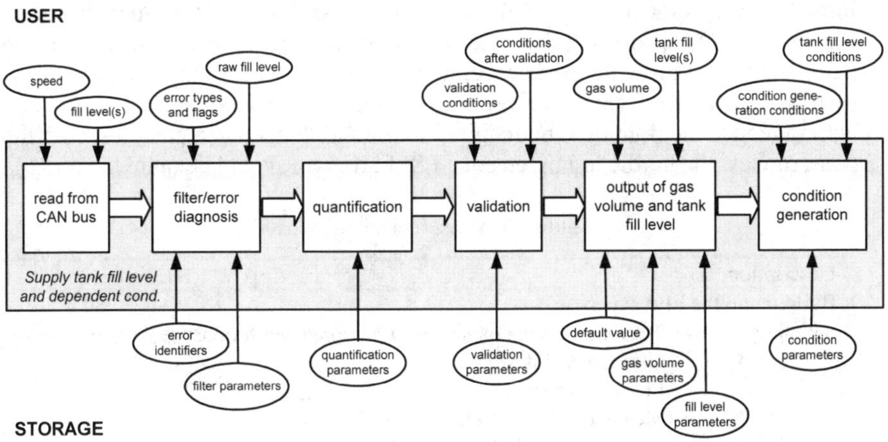

Fig. 7.7. Schematic diagram

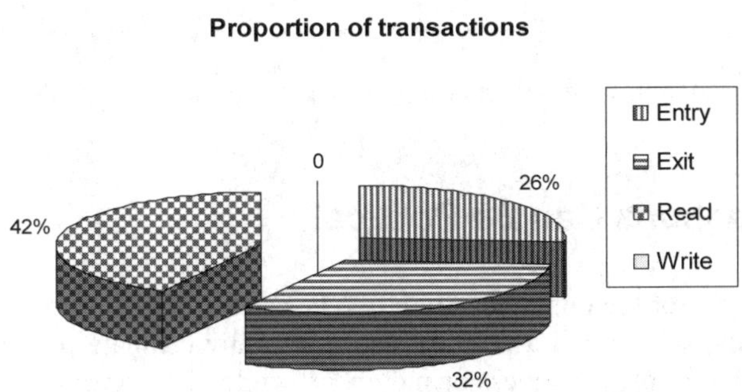

Fig. 7.8. Proportion of transactions

Our knowledge increased step-by-step by measuring the given software components. Functional definitions (at the end of design phase) were the source of information for the measurement. The design documents were complete, and thus all the data required could be found in the documents. As mentioned before, because of a lack of knowledge with respect to the notation style it was difficult and took a lot of effort to extract the desired information. Table 7.5 shows the effort spent for the measurements (which was the effort of two people).

Once again, particularly the understanding of the functional descriptions was difficult and a lot of effort had to be spent on this task. An FFP counter who is familiar with the block diagram notation should be able to extract the required information very quickly (expected mean value: less than one hour per functional description). The effort will decrease with an increasing number of measurements (e.g., because of growing experience, trust in necessary decisions, etc.), as can be seen from our effort data. The recognized, typical measurement scheme should help to reduce the training time required for new FFP counters, and thus from this point of view the hurdle to implement a FSM program should be quite low.

Table 7.5. Measurement effort data

Description		Effort
Building up the FFP expertise		80 h
including	• Training to understand the functional definitions (2 persons, 3 days)	40 h
	• FFP consulting	10 h
	• Measurement of reference software component (supply tank fill level and dependent conditions) as first measurement together with measurement expert (novice in the area of embedded system as well)	5 h
Measurement of three additional, comparable components consisting of 3, 4 and 10 pages (total)		12 h

The presented approach will encourage users to implement a FSM program.

7.5 Estimations Can Be Political

A great obstacle for the implementation of a fair estimation culture is so-called political estimations. We call a political estimation any estimate provided with the prime objective to prove a guess or judgment, while obscuring reality. Especially in large organizations there may be many reasons for this, e.g., lust for power, human vanity and others. The following list presents some associated problems [Bund04].

- Estimation is often mistaken for bargaining. Missing historical data often result in the dictation of unrealistic deadlines.

- The size of the project is often obviously/consciously wrongly estimated (trimmed estimations).
- When cutbacks of the IT project occur(e.g. budgets or deadlines) the estimation is often erroneously trimmed according to the cutbacks instead of by reducing the other primary goals (quality, functionality, costs, time).
- Voluntary unpaid overtime will be planned but not considered in the estimation.
- Goal conflicts often arise from another irrational factor, namely human vanity. The desire for success and acknowledgement often leads to "turf wars" in the IT project environment to the end that project leaders must consider power politics in the environment of their IT project.
- There is a widespread prejudice that application systems, software and hardware cost more in the host environment than in client/server (C/S) applications for software or hardware. This leads to more bargaining in the C/S environment instead of estimations and thus necessitates more effort to convince management that C/S environment costs much the same as the host environment.

A main cause for this underestimation is the fact that often a political estimation is done instead of a realistic one. In reality, the effort of an IT project is often underestimated in order to gain approval for the initiation and performance of this IT project. What a crazy world: here the decision makers are not guided by the estimations, but the effort estimators are guided by the criteria for decision making. The practical result is that the effort is not estimated but is determined by bargaining.

Political estimations and project decisions not based on facts definitely ruin trust in a company. Management and staff should thus avoid these obstacles in order to foster a good estimation culture.

7.6 Establishing Buy-In: The Estimation Conference

Estimations can be done by different individuals and the average of their estimations can be used. But there exists an approved alternative: an estimation conference. Several persons from the project team (e.g., leaders of parts of the project) discuss together, how to estimate the estimation object in view of the total IT project. This leads to an estimation that is accepted by all involved persons, which is more objective than the above-mentioned average and hence can be better defended against other opinions. The results may not differ very much, as we found in some cases [Bund00a].

Another benefit of the estimation conference is that the involved estimators gain awareness of the uncertainties and possible risks of the IT project. Furthermore they all get the same information. An estimation conference is a team-building experience. An estimation conference also promotes the estimation culture in an organization, since it helps to solve acceptance problems by finding a consensus through discussions in a team. These benefits can often be gained in only one two-hour estimation conference!

7.7 Estimation Honesty

Estimation is a process that is closely bound up with resistance: not wanting to estimate, not wanting to commit oneself, and, last but not least, not wanting to be measurable. In order to overcome these acceptance problems, estimations should never and by no means be used in relation to people but only in relation to processes or products. This is the cause of the question of estimation honesty: one estimation for the steering committee, one for the boss and the right (?) one for the actual user.

Project managers often do not like to estimate because they like to map the progress of their project. This desire can only be overcome by education and repeated information about the benefits of estimation. It is evident for project mangers that their acceptance of an estimate is their commitment and that their success will be measured by achieving this goal. A possible motivation in this case is a financial bonus for success.

On the other hand, organizations must clearly express their opinion about the sense of manipulated estimations or lies on time sheets or unrealistic Gantt charts or time schedules.

7.8 Estimation Culture

A lasting estimation culture can only be fostered if the estimation process is clearly defined and transparently performed and thus estimation honesty is promoted. The development of an estimation culture evolves in following phases:

1. **Problem**. Estimation is not viewed positively.
2. **Awareness**. Management and staff become increasingly aware of the estimation theme yet do not start to handle it systematically.
3. **Transition**. Transition from viewing estimation as management task to viewing it as a team task.
4. **Anticipation**. Transition from subjective estimation to measuring and use of metrics and tools.
5. **Chances**. Positive vision of estimation; everybody is responsible for it.

A good estimation culture can prevent management and project leaders from playing political games with estimation and promotes motivated and effective project teams. A good estimation culture is also a positive vision of estimation, which is the responsibility of every staff member. Its foundation can be built by sound training.

7.9 The Implementation of Estimation

The implementation of estimation is an innovative project and hence must be planned and performed like any other IT project. It is the foundation of successful communication as well as for monitoring and improvement of project management processes. As in all innovative projects, the focus has to be directed to acceptance problems.

The king's road to gain acceptance consists of information, training and participation of all involved persons, as mentioned at the beginning of this chapter. In addition, there is need for enough time since awareness for the innovations to be fostered. If this cornerstone is omitted during the implementation of an IT metrics program, then it has a good chance, like half of all software metrics initiatives, to be abandoned early and without success. An IT metrics program is a strategic project and not extra overhead, which is only seen as a necessarily evil.

A roadmap for successful implementation of estimation should consider the following stations (Fig. 7.9) [Bund00a].

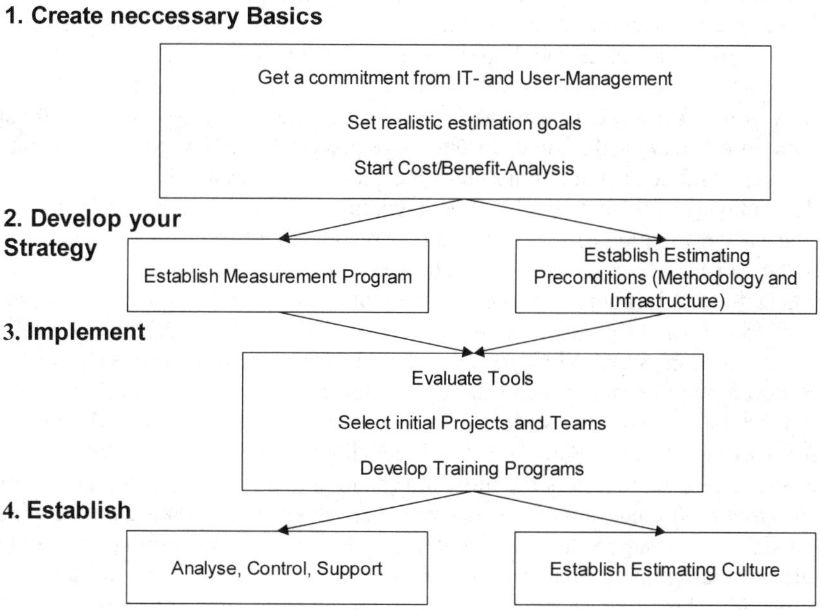

Fig. 7.9. A roadmap for successful implementation of estimation

1. **Building the foundation**. Define the goals and propagate them. Define a standard process. Be informed and gain a market overview. Search for projects with which to start the metrics initiative,. which are typically the strategic projects with at least three months duration and more than one person-year of effort, in order that the implementation of estimation can show the benefits.

2. **Strategic planning**. Foster the transition by training about estimation, for creation of awareness and understanding as well as for motivation and expertise. This is very helpful for knowledge transfer with other users and elimination of fears of the involved staff. Stay on course: Manage resistance and document first experiences. Check consistency via inspections. Improve the processes by development of standards and IT metrics, knowledge transfer and comparison with other users.
3. **Implementation**. This is accomplished by planning, and by budgeting, scheduling and resource coordination. Establish precedence. Define structure, process, methods and tools
4. **Establish the concept**.

A successful implementation in a large organization with about 500 IT developers was done over three years by two persons who worked as the competence center. During this process a method and tools were chosen, and a number of presentations for managers and project leaders were given, an estimation manual was developed, and about 90 persons visited training sessions. As the result at least one person in each developer team got a training in function point counting and estimation. The function point counting of all application systems was performed in a tool-based manner and with assistance of the competence center. The staff of the competence center coached all function point counts and assisted the project leaders in tool-based documentation. For some of these IT projects there already existed an estimate at this time. In one large project the estimation was repeated after a year, and hence the requirements creep could be measured.

The analysis of the data enabled the development of a function point prognosis for the early estimation of function points, which are the basis for estimation using only the number of inputs and outputs of a new development project. The function points that are to be counted in the requirements phase can thus be calculated with a regression formula in advance, with an error of 15% at the time of the project start. In addition, some Microsoft Excel tools for estimation and data analysis were developed in order to assist the project leaders. There also were four project post mortem calculations, which were delivered to the International Software Benchmarking Standards Group (ISBSG) benchmarking database [ISBS98].

Management support was the most important success factor for the implementation process. It consisted of several measures. From the beginning on there was the insight of managers that the implementation of a sound estimation method would bring an immense benefit for processes and quality of project management. Additionally, for three years, two persons had enough time (one full time, the other part time) to gain qualifications and to build up a competence center. This competence center could always involve the developers and project managers in meetings and presentations. After a two year break another two part-time employees joined the competence center.

The three-day training for one person from each group of developers was always done with external consultants. Manpower bottlenecks in function point counting were also settled with external consultants.

The breakthrough of the implementation came with the final function point counting of all application systems. The achievement of this goal was connected with 20% of the annual bonus of the managers of each development department. This led to a huge number of questions from project managers. Experiences in the British organization were much the same. They were able to increase the productivity of application development in one year from 11 to 13 function points per person-month because this goal was also connected with the financial bonus of the project managers.

Continuing questioning from management increased the awareness of managers and project managers for estimation. They realized that function point counting and estimation were more and more integrated in the project life cycle and were no longer neglected or viewed as overhead. The competence center accompanied the whole process with many presentations, discussions, reports and work on routine tasks.

To sum up, there are only few technical challenges for successful implementation of software measurement, but there are many psychological challenges. The following pages introduce answers to frequently asked questions from beginners and discuss the benefits of a competence center.

7.10 Estimation Competence Center

Practical experience demonstrates that it is useful to have central support and qualified and competent personal for estimation available for the organization. This is the only guarantee for central collection, documentation and analysis of the gained estimation experience in order to learn from it. The elaboration of an estimation or metrics database and the development of standards for the improvement of the knowledge base with tool support are necessary and important measures.

Such a competence center can support the dissemination of experiences through continuous publication of results, experiences, reports from conferences, knowledge transfer with other organizations and other news about estimation This improves the communication about estimation and fosters acceptance since the staff feels informed and involved.

The benefits of a competence center are many:

1. **Gaining experience in estimation**. Experienced experts are always available in the organization for all questions about estimation. Often certified function point counters (CFPS, certified function point specialists) are among them.
2. **Independent estimations**. A competence center is independent of the projects that are to be estimated.
3. **Collection of experiences**. Historical data can be collected, and a metrics database and new knowledge can be recognized through the analysis of this data.

However, reasons also exist why estimation should not be done exclusively by a competence center. Specialists for estimation are a scarce resource and thus should work as little as possible on projects. On the other side, the project managers are in closer contact to the problem and thus can better manage the expectations of the users. This is the reason for the alternative, to qualify individuals decentrally for the role of estimation coordinator of a department. These coordinators are then responsible for the organization and elaboration of the estimations and function point counts of their department, for planning and elaboration of all necessary measurement of figures and indicators as well as the calculation of metrics. They are thus the ideal partners for a small competence center. Table 7.6 and Table 7.7 show possible role descriptions for a function point coordinator and a function point counter [Bund04].

Table 7.6. Function point coordinator role description

Role aspect	Explanation
Important Interfaces	Competence Center
Responsibility	Planning of FP counting and FP counting for his department
Coordination	Planning and organization of application-, project- and maintenance task counts
Quality Assurance	Planning and organization of quality assurance of the FP counts by the competence center
Tasks	Administration of the FP counts of his department: applications, projects, maintenance tasks Annual actualization of the application counts and the according Function Point Workbench Master Files
Controlling	Controlling of FP counts and the FP Workbench
Communication	Communication with colleagues, managers and the competence center
Necessary Knowledge	Function Point Courses 1 to 3
Necessary Skills	Function Point Workbench

Table 7.7. Function point counter role description

Role aspect	Explanation
Important Interfaces	Function Point Coordinator
Responsibility	FP counting for his Department: application-, project- and maintenance task counts
Coordination	N/A
Quality Assurance	N/A
Tasks	FP counting and documentation in the Function Point Workbench
Controlling	N/A
Communication	Communication with his function point coordinator
Necessary Knowledge	Function Point Courses 1 and 2
Necessary Skills	FP counting according to IFPUG 4.1, Function Point Workbench

7.11 Training for Estimation

Training for estimation occurs primarily through the exchange of experiences, lectures and workshops at congresses of IT metrics associations. Consultants and trainers are often members of metrics associations and offer training for all aspects of estimation. Many organizations arrange courses for their staff from these consultants or training institutes.

Estimation is often a part of project management training (sometimes not even this). The same holds for (the passive training medium) books. An intermediate approach is interactive learning programs.

The International Function Point User Group (IFPUG),as well as the British UKSMA, and the Dutch NESMA, (IT metrics organizations), each offer certifications for various methods (the IFPUG function point method, the Mark II Method and the NESMA function point method, respectively; see also Chap. 16).

7.12 Hints for the Practitioner

Following questions are frequently discussed in organizations in the context of implementation of estimation

1. The effort for implementation
2. The right moment for implementation
3. The pros and cons for a competence center

The implementation of estimation in a large organization may take about two years. To gain estimation experience and integrate estimation into the project management processes and the consequent introduction of IT metrics for continuing improvement may need another two years.

The cost of an implementation program is often cited as an argument against systematic and professional estimation. Considering the effort for large projects in service organizations and administrations it can be said that only one failed IT project will cost more than all the effort that is necessary to implement and support sound methods for estimation and software measurement [Jone96].

The right moment for implementing estimation is always too late in practical life. A favorable moment is when project management processes or the development environment change. At this moment the estimation tasks can be integrated directly. If the quality of software development is to be guaranteed the motto must be: start any time. Gaining experience and the accompanying learning cycles can thus be started any time.

The selection of the appropriate method of cost estimation based on size or effort prediction depends on different aspects and motivations:

- Carefully investigate your own background on software sizing. Your experience in code size or design elements motivates the appropriateness of cost estimation method. Different sizing techniques are around, such as lines of code, Function Points, use cases, etc.

- FSM methods are successful if they are defined the functional system model or the system architecture. But, the quality of estimation was determined through the experience background for mapping the "points" to the effort or size unit. An example of experience is described in Chap. 13.
- COSMIC-FFP applicability depends on the following experience for a successful migration like considering the domain of software systems (e.g., embedded), using the given experience in FFP application for some well-known application domains, and defining the strategic process for the stepwise use of the FFP method based on the handbook.
- A helpful strategy is given by designing tool-based support for FP counting, aggregation and exploration.
- Finally, it also depends on your own empirical background for use of the FFP method in decision making in different areas of management.

7.13 Summary

In this chapter we presented some recent approaches in cost estimation including size and effort estimation. The selection of a FSM method is affected by several influencing factors such as the software's functional domain and the particularities of the software development process.

A functional size measurement standard COSMIC FFP is described and discussed in the application of embedded system development. Functional definitions (at the end of design phase) are the source of information for the measurement. The recognized, typical measurement scheme helps to reduce the training time required for new FFP counters. The essential characteristic of the COSMIC FFP is the simplicity and flexibility of the application. The success in using this method is supported by extending the experience base in further industrial applications.

8 Project Control

To really trust people to perform,
you must be aware of their progress.
—Watts S. Humphrey

8.1 Project Control and Software Measurement

Project control is defined as a control activity concerned with identifying, measuring, accumulating, analyzing and interpreting project information for strategy formulation, planning and tracking activities, decision-making and cost accounting. As such it is the basic tool for gaining insight into project performance and is more than only ensuring the overall technical correctness of a project [ISO97a, ISO97b, ISO02, DeMa82].

Many R&D projects are out of control. Different studies suggest that roughly 75% of all started projects do not reach their original targets [Gart02]. For each project there is an average sum of roughly 1 Mio Euro that is spent in excess before the project is terminated – for good or bad. On average a project that is cancelled takes 14 weeks of the 27 weeks of average project duration. Only half way through a flawed project is it decided to cancel it. The interesting aspect is, that by 6 weeks before that termination it is clear to all participants that the problem cannot be cured. That is, in the average cancelled project 20% of time and resources are completely wasted because people do not acknowledge facts.

Only 25% of all companies periodically review their project progress. Often projects are even trapped in a vicious circle that the management involved (including sales or marketing) are aware of this, and in anticipation keep requirements overly volatile to negotiate further trade-offs with customers.

We need a way to determine if a project is on track or not. There is a saying that "you cannot control what you cannot measure". Because there is little or no visibility into the status and forecast of projects, it is apparent that some common baseline metrics need to be implemented for all projects in an organization. Such core metrics would provide visibility into the current versus planned status of engineering projects, allowing for early detection of variances and time for taking corrective action. Metrics reduce "surprises" by giving us insight into when a project is heading towards trouble, instead of discovering it when it is already there. Standardized metrics provide management with indicators to control projects and evaluate performance in the bigger picture.

Many organizations that consider software development as their core business often have too much separation between business performance monitoring and evaluation and what is labeled as low-level software metrics [Gart02, Royc98, Pfle97, McGa01]. Similar to a financial profit and loss (P&L) statement, it is necessary to implement a few core metrics to generate reports from different projects that can easily be understood by nonexperts. If you maintain consistency across projects, you can easily aggregate data to assess business performance and to assist with estimating, culminating in a kind of engineering balance sheet. This allows for better predictability of future projects and quantification of the impact of changes to existing ones.

The basic activities within software project management can be clustered as

- tendering and requirements management
- estimation and costing
- resource management
- planning and scheduling
- monitoring and reviews
- product control

Much has been written on those parts related to classic project management, however the monitoring aspect is often neglected. We will therefore focus on this part and call it "*project control*" to distinguish from other financial control activities (e.g. corporate budget) [DeMa82]. Often software managers have all technical background but lack the exposure to management techniques. We will thus look here to some basic techniques to track and control projects. Most key techniques in software project control were driven by classic management.

> Project control answers few simple questions derived from the following management activities:
>
> **Decision-making**. What should I do?
>
> **Attention directing**. What should I look at?
>
> **Performance evaluation**. Am I doing good or bad?
>
> **Improvement tracking**. Am I doing better or worse than last period?
>
> **Planning**. What can we reasonably achieve in a given period?
>
> **Target setting**. How much can we improve in a given period?

Project control is a classic control process as we see it in many control systems. Most important is the existence of a closed loop between the object being controlled, the actual performance metrics and a comparison of targets versus actuals. Fig. 8.1 shows this control loop. The project with its underlying engineering processes delivers results, such as work products. It is influenced and steered by the project targets. Project control captures the observed metrics and risks and relates them to the targets. By analyzing these differences specific actions can be taken to get back on track or to ensure that the project remains on track. These actions serve as an additional input to the project besides the original project targets. To make the actions effective is the role of the project manager.

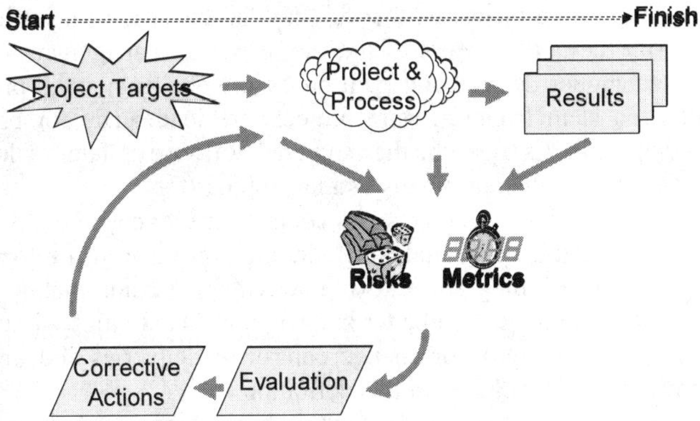

Fig. 8.1. Project control starts with project targets. It extracts metrics and risks and ensures that corrective actions are taken

In this chapter we show how a software metrics program is introduced to reinforce and support project control for software projects. Our motivation for building such a corporate software measurement program is to embed it within the engineering control activities in order to align the different levels of target setting and tracking activities. The close link of corporate strategy with clearly specified business goals and with the operational project management ensures the achievement of overall improvements. We therefore recommend coordinating the metrics program with a parallel software process improvement initiative to ensure that goals on all levels correspond with each other. Often though, the metrics program is actually stimulated by an ongoing process improvement program. Improvement programs absolutely need underlying and consistent project metrics to follow up progress of the improvement activities.

The chapter is organized as follows. Section 2 gives a brief introduction to project control and how it fits into the framework of project management as the major tool for decision-making in software project management. Hints for the practitioner and experiences with software metrics introduction that hold especially from the perspective of organizational learning are provided in Sect. 3. Finally Sect. 4 summarizes this chapter.

8.2 Applications of Project Control

8.2.1 Monitoring and Control

Software projects do not fail because of incompetent project managers or engineers working on these projects; neither do they fail because of insufficient technology. Primarily they fail because of the use of wrong management techniques. Management techniques derived and built on experience from small projects that often do not even stem from software projects are inadequate for professional software development. As a result, the delivered software is late, of low quality and of much higher cost than originally estimated [Gart02].

Project control of software projects is a control activity concerned with identifying, measuring, accumulating, analyzing and interpreting project information for strategy formulation, planning and tracking activities, decision-making, and cost accounting. Further (perhaps even better known) control activities within software projects, such as configuration or change control of deliveries and intermediate working products are not included in this definition.

It is obvious that dedicated management techniques are needed because software projects yield intangible products, and often the underlying processes for creating the products are not entirely understood. Unlike other engineering disciplines at universities, software engineering education until recently meant primarily design and programming techniques instead of proper project management.

Fig. 8.2 provides an overview on the measurement process seen from a project perspective. Four steps are visible in each project, namely selecting metrics, collecting and analyzing them and finally implementing decisions derived from the metrics analysis. Each of the boxes describes one process step. The responsible for executing the respective process is described in the upper part of the box. A metrics team that is active across all different projects ensures coherence of the measurement program.

The metrics team is instrumental in communicating and training on software measurement. In less mature organizations it helps in collecting and analyzing metrics. In more mature organizations it helps to share best practices and advance in new analysis methods and statistical techniques. It should however never get trapped into "outsourcing" measurement activities. Implementing effective project control is the key responsibility of each single project manager.

Several repetitive stages can be identified in project control and the related measurement and improvement process (see also Fig. 8.2):

- Set objectives, both short- and long-term for products and process
- Forecast and develop plans both for projects and for departments
- Compare actual metrics with original objectives
- Communicate metrics and metrics analyses
- Coordinate and implement plans
- Understand and agree to commitments and their changes
- Motivate people to accomplish plans

- Measure achievement in projects and budget centers
- Predict the development direction of process and product relative to goals and control limits
- Identify and analyze potential risks
- Evaluate project and process performance
- Investigate significant deviations
- Determine if the project is under control and whether the plan is still valid
- Identify corrective actions and reward/penalize performance
- Implement corrective actions

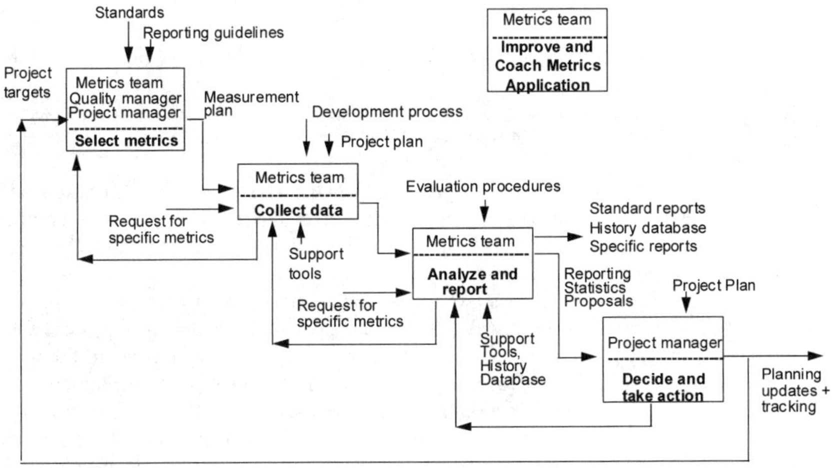

Fig. 8.2. Process overview for an integrated measurement program covering project control and process improvements

Different control objectives request different levels of metrics aggregation. Individual designers or testers need progress metrics on their level of deliverable work products and contribution to the project. Group leaders and functional coordinators need the same information on the level of their work area. Department heads request metrics that relate to time, effort and budget within their departments.

Project managers on the other hand look much more on their projects' individual budgets, schedule and deliverables to have insight in overall performance and progress. Clearly all users of metrics need immediate insight into the lower and more detailed levels as soon as performance targets are missed or the projects drift away from schedule and budget. Easy access to the different levels of information is thus of high importance.

The single best technology for getting some control over deadlines and other resource constraints is to **set formal objectives for quality and resources in a measurable way** [Royc98, Fent97, Eber96, Star94]. Planning and control activities cannot be separated. Managers control by tracking actual results against plans and acting on observed deviations. Controls should focus on significant deviations from standards and at the same time suggest appropriate ways for fixing the problems. Typically these standards are schedules, budgets and quality targets established by the project plan. All critical attributes established should be both measurable and testable to ensure effective tracking. The worst acceptable level should be clear although the internal target is in most cases higher.

Control is only achievable if measures of performance have been defined and implemented, objectives have been defined and agreed, predictive models have been established for the entire life cycle, and the ability to act is given. The remainder of this section will further investigate examples for each of these conditions (Table 8.1).

Table 8.1. Appropriate metrics are selected depending on the process maturity (CMM level).

CMM Level	Maturity description	What it means for metrics
5	Continuous improvements are institutionalized	Control of process changes; assess process innovations and manage process change; analysis of process and product metrics; follow through of defect prevention and technology / processes changes
4	Products and processes are quantitatively managed	Process metrics to control individual processes; quantitative objectives are continuously followed; statistical process control; control limit charts over time. Objectives are followed on process level; control is within projects to immediately take action if limits are crossed
3	Appropriate techniques are institutionalized	Metrics are standardized and evaluated; formal records for retrieving project metrics (intranet, history database); automatic metric collection; maintain process database across projects. Objectives are followed on organizational level
2	Project management is established	Few reproducible project metrics for planning and tracking (contents, requirements, defects, effort, size, progress); profiles over time for these metrics; few process metrics for process improvement progress tracking. Objectives are followed on project basis
1	Process is informal and ad hoc	Ad hoc project metrics (size, effort, faults); however, metrics are inconsistent and not reproducible.

The influence of metrics definition and application from project start (e.g., estimation, target setting and planning) to steering (e.g., tracking and budget control, quality management) to maintenance (e.g., failure rates, operations planning) is very well described in the related IEEE Standard for Developing Software Life Cycle Processes [ISO97a, ISO97b, ISO02]. This standard helps also in defining the different processes that constitute the entire development process including relationships to management activities.

One of the main targets of any kind of measurement is that it should provide an objective way of expressing information, free of value judgments. This is particularly important when the information concerned is "bad news", for instance related to productivity or cost, and thus may not necessarily be well received. Often the observed human tendency is to ignore any criticism related to one's own area and direct attention to somebody else's. Testing articulates that "the design is badly structured", while operations emphasize that "software has not been adequately tested". Any improvement activities must therefore be based on hard numerical evidence. The first use of metrics is most often to investigate the current state of the software process. On CMM Levels 1 and 2 basically any application of metrics is mainly restricted due to nonrepeatable processes and thus a limited degree of consistency across projects.

A selection of the most relevant project tracking metrics is provided in Fig. 8.3, Fig. 8.4 and Fig. 8.5. These metrics include milestone tracking, cost evolution, a selection of process metrics, work product deliveries and faults with status information. We distinguish three types of metrics with different underlying goals.

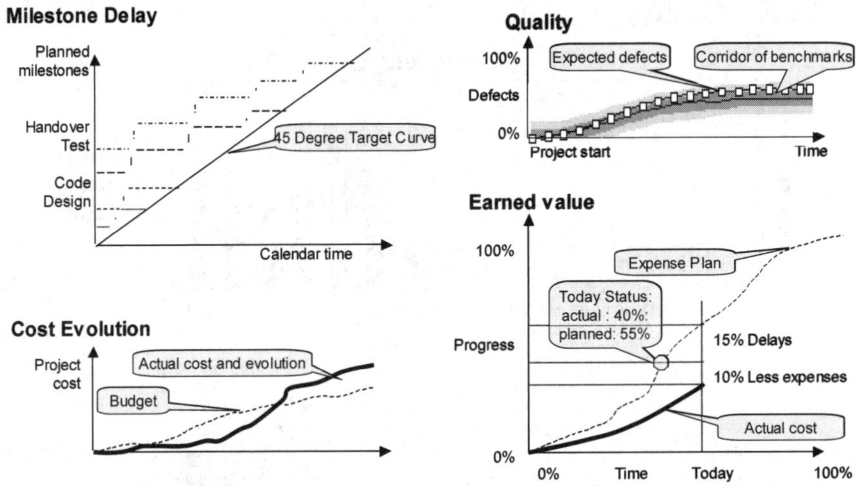

Fig. 8.3. Metrics dashboard (part 1): Overview metrics on schedule, cost, quality and content or earned value

Fig. 8.3 shows the high-level project tracking metrics that should be at the core of each project control toolset. They include milestones (planned versus achieved), cost evolution, quality status and earned value analysis. All these metrics are combined with the latest outlook and the original plan. Fig. 8.4 shows the classic tracking metrics that clearly serve as a more detailed view below what is showed in Fig. 8.3.

Such work product-oriented tracking is not enough for tracking a project, though we still see those metrics mostly used in software projects. Often this is simply because they are trivial to collect. Fig. 8.5 is more advanced and links process performance with project performance. Different core metrics and process indicators are combined to get a view into how the project is doing and how it performs versus the estimated process behaviors. It not only reveals under-performing projects easily, but it also helps to see risks much earlier than with after the fact tracking alone. In-process checks are always better than waiting until it is too late for corrections.

Such tracking metrics are periodically updated and provide an easy overview on the project status, even for very small projects. Based on this set of metrics several metrics can be selected for weekly tracking work products' status and progress (e.g., increment availability, requirements progress, code delivery, defect detection), while others are reported periodically to build up a history database (e.g., size, effort). Most of these metrics are actually byproducts from automatic collection tools related to planning and software configuration management (SCM) databases. Project-trend indicators based on such simple tracking curves are much more effective in alerting managers than the delayed and superficial task-completion tracking with PERT charts.

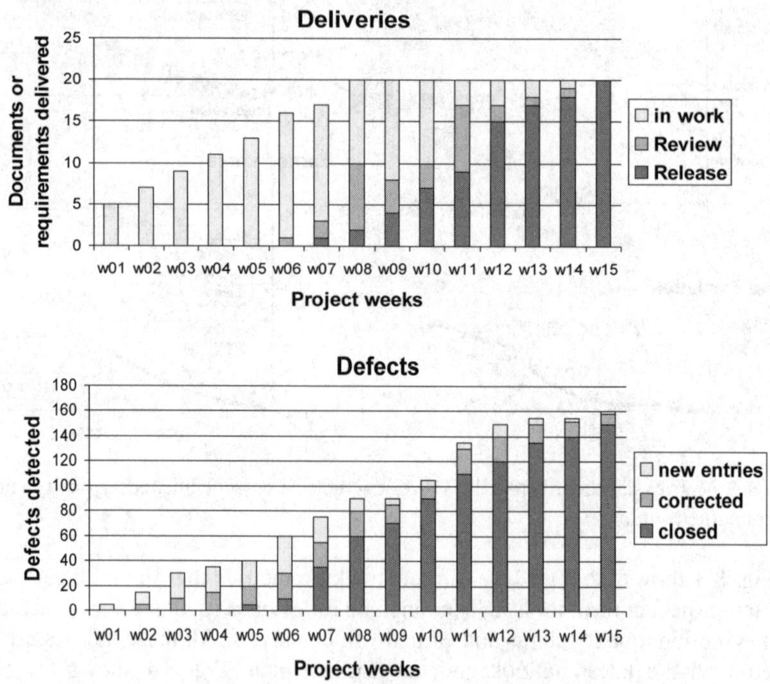

Fig. 8.4. Metrics dashboard (part 2): Work product metrics on delivery and quality for a project over project time. Status information is indicated with different shades

Effective project tracking and implementation of immediate corrective actions requires a strong project organization. As long as department heads and line managers interfere with project managers, decisions can be misleading or even contradictory. Frequent task and priority changes on the practitioner level with all related drawbacks are the consequence. Demotivation and inefficiency are the concrete results. A project or matrix organization with dedicated project teams clearly shows better performance than the classic line organization with far too much influence of department leaders.

Project managers must work based on defined roles and responsibilities. They are required to develop plans and objectives. Measurable performance and quality targets are defined within the project (quality) plans and later tracked through the entire project life cycle. Project managers report project and quality progress using standardized reporting mechanisms, such as fault removal efficiency or progress versus schedule in terms of deliverables (similar to the curves and completeness status in Fig. 8.3, Fig. 8.4, Fig. 8.5).

Metrics	targets	actuals	comment
size [KLOC]			
effort [PY]			
time to market [months]			
tested requirements [%]			
design progress [% of est. effort]			
code progress [% of est. size]			
test progress [% test cases]			
inspection efficiency [LOC/h]			
effort per defect in peer reviews [Ph/defect]			
effort per defect in module test [Ph/ defect]			
effort per defect in test [Ph/ defect]			
defects detected before integration [%]			
number of defects in design			
number of defects in peer reviews			
number of defects in module test			
number of defects in test			
number of defects in the field			

Fig. 8.5. Metrics dashboard (part 3): Example with in-process metrics comparing actuals with targets

Committing to such targets and being forced to track them over the development process ensures that project managers and therefore the entire project organization carefully observe and implement process improvement activities.

Test tracking is a good example of how to make use of tracking metrics. Test results can be used to suggest an appropriate course of action to take either during testing activities or towards their completion. Based on a test plan all testing activities should be seen in the context of the full test schedule, rather than as independent actions. If the goal is, for instance, how well an integration test detects faults then models of both test progress and defects must be available. Information that supports interpretation (e.g., fault density per subsystem, relationships to feature stability) must be collected and integrated.

A typical test-tracking curve is presented in Fig. 8.6. It indicates that effective tracking combines original plans with actual evolution, outlooks, updated plans and decision guidance, such as curves for early rejection if delivered quality is below expectations. Such previously agreed-upon limits or boundaries avoid inefficient and time-consuming fights between departments when delivery occurred with unsatisfactory quality. Transparent decision criteria followed up with respective metrics certainly serve as a more effective decision support for management. Besides the typical S-shaped appearance, several questions must be answered before being able to judge progress or efficiency. For example, how effectively was the specific test method applied? What is the coverage in terms of code, data relations or features during regression test? How many faults occurred during similar projects with similar test case suites over time?

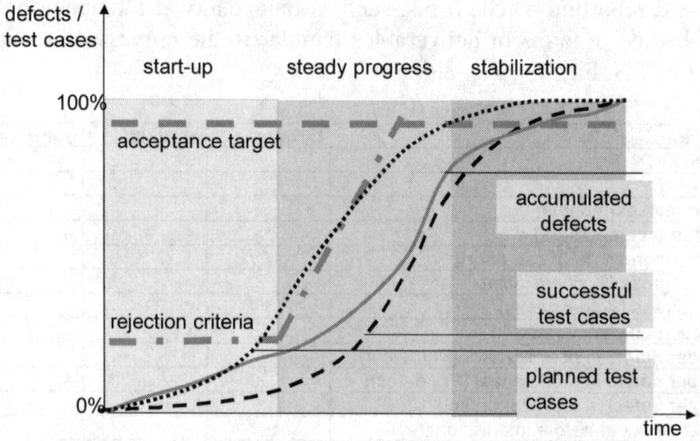

Fig. 8.6. A typical project control exercise: test tracking based on test plans, incoming defects, test progress and various criteria for acceptance and rejection of the test object

Based on such a premise, it is feasible to set up not only release-oriented phase end targets but also phase entry criteria that allow for rejection to module test or inspections if the system quality is inadequate. Related test process metrics include test coverage, number of open fault reports by severity, closure delay of fault reports, and other product-related quality, reliably and stability metrics. Such metrics allow judgments in situations when, because of difficulties in testing, decisions on the nature and sequence of alternative paths through the testing task should be made, while considering both the entire testing plan and the present project priorities. For example, there are circumstances in which full testing of a limited set of features will be preferred to a incomplete level of testing across full (contracted) functionality.

8.2.2 Forecasting

While metrics-based decision making is more accurate and reproducible than so-called intuitive and ad hoc approaches for managing software projects, it should be clear that there are components of uncertainty that ask for dedicated techniques of forecasting:

- Requirements are becoming increasingly unstable to achieve shorter lead times and faster reaction to changing markets. The risk is that the project is built on a moving baseline, which is one of the most often-quoted reasons for project failure.
- Plans are based on average performance indicators and history data. The smaller the project and the more the critical paths that are established due to requested expert knowledge, the higher the risk of having a reasonable plan from a macroscopic viewpoint that never achieves the targets on the microscopic level of individual experts' availability, effectiveness and skills. It was shown in several studies that individual experience and performance contributes up to 70% to overall productivity ranges (see Chaps. 2 and 10) [Hump89, Jone01].
- Estimations are based on individual judgment and as such are highly subjective. Applying any estimation model expresses first of all the experience and judgment of the assigned expert. Even simple models such as Function Points are reported as yielding reproducibility inaccuracy of >30% [Fent97, Jone01]. To reduce the risk related to decision making based on such estimates a Delphi-style approach can be applied that focuses multiple expert inputs to one estimate.
- Most reported software metrics are based on manual input of the raw data to operational databases. Faults, changes, effort, even the task break down are recorded by individuals that often do not necessarily care for such things, especially when it comes to delivery and time pressure. Software metrics, even if perceived as accurate (after all, they are numbers), must be related to a certain amount of error limits, which as experience shows is in the range of 10–20% [Fent97, Jone01].

Forecasts are today an inherent part of any project control. Traditional project tracking looked to actual results versus plans, where the plans would be adjusted after the facts indicate that they are not reachable. This method creates too many delays and is not sufficiently precise to drive concrete corrective actions on the spot. Therefore, predictions are used to relate actual constraints and performance to historic performance results.

Table 8.2 gives an overview on the use of metrics for forecasting. It is important to note that typically the very same underlying raw data is used for both tracking current performance and predicting future results. For instance, for the project management activities, effort and budget are tracked as well as requirements status and task or increment status. This information can also be used to determine risk exposure or cost to complete which relates to forecasting. The same holds for the other phases. In particular, defects and test tracking have a long tradition in forecasting a variety of performance parameters, such as maintenance cost of customer satisfaction.

An example for forecasting in a real project situation is provided in Fig. 8.7. It shows a typical project control question related to managing project risks. Time is running, and the project manager wonders whether he should still spend extra effort on regression testing of some late deliveries. Naturally this can and must be decided based on facts. There are two alternatives, namely doing regression test or not doing it. Each alternative can have three possible outcomes, namely that a critical defect is detected by regression test, a critical defect would be found by the customer, and that there is no critical defect remaining. The respective probabilities are different and are provided in the picture. Clearly the probability of detecting a critical defect when no regression test is run is small compared to the scenario with regression testing. If the probabilities are mapped to the expected outcome or loss (or cost of the outcome), one can calculate a forecasted risk value. The decision is finally rather simple to make, given the big differences in the accumulated cost (or risk) functions.

Good forecasts allow adjusting plans and mitigating risks long before the actual performance tracking metrics would visualize such results. For instance, knowing about average mean time to defect allows planning for maintenance staff, help desk and support centers, or service level agreements.

Table 8.2. Metrics are selected based on the objective to achieve and suited to the respective project phase. Metrics of current status (progress) are distinguished from forecasting metrics (outlook).

Project phase	Progress Metrics	Metrics for Predictions/Outlook
Project management	Effort and budget tracking; requirements status; task/increment status	Top 10 risks and mitigation outlook; cost to complete; schedule evolution
Quality management	Code stability; open defects; in-process checks; review status and follow-up	Remaining defects; open defects; reliability; customer satisfaction
Requirements management	Analysis status; specification progress	Requirements volatility/completeness
Construction	Status of documents, code, change requests; review status; efficiency	Design progress of requirements; cost to complete; time to complete
Test	Test progress (defects, coverage, efficiency, stability)	Remaining defects; reliability; cost to complete
Transition, deployment	Field performance (failures, corrections); maintenance effort	Reliability; maintenance effort

8.2.3 Cost Control

Because it seems obvious that costs in software projects are predominantly related to labor (i.e., effort), it is rare to find practical cost control besides deadline- or priority-driven resource allocation and shifting. The use of cost control, however, is manifold and must exceed headcount follow-up. In decision making cost information is used to determine relevant costs (e.g. sunk costs, avoidable versus unavoidable costs, variable versus fixed costs) in a given project or process, while in management control the focus is on controllable costs versus noncontrollable costs.

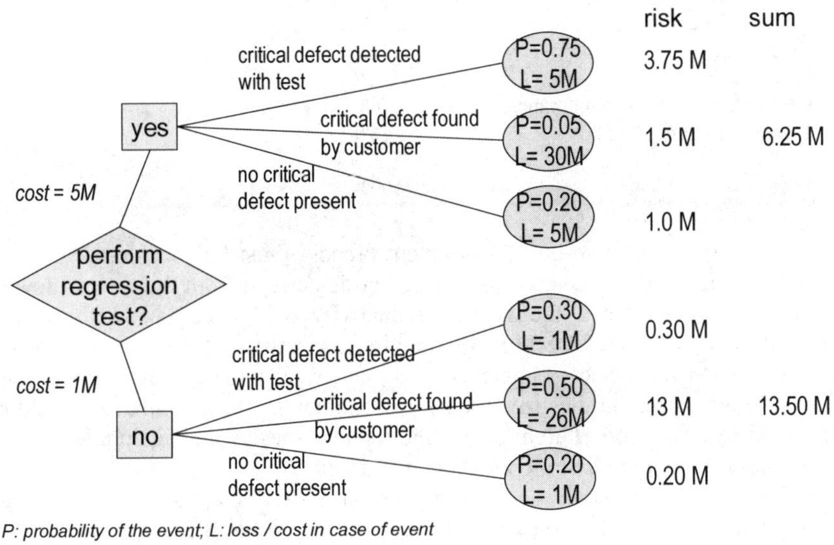

Fig. 8.7. Project control uses the same underlying metrics for progress tracking and risk management

A major step towards decision support is an accounting that moves from head-count-based effort models to activity-based costing. Functional cost analysis and even target-costing approaches are increasingly relevant because customers tend to pay for features instead of entire packages as before. Not surprisingly, cost reduction can only be achieved if it is clear how activities relate to costs. The difference is to assign costs to activities or processes instead of to departments.

Activity-based models allow for more accurate estimates and tracking than using holistic models, which only focus on size and effort for the project as one unit. Effects of processes and their changes, resources and their skill distribution or factors related to each of the development activities can be considered, depending on the breakdown granularity.

An example is given in Table 8.3, which includes a first breakdown to major development phases. The percentages and costs per thousand lines of code (KLOC) are for real-time embedded systems and should not be taken as fixed quantities [McGa01, Jone01]. Typically both columns for percentages and productivity are based on a project history database that is continuously improved and tailored to the specific project situation. Even process allocation might vary; projects with reuse have a different distribution with more emphasis towards integration and less effort for top-level design. Unit cost values are likely to decrease in the long-term as the cumulative effects of technological and process changes become visible.

Table 8.3. Example for activity-based effort allocation

Activity	Percent	Person months per KLOC
Project management	7%	0.7
Analysis, specification	17%	1.7
Design	22%	2.2
Coding	22%	2.2
Integration, configuration management	16%	1.6
Transition, deployment	16%	1.6
Total	100%	10

All activities that form the development process must be considered to avoid uncontrollable overhead costs. Cost estimation is derived from the size of new or reused software related to the overall productivity and the cost per activity. The recommended sequence of estimation activities is first to estimate the size of the software product, then to estimate the cost, and finally to estimate the development schedule based on the size and the cost estimates. These estimates should be revised towards the end of architecture and top level design and again towards end of unit test or when the first increment is integrated.

Although activity-based accounting means more detailed effort reporting throughout each project, it allows for a clear separation between value adding and non-value adding activities, process value analysis, and improved performance measures and incentive schemes. Once process related costs are obvious, it is easy to assign all overhead costs, such as integration test support or tools, related to the processes where they are necessary and again to the respective projects. Instead of allocating such overhead to projects based on overall development effort per project, it is allocated related to activities relevant in the projects. For instance, upfront design activities should not contribute to allocation of expensive test equipment.

While dealing with controlling cost, often the question comes up of which tracking system is to be used. Most companies have rather independent financial tracking systems in place that provide monthly reports on cost per project and sometimes even on an activity base. The reports are often integrated with timesheet systems and relate effort to other kinds of cost. Unfortunately, such financial systems are in many cases so independent from engineering that neither the activities clusters nor the reporting frequency are helpful for making any short-term decisions.

Variance analysis is applied to control cost evolution and lead-time over time. It is based on standard costs that are estimated (or known) costs to perform a single activity within a process under efficient operating conditions. Typically such standard costs are based on well-defined outputs of the activity, for instance, test cases performed and errors found in testing. Knowing the effort per test case during integration test and the effort to detect an error (which includes regression testing but not correction), a standard effort can be estimated for the whole project. Functionality, size, reuse degree, stability and complexity of the project determine the two input parameters, namely test cases and estimated number of faults to be detected in the specific test process. Variances are then calculated as a relative figure: variance = (standard cost – actual cost) / standard cost.

Variance analysis serves to find practical reasons for causes of off-standard performance so that project management or department heads can improve operations and increase efficiency. It is, however, not an end in itself because variances might be caused by other variances or be related to a different target. Predictors should thus be self-contained, such as in the given example. Test cases alone are insufficient because an unstable product due to insufficient design causes more effort in testing.

A major use of cost control metrics combined with actual performance feedback is the tracking of earned value (see also Fig. 8.3). **Earned value** compares achieved results with the invested effort and time. For simplification let us assume that we have an incremental approach in the project with customer requirements allocated to increments. Let us further assume that we deliver increments on a frequent basis, which are integrated into a continuous build. Only if such increment is fully integrated into the build and tested, it is accepted. Upon acceptance of an increment, the status of the respective requirements within this increment is set to "tested". The build, though only internally available, could at any time with low overhead be finalized and delivered to a customer. The value metrics then increases by the relative share of these tested requirements compared to the sum of all project requirements. If, for instance, 70% of all customer requirements are available and tested , the earned value is 70%. Weighting is possible by allocating effort to these requirements. Compared with the traditional progress tracking, earned value doesn't show the "90% complete syndrome", where lots of code and documents are available, but no value is created from an external perspective, because nothing could be delivered to the customer as is.

We can allocate effort to each requirement based on up-front effort estimation. With each requirement that is delivered within an increment the value of the project deliveries would increase by the amount of effort originally allocated to the requirement. The reasoning here is that the effort should correlate with our pricing. This certainly is not reality, however a good predictor for value generated. Why, after all, should one spend a large part of project effort on a small marginal value to the customer? If the value of delivered requirements is bigger than what was supposed to be invested in terms of engineering effort, the project is ahead. If it is less it is behind. The same approach is taken for schedule. Both parameters combined give an excellent predictor for time and cost to complete a project.

Return on investment (ROI) is a critical expression when it comes to development cost or justification of new techniques (see Chaps. 2 and 10) [McGi96, Jone95]. However, heterogeneous cost elements with different meaning and unclear accounting relationships are often combined into one figure that is then optimized. For instance, reducing "cost of quality" that includes appraisal cost and prevention cost is misleading when compared with cost of nonconformance because certain appraisal cost (e.g., module test) are components of regular development. Cost of nonconformance, on the other hand, is incomplete if we are only considering internal cost for fault detection, correction and redelivery because we must include opportunity cost due to rework at the customer site, late deliveries or simply binding resources that otherwise might have been used for a new project.

8.3 Hints for the Practitioner

Start with **few metrics that are mandatory for all projects**. This will help to ramp up fast and to educate on usage and analysis of the metrics in a variety of project situations. Some 10 different metrics should be reported and evaluated. They should be standardized across all projects to allow benchmarking, automation and usability. A **typical suite of project metrics** or core metrics with examples for practical usage is summarized in Table 8.4.

Table 8.4. A minimum metrics suite for project control

Metric type	Examples
Project size	New, changed, reused, or total; in KLOC or KStmt or a functional metric such as function points
Calendar or elapsed time	Estimated end date with respect to committed milestones, reviews and work product deliveries compared with planning data, predictability
Effort and budget	Total effort in project, cost to complete, cost at completion, effort distribution across life cycle phases, efficiency in important processes, cost structure, cost of non-quality, estimation accuracy
Progress	Completed requirements, increment progress, test progress, earned value, requirements status
Quality	Fault estimation per detection phase, faults across development phases, effectiveness of fault detection during development process, faults per KLOC in new/changed software, failures per execution time during test and in the field, reliability estimate

For **maintenance projects** with small new development rates, and for projects that primarily need to continue delivering services without new development, the metrics suite might need to be adjusted to focus on service level agreements and quality. Metrics could include: the SLAs adherence; mean time between failures (MTBF) of different severity (critical, major, minor), which helps to predict the occurrence of customer maintenance requests; average time and effort taken to resolve a defect; maintainability metrics; or load of project resources, which helps in resource allocation.

Project control must make sense to everybody within the organization who will be in contact with it. Therefore, metrics should be piloted and evaluated after some time. Potential evaluation questions include:

- Are the selected metrics consistent with the original improvement targets? Do the metrics provide added value? Do they make sense from different angles and can that meaning be communicated simply and easily? If metrics consider what is measurable but do not support improvement tracking they are perfect for hiding issues but should not be labeled metrics.

- Do the chosen metrics send the right message about what the organization considers relevant? Metrics should spotlight by default and without cumbersome investigations of what might be behind. Are the right things being spotlighted?
- Do the metrics clearly follow a perspective that allows comparisons? If metrics include ambiguities or heterogeneous viewpoints they cannot be used as history data.

8.4 Summary

We have presented the introduction and application of a software metrics program for project control. The targets of project control in software engineering are as follows:

- setting process and product goals
- quantitative tracking of project performance during software development
- analyzing measurement data to discover any existing or anticipated problems
- determining risk
- early available release criteria for all work products
- creation of an experience database for improved project management
- motivation and trigger for actual improvements
- success control during reengineering and improvement projects

Most benefits that we recorded since establishing a comprehensive software metrics program are indeed related to project control and project management:

- improved tracking and control of each development project based on uniform mechanisms
- earlier identification of deviations from the given targets and plans
- accumulation of history data from all different types of projects that are reused for improving estimations and planning of further projects
- tracking process improvements and deviations from processes

Many small and independent metrics initiatives had been started before within various groups and departments. Our experience shows that project control of software projects is most likely to succeed as a part of a larger software process improvement initiative (e.g., CMM Level 2 demands basic project control as we explained in this chapter, while CMM Level 4 and Six Sigma initiatives explicitly ask for statistical process control and process measurement). In that case, the control program benefits from an aligned engineering improvement and business improvement spirit that encourages continuous and focused improvement with support of quantitative methods.

A measurement program must evolve along with the organization: it is not frozen. The measurement process and underlying data will change with growing maturity of management and organization. Measurements must always be aligned with the organization's goals and serve its needs. While raw data definitions can remain unchanged for long times, the usage of the metrics will definitely evolve. What used to be project tracking information will grow into process metrics. Estimation of effort and size will evolve into statistical process control. Setting annual objectives on the senior management level will grow into continuous improvements based on and tracked with flexibly used software measurements.

The good news is that measurement is a one-way street. Once managers and engineers get used to measuring and building decisions on quantitative facts instead of gut feelings, they will not go backwards. This in turn will justify the effort necessary for introducing and maintaining a measurement program, which is around 0.25–2% of the total R&D or IT budget. The higher numbers occur during introduction, later the effort is much less. We measured benefits in the range of over 5% just by having metrics and thus being able to pinpoint weaknesses and introduce dedicated changes, thus improving project plans and their delivery dates. Senior managers used to measurement will drive hard to get trustworthy data, which increasingly they will use to base their decisions upon and show to customers, analysts or at trade shows. **What gets measured gets done!**

9 Defect Detection and Quality Improvement

Quality is not an act.
It is a habit.
—Aristotle

9.1 Improving Quality of Software Systems

Customer-perceived quality is among the three factors with the strongest influence on long-term profitability of a company [Buzz87]. Customers view achieving the right balance among reliability, market window of a product and cost as having the greatest effect on their long-term link to a company. This has been long articulated, and applies in different economies and circumstances. Even in restricted competitive situations, as we have observed with some software products, the principle applies and has, for instance, given rise to open source development. With the competitor being often only a mouse-click away, today quality has even higher relevance. This applies to Web sites as well as to commodity goods with either embedded or dedicated software deliveries. And the principle certainly applies to investment goods, where suppliers are evaluated on a long list of different quality attributes.

Methodological approaches to guarantee quality products have lead to international guidelines (e.g., ISO 9000) and widely applied methods to assess the development processes of software providers (e.g., SEI CMM, [Jone97, Paul95] or CMMI [Aher03, Chri03]). In addition, most companies apply certain techniques of criticality prediction that focus on identifying and reducing release risks [Khos96, Musa87, Lyu95]. Unfortunately, many efforts usually concentrate on testing and rework instead of proactive quality management [McCo03].

Yet there is a problem with quality in the software industry. In talking about quality we mean the bigger picture, such as delivering according to commitments. The industry's maturity level with respect to "numbers" is known to be poor. What is published in terms of success stories is what few excellent companies deliver. We will help you with this book to build upon such success stories.

While solutions abound, knowing which solutions work is the big question. What are the most fundamental underlying principles in successful projects? What can be done right now? What actually is good or better? What is good enough – considering the immense market pressure and competition across the globe? The first step is to recognize that all your quality requirements can and should be specified numerically. This does not mean "counting defects". It means quantifying quality attributes such as security, portability, adaptability, maintainability, robustness, usability, reliability and performance [Eber97b].

In this chapter we look into how quality of software systems can be measured, estimated, and improved. Among the many dimensions of quality we look into defects and defect detection. Within this chapter several abbreviations and terms are used that might need some explanation. CMM is the Capability Maturity Model, which was originally created by the Software Engineering Institute (SEI); CMMI is the integrated Capability Maturity Model. It is the successor to the CMM and covers a much broader scope than the CMM. We will nevertheless for simplicity speak in this book about "CMM", covering the software CMM as well as the CMMI. ROI is return on investment; KStmt is thousand delivered executable statements of code (we use statements instead of lines, because statements are naturally the smallest chunk designers deal with conceptually); PY is person-years and PH is person-hours.

A failure is the departure of system operation from requirements, for instance, the nonavailability of a channel in an exchange. A fault is the reason in the software that causes the failure when it is executed, for instance, a wrong population of a database. The concept of a fault is developer-oriented. Defects and faults are used with the same meaning. Furthermore, $\lambda(t)$ is the failure intensity, and $\mu(t)$ is the amount of cumulative failures that we use in reliability models.

Reliability is the probability of failure-free execution of a program for a specified period, use and environment. We distinguish between execution time, which is the actual time that the system is executing the programs, and calendar time, which is the time such a system is in service. A small number of faults that occur in software that is heavily used can cause a large number of failures and thus great user dissatisfaction. The number of faults over time or remaining faults is therefore not a good indicator of reliability. The term "system" is used in a generic sense to refer to all software components of the product being developed. These components include operating systems, databases, or embedded control elements, however, they do not include hardware (which would show different reliability behaviors), as we emphasize on software development in this chapter.

The chapter is organized as follows. Section 2 summarizes some fundamental concepts of achieving quality improvements and estimating quality parameters. Section 3 describes the basic techniques for early defect detection. Knowing that inspections and module tests are most effective if they are applied in depth to the components with high defect density and criticality for the system, in Sect. 4 we look at approaches for identifying such components. This section introduces to empirical software engineering. It shows that solid rules and concrete guidance with reproducible results can only be achieved with good underlying history data from a defined context. Reliability modeling and thus predicting release time and field performance are introduced in Sect. 5. Section 6 looks into how the return on investment is calculated for quality improvement initiatives. Sect. 7 provides some hints for practitioners. It summarizes several rules of thumb for quick calculation of quality levels, defect estimation, etc. Finally, Sect. 8 summarizes the chapter.

9.2 Fundamental Concepts

9.2.1 Defect Estimation

Reliability improvement always needs measurements on effectiveness (i.e., percentage of removed defects with a given activity) compared to the efficiency of this activity (i.e., effort spent for detecting and removing a defect in the respective activity). Such measurement asks for the amount of remaining defects at a given point in time or within the development process.

But how is the amount of defects in a piece of software or in a product estimated? We will outline the approach we follow for up-front estimation of remaining defects in any software that may be merged from various sources with different degrees of stability. We distinguish between upfront defect estimation, which is static by nature as it looks only on the different components of the system and their inherent quality before the start of validation activities, and reliability models, which look more dynamically during validation activities at remaining defects and failure rates.

Only a few studies have been published that typically relate static defect estimation to the amount of already detected defects independent of the activity that resulted in defects [Cai98], or the famous error seeding, which is well known but is rarely used due to the belief of most software engineers that it is of no use to add errors to software when there are still far too many defects in, and when it is known that defect detection costs several person hours (PH) per defect [Mill72].

Defects can be easily estimated based on the stability of the underlying software. All software in a product can be separated into four parts according to its origin:

- Software that is new or changed.
- Software to be tested (i.e. reused from another project that was never integrated and therefore still contains lots of malfunctions; this includes ported functionality).
- Software reused from another project that is in test (almost) at the same time. This software might be partially tested, and therefore the overlapping of the two test phases of the parallel projects must be accounted for to estimate remaining malfunctions.
- Software completely reused from a stable project. This software is considered stable and therefore it has a rather low number of malfunctions.

The base of the calculation of new/changed software is the list of modules to be used in the complete project (i.e., the description of the entire build with all its components). A defect correction in one of these components typically results in a new version, while a modification in functionality (in the context of the new project) results in a new variant. Configuration management tools such as *CVS* or *Clearcase* are used to distinguish the one from the other while still maintaining a single source.

To statically estimate the amount of remaining defects in software at the time it is delivered by the author (i.e., after the author has done all verification activities, she can execute herself), we distinguish four different levels of stability of the software that are treated independently:

$$f = a \times x + b \times y + c \times z + d \times (w - x - y - z)$$

with

- x: the number of new or changed KStmt designed and to be tested within this project. This software was specifically designed for that respective project. All other parts of the software are reused with varying stability.
- y: the number of KStmt that are reused but are unstable and not yet tested (based on functionality that was designed in a previous project or release, but never externally delivered; this includes ported functionality from other projects).
- z: the number of KStmt that are tested in parallel in another project. This software is new or changed for the other project and is entirely reused in the project under consideration.
- w: the number of KStmt in the total software build within this product.

The factors *a-d* relate defects in software to size. They depend heavily on the development environment, project size, maintainability degree, etc. Our starting point comes from psychology. Any person makes roughly one (non-editorial) defect in ten written lines of work. This applies to code as well as a design document or e-mail, as was observed by the personal software process (PSP) and many other sources [Jone97, Hump97]. The estimation of remaining malfunctions is language independent because malfunctions are introduced per thinking and editing activity of the programmer, i.e., visible by written statements. We could prove in our own environment this independency of programming language and code defects per statement when looking to languages such as Assembler, C and CHILL.

This translates into 100 defects per KStmt. Half of these defects are found by careful checking by the author, which leaves some 50 defects per KStmt delivered at code completion. Training, maturity and coding tools can further reduce the number substantially. We found some 10—50 defects per KStmt depending on the maturity level of the respective organization. This is based only on new or changed code, not including any code that is reused or automatically generated.

Most of these original defects are detected by the author before the respective work product is released. Depending on the underlying personal software process (PSP), 40–80% of these defects are removed by the author immediately. We have experienced in software that around 10–50 defects per KStmt remain. For the following calculation we will assume that 30 defects/KStmt are remaining (which is a common value [Jone96]. Thus, the following factors can be used:

- a: 30 defects per KStmt (depending on engineering methods; should be based on own history data)
- b: 30 × 60% defects per KStmt, if defect detection before start of test is 60%

- *c*: 30 × 60% × (overlapping degree) × 25% defects per KStmt (depending on overlapping degree of resources)
- *d*: 30 × 0.1–1% defects per KStmt depending on the amount of defects remaining in a product at the time when it is reused

The percentages are, of course, related to the specific defect detection distribution in one's own history database (Fig. 9.1). A careful investigation of stability of reused software is necessary to better substantiate the assumed percentages.

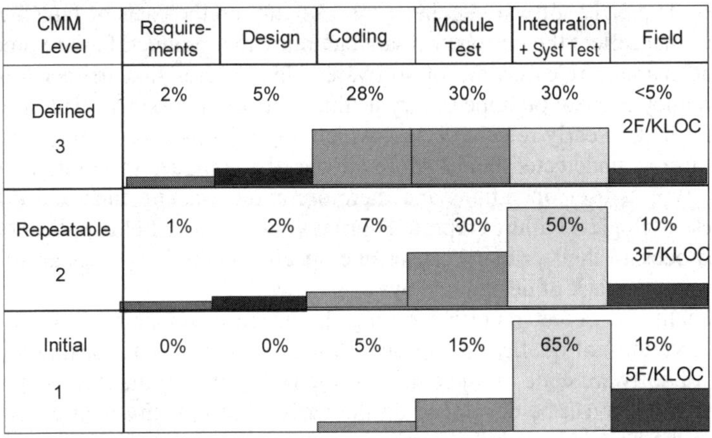

Fig. 9.1. Typical benchmark effects of detecting faults earlier in the life cycle

9.2.3 Defect Detection, Quality Gates and Reporting

Since defects can never be entirely avoided, several quality control techniques have been suggested for detecting defects early in the development life cycle:

- design reviews
- code inspections with checklists based on typical fault situations or critical areas in the software
- enforced reviews and testing of critical areas (in terms of complexity, former failures, expected fault density, individual change history, customer's risk and occurrence probability)
- tracking the effort spent for analyses, reviews, and inspections and separating according to requirements to find out areas not sufficiently covered
- test coverage metrics (e.g., C0 and C1 coverage)
- dynamic execution already applied during integration test
- application of protocol testing machines to increase level of automatic testing
- application of operational profiles and usage specifications from start of system test

We will further focus on several selected approaches that are applied for improved defect detection before starting with integration and system test. The starting point for effectively reducing defects and improving reliability is to track all faults that are detected. Faults must be recorded for each defect detection activity.

Counting faults and deriving the reliability (that is failures over time) is the most widely applied and accepted method used to determine software quality. Counting faults during the complete project helps to estimate the duration of distinct activities (e.g., module test or subsystem test) and improves the underlying processes. Typically software engineer view quality on the basis of faults, while it is failures that reflect the customer's satisfaction with a product. Failure prediction is used to manage release time of software. This ensures that neither too much time or money is spent on unnecessary testing that could possibly result in late delivery, nor that an early release occurs, which might jeopardize customer satisfaction because of undetected faults. More advanced techniques in failure prediction focus on typical user operations and therefore avoid wasting time and effort on wrong test strategies. Failures reported during system test or field application must be traced back to their primary causes and specific faults in the design (e.g., design decisions or lack of design reviews).

The quality of defect reporting during the entire development process determines the validity of quality predictions. Based on fault reports starting with first delivery of software code by the author to the configuration management system, predictive models can be developed on the basis of complexity metrics (see Sect. 4) and on the basis of reliability prediction models (see Sect. 5). As a result, it is possible to determine defective modules or classes during design and field failure rates during testing. This in turn can be used as exit criteria to balance cost of quality with cost of non-quality and with project duration.

Fig. 9.1 shows that in organizations with rather low maturity (i.e., ranked according to the capability maturity model) faults are often detected at the end of the development process despite the fact that they were present since the design phase. Late fault detection results in costly and time-consuming correction efforts, especially when the requirements were misunderstood or a design flaw occurred. Organizations with higher maturity obviously move defect detection towards the phases where they were introduced.

9.3 Early Defect Detection

9.3.1 Reducing Cost of Non-Quality

Quality improvement activities must be driven by a careful look into what it means in the bottom line of the overall product cost. It is not building a sustainable customer relationship to deliver bad quality and ruin one's reputation just to achieve a specific delivery date. And it is useless to spend an extra amount on improving quality to a level nobody wants to pay for. The optimum seemingly is in between. It means to achieve the right level of quality and to deliver in time. And it means to continuously investigate what this best level of quality really means, both for the customers and for the engineering teams who want to deliver it.

We look primarily at factors such as cost of non-quality to follow through this business reasoning of quality improvements. For this purpose we measure all cost related to error detection and removal (cost of non-quality) and normalize by the size of the product (normalize fault costs). We take a conservative approach in only considering those effects that appear inside our engineering activities, i.e., not considering opportunistic effects or any penalties for delivering insufficient quality. To identify the respective metrics we followed a goal-driven approach [VanS00].

Reducing total cost of non-quality is driven by the fault detection distribution (see Fig. 9.1 again). Assuming a distinct cost for fault detection and repair (which includes regression testing, production, etc.) per detection activity allows one to calculate the total cost of non-quality for a distinct project. Obviously the activities of fault detection are taken into consideration and not necessarily the achieved milestone. Milestones in today's incremental development might completely mislead the picture because a distinct milestone could be achieved early, while major portions of the software are still in an earlier development phase. Cost of non-quality in terms of average cost per fault is then calculated based on the respective detection activity. This also supports using a fixed value per fault and activity in a distinct timeframe, because finding a fault with module test including the correction takes a rather stable effort, as well as for instance the detection, correction, regression test, production and delivery during system test.

Three key drivers for achieving the downstream targets were singled out and periodically measured in all projects to improve defect detection during the life cycle. They later coined the underlying engineering rules to establish consistent defect detection processes.

1. Reading or checking speed in inspections or peer reviews. Reducing reading speed during code inspections improves design defect detection effectiveness and thus reduces normalized fault cost and customer-detected faults.
2. Faults found per new or changed statement with module test. Increasing faults found per new or changed statement with module test improves design defect detection effectiveness and thus reduce normalized fault cost and customer detected faults.
3. Test defect detection effectiveness. Increasing test defect detection effectiveness (i.e., percentage of remaining faults being detected during integration) reduces normalized fault cost and customer detected faults.

Our contribution to research in this domain was that we validate several key relationships in real settings with projects based on legacy software [Eber99]. Our contribution for practical development projects is that we propose meaningful and valid approaches to achieve quantitative field performance improvement.

9.3.2 Planning Early Defect Detection Activities

The most cost-effective techniques for defect detection are code reviews and inspections and module test. Detecting faults in architecture and design documents has considerable benefit from a cost perspective, because these defects are expensive to correct. Major yields in terms of reliability, however, can be attributed to better code, for the simple reason that there are many more defects residing in code that were also inserted during the coding activity. We therefore provide more depth on techniques that help to improve the quality of code, namely code reviews (i.e., code reading (COR) and code inspections (COI)) and module test.

There are six possible paths between the delivery of a piece of software from design until the start of integration test (Fig. 9.2). They indicate the permutations of doing code reading alone, performing code inspections and applying module test. Although the best approach from a mere defect detection perspective is to apply inspections and module test, cost considerations and the objective to reduce elapsed time and thus improve throughput suggest to carefully evaluate which path to follow in order to most efficiently and effectively detect and remove faults. In our experience code reading is the cheapest detection technique, while module test is the most expensive. Code inspections lie somewhat in between.

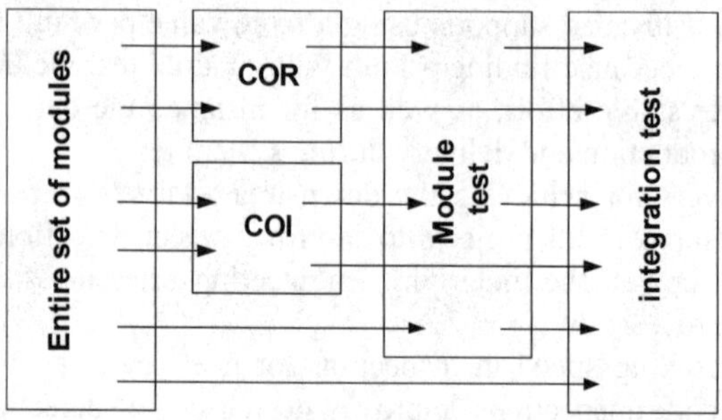

Fig. 9.2. Six possible paths for modules between end of coding and start of integration test

Module test, however, combined with C0 coverage targets have the highest effectiveness for regression testing of existing functionality. Inspections, on the other hand, help in detecting distinct fault classes that can only be found under load in the field.

The target is to find the right balance between efficiency (time spent per item) and effectiveness (ratio of detected faults compared to remaining faults) by making the right decisions to spend the budget for the most appropriate quality assurance methods. In addition overall efficiency and effectiveness have to be optimized. It must therefore be carefully decided which method should be applied on which work product to guarantee high efficiency and effectiveness of code reading (i.e., done by one checker) and code inspections (i.e., done by multiple checkers in a controlled setting). Wrong decisions can mainly have two impacts:

- The proposed method to be performed is too "weak". Faults, which could have been found with a stronger method, are not detected in the early phase. Too little effort is spend in the early phase. Typically in this case efficiency is high, and effectiveness is low.
- The proposed method to be performed is too "strong" or overly heavy. If the fault density is low from the very beginning, even an effective method will not discover many faults. This leads to a low efficiency, compared to the average effort that has to be spent to detect one fault. This holds especially for small changes in legacy code.

Faults are not distributed homogeneously through new or changed code [Wayn93, Eber97a]. By concentrating on fault-prone modules both effectiveness and efficiency are improved. Our main approach to identify fault-prone software-modules is a criticality prediction taking into account several criteria. One criterion is the analysis of module complexity based on complexity metrics. Other criteria concern the amount of new or changed code in a module, and the amount of field faults a module had in the predecessor project.

The main input parameters for planning code inspections are:

- **General availability of an inspection leader**. Only a trained and internally certified inspection leader is allowed to plan and perform inspections to ensure adherence to the formal rules and achievement of efficiency targets. The number of certified inspection leaders and their availability limits the number of performed inspections for a particular project.
- **Module design effort (planned/actually spent).** The actual design effort per module (or class) can give an early impression on how much code will be new or changed. This indicates the effort that will be necessary for verification tasks like inspections.
- **Know-how of the checker.** If specific know-how is necessary to check particular parts of the software, the availability of correspondingly skilled persons will have an impact on the planning of code reviews and code inspections.
- **Checking rate.** Based on the program language and historic experiences in previous projects the optimal checking rate determines the necessary effort to be planned.
- **Size of new or changed statements.** Relating to the checking rate, the total amount of the target size to be inspected defines the necessary effort.
- **Quality targets.** If high-risk areas are identified (e.g., unexpected changes to previously stable components or unstable inputs from a previous project) exhaustive inspections must be considered.
- **Achieving the entry criteria.** The inspection or review can start earliest if entry criteria for these procedures can be matched. Typically at least error-free compileable sources have to be available.

The intention is to apply code inspections to heavily changed modules first, in order to optimize payback of the additional effort that has to be spent compared to the lower effort for code reading. Formal code reviews are recommended to be performed by the author himself for very small changes with a checking time shorter than two hours in order to profit from a good efficiency of code reading. The effort for know-how transfer to another designer can be saved.

For module test some additional parameters have to be considered:

- **Optimal sequence of modules to be tested before start of integration test**. Start-up tests typically can start without having the entire set of new features implemented for all modules. Therefore the schedule for module test has to consider individual participation of modules in start-up tests. Later increments of the new design are added to integration test related to their respective functionality.
- **Availability of reusable module test environments**. Effort for setting up sophisticated test environments for the module test must be considered during planning. This holds especially for legacy code, where often the module test environments and test cases for the necessary high C0 coverage are not available.
- **Distribution of code changes over all modules of one project**. The number of items to be tested has a heavy impact on the whole planning process and on the time that has to be planned for performing module test. The same amount of code to be tested can be distributed over a small number of modules (small initialization effort) or over a wide distribution of small changes throughout a lot of modules (high initialization effort).
- **Achieving the entry criteria**. The readiness of validated test lists is a mandatory prerequisite for starting the module test.

9.4 Criticality Prediction – Applying Empirical Software Engineering

9.4.1 Identifying Critical Components

The distribution of defects among modules in a software system is not even. An analysis of many projects revealed the applicability of the Pareto rule: 20% of the modules are responsible for 80% of the malfunctions of the whole project [Eber97a]. These critical components need to be identified as early as possible, i.e., in the case of legacy systems at start of detailed design, and for new software during coding. By concentrating on these components the effectiveness of code inspections and module test is increased and fewer faults have to be found during test phases (see also Chap. 15).

It is of great benefit towards improved quality management to be able to predict early on in the development process those components of a software system that are likely to have a high fault rate or those requiring additional development effort. Criticality prediction is based on selecting a distinct small share of modules that incorporate sets of properties that would typically cause defects to be introduced during design more often than in modules that do not possess such attributes. Criticality prediction is thus a technique for risk analysis during the design process.

Criticality prediction is a multifaceted approach taking into account several criteria. One criterion is the analysis of module complexity early in the life cycle. There is no common agreement among psychologists what complexity is and what makes some things more complicated than others. Of course, volume, structure, order or the connections of different objects contribute to complexity. However, do they all account for it equally? The clear answer is no, because different people with different skills assign complexity subjectively, according to their experience in the area.

Other criteria concern the amount of new or changed code in a module, and the amount of field faults a module had in the predecessor project, etc. All these criteria are used to build a complete criticality prediction model. Based on a ranking list of criticality of all modules used in a build, different mechanisms can be applied to improving quality, namely redesign, code inspections or module test with high coverage.

Instead of predicting the number of faults or changes (i.e., algorithmic relationships) we consider assignments to groups (e.g., "fault-prone"). While the first goal can be achieved more or less exactly with regression models or neural networks predominantly for finished projects, the latter goal seems to be adequate for predicting potential outliers in running projects, where preciseness is too expensive and is unnecessary for decision support.

Training and test data were taken from previous projects. All modules selected for this experiment were from completed projects. They had been placed under configuration control since the start of coding. Software defects or faults are all deviations from functional requirements that are observed after the specific module had been delivered by the designer as having full functionality. They are recorded within the configuration control system for each module together with several complexity metrics. At this point we do not distinguish faults in terms of potential downstream impact (e.g., cost or performance), as this is difficult to judge during coding. Soft factors, such as designers' experiences are recorded during the design process; however, for privacy reasons they were only temporarily recorded and not for public access.

Having identified such overly critical modules, risk management must be applied. The most critical and most complex, for instance, the top 5%, of the analyzed modules are candidates for a redesign. For cost reasons mitigation is not only achieved with redesign. The top 20% should have a code inspection instead of the usual code reading, and finally at least the top 80% should not get any exception concerning a complete module test. By concentrating on these components the effectiveness of code inspections and module test is increased and fewer faults have to be found during test phases. To achieve feedback for improving predictions the approach is integrated into the development process end-to-end (requirements, design, code, system test, deployment).

Evaluation of the classification approaches is based on [Wads90]:

- low chi-square values, which is equal to reduced misclassification errors
- comparing the two types of misclassification errors, namely type-I errors ("fault-prone components" classified as "uncritical components") and type-II errors ("uncritical components" classified as "fault-prone components").

The goal obviously must be to reduce type-I errors at the cost of type-II errors because it is less expensive to investigate some components despite the fact that they are not critical compared to labeling critical components as harmless without probing further.

Fuzzy classification proved to be especially effective in the early identification of critical components. This was underlined in some studies we performed. If software engineering expert knowledge is available we recommend fuzzy classification before using learning strategies that are only result-driven (e.g., classification trees or mere neural network approaches). However, we see the necessity of such approaches when only a few guiding principles are available and sufficient project data can be utilized for supervised learning. Fuzzy classification was combined with genetic algorithms to improve type-I misclassifications, while preserving the maximum chi-square. A natural limit of prediction correctness was detected as the two data sets belonged to two entirely different populations.

It must be emphasized that using criticality prediction techniques does not mean attempting to detect all faults. Instead, they belong to the set of managerial instruments that try to optimize resource allocation by focusing them on areas with many faults that would affect the utility of the delivered product. The trade-off of applying complexity-based predictive quality models is estimated based on

- limited resources are assigned to high-risk jobs or components
- impact analysis and risk assessment of changes is feasible based on affected or changed complexity
- gray-box testing strategies are applied to identified high-risk components
- fewer customers reported failures

9.4.2 Practical Criticality Prediction

The process for criticality classification and validation is shown graphically in Fig. 9.3:

1. Provide a list of all modules (or classes in object-oriented languages) at the start of the project, during design and at the end of module test.
2. Provide a fault history classification for each module on the lists. A root cause analysis might be added for high-ranking faults that allows for a Pareto-based mitigation list.
3. Provide a change history classification (i.e., number of compiles or number of deliveries).
4. Provide a complexity classification as indicated in previous sections.
5. Finalize a comprehensive criticality list that takes into account the different inputs from steps 2–4 mapped on the appropriate input list. Before the final rank-

ings are presented to decide on further actions, the validity of the lists must be evaluated (e.g. screening on reasonable modules, outliers, potential misleading effects, etc.). The goal of screening is not to filter out what is thought to be unchangeable, but rather to question undesired influences from history. Of course, screening and ranking must primarily ensure that type I prediction errors are at the lowest feasible levels.

6. Prepare suggestions based on ranked critical modules. Typical approaches include redesign of a few highest ranked modules according to a simultaneous classification (i.e., the top modules must rank high in all three lists simultaneously). Redesign includes reduction of size, improved modularity, etc. Application of thorough module test with high C0 coverage should be applied to high runners according to independent classification (i.e., the top modules of all three approaches are grouped). Details of complexity metrics must be investigated for the selected modules to determine the redesign approach. In all cases it is typically the different complexity metrics that indicate which approach in redesign or test should be followed.
7. Validate and improve the prediction model based on post mortem studies with all collected faults and the population of a "real" criticality list. Then the actual fault ranking is compared with the predicted ranking. The reasons for deviations are investigated and the automatic classification approaches used are tuned. The rules for screening are improved to ensure that type-II prediction errors will be reduced the next time.

Our experiences show in accordance with other literature [Evan94b] that corrections of faults in early phases is more efficient, because the designer is still familiar with the problem and the correction delay during testing is reduced.

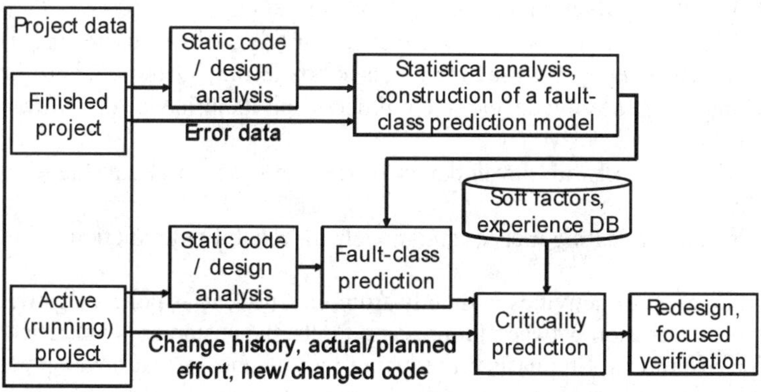

Fig. 9.3. Criticality prediction for source code based on static code analysis and code history

9.5 Software Reliability Prediction

9.5.1 Practical Software Reliability Engineering

Software reliability engineering is a statistical procedure associated with the test and correction activities during development. It is further used after delivery, based on field data, to validate the prediction models. Customers of such prediction models and the resulting reliability values are development managers who use them to determine the best suitable defect detection techniques and to find the optimum delivery time. Operations managers use the data for deciding when to include new functionality in a delivered product that is already performing in the field. Maintenance managers use the reliability figures to plan resources they need to deliver corrections in due time according to contracted deadlines.

The current approach to software reliability modeling focuses on the testing and rework activities of the development process. On the basis of data on the times between occurrences of failures, collected during testing, we attempt to make inferences about how additional testing and rework would improve the reliability of the product and about how reliable the product would be once it is released to the user.

Software reliability engineering includes the following activities [Musa87, Lyu95, Musa91]:

- selecting a mixture of quality factors oriented towards maximizing customer satisfaction
- determining a reliability objective (i.e., exit criteria for subsequent test and release activities)
- predicting reliability based on models of the development process and its impact on fault introduction, recognition and correction
- supporting test strategies based on realization (e.g., white box testing, control flow branch coverage) or usage (e.g., black box testing, operational profiles)
- providing insight to the development process and its influence on software reliability
- improving the software development process in order to obtain higher quality reliability
- defining and validating metrics and models for reliability prediction

The above list of activities is mainly from the customer's point of view. When making the distinction between failures and faults, the customer is interested in the reduction of failures. Emphasis on reducing failures means that development and testing is centered towards functions in normal and extraordinary operational modes (e.g., usage coverage instead of branch coverage during system testing, or operational profiles instead of functional profiles during reliability assessment). In this section we will focus on the aspect of reliability modeling that is used for measuring and estimating (predicting) the reliability of a software release during testing as well as in the field.

Such models use an appropriate statistical model, which requires accurate test or field failure data related to the occurrences in terms of execution time. Several models should be considered and assessed for their predictive accuracy, in order to select the most accurate and reliable model for reliability prediction. It is of no use to switch models after the facts to achieve best fit, because then you would have no clue about how accurate the model would be in a predictive scenario. Unlike many research papers on that subject, our main interest is to select a model that would provide in very different settings (i.e., project sizes) of the type of software we are developing a good fit that can be used for project management. Reliability prediction thus should be performed at intermediate points and at the end of system test.

At intermediate points, reliability predictions will provide a measure of the product's current reliability and its growth, and thus serve as an instrument for estimating the time still required for test. They also help in assessing the trade-off between extensive testing and potential loss of market share (or penalties in case of investment goods) because of late delivery. At the end of development, which is the decision review before releasing the product to the customer, reliability estimations facilitate an evaluation of reliability versus the original set targets. Especially in communication, banking and defense businesses, such reliability targets are often contracted and therefore are a very concrete exit criterion. It is common to have multiple failure rate objectives.

For instance, failure rate objectives will generally be lower (more stringent) for high failure severity classes. The factors involved in setting failure rate objectives comprise the market and competitive situation, user satisfaction targets and risks related to malfunctions of the system. Life-cycle costs related to development, test and deployment in a competitive situation must be carefully evaluated, to avoid setting reliability objectives far too high.

Reliability models are worthless if they are not continuously validated versus the actually observed failure rates. We thus also include in our models, which will be presented later in this section, a plot of predicted versus actually observed data.

The application of reliability models to reliability prediction is based on a generic algorithm for model selection and tuning:

1. Establish goals according to the most critical process areas or products (e.g., by following the quality improvement paradigm or by applying a Pareto analysis).
2. Identify the appropriate data for analyzing faults and failures (i.e., with classifications according to severity, time between failures, reasons for faults, test cases that helped in detection, etc.).
3. Collect data relevant for models that help to gain insight into how to achieve the identified goals. Data collection is cumbersome and exhaustive: Tools may change, processes change as well, development staff are often unwilling to provide additional effort for data collection and – worst of all – management often does not wish for changes that affect it personally.
4. Recover historical data that was available at given time stamps in the software development process (for example, fault rates of testing phases); the latter of these will serve as starting points of the predictive models.

5. Model the development process and select a fault introduction model, a testing model and a correction model that suit the observed processes best.
6. Select a reliability prediction model that suits the given fault introduction, testing and correction models best.
7. Estimate the parameters for the reliability model using only data that were available at the original time stamps.
8. Extrapolate the function at some point in time later than the point in time given for forecasting. If historical data is available after the given time stamps it is possible to predict failures.
9. Compare the predicted fault or failure rates with the actual number of such incidents and compute the forecast's relative error.

Finally, this process can be repeated for all releases and analyzed to determine the "best" model.

9.5.2 Applying Reliability Growth Models

Reliability growth models assume that when a failure occurs there is an attempt to remove the design fault that caused the failure. After the correction the software is set running again, to eventually fail yet again because of another fault. When the defect is removed without causing a new fault, and under the assumption that the number of defects is limited, reliability will grow over time. The successive times of failure-free working are the input to probabilistic reliability growth models, which use these data to estimate the current reliability of the software under study, and to predict how the reliability will further improve in the future.

Many software reliability prediction models are based on some kind of Poisson processes [Musa87, Lyu95, Musa91]. Poisson processes are well known in all fields that deal with events that occur at random and independently from each other. Applications include the occurrence of phone calls in a switching system or their individual length. Both situations have been extensively investigated in traffic theory with the result that they follow typical (Poisson) distributions that are not normal but skewed, and which depend on several parameters. Naturally, the occurrence of failures and of phone calls can be compared, providing a basis for the definition of reliability models. Poisson models are based on a set of assumptions that are as follows (with time t, failure intensity $\lambda(t)$ and cumulative failures $\mu(t)$):

- Cumulative number of failures at the beginning is $\mu(t) = 0$.
- Failures are independent of other events or of history.
- The probability of occurrence of a failure in a given small time interval is negligible and is the same for a second occurrence in the same small time interval.

An important property of the Poisson process is its additivity, which says that mutually independent Poisson processes with intensities λ_i can be superimposed to create an overall Poisson process with intensity λ, where λ is the sum of all λ_i .

Formally both the failure intensity $\lambda(t)$ and the collection of all failures at time t, $\mu(t)$, are Poisson distributed random variables.

A model with constant failure intensity, a homogeneous Poisson process, is applicable during field operations without fault corrections. On the other hand, if corrections are made in response to failures, such as during testing or when new releases are introduced to the field, then a nonhomogeneous Poisson process (NHPP) is appropriate. In the latter case the failure rate decreases over time with corrections being provided (including the consideration of defective corrections). The second approach to a decreasing failure rate is divided into two basic models [Musa87, Lyu95].

- Infinite failure models like the logarithmic nonhomogeneous Poisson execution time model (LNHPP).

$$\lambda(\mu) = \lambda_0 \exp(-\theta\mu)$$

  Other representatives are the Littlewood-Verrall model and the Weibull process model.

- Finite failure models like the basic exponential nonhomogeneous Poisson execution time model (ENHPP).

$$\lambda(\mu) = \theta(\mu_0 - \mu)$$

  This function assumes a linear decrease in intensity with each detection (and correction) of a failure. Other representatives are the expanded exponential S-shaped Yamada-Osaki model or the Crow model.

For a distinct subset of tests during subsystem and system test, an ENHPP model can approximate the reported fault rates with good accuracy. In order to validate forecasts made in the past, rates reported after the time that the forecast was made can be compared with the ones that were extrapolated (Fig. 9.4).

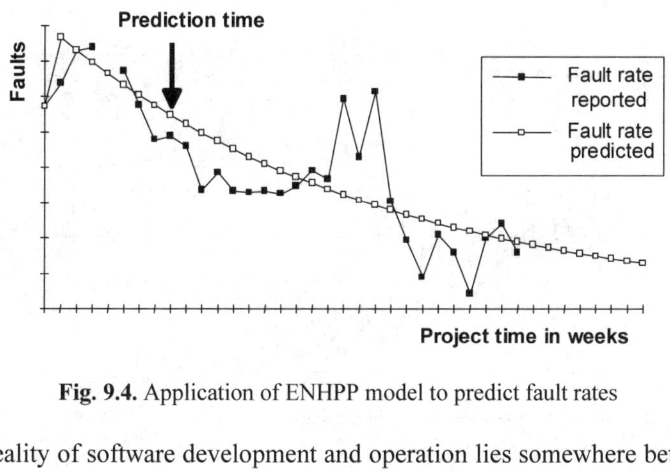

Fig. 9.4. Application of ENHPP model to predict fault rates

The reality of software development and operation lies somewhere between the two formal models. Failures may occur as a result of interaction between several faults (e.g., two fatal faults are in immediate sequence, leaving the correction of only one of them without any effect on the failure rate). Another phenomenon that we observed within communication systems is load-dependent failures that typically occur after the same parts of the code have been executed several times. In this case the individual fault processes are not Poisson distributed as long as the execution or load sequence by itself is not a Poisson process. This pattern often causes communications software to fail once the environment changes (e.g. workload or equipment changes), although the software seemed to operate fault-free during test.

Software failures are gathered and faults are detected from time to time based on an analysis of cumulated failure descriptions, thus resulting in the detection of faults that have caused between none and several different failures. Delayed fault detection and correction or cumulated corrections of software (which is common in huge systems with several million statements) are, of course, non-Poisson distributed. To make things easier, theory provides a law of huge numbers: as time and thus failures approach infinity in such a way that the arrival of any failure is very unlikely (i.e., in the field), superimposed occurrences $\mu(t)$ converge to a Poisson process.

The overall goal is, of course, not to accurately predict the failure rate but to be as close as possible to a distinct margin that is allowed by customer contracts or available maintenance capacity. An example for a practically used combined reliability profile summarized from various models is showed in Fig. 9.5.

9.6 Calculating ROI of Quality Initiatives

Quality improvement is driven typically by two overarching business objectives:

- improving the customer-perceived quality
- reducing the total cost of non-quality

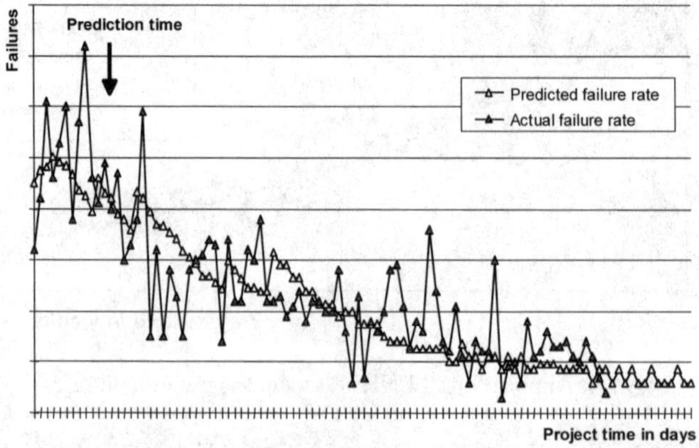

Fig. 9.5. Predicted field failure rate of several increments

Improving customer-perceived quality can be broken down to one major improvement target, namely to systematically reduce customer detected faults. Reducing field defects and improving customer-perceived quality almost naturally improves the cost-benefit values along the product life cycle. Investments are made to improve quality, which later improve the customer satisfaction. Therefore the second objective of reducing the cost of non-quality comes into the picture: this is the cost of activities related to detecting defects too late. Both aspects contribute to reduced product cost and therefore improve the bottom line.

Return on investment (ROI) is a critical, yet often misleading expression when it comes to development cost or justification of innovative technologies [Wayn93]. Too often heterogeneous cost elements with different meaning and unclear accounting relationships are combined into one figure that is then optimized. For instance, reducing the "cost of quality" that includes appraisal cost and prevention cost is misleading when compared with cost of nonconformance because certain appraisal costs (e.g., module test) are components of regular development. Cost of nonconformance (cost of non-quality) on the other hand is incomplete if we only consider internal cost for fault detection, correction and redelivery because we must include opportunity cost due to rework at the customer site, late deliveries or simply binding resources that otherwise might have been used for a new project.

ROI is difficult to calculate in software process improvement. This is not really due to not having collected effort figures but rather because it is necessary to distinguish the actual effort figures that relate to investment (that would have otherwise not been done) and the returns (as a difference to what would have happened if it had not been invested). At Alcatel in the past years we built a set of ROI calculations related to software process improvement.

The following rules should be considered for calculating ROI effects:

- Samples should consider projects before and after the start of the improvement program to be evaluated with ROI.
- Controlling should be able to provide history data (e.g., effort).
- Aggregated or combined effort or cost figures must be separated (i.e., prevention, appraisal cost, cost of nonperformance, cost of performance – which are typically spent in any case).
- Include only those effects that trace back to root causes that were part of the original improvement planning.
- Check cost data for consistency within one project and across projects.

ROI is most efficiently presented according to the following flow:

1. Current results (these are the potentials, i.e., problems, cost; causes)
2. Known effects in other (competing) companies (i.e., improvement programs in other companies, benchmarking data, cost-benefit estimation for these companies)
3. ROI calculation (calculate cost of quality per month for several sample projects; calculate the savings since start of the improvement program; extrapolate these savings for all affected projects, which is benefit; compare the benefit

with the cost of the improvement program, which is ROI; never include the cost of performance since this is regular effort)

We had the following experiences with ROI calculations:

- It is more accurate and far easier to collect different effort figures during a project than afterwards.
- Activities related to distinct effort figures must be defined (activity-based costing helps a lot).
- Cost and effort must not be estimated, but rather collected in projects (typically the inputs to the estimation are questioned until the entire calculation is no longer acceptable).
- Detailed quality costs are helpful for root cause analyses and related defect prevention activities.
- Tangible cost savings are the single best support for a running improvement program.
- Cost of nonperformance is a perfect trigger for a process improvement program.
- Obvious management and software engineering practices are typically not ROI topics.
- There are many "hidden" ROI potentials that are often difficult to quantify (e.g., customer satisfaction; improved market share because of better quality, delivery accuracy and lower per feature costs; opportunity costs; reduced maintenance costs in follow-on projects; improved reusability; employee satisfaction; resources are available for new projects instead of wasting them for firefighting).
- There are also hidden investments that must be accounted (e.g., training, infrastructure, coaching, additional metrics, additional management activities, process maintenance).
- Process metrics are mandatory for following up and reinforcing changes (i.e., without metrics no improvement, and without improvement no metrics).

Not all ROI calculations are based on monetary benefits. Depending on the business goals, they can as well be directly presented in terms of improved delivery accuracy, reduced lead time or higher efficiency and productivity.

For early defect detection, we will try to provide detailed insight in an ROI calculation (Table 9.1). The data that are used for calculations result from average values that have been gathered in our project history database. We will compare the effect of increased effort for combined code reading and code inspection activities as a key result of our improvement program. The summary shows that by reducing the amount of code to be inspected per hour by more than a factor of three, the efficiency in terms of faults detected increased significantly. As a result the percentage of faults detected during coding increased dramatically. While reading speed reflects only the actual effort spent for fault detection, the effort per KStmt includes both detection and correction, thus resulting in around 3 PH/Fault, which seems stable.

Given an average-sized development project and only focusing on the new and changed software without considering any effects of defect-preventive activities over time, the following calculation can be derived. The effort spent for code reading and inspection activities increases by 1470 PH. Assuming a constant average combined appraisal cost and cost of nonperformance (i.e., detection and correction effort) after coding of 15 PH/Fault, the total effect is 9030 PH less spent in year 2. This results in a ROI value of 6.1 (i.e., each additional hour spent on code reading and inspections yields 6.1 saved hours of appraisal and nonperformance activities afterwards).

Effects of applying complexity-based criticality prediction to a new project can be summarized as follows: 20% of all modules in the project were predicted as most critical (after coding). and these modules contained over 40% of all faults (up to release time). Knowing that at least 60% of all faults can be detected until the end of module test and fault correction during module test and code reading costs less than 10% compared to fault correction during system test, 24% of all faults can be detected early by investigating 20% of all modules more intensively with 10% of the effort compared to fault correction during system test, therefore yielding a 20% total cost reduction for fault correction.

Additional costs for providing the static code analysis and the related statistical analysis are in the range of few person hours per project. The tools used for this exercise are off-the-shelf and readily available (e.g., static code analysis, spreadsheet programs).

Table 9.1. ROI calculation of process improvements with focus on code reading / inspections (defect prevention activities are not considered for this example)

	baseline	year 1	year 2
Reading speed [Stmt/PH]	183	57	44
Effort per KStmt	15	24	36
Effort per Fault	7.5	3	3
Faults per KStmt	2	8	12
Effectiveness [% of all]	2	18	29
Project: 70 KStmts. 2100 Faults estimated based on 30 defects per KStmt			
Effort for code reading or inspections [PH]	1050		2520
Faults found in code reading/inspections	140		840
Remaining faults after code reading/inspections	1960		1260
Correction effort after code reading/inspections [PH] (based on 15 PH/F average correction effort)	29400		18900
Total correction effort [PH]	30450		21420
ROI = saved total effort/additional detection effort			6.1

9.7 Hints for the Practitioner

We advocate at many places in this book to build your own history database. However, everybody initially is at the point where bootstrapping a certain initiative needs some concrete data – before even building a history database. Where do you get such initial data? We started looking into books and conference proceedings, cost estimation tools, lots of own project lessons learned, and gradually extracted some simple rules of thumb that we could use even in situations where no historic information was accessible.

This section summarizes some quality-related rules of thumb in software projects. It is far from complete and certainly is not as scientific and supported by experiments as some later parts of this chapter – but it is a start. The data stems from our own history databases and also from a number of external sources, such as estimation tools, project management literature, etc. [Eber96, Jone97, Musa87, Lyu95, Jone01, McCo98, Royc98, Fent97].

The amount of remaining defects at code completion (i.e., code has been finished for a specific component and has passed compilation) can be estimated in different ways. If size in KStmt or KLOC is known, this can be translated into remaining defects. We found some 10—50 defects per KStmt depending on the maturity level of the respective organization. This is based only on new or changed code, not including any code that is reused or automatically generated.

Defect detection and correction – after the activity where the defect was introduced – costs around 30—70% of total engineering (project) effort. This is what we call cost of non-quality. It is by far the biggest chunk in any project that can be reduced to directly and immediately save cost!

Defect detection by means of inspection is the least expensive of all manual defect detection techniques. We found some 1—3 person hours per defect for inspections and peer reviews. Before starting peer reviews or inspections, all tool-supported techniques should be fully exploited, such as static and dynamic checking of source code. Module test comes after peer reviews, as it detects other defect classes and needs some 2—10 person hours per defect.

Defect detection is roughly 30% per distinct defect detection (quality control) activity. That translates into 30% of defects remaining at a certain point of time can be found with a new defect detection technique. This is a cascading approach, where each cascade (e.g., static checking, peer review, module test, integration test, system test, beta test) removes some 30% of defects. It is possible to exceed this number slightly towards 40—50% but at dramatically increasing cost per defect.

If 30% of defects are removed per detection activity then 70% will remain. Remaining defects at the end of the project thus equal the amount of defects at code completion times 70% to the power of independent detection activities (e.g., code inspection, module test, integration test, system test, etc.).

Typical release quality of software is 90% of all initial defects at code completion will reach the customer. Depending on the maturity of the software organization, the following defects at release time can be observed: CMM Level 1: 5—60 defects/KStmt; Level 2: 3—12 defects/KStmt; Level 3: 2—7 defects/KStmt; Level 4: 1—5 defects/KStmt; Level 5: 0.5—1 defects/KStmt. Don't expect high quality in external components from suppliers on low maturity levels, especially if not explicitly contracted.

Improving release quality needs time: 5% more defects detected before release time translates into 10—15% more lead-time in the project.

Corrections create some 5—30% of new defects depending on time pressure and underlying tool support. Especially late defect removal on the critical path to release cause many new defects because quality assurance activities are undermined and engineers are stressed. This must be considered when planning testing/validation or maintenance activities.

The amount of necessary test cases can be estimated by functionality and translates roughly into 0.3—1 test case per Function Point. For procedural languages such as C, this translates into 3—7 test cases per KStmt.

At least 30% of all test cases are redundant. This is an excellent business case in itself towards applying better test management and test coverage tools. Orthogonal test case arrays help in reducing test redundancies.

Software strictly follows the Pareto principle. As a rule of thumb, 20% of all components (subsystems, modules, classes) consume 60—80% of all resources. 20% of all components contain 60% of all effective defects. 20% of all defects need 60—80% of correction effort and 20% of all enhancements require 60—80% of all maintenance effort.

9.8 Summary

Quality improvement such as increased reliability and maintainability are of utmost importance in software development. In this field, which was previously ad hoc and unpredictable rather than customer-oriented, increasing competition and decreasing customer satisfaction have motivated many companies to put more emphasis on quality. The software industry's problem is that the maturity with respect to "numbers" is poor. While solutions abound, knowing which solutions work is the big question.

We have introduced in this chapter to several practical techniques for analyzing and improving software quality. They are based on ideas of measurement, quantification, and feedback. All your quality requirements can and should be specified numerically. This means quantifying qualities such as security, portability, adaptability, maintainability, robustness, usability, reliability, and performance. Based on experiences in our projects as well as external benchmarking studies we have summarized some rules of thumb for practitioners. This allows introducing quality metrics without exhaustive upfront internal data collection. Of course, these rules of thumb do not relieve using own metrics for improving accuracy.

10 Software Process Improvement

They always say time changes things,
but you actually have to change them yourself.
—Andy Warhol

10.1 Process Management and Process Improvement

Today, software is a major asset of many companies. R&D investments primarily go into software development for a majority of applications and products. To stay competitive with software development, many companies are putting in place orchestrated improvement programs of their engineering processes and the underlying engineering tools environments. Often the improvement programs also include a broader perspective into reengineering existing R&D processes.

We call such comprehensive engineering process improvement approach "e-R&D" following the notation of business process improvement and e-business initiatives. The term e-R&D also means enabling of interactive R&D processes and allows increasingly collaborative work independent of location. e-R&D can be broken into three implementation tracks:

- strengthened process capability
- visibility
- workflow integration

Strengthened process capability is key to e-R&D. If you do not know where you are and where you want to go, change will never lead to improvement. Effective process improvement is achieved by using the well-known Capability Maturity Model (CMM or CMMI), originally issued by the Software Engineering Institute [Paul95, Aher03]. This model provides a framework for process improvement and is used by many software development organizations. It defines five levels of process maturity plus an improvement framework for process maturity and as a consequence, quality and predictability.

This model must be combined with a strong focus on business objectives and metrics for follow-up of change implementation. Otherwise, the risk is high that too much attention is focused on processes and not enough on what is essential for customers and shareholders. For instance, several years ago, Alcatel's voice networks business unit primarily focused on field quality improvement. Later, rapidly changing markets pushed the carriers to offer new services at a rapid pace, so we cut cycle time. Such a shift of priorities in a consistent and sustainable way is only achieved with a strong organizational process focus. Alcatel would not have achieved it without being on CMM Level 3 in that business unit.

Are processes and engineering tools related? That is perhaps the major difference between process improvement as it is described in the theoretical literature and e-R&D for practical usage. e-R&D takes a more comprehensive view. Processes without adequate tool support remain theoretic. The objective is to improve visibility in engineering and master a variety of workflows and external interfaces related to R&D. e-R&D must bridge the needs of process improvement with adequate tool support – but without tightly coupling them.

These workflows together describe how software engineering work products are gradually generated and further on embedded in products or services. They indicate the link to corporate business processes and specific tools environments. Some workflows are entirely internal to engineering, while others are at the boundary to other functions. Service request management exemplifies such a workflow and related interfaces. Service requests result from field operations and are treated within R&D for corrections that are again deployed to the field.

Being able not only to reuse information but also to embed the respective processes in more integrated workflows for specific tasks generates immediate returns by making engineers more flexible, and it reduces friction caused by manual overhead at the boundaries of those tools and processes. A simple business case could be constructed by taking the time and effort necessary to move engineers from one project to another. Having standard workflow management around a standard product life cycle reduces the learning effort to real technical challenges, instead of organizational overhead.

Emphasis, however, is given towards setting and dealing with quantitative objectives and thus making progress of the improvement initiative visible. As such our experiences are to a lower degree targeted towards the failing improvement initiatives with their specific problems during the first months after the assessment, but rather for those with sufficient breadth – especially on the upper management side – to continuously stretch the targets and thus never stop pushing for improvements.

Although we focused from the beginning on many key process areas (KPAs) in parallel and not so much on the leveraged approach of the CMM, the clear objective typically is during the first years of such an initiative to improve predictability and customer-perceived quality, and to lower the cost of non-quality.

Why do software organizations embark on the CMM? There are several answers to this question. Certainly it is all about competition. The trend in the industry as a whole is growing towards higher maturity levels. Companies have started to realize that momentum is critical: If you stand still, you fall behind! The business climate and the software marketplace have changed in favor of end users and customers. Companies need to fight for new business, and customers expect process excellence.

Outstanding companies certainly do not embark on process improvement because they collect “certificates”. It is all about business: Your competitors are at least at this same place (or ahead of you). The goal is to further improve planning and decision making, lower costs, increase adherence to schedule and improve product quality.

Most industry results published describe the background of such a program with too much focus on the assessment and improvement framework [Chri03, Aher03, Muta03, Wohl95]. The published results of SPI initiatives within CMM L5-ranked Boeing Defense and Space Group [Wigl97] and a group within Motorola [Eick03] surely help us to understand the value of moving on the long path towards CMM L5. As one senior manager from a level-5 company said in a workshop: "The most valuable asset in our process improvement initiative is that all these engineers still remember how awful it was when we were still at Level 1".

Several studies investigate the added value of a SPI program from a quantitative perspective [McGi96, McGa01, Dekl97]. They try to set up a return on investment (ROI) calculation that however typically takes average values across organizations and would not show the lessons learned in sufficient depth within one organization. It has been shown in these studies that the CMM is an effective roadmap for achieving cost-effective solutions. It has, by the way, not yet been proven for the CMMI, which still is in its infancy [Aher03].

Key terminology in this chapter is briefly explained here. A policy is a high-level but concrete commitment that each process has to follow. It is sufficiently abstract to be used independently of environmental changes in the business unit. An example of a policy is the directive to only start a project if the resources are identified and assigned.

A process is a sequence of steps performed for a given purpose, for example, the software development process. The process follows the guidance provided by enterprise or business unit policies. A work product or artifact is the outcome of a process. It can be intermediate and internal to a process or it can be delivered to another process. A process document is a description of objectives to be achieved with the process, the inputs and outputs of the processes, the steps that transform inputs into outputs, and actors responsible for certain steps of the process. A process is typically hierarchically described. A process element is one piece of a process on a lower level, typically used to model a specific aspect or step of a more complex process.

Process diversity refers to processes or workflows that follow the same set of higher-level policies, but implemented in different ways. Managing process diversity is primarily achieved by manual or automatic instantiation of such processes for a concrete environment and its specific conditions. The topic of process diversity and different approaches to dealing with it has been evaluated and described in [Lind00, Eber03b].

The CMM is the Capability Maturity Model, for a decade the de facto standard of software process improvement [Paul95]. It is structured into five levels of growing maturity (Table 10.1). Each level as of Level 2 consists of several KPAs.

The CMMI is the integrated CMM [Aher03]. The CMMI is gradually replacing the CMM, as it covers a wider range of process areas and application domains. In this book we do not distinguish the two frameworks in detail and for simplicity talk about "CMM". SPI is software process improvement. In this context we do not distinguish much between hardware and software systems regarding business

processes and the underlying management processes in portfolio and project management. An EPG is the engineering process group, sometimes also referred to as SEPG for software engineering process group. It is the team of people responsible for implementing changes to engineering processes.
The chapter is organized as follows. Section 2 provides an overview on process improvement and summarizes the fundamental background. Section 3 introduces the topic and background of managing processes and process diversity. Section 4 looks on the business perspective and underlines what rewards to expect from process improvement. Section 5 provides practical hints for practitioners and section 6 summarizes the major lessons from process management and improvement.

Table 10.1. The five maturity levels of the CMM and their respective impact on performance (based upon [Paul95])

CMM Level	Title	Focus	Key Process Areas
5	Optimizing	Continuous process improvement on all levels	Process change management Technology change management Defect prevention
4	Managed	Predictable product and process quality	Quality management Quantitative process management
3	Defined	Standardized and tailored engineering and management process	Organization process focus Organization process definition Product engineering Integrated product management Intergroup coordination Training program Peer reviews
2	Repeatable	Project management and commitment process but still highly people-driven	Requirements management Project planning Project tracking & oversight Subcontract management Quality assurance Configuration management
1	Initial	Heroes and massive effort with chaotic results	

10.2 Software Process Improvement

10.2.1 Making Change Happen

Process improvement has primarily to do with implementing changes. Successful process improvement is successful change management. Success is what is visible in the top and bottom lines. We look here primarily at what can be influenced directly within R&D process improvement, which impacts the bottom line more than the top line. Inefficiencies can be attacked, rework can be reduced, customer satisfaction can be improved, and effectiveness and productivity can be enhanced.

Successful change management impacts the "people side" of business. Technology typically can be changed with a new product or at project start, or can be facilitated with dedicated training and tools. However, it is more difficult to overcome obstacles that result from the people working with this technology, who might have been working for years in a specific way. Suddenly these previously successful ways of working (i.e., what we call processes) prove obsolete. These changes are difficult in many dimensions. From an individual perspective, engineers fear that with defined processes they can be replaced easier or their work could be outsourced. Managers realize that they not only need to understand new ways of working but they also need to learn new ways of managing people and innovation.

On an individual level, behaviors have to change. On a corporate level, culture has to change. Cultural change is still a phenomenon dealt with mostly within business outside the software engineering and IT world [Harv93, Pete88, Binn95]. In particular, the latter study outlines with lots of practical insight from several organizations (among them none with software as their core business) that the more successful leaders are in giving clear direction and being forthright, the more they encourage people to take responsibility and to express their true thoughts and feelings.

Successful process improvement means that results are tangible, are in line with expectations, provide business value and are sustainable – even if management attention is reduced (Fig. 10.1). At the top of the picture we summarize the starting point of any change program, namely knowing what one's own situation is (by means of an assessment) and knowing what the objectives are for the changes. This has often been summarized as the combination of a map (i.e., knowing one's own position) and a goal (i.e., knowing where you want to go to). The two belong together like two sides of that one coin of successful process improvement.

Process improvement is a journey – typically without an end. It is a journey because there are many intermediate targets. It has no clearly defined end, since there are always companies eagerly waiting to take your business. It is not just a few months of effort and then comes the next wave of new things. In fact, process improvement is the commitment to continuous changes, as it is asked from all doing business in the software arena. To wait and rest on one's achievements too long typically means to see a new competitor entering the picture. The entry barriers are so low that success and loss are only a few months (and sometimes mouse clicks) apart.

This journey is best portrayed by a cyclic endeavor of iterative improvements. We start at the top with establishing sponsorship. This is key to any change, as it means that the responsible highest management makes a personal commitment to making the change happen. From this executive sponsorship stem the business objectives that the changes should achieve. The next step is the assessment. Typically assessments follow a well-defined formalized scheme (e.g., CMM CBA-IPI assessment or CMMI SCAMPI method [Aher03]).

The assessment generates a snapshot of one's own current situation, and how that relates to the objectives. Gaps are identified as are next steps. From those gaps a concrete action plan is derived that serves as the basis for making the change initiative into a concrete project. The action plan must be implemented in the form of a regular project, or there will be a continuous lack of resources and insufficient management follow-up. The last piece in this iteration is the continuous tracking of actual improvement performance versus original objectives and versus project milestones. Here is where metrics come very much into the picture to make changes tangible and to identify what works and what needs still more effort and focus.

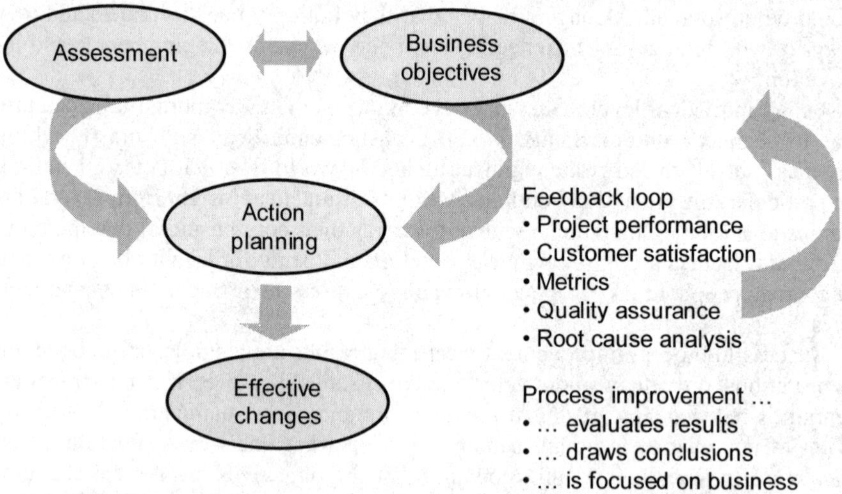

Fig. 10.1. Effective and sustainable changes result from knowing the objectives and the current situation

We talk a lot about the different levels of the CMM or CMMI. Let us briefly and informally characterize them since they impact the way we address change management in this chapter (Table 10.1). There are five levels, of which Level 2 is the most difficult to reach with respect to culture changes in the organization. The major culture change from an ad hoc behavior on Level 1 to the controlled behaviors per project on Level 2 is as follows:

- joint commitments are made within the scope of a project
- project plans become increasingly realistic
- the whole project team reviews and has input to the plan
- estimates are made by teams of developers
- schedules made by project managers comprehend real work time

Towards Level 3 we see another pattern, that of generalizing changes so that they impact the entire organization. This means:

- the organization adopts a standardized process framework
- a common professional culture emerges

- the culture is carried by all engineers and driven by increased pride in the organization
- development and training is achieved through using process assets
- focus on performance improvement with clear business perspective
- customers feel with each contact a coherent and focused way of working
- less rework and cost of non-quality allows the organization to focus on new development
- motivated personnel stay with the organization

Towards Level 4 we see again a substantial change in culture, this time from the organization back to projects and directly linking performance improvement targets to process improvement. This is where profound process knowledge is consistently visible on all levels and in all functions and roles. Level 5 finally looks into continuous improvements that are driven by empowered teams and individuals.

10.2.2 Setting Reachable Targets

Process improvement needs software measurement. Fig. 10.2 shows the dependencies between the execution of a process, its definition and the improvements. Improvements are only feasible if they relate to measurement. Processes must be judged whether they are good or bad, or whether they are better or worse than before. To make change sustainable, it must be based on realistic targets.

The interaction of objectives and feedback is obvious in day-to-day decision making. Different groups typically work towards individually controlled targets that build up to business division-level goals and corporate goals.

The example of improving maintainability indicates this hierarchy. A department or business division-level goal could be to improve maintainability within legacy systems, as it is strategically important for all telecommunication suppliers. Design managers might break that down further to redesigning exactly those components that are at the edge of being maintainable. Project managers, on the other hand, face a trade-off with time to market and might emphasize on incremental builds instead. Clearly both need appropriate indicators to support their selection processes that define the way towards the needed quantitative targets related to these goals. Obviously, one of the key success criteria for SPI is to understand the political context and various hidden agendas within the organization in order to make compromises or weigh alternatives.

Objectives related to individual processes must be unambiguous and agreed upon the respective groups. This is obvious for test and design groups. While the first are reinforced for finding defects and thus focus on writing and executing effective test suites, design groups are targeted to delivering code that can be executed without defects. Defects must be corrected efficiently, which allows for setting up a quantitative objective for a design group, that is, the backlog of faults it has to resolve. This may uncover one of the many inherent conflict situations embedded in an improvement program. Setting an overall target of reducing defects found by the customer of course triggers immediate activities in design, such as improved coding rules, establishing code inspections, etc. Finding such defects up front means better input quality to integration test that as a result might not be able to still accomplish efficiency targets, such as a distinct rate of faults per test case. Besides reaching test coverage, a successfully running test case has little worth from a cost reduction perspective, which shows the inherent dilemma of conflicting goals.

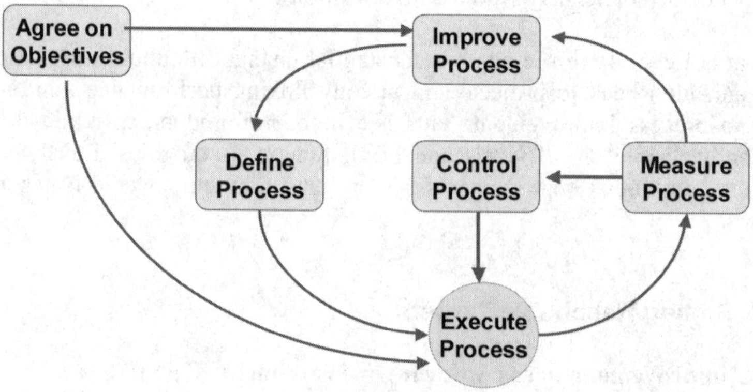

Fig. 10.2. Process improvement is based on upon process measurement

A goal-oriented measurement approach (see Chap. 3) ensures that process improvement is embedded in a closed feedback loop (see Fig. 10.3). Goals are business-driven and are translated into annual targets or key performance indicators. They are reflected in and tracked with scorecards. A history database captures process, product and project information. It helps with tailoring processes and with setting specific process and project targets. It also facilitates setting control limits for statistical process control. The feedback loop is built upon measurements from processes that are analyzed versus control limits and compared with targets.

It is important to consider different perspectives and their individual goals related to promotion, projects and the business. Most organizations have at least four such perspectives: those of the practitioner, the project manager, the department head and senior management/executives. Their motivation and typical activities differ greatly and often create confusing goals. Generally senior management and practitioners support improvement programs because they feel the needs on a daily basis. This is less true for middle management that has to make improvements happen within conflicting goals and commitments. Projects are still running with agreed-upon deadlines and available resources, while impetus for change might require specific additional resources at a given moment. The yield of any improvement initiative can be substantially lowered if preconditions are not satisfied in the day-to-day project work. For instance, asking for inspections before estimation and planning are adapted might result in superficial preparation and document reading, thus not detecting all defects that could have been found and, in addition, provoking review findings that are never closed.

Lack of buy-in of middle management to our experience has two crucial effects. First, they definitely put medium-term improvement at a lower priority because they are measured according to short-term project results. Second, they might even send conflicting signals to engineers. Often the traditional reward systems stem from hierarchical organizations that disempower teams charged with executing cross-functional processes. Reuse is an example that continuously creates such discussions. When a project incurs expenses in order to keep components maintainable and to promote their reusability, who pays for it and where is this trade-off recorded in a history database that only compares efficiency of projects and thus of their management? Obviously, another critical success factor is to make existing management processes compatible with redesigned business processes. This includes measuring middle management towards achieving realistic and quantified improvements objectives – in other words to leave the classic functional line- or project-oriented merit rating.

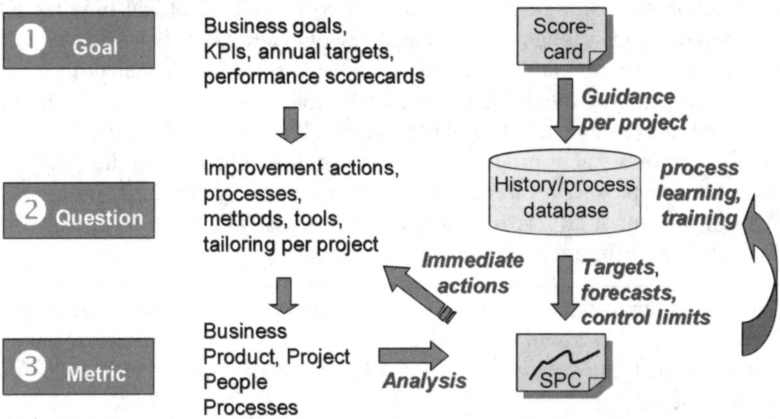

Fig. 10.3. Goal-oriented measurement ensures that process improvement is embedded in a closed feedback loop

Before moving to the second part of effective change, namely feedback, we should spend a word on planning change. Change should be undertaken in a timely way. It should not be forced so fast that it is obvious to engineers that the targets cannot be reached. There should, however, never be a situation where people wait and wonder what will happen next. This situation typically occurs during the initial period when an assessment has just been finished and workgroups struggle to implement process changes. After having achieved some first benefits, again the risk is high to lose momentum because, after all, change is painful – as it runs in parallel with regular work – and having achieved some goals signals to many involved parties to concentrate more on project work.

Knowing that accurate planning is necessary to make change happen, it is somewhat of a relief to also realize that planning is a motivating activity. Doing the planning makes the targets more concrete, and accomplishing them is suddenly seen as possible, and even inevitable. Planning is the translation of the scorecard principle towards reachable individual targets. The vehicle is working groups for the operational change management and task forces for macro changes, who based on some high-level business goals establish the plan and later follow it. Seldom are people more motivated to work than just after they have finished their own planning.

10.2.3 Providing Feedback

Managing and tracking SPI is done on different levels of abstraction. Senior management is interested in the achievements compared to business goals and related to what has been invested in the program. Related objectives include the effectiveness of fault detection because the obvious relationship to cost of quality is directly related to the common business goal of cost reduction. Lead-time reduction and effort reduction is related to reduced rework and as such is also related to fewer defects and early fault detection. On the project level, managing process improvements asks for specific process metrics that compare efficiencies and thus relate on the operational level to achieving the business goals. Several achievements of our improvement program can be attributed to increasing the visibility of project status, improved awareness of work products quality and setting result-oriented improvement targets for each major process. Thorough technical control satisfies all these different needs for effective feedback.

> Questions such as "**are we doing better or worse?**" will provide feedback from the currently running R&D or engineering projects where changes should be institutionalized to the respective workgroups responsible for making change happen.

The feedback loop within a process improvement initiative, which we already know from Fig. 10.1 and Fig. 10.2, is detailed in Fig. 10.4. On the left side we have the classic improvement activities, such as periodic assessments and dedicated working groups that would implement specific changes. They certainly influence the way requirements are managed (e.g., CMM Level 2), how development and engineering processes are improved, what quality objectives could be set and to which degree technology and infrastructure need to be addressed. This is all input to the functional organization that is responsible for implementing the regular engineering projects. They are continuously tracked by means of project tracking and oversight metrics, which are not only used to monitor and manage projects, but also to provide feedback to the working groups on the progress of change institutionalization. Root cause analysis of defects or in-process quality checks provide further information on what is going right and what is going wrong.

Unfortunately, many organizations that consider software development as their core business strictly separate between business performance monitoring and evaluation on one hand and what is labeled software metrics on the other hand [Pfle97]. Our motivation while building up a corporate SPI program was to link it with the corporate technical control in order to align the different levels of target setting and tracking activities. Only the close link of corporate strategy with clearly specified business goals and with the operational project management helps in achieving overall improvements. We therefore linked the operational metrics program for development and project management with our SPI initiative to ensure that objectives on all levels correspond with each other.

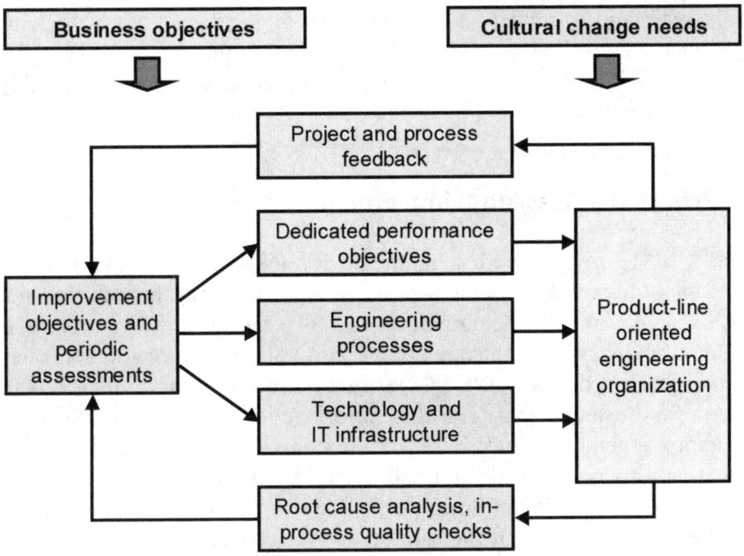

Fig. 10.4. Process improvement activities need feedback loops from actual project and process performance

> Metrics need to make sense to everybody within the organization who will be in contact with them. Therefore the metrics should first be piloted and then evaluated after some time. **Potential evaluation questions include**:
>
> Are the selected metrics consistent with the original improvement targets? Do the metrics provide added value? Do they make sense from different angles and can that meaning be communicated without many slides?
>
> Do the chosen metrics send the right message about what the organization considers relevant? Metrics should spotlight by default and without cumbersome investigations of what might be behind. Are the right things being spotlighted?

Do the metrics clearly follow a perspective that allows comparisons? Do they avoid ambiguities or heterogeneous viewpoints, thus allowing to be used as history data?

With such premises it is feasible to set up not only release-oriented phase end targets but also phase entry criteria that allow for rejection to validation activities (such as reviews or integration) if the system quality is inadequate.

There are two major reasons for project failure that can be observed in many organizations. First and most important is the fact that we commit to inadequate estimates prematurely, stick to original budgets and schedules even if requirements change, let requirements change until well into integration, and still rarely update the estimates to match reality. The other major reason is insufficient navigation of managers in the sea of data that modern communication and reporting tools produce. Without navigation and adequate metrics managers invariably veer off in wrong directions.

10.2.4 Practically Speaking: Implementing Change

Since the CMM provides both a guideline for identifying strengths and weaknesses of the software development process and a roadmap for improvement actions, Alcatel like many other organizations also based its SPI activities on the CMM. Periodically assessments are conducted in all major development sites. The direct findings according to the CMM are analyzed according to their prospective impacts on the business goals and then prioritized to select those areas with the highest improvement potential. Based on this ranking a concrete planning of improvement actions is repeatedly refined, resulting in an action plan with detailed descriptions of improvement tasks with responsibilities, effort estimates, etc. Checkpointing assessments of the same type are repeatedly done to track the implementation of the improvement plan.

With process change management becoming a management function and SPI as a project receiving high priority in the context of all engineering projects, real authority is given to the SPI program. For the same reason, engineering process groups (EPGs) are typically rather small, while at the same time part-time contribution of experts in various areas fosters buy-in and sustainable culture change. To avoid the prevailing attitude that nothing is worse than a six-month old slogan, senior management should make explicit that any change needs within engineering (e.g., efficiency improvement, elapse time reduction, etc.) would be covered under one process improvement (project) umbrella. All this is the life insurance for your SPI initiative.

Reaching CMM Level 3 cannot be an end, as many KPAs on the levels four and five ensure institutionalized process focus. Remaining on a CMM Level 3 would definitely derail the organization with the first bigger technology change. Also, level 3 keeps practitioners and the projects unsatisfied, as they cannot and should not directly influence processes on their respective operational level.

Achieving the high maturity levels empowers individuals and guarantees continuous improvements – bottom-up

10.2.5 Critical Success Factors

The approach of critical success factors allows you to keep the focus on resolving concrete issues by decomposing goals into activities. It also ensures that within complex decision processes, such as in regular project reviews, the relations between day-to-day tasks and the SPI program and its objectives are not lost.

> We identified several critical success factors related to a process improvement program.
>
> Commitment and motivation from the senior management to the engineers;
>
> Treating process improvement as a project;
>
> Short-term results that immediately show measurable achievements in running projects;
>
> Sustainable results even if pressure would be loosened;
>
> Continuous change within and across processes.

What does it mean concretely that there is a push and concrete commitments behind changes? It is definitely not what we faced in a change initiative in one of our development centers some years ago. An improvement program with heavy emphasis on quality improvement was installed. Both external and in-house consultants were hired for coaching. Management said that they "empowered" team leaders and gave priority to quality. The initiative, however, never flew as the push was lacking, and all management cared about was output and preserving their own stakes. Senior management never walked their talk and in critical situations made the same wrong decisions as before.

"Push" means that management plays an active role in setting overall targets and then continuously reviews results. Tom Peters specified such reviews as "during each staff meeting, go around the table posing the questions: What have you changed lately? How fast are you changing? Are you pursuing bold enough change goals? to each colleague. Do it ritualistically. Make these simple questions a prime element in your performance appraisal system, as well as in your informal monthly sit-down appraisal" [Pete88]. In our case such reviews are carried out on a monthly base with the respective vice president, the institutionalization or deviations are questioned in the respective project reviews, and customers are part of the feedback loop.

10.3 Process Management

10.3.1 Process Definition and Workflow Management

Successful processes are not static. Processes must be managed. They must be easily accessible for the practitioners and managers. They must integrate seamlessly, and they must not disturb or create overhead. Process improvement will fail if we do not consider these basic requirements. Process improvement will also fail if we try to make the development processes completely uniform across large organizations. By focusing on the essence of processes, integrating processes elements with each other and providing complete tools solutions, organizations can tailor processes to meet specific needs and allow localized and problem- or skill-specific software practices, while still ensuring that basic objectives of the organization are achieved. This is what we call here managed process diversity.

Practitioners do not look for heavy process documentation, but rather for process support that exactly describes what they have to do at the moment they have to do it. Different products or components and various parameters such as system size or type of development paradigm ask for a carefully balanced approach of process documentation and maintenance. Modular process elements must be combined according to a specific role or work product to be delivered. Still the need for an organizational process, as described by CMM L3, is strongly emphasized and reinforced [Paul95].

In implementing a homogeneous workflow support, we started with an inventory, how we managed processes and their tailoring to specific settings. Processes were agreed by the experienced practitioners for years and were approved by an organization-wide process control board. This ensures that on the level of process, policies, or commitments, no difference exists. On lower levels, however, the implementation of these processes or policies varied dramatically primarily because of cultural and legacy reasons. The need prevailed that from a sales or overall engineering perspective, we had to provide a solution to our customers that integrated various components. These components are individually assembled and then integrated according to the specific network topology and market requirements an operator faces. For instance, two components might have the same requirements management process, but two different tools in place. This means that whenever we need to track progress of a product that integrates these two components, specific interfaces were necessary to get the complete picture. This situation was even worse if they applied different change management tools. In such cases the entire metrics suite and traceability approaches were replicated for both components.

Even if the components are not integrated and are never intended to be integrated, such as two competing products, there can still be a trade-off in aligning procedures or tools, which can build upon synergy. Scalability applies for license cost of tools as well as for training. Managed process diversity, for instance, allows for easier moving of engineers from one product to another, as long as the role descriptions and the procedures are aligned.

Having the concepts for managing process diversity within the software development, the next step is to seamlessly integrate R&D workflows, such as software development or software maintenance with their (e-)business counterparts, such as customer relationship management or service request management. Collaborative product commerce (CPC), specifically from an end-to-end perspective, will help that engineering processes integrate with the interfacing business processes. Examples include configuration management for software artifacts, and how they relate to the overall product data management. or software defect corrections, and how they relate to overall service request management as part of the enterprise CRM solution. Product life cycles, though necessary as a foundation, are insufficient if not integrated well with non-SW-related business processes.

Fig. 10.5 details how such factors not only characterize the project complexity and thus the management challenges, but also how they determine the level of process integration and workflow management. Various project factors determine different approaches to manage the involved software processes. Workflow management systems offer different perspectives to allow for instance navigation based on work products, roles or processes.

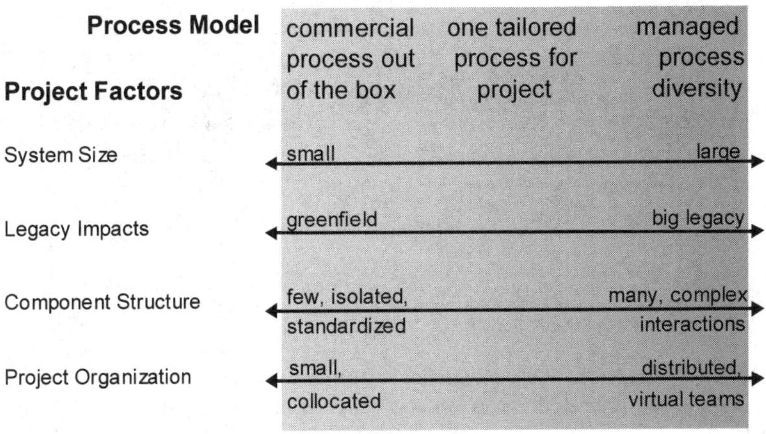

Fig. 10.5. Different solutions for process diversity

Navigation is realized with HTLM hyperlinks as shown in Fig. 10.6. A lifecycle picture shows the global overview of the processes, and many embedded hyperlinks allow navigating with a few clicks to the final element in which the reader is interested. Compared with static process models of the 1980s, which typically used standard data modeling languages, the currently available workflow systems provide nicely visualized flows that hide as much as possible anything that is not relevant for a specific view. Usability is key and not formalism.

The perceived conflict between organizational process and individual tailoring can be resolved by a tailorable process framework [Eber03b]. Such a framework should be fully graphically accessible and allows the selection of a process applicable for components as well as an entire product based on selecting the appropriate parameters that characterize the project. The framework allows for automatic instantiation of the respective development process and product life cycle, a project quality plan or specific applicable metrics, based on modular process elements such as role descriptions, templates, procedures or check lists, which hyperlink with each other.

Usability of any workflow support system is determined by the degree to which it can be adapted or tailored towards the projects' needs. There are organizational and project-specific environmental constraints, which make it virtually impossible to apply the workflow system out of the box. Adaptation is achieved by offering a set of standard workflows, which are selected (e.g., incremental delivery versus grand design; parallel versus sequential development; development versus maintenance). On a lower level, work products are defined or selected out of a predefined catalogue. The process models should distinguish among mandatory and optional components.

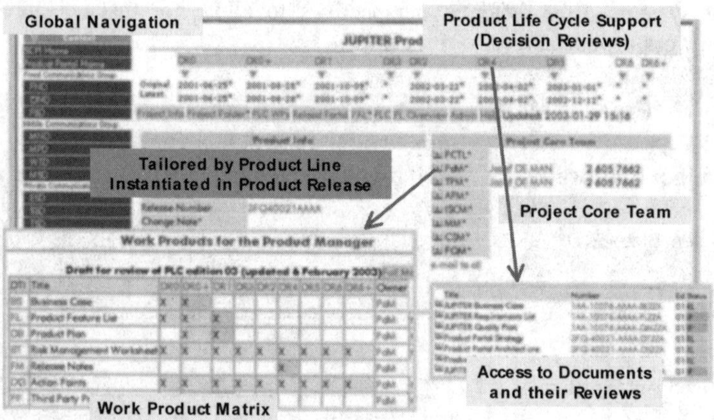

Fig. 10.6. Hyperlinks facilitate integration with other tools and processes. This instance shows the project dashboard that is automatically set up and prepopulated upon approved project

Process diversity and tailoring of processes happens on various levels. A small example shows this approach. To successfully deliver a product with heterogeneous architecture and a mixture of legacy components built in various languages, certain processes must be aligned on the project level. This holds for project management, configuration management and requirements management. Otherwise it would, for instance, be impossible to trace customer requirements that might impact several components through the project life cycle.

On the other hand, design processes and validation strategies are so close to the individual components' architecture and development paradigms that any standard would fail as well as all standards for one design or programming methodology have failed in the past. To make the puzzle complete, for efficiency reasons, the manager of that heterogeneous project or product line surely would not like it if within each small team the work product templates or tool-based workflows were redefined. Many workflow systems for unified processes fail on such low-level process change management. They do not allow integrating process needs on different levels into a hierarchy with guided selection.

10.3.2 Quantitative Process Management

Integration of process tailoring, software measurement, history databases, and analysis of metrics with the statistical control of metrics will facilitate quantitative process management. Quantitative process management involves establishing goals for the performance of the process, taking measurements of the process performance, analyzing the resulting metrics, and making process adjustments to maintain process performance within acceptable limits. This means that the software organization collects process performance data from the software projects and uses these data to characterize the process capability of its processes. It's understood that not only processes are variable, but that understanding variation is the basis for management by fact and systematic improvement. It means to quantitatively understand the past, control the present and predict the future.

Quantitative process management builds upon statistical techniques to identify process anomalies, to eliminate them and to ensure the processes will remain within what is asked by business needs (Fig. 10.7).

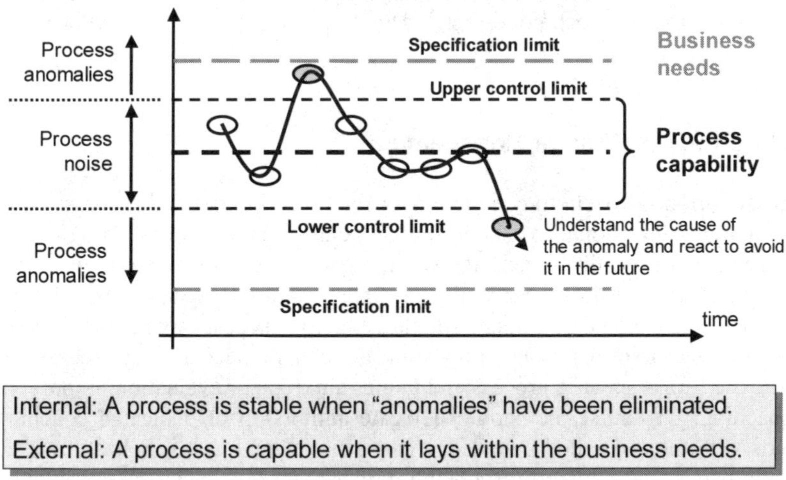

Fig. 10.7. Quantitative process management

We see in Fig. 10.7 several dots resulting from process behaviors over time, for instance, field quality in different projects. The business needs determine specification limits, such as a maximum of defects in the field. Often these specification limits are asymmetric. In our example of field defects a lower specification limit could be impacted by time to market, thus indicating that the product must have the right quality. The process behaviors determine control limits. Depending on the stability of the process, these control limits are inside the specification limits and allow adjustments, such as in case a higher quality level is asked. For immature organizations, the control limits (which control?)are mostly outside the specification limits and the organizations are clueless on how to adapt processes (which processes?) towards reaching specification limits. The process is not capable. This explains why the CMM has in its name the word capability.

Predictability is a good indicator for the process maturity of an organization. While on lower maturity levels the objective is to get the projects done in time and budget – but with substantial variances, it evolves towards CMM L3 to the ability to predict cost, schedule, and defects based on past performance. On higher maturity levels upper and lower boundaries are defined for the expected performance. Estimates actively deal with the uncertainties and acknowledge this by intervals instead of point estimates.

Low maturity organizations often collect metrics just to show data. We often faced situations where neither practitioners nor their management really used the data. They would bring their reports and when asked questions had no idea how the data points relate to each other. This is a waste of effort. Deciding to measure implies the effort to evaluate and execute from what is measured (Fig. 2.1). The analysis techniques include gap analysis between estimates and actual performance, correlations within the quantitative data, trends analysis, classification, partitioning, identification of outliers, and analysis of rationale of such outliers, various SPC (Statistical Process Control) techniques, including process stability analysis and various analysis techniques related to statistical models for product/service characteristics.

10.3.3 Process Change Management

Processes are not frozen; they evolve over time. Having defined processes on any level of an organization also asks for process change management. Process change management is typically an activity of the organization, however will also happen within individual projects, especially in higher maturity organizations. To facilitate change, any process element should refer to a process owner who typically serves as focal point for change proposals and change decisions. A process owner is the expert for a specific process and guides any type of evaluation, improvement or coaching. Of course, he should delegate authorship or dedicated coaching to experts with more detailed knowledge and experience, but it is helpful to identify a single person with overall responsibility to whom people can ask questions and to whom they can suggest improvements. Any single instance of a process element should be placed under configuration control, which allows managing change in the context of several parallel projects. The latter is particularly relevant to avoid uncontrolled mushrooming of variants, thereby creating situations where an engineer would suddenly have to deal with two versions of the same process. It is for this reason that quality audits always ask for defined time stamps related to process selection.

Tailoring and assembling process elements is outlined in Fig. 10.8. Project parameters (horizontal axis) drive the applicability and assembling of process characteristics (vertical axis). By relating the elements to criteria on a generic level, individual adaptation is far easier than doing this repeatedly for each project. Both the elements and their links are subject to change, which is controlled and managed by a process control board. Many process elements are related by their inherent semantics that already predefine many internal relationships. For instance, depending on the permission to allow or to prohibit late requirements changes, the workflow is impacted at many places. This should not be identified for each single project again and again. Instead the hooks are foreseen in the respective estimation, planning or design processes to integrated requirement changes or late requirements, which in one case are activated and in the other case are not visible.

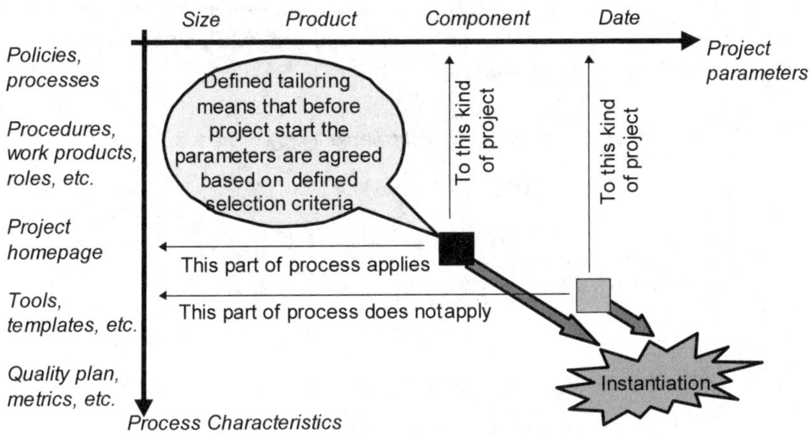

Fig. 10.8. Assembling a specific process instance based on building blocks and project parameters

Managing process changes of course depends on process maturity. On lower CMM levels, it is centrally governed, while on higher levels, tailoring and change management – within a defined scope – increasingly is going back into the projects and teams.

10.4 Measuring the Results of Process Improvements

In this section we will show how process improvement and the respective process measurement relates to concrete ROI tracking. To be more concrete, we will again take an example from one of Alcatel's business divisions during the nineties. At the beginning of the software process improvement program the focus was on four areas closely related to our overall business goals:

1. improving the customer-perceived quality
2. improving schedule predictability
3. reducing the total cost of non-quality
4. reducing the cycle time

Although these four objectives are somehow related, it is clear that priorities must be given to ensure reproducible decisions in case of conflicts. The order given above reflects these priorities at the start of the SPI program.

Some results of this software process improvement program can be seen in the following figures. Note that we follow the principles indicated earlier, such as starting to measure *before* changes are implemented. Increasing design defect detection effectiveness over a three-year timeframe is indicated in Fig. 10.9. Design defect detection effectiveness is the percentage of all defects that are detected before the start of integration test. Before starting the improvement program 17% of all faults were detected before the start integration test, while after three years almost two thirds of all faults are detected up front.

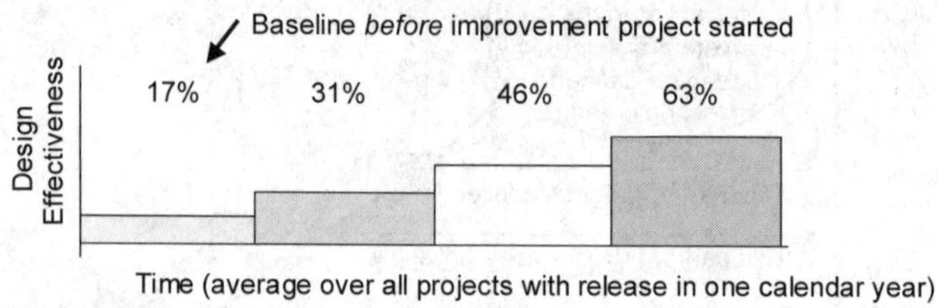

Fig. 10.9. Design defect detection effectiveness over four years

As a consequence, we could reduce defects in the field (after handover to the customer) by more than 20% year after year during this initiative! Besides better overall quality, this of course directly impacts productivity and predictability. Schedule predictability (i.e., achieving the planned delivery date) improved (Fig. 10.10) dramatically. These are typical achievements that you obtain when moving from CMM Level 1 to CMM Level 3. But different from a theoretical lecture, we have shown in this chapter *how* such improvements are implemented to achieve the results.

Process diversity relates to cost management. Processes can be individually sufficient and perfectly fitting in some overall objectives related to process maturity, while still not positively impacting productivity and throughput of the entire organization. We found, for instance, that at a given time frame a state-of-the-art commercial CM system was introduced for more than five components within several business divisions in parallel without knowledge of each other. The process objectives, which were long-since agreed upon, were always guiding the introduction, but the set up, the definition of procedures, roles or delivery mechanisms and even the link to standard metrics and standard problem management was reinvented in each single case. Synergy as it is intended within most companies cannot grow with such lack of organizational learning.

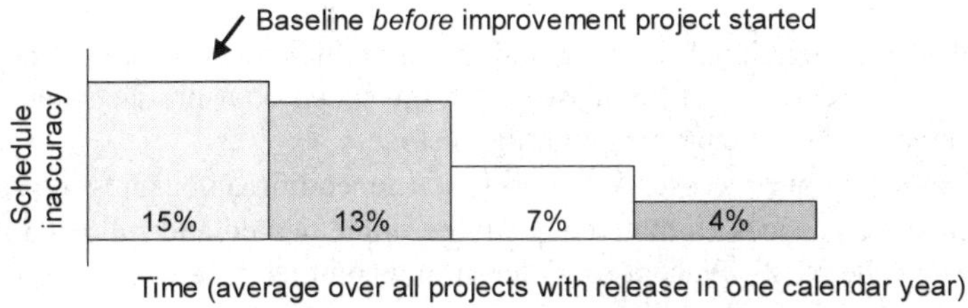

Fig. 10.10. Schedule inaccuracy (in terms of achieved delivery date versus plan) over four years

10.5 Hints for the Practitioner

A key question that any process improvement activity must answer is, whether the organization can demonstrate actual business benefit. An improvement that after some months doesn't show sustainable value is badly managed. As the Baldrige award suggests, if the business results are not measurably visible as improvement trends, it signals an approach or deployment problem, perhaps resulting from a focus on getting a "level" or "certificate" rather than achieving business objectives.

Successful process management and process improvement within the full scope of e-R&D is based upon a few principles:

- **Process improvement must always be driven from clear business objectives**. Never start a process improvement activity with unclear objectives, or by simply telling that a certain CMM level must be achieved. It will fail and deliver mediocre results.
- Improve R&D project performance based on the criteria of predictability, quality and productivity.
- **Reinforce accountability** through usage of concrete planning and progress tracking instruments. Progress is what is measurable.
- **Line up processes with business needs** and reinforce continuous learning and improvement driven by the ever-changing business environment.
- **Continuously challenge existing behaviors**. Use external benchmarks to stimulate better performance.
- Facilitate virtual teams across your projects that communicate and interact with an increasingly integrated workflow system. Projects get smaller and teams will be more distributed and mobile than ever. Prepare for such flexibility.
- Improve efficiency by using standard processes and the technology and tools that best support these processes.

- Integrate and interface with heterogeneous R&D tool suites. Do not rely on specific tools and vendors. Decouple processes from tools to be able to make changes without much overheads. The time of integrated and heavy CASE suites is over.
- Stimulate organizational learning and avoid architecture- or project-dependent isolation. Processes must be innovated at the speed your products and services are innovated. Don't engrave anything in stone.
- Allow tailoring of processes and workflows depending on business needs.
- Introduce lean processes that can easily be implemented and followed through, such as a "checklist" concept for determining completeness of milestones.
- Integrate workflows by using standard interfaces and the same configuration management for process elements and work products. Web services can facilitate simple interfaces.
- Interface with other critical business processes and workflows based on a general e-business strategy and quality management system (e.g. operations, services, supply chain management, procurement, etc.).
- Above all, **treat any improvement or innovation initiative as a project** on its own with allocated resources, committed milestones, a project plan and periodic follow-up. Change is not for free, and to assume that it somehow will get done means nothing else than that management is not committed.

Measuring results of process improvement and thus making the business cases for your own improvement projects can build upon the following insights:

Improved quality. We can directly address the customer needs by linking dedicated improvement objectives, such as return rate, via the CMM to process changes in R&D. This is actually the strength of CMM Levels two and three. Two-digit quality improvements year over year are feasible if the CMM is applied and closely followed up in engineering projects.

Reduced cycle time. The efficiency and effectiveness of engineering processes directly impact engineering cycle time. For instance, earlier defect detection means faster and more comprehensive defect correction. A defect found during development costs less than 10% to correct compared to detection during test. Your focus here should be on defect phase containment. Build the necessary checks to ensure that work products have the right quality level before being passed on to the next process step. Cycle time reduction builds upon a consistent product life cycle and process repository, which allows instrumenting and tuning processes to needs.

Improved engineering flexibility. With decreasing size and duration of projects, engineers need to be flexible to quickly start working in new environments. While technical challenges cannot be reduced, the organizational and administrative overhead must be managed and limited. Agreeing and reinforcing one consistent and overarching product life cycle across the company ensures that you can deliver solutions independently of where the components come from. Increasingly components come from various suppliers, including freely available software. The life cycle offers the framework for all projects to have a minimum set of decision gates. Engineers can faster move to new projects or other departments if some basic process framework applies to the entire company.

Reduced overhead. Links to the management system with its process and role descriptions, document templates are embedded in the workflow support system, presenting engineers with immediate process support when and where they need it. Long process descriptions are replaced by pictorial overviews and automated interfaces. For example, clicking on a work product name can activate an interface to a document management system, and administrative data such as the document number are automatically derived from the project context. Less overheads facilitate that work products are kept consistent when changes occur.

Improved communication. Information is presented in a consistent way for all projects, avoiding replication of data and reducing search time. A standardized workflow and product life cycle management system can easily offer a dashboard with immediate visibility on key data and responsibilities contributing to an increase awareness of accountability. If you don't have such workflow system at hand, build nevertheless the project dashboard. Standardizing one management part of the process (such as project metrics) and automating it will increasingly grow towards alignments and standardization of other tools and processes.

Improved alignment of process and tools. With process asset libraries linked to tools, we are able to filter out and evaluate scenarios of how process change impacts tools, or where tool changes would impact processes. So-called "best-practices" can be communicated with related tools and procedures to move up engineering effectiveness and learn from the best in class in your company. Interfaces to tools and their user guides can now be embedded in the process support environment.

Easier generation of training plans. With the advent of managed process diversity, aligned training plans and closer follow-up of skill evolution has been achieved. Increasingly, project roles and also specific work product templates or process-related roles are standardized and can be reused, thus facilitating more consistent skill and human resource management.

10.6 Summary

Process improvement drives productivity improvement and thus frees resources for innovation. We have tried with this chapter to close the gap and to avoid focusing only on theoretically describing improved processes or only introducing a software engineering tools suite. e-R&D is a comprehensive view of process improvement, starting from the basics of culture change towards more accountability and building upon a number of integration mechanisms to ensure that technology effectiveness keeps pace with process maturity.

Process management is necessary to ensure having the right processes. Too narrow an implementation of ISO 9000 or CMM bears the risk that processes specify in all detail what needs to be done. Especially big organizations believe that processes can control everything. They loose flexibility and will be overrun by small new entrepreneurs with much more agility. We have observed organizations that would treat the certifications as the goal, rather as a step in achieving real goals. Process improvement and frameworks like ISO 9000 or CMM are always and only tools to an end. They are important tools and within software engineering they will definitely deliver results. However, the goal is better performance in projects and products.

Depending on market requirements and technology change, processes are different even within one organization. Process definition and process reinforcement should be as high as necessary to ensure quality, predictability and productivity, and as low as feasible to preserve flexibility and agility. Each single process must be judged on the cost it creates versus the benefit it yields. Processes need commercial justification, which is impossible if they are not even defined. Once organizational maturity approaches a certain level (i.e., CMM L3), the real challenge is how much to document and what to automate. While a lot has been written about documentation and process improvement, not much is available on practical experiences with introducing workflow management.

Two elements are critical to making a change successful: *setting objectives* – defining what specific change should occur and setting targets for attaining that change – and *providing feedback* – as the effort to change is underway, those changing must receive concrete information about their progress in achieving the goals. **Where there are objectives and feedback, both the commitment to change and the likelihood that change will in fact occur are much higher**.

11 Software Performance Engineering

Measurement is an excellent abstraction mechanism
for learning what works and what doesn't.
—Victor Basili

11.1 The Method of Software Performance Engineering

Software performance engineering can be defined as a collection of methods for the support of performance-oriented software development of application systems along the entire software development process to ensure appropriate performance-related product quality. It uses a systems engineering perspective to ensure a comprehensive view on performance requirements. It extensively uses software measurements to define, implement and monitor performance objectives. Software performance engineering can be described as a kind of aspect-oriented software development.

Software performance engineering becomes an interface between software engineering and performance management. It is not a relaunch of long-standing performance management methods as other engineering approaches that were successfully used in the area of telecommunications. Performance engineering analyzes the expected performance characteristics of a software system in early development phases. In the system analysis, software developers, customers and users define performance characteristics as service level objectives in addition to functional specifications (Fig. 10.1).

> Performance has to be determined and quantified by performance metrics. They are specific product metrics that can be derived from different system levels and perspectives. Internal and external perspectives are often distinguished.
>
> Internal performance metrics refer to operation times, e.g., the number of operations per time unit, to transfer ratios, like the number of transferred bytes per second, or to the utilization of system resources, like CPU or RAM.
>
> External performance metrics reflect the outside behavior of the software system with regard to executed functions. The metrics often refer to response times of concrete application functions and to the throughput.

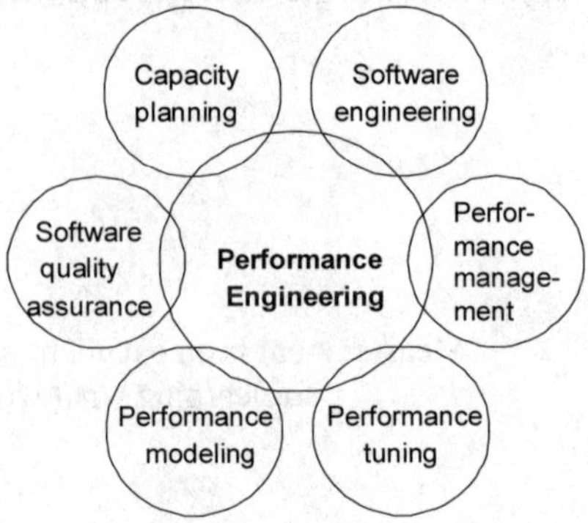

Fig. 11.1. Use of existing concepts from other disciplines

A mix of varied quantified metrics describes the performance characteristic of an IT system. The negotiations of developers, customers and users should be based on suitable and justifiable cost performance ratios [Folt01]. Performance engineering already provides instruments for this phase, like rules of thumb. Unrealistic developments can be discontinued early or can be renegotiated. The quantified performance metrics have to be refined in the system design and implementation phase.

Concrete application functions and interfaces can be evaluated at this time. The software development process should allow a cyclic verification of the performance characteristics. They will be analyzed in the respective phase of the software life cycle in the available granularity. In the first phases estimations have to be used that are often based on rules of thumb. In further development phases analytical and simulative models can be used. If prototypical implementations of individual program components are already available, measurements can be executed.

The quantified metrics should be continuously compared with the required performance characteristics. Deviations lead to an immediate decision process. Performance engineering uses existing methods and concepts from the areas of performance management, performance modeling, software engineering, capacity planning, and performance tuning as well as software quality assurance. It enlarges and modifies them by performance-related analysis functions (see Fig. 10.1). However, the performance metrics are only as exact as the basis data of the models. In order that the calculations be concrete and realistic as possible, the set up of a performance database is imperative.

Since a lot of performance data can be collected in the productive operation of a software system by benchmarking and monitoring, it should be ensured that these data are stored in the database for further performance engineering tasks in future development projects. The quality of the performance evaluation depends decisively on the maturity of the development process (see also the approach of a Performance Engineering Maturity Model (PEMM) in [Schm00b]). However, critical software components are analyzed until the end of the implementation phase. The complete test environment is available within the phase of the system test.

If prototypical implementations were not used within the design and implementation phase, the fulfillment of the performance requirements can be verified with the help of load drivers, e.g., by synthetic workload, in the system test phase. The real production system is available in the system operation phase. Often performance analyses are performed again in pilot installations over a certain time period, since the analysis is now based on real workloads conditions. Thereby, an existing system concept can be modified again. The workload of the system often increases with a higher acceptance. That is why reserves should be considered within the system concept. The proposed procedure has to be adapted to domain-specific environments. Because of the scope of the tasks, specialists should support performance engineering.

In subsequent development projects these tasks are handed over step-by-step to the software developers. Their task spectrum widens to a long-term perspective. The integration can essentially be simplified if software developers have already learned these principles in their academic education.

11.2 Motivation, Requirements and Goals

11.2.1 Performance-related Risk of Software Systems

The performance characteristics of a software product are frequently considered only at a much later point in the development process, typically during testing or in the phase of deployment. This approach, known in the literature as the "fix it later approach", repeatedly leads to major problems (redesign, the use of more powerful hardware than anticipated, delayed introduction, and so on), since the possible performance characteristics are already defined at early stages of development by design decisions regarding hardware and software architecture. The efficient operation of business processes depends on the support of IT systems. Delays in these systems can have fatal effects for the business. The following examples clarify the explosive nature of this problem:

- The planned development budget for the luggage processing system of the Denver, Colorado airport increased by about US$ 2 billion because of inadequate performance characteristics. The system was only planned for the terminal of United Airlines. However, the system was enlarged for all terminals of the airport within the development without considering the effects on the system's workload. The system had to manage more data and functions than any comparable system at any other airport in the world at the time. In addition to faulty project management, inadequate performance characteristics delayed the opening of the airport by 16 months. A loss of US$ 160,000 per day was recorded.

- An IBM information system was used for the evaluation of individual competition results at the Olympic games in Atlanta, Georgia. The performance characteristics of the system were tested in advance with approximately 150 users. However, more than 1,000 people used the system in the production phase, and the system collapsed under this workload. The matches were delayed and IBM suffered image losses, whose immaterial damages are hard to determine. These examples show that the evaluation of the performance characteristics of IT systems is important, especially in highly heterogeneous system environments.

However, active performance evaluations are often neglected in the industry. The quality factor performance is only analyzed at the end of the software development process. Then performance problems lead to costly tuning measures, the procurement of more efficient hardware or to a redesign of the software application. As the performance of new hardware systems increases, especially complex application systems based on new technologies, e.g., multimedia data warehouse systems or distributed systems, they need an explicit analysis of their performance characteristics within the development process. These statements are also confirmed by an examination of Glass. He identified performance problems as the second most frequent reason of failed software projects in an extensive analysis [Glas98].

11.2.2 Requirements and Aims

The performance characteristics of a system have to be considered within the whole software development process. Performance has to be given the same priority as other quality factors like functionality or maintainability. However, a practicable development method is necessary to assure sufficient performance characteristics. Extensive and cost-intensive tuning measures, which are a major part of most development projects, can be consequently avoided. The operation of highly critical systems, e.g., complex production planning and control solutions, depends on specific performance characteristics, since inefficient system interactions are comparable to a system breakdown because the subsequent processes are affected. However, the system users' work efficiency is impaired with inadequate response times, causing frustration. Additionally, software ergonomic analyses show that users who have to wait longer than five seconds for a system response initiate new thought processes. Controlled cancellations of the new thought processes and the resumption of the old condition take time and lead to lower user productivity.

The development method has to determine performance characteristics early within the development process to minimize performance-entailed development risks. A structured performance analysis is necessary. It should be supported by a process model, which has to be integrated within the existing company-specific software development process. The application of this method should also not be isolated from the development process, since additional activities that accompany the software development process are usually neglected in the face of staff and time problems.

The fused models should not become an inefficient complex; an economic application must still be guaranteed. Expenditures should have a justifiable relationship to the total project costs [Scho99]. The height of the expenditures is often based on empirically collected data and knowledge. The deployment of qualified employees who have a high level of knowledge in the areas of software engineering and performance analysis is imperative. However, methods and technologies must be shaped in a way that they are to be handled for the developer.

11.3 A Practical Approach of Software Performance Engineering

11.3.1 Overview of an Integrated Approach

The aim of software performance engineering (SPE), as mentioned before, is primarily to ensure that the performance of an information system – in terms of the response time, throughput and technical process run times – is taken into account from the early phases of development. The vision is to develop information systems that, based on the specification of a defined load model and the resulting resource consumption, are able to provide the performance attributes demanded by future users based on specific application functions.

Although SPE should be considered as a process integrated into software engineering, it cannot be considered entirely separately from other performance-related tasks within the life cycle of an IT system. Software performance engineering builds especially on the data measured for performance management and benchmarking and utilizes methods – such as workload, performance and cost estimation models [Schm00a] – which can, to a certain extent, be compared with those used in capacity planning.

11.3.2 Establishing and Resolving Performance Models

The need for performance-related modeling variables in the context of software development will be illustrated below based on the procedure that [Smit90] has proposed for SPE. The aim is to transform scenarios (use cases) from the subsequent software system into suitable performance models. Assistance with this procedure for creating the model and then analyzing performance is offered by the SPE·ED tool [SPEE98].

In order to take both software and hardware properties into account, a combined software and hardware model is needed. Whereas software models are currently usually created based on rather informal notation such as Unified Modeling Language (UML), hardware systems in the environment of performance assessment are traditionally modeled using queue models or Petri nets.

The first step is to identify performance-critical scenarios that pinpoint the interaction or exchange of messages between the objects in the software system and that are involved in executing a specific user function. Assuming that UML notation is used, these should be represented in detail using sequence diagrams (isolated message sequence charts can be used too). The next step is to transform the diagrams into "execution graphs", which, amongst other things, may be made up of elementary nodes, branch nodes, repetition nodes, apportionment nodes or nodes that represent parallel processes (Fig. 11.2).

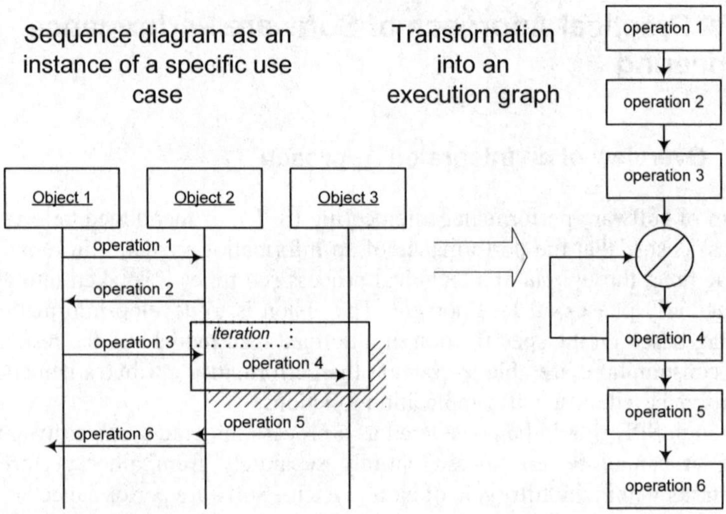

Fig. 11.2. Transformation of sequence diagrams into execution graphs

Once the execution graphs have been created, the nodes contained in the model must be quantified with regard to their resource consumption. Aspects that must be specified may include the CPU instructions needed for the nodes or the number of input and output operations performed to transfer data from and to the hard disk system or network (Fig. 11.3).

The specified sequence of resources is based on the hardware system used in the model in each case. This must also be specified in terms of the achievable operating times (service time) for resources such as the CPU, the available throughputs for hard disks used and the network capacity.

Another step to be performed is to specify the load model. This entails defining job details – such as number of jobs per second, arrival time distributions (e.g., exponential) or the number of users and appropriate thinking time – for the model.

The technical resolution of the model that has been established, based on an analytical or simulated resolution procedure, requires the use of a suitable tool.

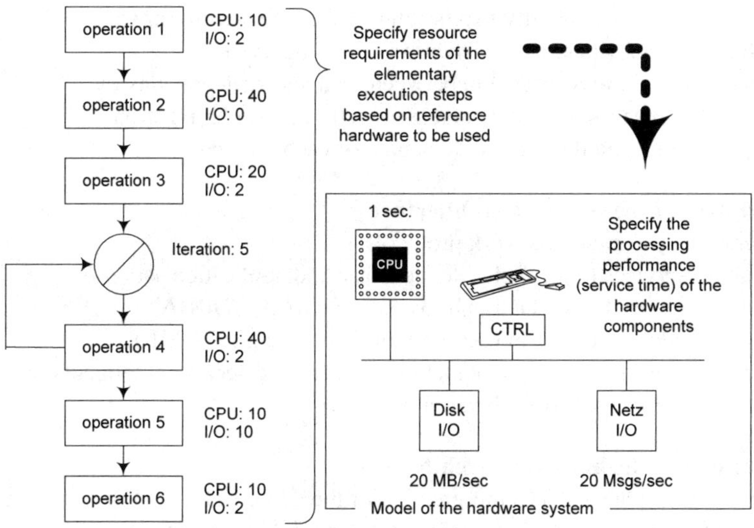

Fig. 11.3. Defining resource requirements based on reference hardware

The SPE ED tool used for modeling – one of the few tools commercially available – provides the option of a software-based view during performance modeling. Possible performance information, for instance, relates to the time behavior (total duration and execution time of the individual nodes), best-case and worst-case analyses, average values and hot-spot analyses for the individual components of the scenarios. This therefore allows you to estimate the extent to which a chosen software architecture will actually be able to meet performance expectations. You will usually find either architecture-based tools (e.g., SES-Strategizer), which only permit process-related conclusions about the software system to be investigated, or software modeling tools (e.g., Telelogic Tau), which fail to take the hardware resources into account and therefore only allow relative performance analyses. More information on the comparison of various modeling tools can be found, for instance, in [Schm01a].

11.3.3 Generalization of the Need for Model Variables

Regardless of the specific models, methods and tools used for performance modeling, it is necessary to access information and modeling variables that are able to describe the system – made up of hardware and software – with regard to its performance properties. In the context of performance models, the following basic information that is needed can be determined.

Workload (classes of elementary jobs)

- number and type of job classes (online, interfaces, batch)
- load profiles over periods in time (frequency of execution of job classes)

- job volumes (data quantity that is submitted to the system for each job)
- output volumes (quantity of data returned to the user)
- complexity of and relationship between read and write job classes
- proximity of accesses to the database (cache vs. synchronization)
- response time and throughput demands for each job class

Description of the software architecture
- operating system and network protocols
- standard services (e.g., Web, file, database and application servers)
- middleware used (e.g., DCE, ODBC, JDBC, RMI, CORBA)
- design models of client and server components (e.g., in UML)
- aspects regarding the implementation of client and server components
- mapping job classes to application processes

Description of the hardware architecture
- hardware systems used (representation of the CPU, HD, RAM, structure, etc.)
- network systems used (sketch of the LAN or WAN properties)
- I/O controllers and network controllers used
- special controllers (e.g., audio and video cards)

Description of the performance capability

Once the load and the hardware/software architecture have been described, it is still necessary to quantify the performance of the hardware and software components used, for instance, in the form of "service rates" or possible throughput rates. Modeling tools, such as SES-Strategizer, contain templates for this allowing entire server systems to be mapped with regard to essential resources (CPU, I/O, memory, network). In the case of the processor, for instance, performance is often described in terms of the number of instructions that can be executed per time unit or in terms of results of standard benchmarks such as SPECint95 or tpmC (TPC-C, by the Transaction Processing Council).

Description of the load behavior

The next step is to assign resource requirements to specific model elements or application system processes that are met via jobs submitted for processing. For a specific component in the design model or a server process, therefore, it must be determined how many CPU instructions, I/O activities or network accesses are needed in order to provide the functionality concerned. These steps require fairly detailed knowledge of the operating system concerned because such variables can only be determined with the help of monitoring systems (e.g., system activity reporter (sar)).

11.3.4 Sources of Model Variables

We will now provide a summary of the sources from which model variables can be obtained.

Model variables from operational systems

It is possible to obtain model variables from systems that have already been implemented. Typically, this is done as part of performance management tasks. These tasks are only of interest for software development if the recorded consumption of resources such as CPU, main memory, hard disk requirements, I/O system, and network bandwidths can also be assigned to technical application functions. In addition, it is also necessary to know the load parameters mentioned in the previous section as well as the hardware and software architecture.

Model variables based on prototypes (individual benchmarks)

In the case of new technologies, such as applications servers, models cannot be used until sufficient experience of generating meaningful performance model variables has been gained. In order to build up experience with regard to the performance of new technologies, therefore, it is necessary to carry out measurements on real systems or appropriate prototypes. This task especially lends itself to using load driver systems in order to gather suitable data with prototypical implementations. Only in this way can reproducible performance data be obtained based on a defined load profile.

Model variables based on standard benchmarks

In the area of server systems you can usually obtain performance specifications from benchmark organizations. In addition to allowing you to conduct a relative comparison of computer systems, these allow you to estimate the necessary resources based on your own application, providing these resources and the load used can be largely compared with the benchmark application. Corresponding metrics are used in performance modeling, for instance, with BEST/1 as model variables, especially for the task of characterizing CPU performance. Manufacturer-independent benchmarks are offered by organizations such as TPC, SPEC and BAPCo (for further information see also Chap. 16). Information on the results of these benchmarks can be found in [Idea00].

Model variables based on datasheets for hardware systems

Using datasheets is a particularly good idea when it comes to describing the performance properties of network controllers (data throughput), bus systems or hard disk systems being used. In the case of a hard disk system, for instance, the following performance attributes play a role:

- Properties of the disk controller (e.g., typical available bandwidth in MB/s, cache hit rates for any available read and write cache)
- Properties of the connected disk drives (e.g., search times – positioning of the R/W head above the required track, rotation delay – positioning of the R/W

head within the track, transfer rate – transmission of data between the controller and disk drive, memory capacity of the hard disk systems).

Instrumentation based on measurement points introduced during development is crucial for recording the time behavior and resource consumption of entire application functions through to elementary functions of individual software components (e.g. method calls from objects). One practical alternative solution is offered by Application Response Measurement Applications Programmers Interface ARM-API, a quasi-standard drawn up by the Computer Measurement Group. It can be used to include measurement points in both C++ applications and Java applications (as of version 3.0 of ARM-API).

11.3.5 Performance and Software Metrics

Because new information systems are becoming more and more complex, the empirical assessment of architectures and software systems is becoming increasingly important. In order to allow the entire life cycle of an information system to be evaluated in terms of quality and quantity and be iteratively optimized, software engineering makes use of metrics. The process of quantifying the attributes of software engineering objects and components in relation to specific measurement goals, possibly by using measurement tools, is referred to as "software measurement". The basic idea behind software measurement is to record valid metrics in order to achieve an empirical assessment of the process, the resources used, and the actual product.

Numerous analyses (e.g., [Smit98], [Schm00a]) have demonstrated there to be a problem in that only very vague ideas of the information system to be developed exist in the early stages of development. As a result, the application of precise procedures for resolving the model is usually pointless at the beginning of a performance analysis. Instead, successive attempts should be made to obtain relevant information using the simplest means in each case (assumptions, rules of thumb, trend analyses, analytical models, and simulation models; Fig. 11.4).

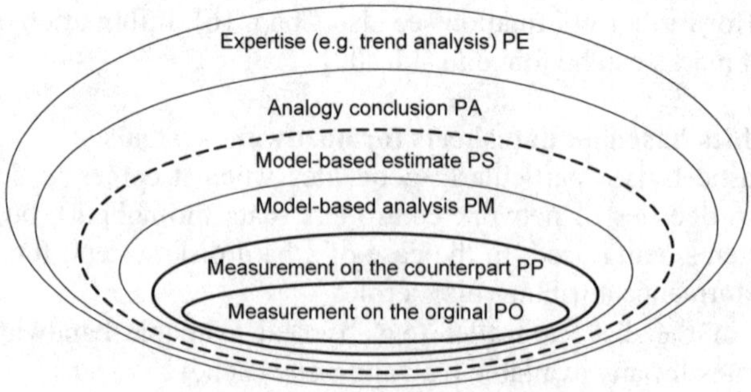

Fig. 11.4. Performance-based layer model

To formalize this approach, Norton [Nort00] has suggested using an adapted spiral model as defined by Boehm [Boeh88]. The spiral model processes, which should be iterated, are planning, development, evaluation and presentation.

> The spiral model for performance metrics introduction, which should be iterated, consists of following steps:
>
> **Planning**. Implementing the goals with the least effort
>
> **Development**. Deriving suitable performance data
>
> **Evaluation**. Verifying and validating the results
>
> **Presentation**. Evaluating whether customer requirements have been met

Empirical data relating to the performance properties of an IT system may be obtained, for instance, by applying the empirical layer model specified in Fig. 11.5. Emulating the work in [Dumk00b], we have extended this model, putting it into concrete terms. In order to draw empirical conclusions about the "next level in" (the *i*-1th level), the following general connection can be deduced based on a software system or software component *k:*

$$(\textit{performance behavior}\ (k))_{i} =$$

$$(\text{correction factor} \times \text{performance determined}^{\text{correction exponent}})_{i+1}$$

The accuracy of the "performance determined" decreases as the number of layers increases because of abstracting from the underlying original system. Existing comparative data often has to be used for subcomponents of a software system in the early development stages due to a lack of alternatives (Table 11.1).

Table 11.1. Examples of possible transformation forms

Transformation	Description
PP → PO	Performance Counterpart – The application of data regarding the performance behavior of a network-based application under laboratory conditions through monitoring as an initial assessment for real practical implementation
PM → PO	Performance Model – The model-based performance analysis, based on analytical or simulated resolution procedures, of a client/server application as the starting point for assessing the performance of distributed systems
PS → PO	Performance Estimate – The use of an estimation model (rules of thumb) for characterizing the performance properties of a generally known technology such as file or database server systems
PA → PO	Performance Analogy – Application of the key performance figures of a LAN for estimating the application characteristics in a WLAN
PE → PO	Performance Expertise – The application of general trend data regarding performance development for network-based platforms as a basis for estimating the performance of the software system to be developed

The main point of interest of software performance engineering is to find or generate manageable relationships between the layers in order to support appropriate error rectification. If the transformations that have been presented are carried out step by step, this corresponds to the successive accumulation of performance experience relating to a new system to be developed that Norton [Nort00] proposed in the context of his spiral model. We do not intend to look any further here at other time-based, multivariate or reflexive aspects.

11.3.6 Persistence of Software and Performance Metrics

In order to establish such dependencies, we need statistical evaluations (such as correlation analyses) that are able to take both performance metrics and software metrics into account. Both at universities and in the industrial environment, software metrics and performance metrics are usually stored separately and are partially redundant, making it difficult for complex connections between these metrics to be proven. The aim, however, should be to set up a control loop covering the entire software life cycle. On the one hand, this means that software developers should be given access to performance data for live information systems so that such practical knowledge regarding the performance engineering process can be taken into account. On the other hand, potential operators of new information systems should be given access to performance metrics relating to software development, for instance, to allow them to conduct forward-looking system planning (e.g., regarding necessary network expansion for the implementation of new application types). It goes without saying that each of these groups of users is only interested in a limited section of the data available. For example, application developers are only interested in metrics regarding application types that can be compared to a certain degree with the applications that they are developing (Fig. 11.5).

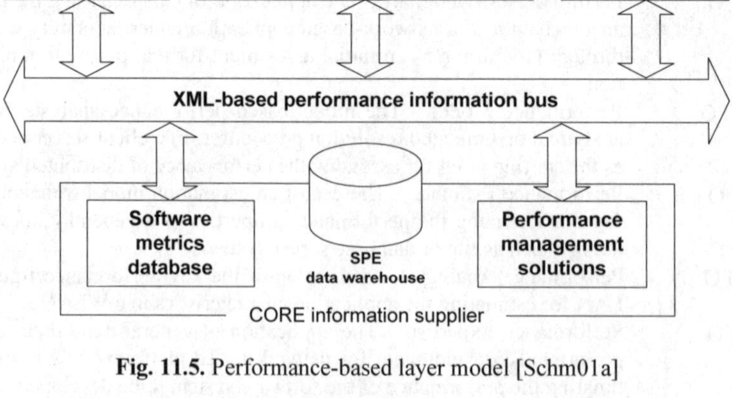

Fig. 11.5. Performance-based layer model [Schm01a]

With a view to integrating the various data storage systems, it would be a good idea to define a standardized interface (e.g., in the form of a CORBA-IDL or via an XML-based interface) for the automatic exchange of performance metrics/knowledge. The idea of defining an exchange format for performance-related data was first raised by Smith [Smit94], who proposed a "Performance Model Interchange Format". An initial proposal for a suitable exchange format, but designed especially for performance models, can be found in [Smit99]. Data exchange between heterogeneous systems, which in view of the wide variety of possible sources is the probable scenario for performance-related data, particularly lends itself to using XML as the data exchange format.

An XML-based interface has the advantage that it can be used pretty much regardless of programming languages and platforms, therefore allowing an automated control loop to be established covering the entire software life cycle. This interface could then be used not only for software development environments and performance management solutions for the purpose of exchanging data, but also for the consistent management of performance-related data within suitable repositories or metrics databases. In this way, for instance, data and metrics that are obtained via benchmarking, modeling or monitoring as well as general hardware and software metrics could be taken into account and added to an automatic control loop. Based on such superior metrics, it would be possible to perform tasks such as validating models or carrying out statistical analyses to identify dependencies between general software metrics (product, resource, process) and performance metrics. A general proposal and the prototypical implementation for storing measurement variables are described in [Folt00].

11.4 Case Study: EAI

Enterprise application integration (EAI for short) solutions require sufficient performance both in terms of time/resource behavior and supported scalability. In this respect, steps must be taken to ensure that sufficient performance is built into the communications requirements of the applications when developing EAI systems, and that the data required in equal part by all applications can be written and read efficiently. This section provides an overview of the approach adopted for EAI performance analysis and highlights possible results obtained as part of a benchmark test under consideration of the ISO 14756 standard.

11.4.1 Introduction of a EAI Solution

By way of introduction, an outline overview of EAI solutions is provided using the following definition (based on [Juri01b]):

> *EAI allows data and business processes to be used company-wide on the basis of network-based applications or data sources. Early software programs, such as inventory*

and personnel management, sales systems and database systems, were developed largely independently of each other without account being taken of the potential interactions between those systems. They were developed using the technologies of the day and were tailored to meet specific customer needs, this resulting frequently in proprietary systems. With the increasing growth of companies and the realization that application data and functions could be exchanged and used company-wide, there was an investment in corresponding EAI solutions.

The provisioning of EAI solutions is currently one of the major challenges facing the IT industry. One of the key arguments for developing such solutions revolves around the potential for implementing efficient, high-quality integrated business processes to reduce dramatically the time-to-market of associated products, for example. The performance of business processes supported by an EAI system depends on a multitude of factors. These factors include the degree of distribution, the transmission capacity of the networks utilized, the degree of process automation, the potential number of users that can work on the system, the performance of existing systems and systems that will be developed from scratch or even the hardware architecture utilized.

The selected software design of the integration applications used also has a major impact on performance. These applications are typically used to store reference and master data permanently that can be provided to all the applications involved in the integration, to monitor and control supported business processes, integrate user interfaces via relevant web portals and to integrate heterogeneous system environments using standardized middleware solutions such as message-oriented middleware (MOM) and Common Object Request Broker Architecture (CORBA). As part of the EAI solution analyzed here to determine its performance characteristics, only MOM technology has been used to date. MOM technology works primarily on an asynchronous basis (transmission of XML messages) and is based on IBM's MQ Series product.

The primary objectives of the performance analyses conducted were:

- to analyze the performance behavior of the overall application
- to identify potential bottlenecks in relation to any developed software components
- to identify the performance behavior of individual system components
- to determine resource requirements in relation to hardware and software services

11.4.2 Available Studies

At present there is relatively little research work that looks explicitly at the performance characteristics of EAI solutions. One reason is that these solutions are so complex coupled with the fact that an EAI solution may be broken down into various subaspects that, when looked at individually, have no direct bearing on the EAI system per se. Research that deals with the performance characteristics of

EAI solutions therefore tends to focus especially on those technologies that can be used as part of EAI and less on complete solutions.

- Relevant research can be found for example in [Krai00]. This research analyzes the possibility of prioritizing messages to implement user class-specific response times within the MQ Series message backbone.
- The issues of EAI solution performance and scalability based on J2EE-compliant integration architectures are tackled in [Juri01b]. Juric looks at the various aspects of developing solutions to meet performance needs and includes notes on devising an efficient design for the subsequent application as well as observations on tuning aspects of an integration infrastructure.
- The performance analyses provided by IBM covering the MQ Series technology have proved very useful. This information enabled initial estimates to be made both of the performance behavior of message transmission and also of the MQ Series Integrator components used [Dunn00].
- A performance analysis of so-called global straight-through processing (GSTP) solutions can by found under [Czac01]. The analyzed solution was realized by the use of queuing (MQSeries) and message broker (MQSeries Integrator) technology from IBM. A realistic simulation of a GSTP workload was implemented and tested under high message rates to gain an in-depth understanding of the STP design and performance issues.

11.4.3 Developing EAI to Meet Performance Needs

This section sets out to highlight the approach adopted to developing system architecture in order to meet performance needs while outlining the nature of an EAI load model. As opposed to the way in which a load model is derived from user interactions for a conventional software application, an EAI load model results from the communications requirements of the subapplications that need to be integrated.

Overview of steps taken

Within the context of the telecom-based EAI project that underpins this example, an interactive approach to performance-oriented architecture development was adopted. The steps listed below were initiated at an early stage of the project.

1. Performance requirements and load profile

The interaction behavior between the integrated applications had to be predicted to determine the communications load profile. To this end, the following assessment model was adopted and used to analyze each interface:

- communications profile incl. performance requirements (throughput/latency)
- volume of data per communication
- type of synchronization
- determine priority classes in relation to individual interfaces
- determine persistency and transaction requirements

- determine performance requirements
- identify impact of inefficient communications relationships

2. Identifying and initially assessing components that affect performance
This involves in particular identifying potential performance bottlenecks associated with specific technologies (e.g., CORBA, MOM) and products (e.g. MQS/MQSI), and highlighting suitable alternative solutions to optimize performance. Selected examples of such factors include:

- use of persistent versus non-persistent messages
- impact on performance of the transaction backup process used
- processing performance/performance of source and target systems
- performance of functions associated with the MQ Series Integrator component (MQSI for short)
- system architecture characteristics (HW, NW, system components)
- number of messages written to a queue/read per time unit
- connection of a reference database via an interaction application

3. Setting up an equivalence or analogy model
This stage involves drawing up a generalized load model (types of messages in relation to time intervals). At the same time, based on the performance behavior of analyzed reference implementations (e.g., using available benchmarks for the selected integration product) conclusions can be extrapolated about the performance behavior of the actual integration application using the simplest procedures.

- use and disclose analogy procedures
- identify potential error sources and assess possible inaccuracies:
  - unclear requirements,
  - rule-based functions within the MQSI that are difficult to predict,
  - application scalability within the planning time frame,
  - performance (throughput) of the persistence mechanisms used.
- Represent and delineate the analyzed application layers

4. Performance analysis
Measurement-based performance analyses (so-called benchmarks based on the application itself) provide a far more accurate assessment of the performance behavior than the analogy procedures discussed in the previous section. Since there is still very little research on the performance behavior of EAI solutions, explicit performance analyses need to be included as part of developing this kind of system.

For our benchmarks we used the T-Systems performance tool, s_aturn, which is available for the Solaris and Linux platforms. It supports performance analyses in accordance with ISO 14756 "Measurement and Rating of the Performance of Computer-based Software Systems". This standard, which has existed since 1991, describes an evaluation process for time characteristics of IT systems from the end users' point of view. The standard considers the whole system consisting of hardware and software. It follows the "black box" principle and provides measurements available at the user interface.

Measurement of performance according to ISO is performed in three stages [ISO97c]:

1. demand profile drawn up
2. measurements made
3. ISO assessment factors evaluated and assessed

Performance requirements and implied risks

To justify the costs associated with the performance analyses that need to be conducted, the use of a "performance risk analysis" as per [Schm01b] has proven useful. As part of interviews with the customer, developer and operator, the interfaces used within the EAI solution are analyzed and potential performance losses are assessed in terms of their secondary financial effects. Potential effects relate both to a loss in respect of the supported business process (primary risks, such as fewer customers served than envisaged, revenue expectations, image tarnished, etc.) and to the development and subsequent live operation (secondary risks). It may well often prove difficult to assess the subsequent load profile realistically and what impact inefficient system behavior may have. A successful outcome can therefore only be ensured by adopting a gradual approach and carrying out multiple assessments.

Developing an EAI-compliant load model

An abstract load model needs to be developed to set up performance models and conduct benchmark tests. The aim is to combine the identified interfaces to form abstract communications interface types (CT_n for short). In this respect the volume of data to be transmitted (peak values) and, where necessary, existing critical requirements relating to performance are taken into account. A potential approach to this task could include the following types:

- CT_1: up to 1 KByte/s (performance non-critical)
- CT_2: up to 100 KByte/s (performance critical)
- CT_3: implementation unclear (more than 100 KByte/s)

By utilizing the combined performance characteristics of the individual interfaces, these characteristics can be mapped to the corresponding benchmark values (the graphic shows the throughput of the integration interface for MQ input/output – queue portion, as can be seen from [Dunn00]) in relation to the integration software used. Clustering individual interfaces to create interface types will yield the lacking information relating to the time/quantity structure of the relevant communications requirements.

Expected results

Based on the aforementioned abstract communications load model, the application benchmark is conducted using the actual application. As part of this, the communications load generated on the message bus is simulated so that the achievable performance in terms of response time and throughput of the bus system and the integration application can be determined based on a given use of resources. The model-based assumptions can be verified (response times, throughput, resource consumption) using these tests, while other findings can be adopted in corresponding design guidelines governing the message bus.

If customer-relevant performance bottlenecks are identified in the test, the following action needs to be taken to resolve these shortcomings:

- Specify hardware requirements and stipulate required scalability.
- Identify tuning-relevant characteristics of the SW components involved.
- Prepare and implement the prioritization of potential interfaces.
- Optimize the communications interfaces between the components.
- Specify network requirements.
- Adapt user requirements depending on costs.
- Draw up alternative architecture proposals (worst case: system redesign).

Customer performance requirements of the complete EAI architecture can only be ensured if issues relating to performance behavior of the subsequent EAI solution can be included from an early stage of development. This means that communications load profiles in relation to the interfaces used need to be available; this technical information must be provided by the subapplications that need to be integrated.

11.5 Costs of Software Performance Engineering

To derive the costs of necessary SPE tasks we propose the use of a risk-driven approach. To develop and introduce information systems that meet both functional and qualitative requirements, it is necessary to plan appropriate technical and human resources to implement the tasks involved. In general, it is easy to understand that a system with high quality requirements involves greater costs than one with lower quality requirements. However, if one examines the quality feature of space- and time-related efficiency (performance in general) as defined by the ISO 9126 quality standard, it then becomes more difficult to make an assessment. It is necessary to apply software performance engineering (SPE) methods during the entire software development process to guarantee this quality feature.

11.5.1 Performance Risk Model (PRM)

The so-called *Performance Risk Model* (PRM) considers three areas involved (business process, development, operational environment), where the occurrence of a performance risk leads to potential losses (Fig. 11.6). These include primary risks R_{pG} arising in connection with the business process, and secondary risks R_{s} that arise in the context of development R_{sE} and the operational environment R_{sW}. The evaluation model presented below is for determining the potential risks in the areas affected.

We pursue two approaches to quantify the risks in a monetary context. One for the primary risks $R_{\mathrm{pG}i}$ (business process) and another one for the secondary risks $R_{\mathrm{sE}i}$ (development) and $R_{\mathrm{sW}i}$ (real operation). The total risk R (in Euro) is the summation of determined primary and second risks weighted via the entry probability p_i.

$$R[euro] = \sum_{i=1}^{n} p_i R_{pG_i} + \left\{ \sum_{i=1}^{n} p_i R_{sE_i} + \sum_{i=1}^{n} p_i R_{sW_i} \right\}$$

The overall risk R (in Euro) is made up of the summation of primary and secondary risks weighted using the probability of occurrence p_i.

The valuation model should be applied several times in the course of the life cycle of an IT solution, in the form of checklists to be filled in for each risk criterion. This enables risks involved in the business process to be recognized during an SIB (Strategic Information Planning, cf. Business Process Reengineering) for the first time. However, risks that refer to SW development and subsequent active operations are not recognized until the beginning or during the actual development project.

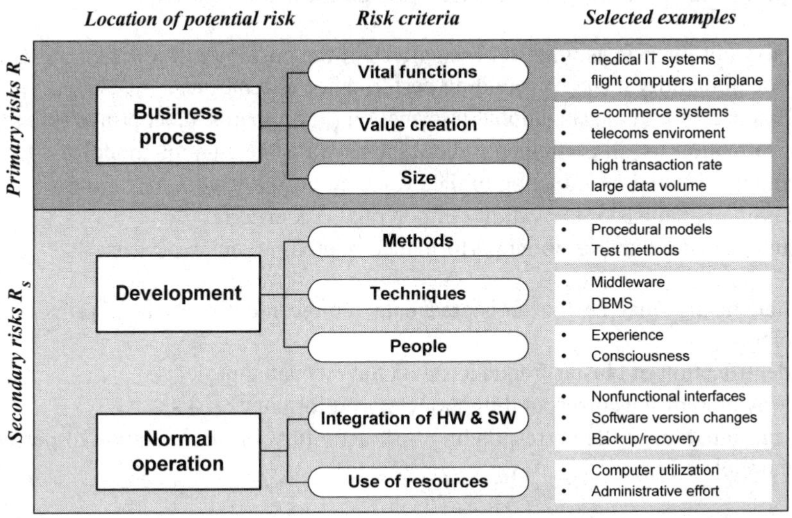

Fig. 11.6. Overview of the performance risk model

11.6 Hints for the Practitioner

When the full software life cycle is considered, a performance management tool chain (tools for measurement, short term analysis, long term analysis, performance prediction) should be implemented immediately before and during operational use to answer the following performance-relevant questions:

- to generate performance-relevant information concerning software components/architectures through prototype benchmarks
- verification of required service levels based on the whole IT system using performance benchmarks
- definition of tuning measures for efficient production, consideration all software and hardware components of the system
- support in capacity planning for changing load profiles are impending migrations

The performance measurements gathered from production systems can then be used as input parameters for modeling tools, when the same software components are to be used for newly developed software systems.

We recommend a stepwise approach for building a performance risk model:

1. Provide a project-specific checklist (similarly a tailoring activity).

- determination of potential risk categories in dependence on affected fields
- specialization of the risk categories through the actual risk criteria

2. Carry out interviews with representatives of the customer, developer and operator side to identify the corresponding performance risk metrics.

- identification of organizational information (participants, date, project-phase)
- Information for all participants about the used PRM valuation model
- contents-related introduction of the project to be analyzed
- common analysis of the validity of potential risk criteria
- summarizing remarks about performance-related project experiences

3. Statistically analyze the registered data for the identification of primary risk problems.

- identification of cluster frequencies via the evaluated projects
- derivation of the corresponding monetary performance risks
- determination of the corresponding SPE activities for minimization of performance-related risks

4. Verify the valuation model and identify potential improvements both of the valuation model and of the employed checklist procedure.

The use of models to analyze the performance of an information system irrespective of the special solution method requires the following steps:

1. Analysis of the technical load requirements and identification of job classes as the basis of the load model. The performance requirements of later users must adhere to the job classes.
2. Allocation of technical job classes to processes in the application system and calculation of the interactions between them.
3. Recording of the resource consumption of the identified processes with regard to computer and network systems used or to individual components.
4. Reproduction of the components of the information system critical for the performance of the overall system in a model.

5. Execution of the performance model with the requisite and increased load profiles and constant and altered system resources.
6. Evaluation of identified performance metrics using statistical methods.
7. Model validation by means of performance metrics measured in operation from applications or using prototypical benchmarks. A successive improvement of the results of models should be possible as a result.

The application of performance models for a particular technology is only possible if there is sufficient performance experience. For new technologies, this can only be gained by running prototypical performance tests and successively building up empirical results from information systems in active operation. An exclusively theoretical examination will not lead to any result that is usable in engineering terms in this case.

Other important sources of performance metrics are benchmarks. Well known benchmarks for hard- and software-systems can be found by the Standard Performance Evaluation Cooperation (SPEC) and the Transaction Processing Performance Council (TPC). For further information see also Chap. 16.

11.7 Summary

This chapter has shown an overview about a practical way for the implementation of a software performance engineering process. After a motivation for SPE-related activities, an overview about necessary tasks was given. In this context, we explained the necessary preconditions for successful SPE activities, like the required metrics, potential sources of metrics and so on. Furthermore we have given an overview about a case study for the investigation of the performance behavior of an enterprise application integration solution. Finally, for the realization of SPE activities we proposed a risk-driven approach. This approach provides the possibility to explain potential benefits for the project management.

The idea proposed in this chapter of deriving the costs required to realize performance engineering tasks from potential risks has the advantage of enabling risks to be made transparent and of putting these into monetary terms as far as possible. On the basis of assessed risks it should be easier for project management to integrate SPE tasks into the time schedules and costs of project plans and estimate their added value. Moreover, the selection of actual SPE methods is supported by the definition of a cost framework.

12 Service Level Management

The only Zen you find on the tops of mountains
is the Zen you bring up there.
—Robert Pirsig

12.1 Measuring Service Level Management

Although the area of network and system management has experienced a regressive trend over the past two years, the use and management of service level agreements can, according to [Gart02], most certainly be considered an enabler technology for market growth in the area of service-based integration solutions. The use of service level agreements is not yet taken for granted even in the case of traditional IT solutions.

An analysis has shown that service level agreements that are comprehensible and, most importantly, measurable by the customer are concluded for only 5 to 10% of all applications. You may well ask why this low regard for SLAs (SLAs) actually needs to be changed for Web service-based applications.

The following properties inherent in such architectures and the disadvantages associated with traditional technologies explain poor usage of measurements:

- Web service-based applications are designed for use across various companies, whereas previous applications were primarily used within a single company.
- Current pressure on costs is giving rise to customer demand for transparent costs for service provision, and Web service-based applications support this goal.
- Up to now, SLAs have been primarily based on resource-related measurement variables that were generally incomprehensible to customers in the context of the functions they used.
- In the case of Web service-based applications, the main focus is on the interaction chain involving measurement variables that are based on functions or business processes and that take the actual customer benefit into account.
- Commercial application systems based on integrated Web services urgently require the services used to be subject to quality assurance (efficiency, security, availability, etc.).

As SLAs for Web service-based solutions can also be concluded "on demand", i.e., at run time, this gives rise to further requirements for the underlying technology, the content of agreements, SLA monitoring and also the measures that need to be drawn up during development. Whereas SLAs used to have a predominantly technical orientation and were mostly the domain of the operators of IT solutions, Web service-based solutions also require system integrators to take account of the use of SLAs during development. Only if the issue of SLA management is explicitly addressed in development can SLAs that are comprehensible for customers and backed up by measured values be concluded later during actual operation [Dunc01].

For the operators of IT solutions, this situation is associated with a changeover from system management to service management. This is the only way to take better account of the business process supported.

After providing an introduction to Web service technology, this part primarily aims to describe the topic of SLA management in such environments. In this context, we highlight the general contents of SLA agreements, describe the interaction chain for service provision that arises in Web service-based solutions, and provide a brief explanation of the opportunities offered by the WSLA (Web service level agreements) framework that IBM has developed especially for Web services. Within the various sections we will also look at development tasks – an aspect that is usually neglected but without which the authors consider efficient SLA management to be impossible.

12.2 Web Services and Service Management

12.2.1 Web Services at a Glance

Web service-based solutions entail using the Internet as middleware for implementing business to business (B2B) applications. This could not be done very easily using previous middleware solutions such as CORBA, RMI or DCE. The rigid coupling and predominantly synchronous communication methods made it necessary to resolve the communications relationships right at the time of development.

Using Web service technology, applications are able to communicate with one another easily and at low cost via the Internet, regardless of the technology used. This is made possible by using the HTTP-based Simple Object Access Protocol (SOAP), which, using HTTP, can also be routed across, firewalls. By means of Extensible Markup Language (XML) and XML-based messages it is possible to achieve both asynchronous and quasi-synchronous communication.

Based on the Web-Service Description Language description, applications located on the Internet are able to specify services of their own and publish them in suitable directories, for instance, Universal Description Discovery and Integration (UDDI). Central UDDI business registries are currently operated by companies such as IBM and Microsoft. In order to access a specific Web service, the initiating system requires its WSDL description, which can also be queried at runtime via UDDI (Fig. 12.1).

Advantages expected from using Web services:

- simpler and less costly than dedicated integration frameworks
- higher degree of standardization
- synchronous and asynchronous communication model via company boundaries
- support of the component paradigm
- simple means of communicating across firewalls
- widespread acceptance in industry
- bridge between different technology approaches, such as J2EE and .net.

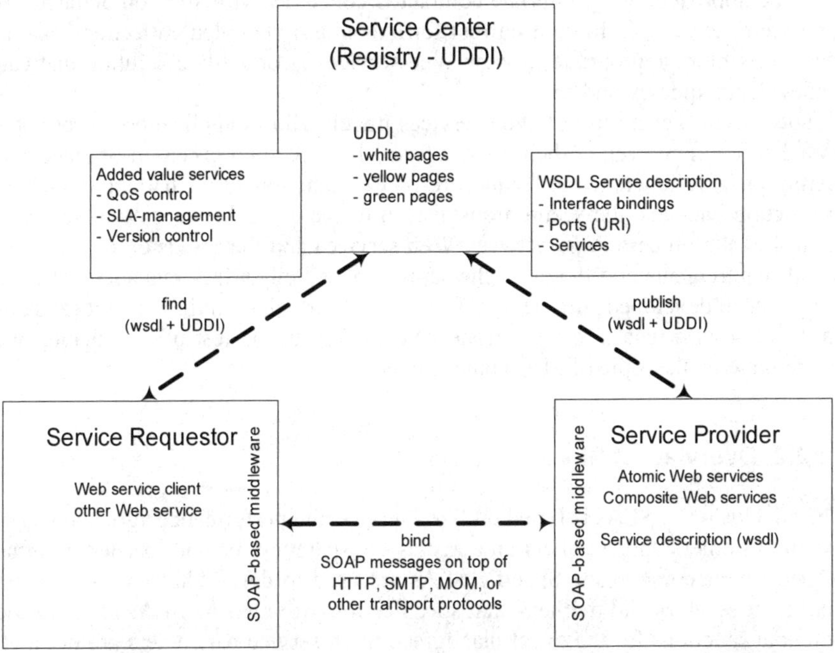

Fig. 12.1. Web service architecture model [Alon04]

Web services can be viewed as technical components that reside on the Internet [Turo02], with it being possible to develop entire application systems based on a loose coupling. A Web service should constitute a clearly identifiable part of the business or service process that is being supported. This means that the interface for a Web service is coarsely granular in nature, although no quantifiable dimensions for this feature can be given at present due to a lack of experience. In the case of the requirement for the functions offered by a Web service to be supported by suitable SLAs, this characteristic is especially important because this means being able to restrict the variety of potential SLAs. The authors believe that such an interface should contain five to ten business functions (excluding elementary functions).

The live operation of a Web service can largely be compared with that of other applications. The essential difference involves use on the Internet of commercially offered Web services, in which case the provider concerned is responsible for the functional and nonfunctional aspects. For this reason, agreements regarding quality of service are needed between the provider and potential users of the Web service.

A distinction can be made here between a static and a dynamic approach. In the case of static agreements, functional and nonfunctional aspects are determined in their entirety at the time when live operation commences, whereas in the case of a dynamic approach, an appropriate contract is concluded virtually "on demand" at the time of execution. In their current form as loosely coupled collections of services, it is more appropriate to view Web services as an ad-hoc solution that can be developed quickly and easily.

The present generation of Web services merely allows applications to be integrated at function level. In their present form, they are not transaction-oriented and merely provide fundamental "request/response" functionality. Challenges such as transaction backups, the secure transmission of messages between Web services, control of the process logic between Web services and the provision of nonfunctional requirements and therefore the support of effective SLA management have not yet been developed sufficiently. There are nevertheless initial attempts at standardization with regard to these issues [Schm03a]. In the rest of this chapter we concentrate on the topic of SLA management.

12.2.2 Overview of SLAs

The conclusion of SLAs is based on fixed service and performance agreements between customers and suppliers and creates transparency for both parties in terms of performance and costs. Specific SLAs are used to define the type, scope and quality of services and to check that specifications are met. As SLAs also include potential sanctions for the event that agreed-upon service parameters are not met, the specifications made in them have a significant effect on the commercial success of a company providing services for a customer.

As part of SLA management for Web service-based applications, a service level agreement must be concluded in addition to providing the actual Web service.

The following specifications are required [Hein02, Kell03]:

- Partners involved and the validity of the agreement, i.e., the period over which the service is to be provided
- Specification of the contract components and procedure for any necessary modifications
- Specification of the functional scope and quality of the service to be provided
- Definition of the SLA parameters with which provision of the service will be proved

- Specification of the procedure for determining/calculating the SLA parameters
- The consequences of contract disruptions and legal basis
- Settlement arrangements

> In the context of service-oriented architectures, the benefits of successful service level management can be described as follows:
>
> The number of conflict situations within supplier relationships can be reduced, resulting in enhanced customer satisfaction.
>
> The resources used in order to render the service (hardware, personnel, licenses) can be distributed at a detailed level by the provider and therefore used in such a way as to optimize costs.
>
> Problems can be identified speedily by service level monitoring and the associated cause determined.
>
> Costs can be made more transparent – on the one hand, the customer only wants to pay for services actually used, while on the other hand, plausible pricing can be guaranteed.

It is obvious that the contents described for a service level agreement may vary significantly in terms of the precise details. In the case of Web service-based applications, it is especially necessary to maintain the relationships between the Web services involved in providing the service and to promote a broad standardization of possible SLA agreements. Both aspects of syntax and aspects of semantics need to be considered. Only the aspects of syntax can be dealt with today by using a technology-independent language such as XML.

One example is the task of interpreting the availability of a Web service that is specified as being 98%. Users may well ask questions such as whether this takes maintenance time into account, whether it is based on round-the-clock operation, and how potential downtime (i.e., recovery time) is dealt with. This flexibility must be explicitly taken into account during development, and the Web service interface must be supplied with this information. In addition, monitoring must be supported by suitable measurement points so that potential bottlenecks or infringements of the SLA can actually be identified. It is only if these aspects are taken into account when developing a specific Web service that SLA management can be implemented for such a solution.

12.2.3 Service Agreement and Service Provision

Fig. 12.2 illustrates the interaction chain of a Web service-based application. We have specified different instances of SLAs here – an Operation Level Agreement (OLA) in the context of an internal service, a Underpinning Contracts (UC) in the case of a subcontracted service, and an SLA with regard to the actual user. Although Web services can also be used directly by appropriate end users, we will proceed by assuming the integration (loose coupling) of Web services to form new application systems. This means that it would actually be more appropriate to speak of UCs rather than SLAs.

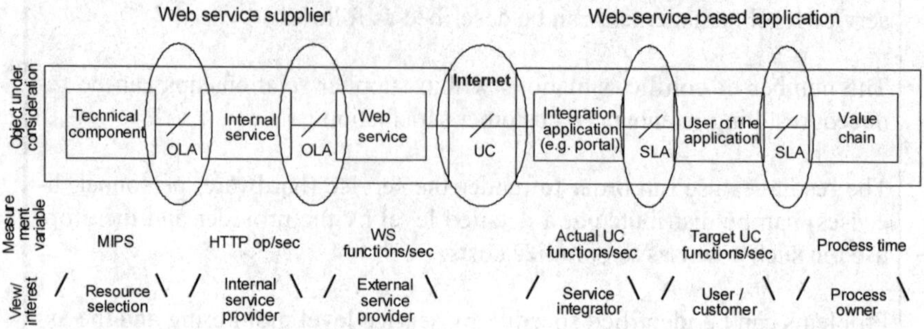

Fig. 12.2. Service level-based interaction chain

Now that the interface in question has been identified in the interaction chain as a whole, we intend to look at the potential procedure for a service level agreement. The scenario shown in Fig. 12.3 is based on the lifecycle of an SLA that [Debu03] illustrated in the context of a multi-provider environment.

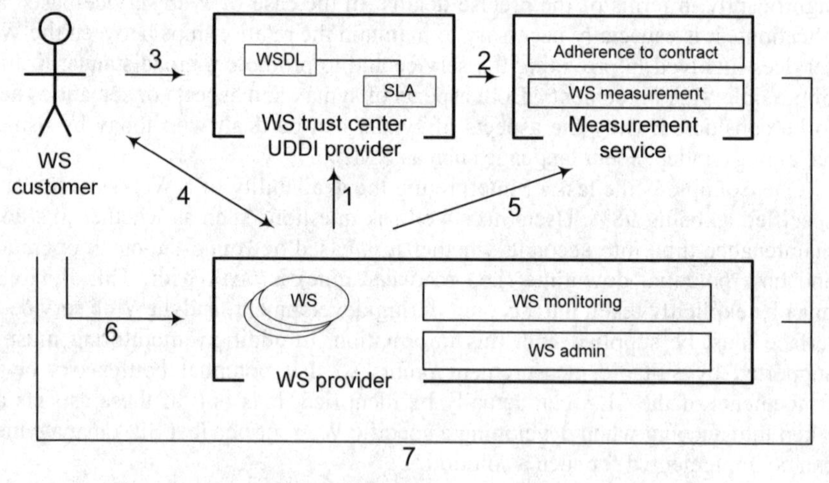

Fig. 12.3. Scenario for using an SLA-supported Web service

The individual steps performed here are as follows:

1. Publication of an available Web service from the provider side, including possible SLA conditions.

2. Inclusion of a measurement service. Based on the measurement service it is possible to observe the functional and nonfunctional behavior (e.g., availability, performance) of the used Web service.
3. Customer query (also a requirement from a specific integration application) with regard to a specific Web service from an independent supplier.
4. Conclusion of a contract between the customer (human or technical) and the Web service provider.
5. Activation of the measurement service for monitoring adherence to the contract. Observation of specific attributes like the availability.
6. Use of the Web service within the customer's own application. The use of the Web service can be also motivated by a dynamic request.
7. Billing of the services provided, taking the SLA specifications into account. Achieved or not achieved service levels form the basis for bonuses or contractual penalties.

12.3 Web Service Level Agreements

In order for the requirements described above to be implemented technically, a commercially available solution is required. We will now provide a brief introduction to the WSLA framework that IBM developed for the purpose of service level management in Web service-based environments. The WSLA framework is part of the IBM Web Service Toolkit (here version 3.2). The following descriptions have been drawn up using [Kell03] and [Debu03] as well as a practical test implemented in this environment [WSTK02].

12.3.1 WSLA Schema Specification

The XML-based WSLA schema specification offers a generic basis for a specific SLA language description. Based on experience, the following structural elements are taken into account here [Kell03]:

Parties section

- Information regarding the contract parties (e.g., contact persons)
- Any subcontractors involved by the supplier

Service description section

- Definition of the SLA parameters used
- Assignment of the SLA parameters to the services used
- Procedure for determining (measuring/calculating) the SLA parameters

Obligations

- Conditions to be adhered to
- Procedure for dealing with infringements of SLA parameters

12.3.2 Web Services Run-Time Environment

The run time environment includes a deployment service (for installing and configuring the technical environment), a measurement service (for measuring the quality of service QoS), and a condition evaluation service (for identifying contract infringements). Using these services together with the proposed roles – the party using the service (service customer), the party offering the service (service supplier) and an independent third-party supplier (service hub) – the various tasks in the process of offering and using Web services are covered. The procedure used is tailored to the typical classification of the marketing of conventional products. The process begins with the provider of a service, referred to here as the *service supplier*, whose range of tasks include developing, producing and offering the service. The result is the service, which can be accessed and used on the Internet via a URL. The producer does not have a direct connection to the customer in this model.

The *service hub* is responsible for making contact with the customer and actually processing the business transaction. This party can be viewed as a product dealer. The service supplier makes usable services available to the service hub by registering the services in a database. A UDDI directory service could be used for this task, for instance. In the case of the Web service run time environment from IBM, this task can be carried out using a Web browser-based interface. The data required includes a brief description and the WSDL definition of the service. A reference to a demonstration page can also be specified as an additional option.

The WSDL information is specified in the form of a URL, via which the actual document can be obtained. The service hub can now create offerings for a customer. A name and the corresponding registered service are then defined for this. In addition, other properties can be defined and the usage period can be specified. For instance, an SLA can be defined for a required performance level and, in terms of measurement technology, can be based on the throughput volume. For instance, the throughput may be measured in terms of accesses per minute. It is possible to define upper and lower limits that the customer can select later.

The performance level determines the priority for adherence to the restrictions. The offering can then be presented to the user by the service hub activating it. Services that have already been sold provide the hub with information on service usage, for instance, the frequency of the application and the costs involved. So that a customer is able to work with a service, the service hub and the service requester as the user draw up a contract. The customer thereby accepts the offer and determines other details such as the means of payment, the service model and the expected number of accesses per minute. In addition, the run time of the agreement can be adjusted. Once the contract has been activated, the user can now access the service in the demonstration environment using a browser (Fig. 12.4).

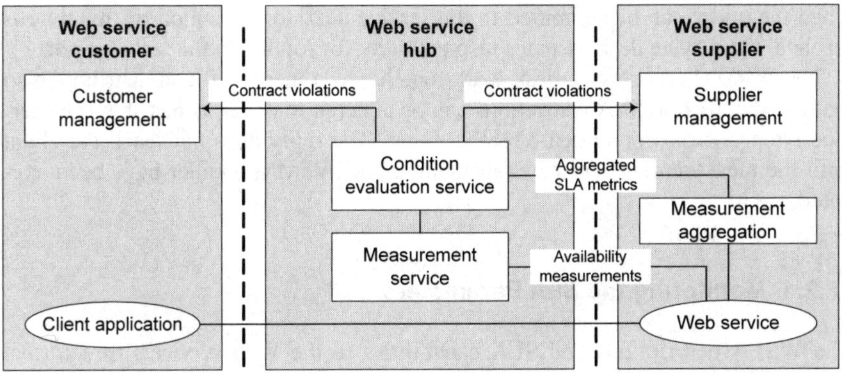

Fig. 12.4. Overview of the WSLA framework run time environment [Debu03]

12.3.3 Guaranteeing Web Service Level Agreements

The technical implementation is realized by Web Service Level Agreements (WSLA) for defining and monitoring SLAs. The run time control is carried out within the Web service management middleware (WSMM) in order to guarantee a service. Another aspect is the service desk, via which several services can be grouped together automatically and therefore used together. The possible functions allow users to autonomously create, compile, manage, route and search Web services as well as to switch between them.

The advantage for clients is that this system reduces the complexity of the connection, the interoperability, the distribution and the combination of various heterogeneous Web services. The three-layer architecture that maps the respective roles intercommunicates via SOAP messages.

For the client it does not matter whether the partner with whom he communicates is a hub or the service itself because the access is the same. This supplier level is divided into two layers in the architecture: the hub and the service supplier. A client communicates with the hub, which assumes responsibility for identifying the client, executing the auxiliary services, and forwarding data to the correct service. This is done in a type of pipeline.

When a client sends a query to the hub, a profile service, started by a handler, assigns the client a profile ID for further processing. The value is inserted in the message context so that the ID can be used by other handlers. The next step entails a contract service checking the client's authorization to access a particular service. A measurement service is then prepared to determine the performance. The query is saved in the subsequent management request service for statistical purposes. The concluding Web service management middleware controls the time at which the data is forwarded to the actual service. The contract ID is queried for this, allowing the associated WSLA conditions to be evaluated. Based on these performance requirements and the current load of the service supplier, the WSMM decides when the query can be submitted to the service desk for execution. If this time is reached, the service desk assumes responsibility for routing to the actual service.

The WSMM and service desk work together as a means of load distribution so that the specified WSLA restrictions can be adhered to as far as possible. The service's reply is not forwarded directly, either. The reply does not reach the client until the measurement service, management and WSMM handler have been executed.

12.3.4 Monitoring the SLA Parameters

The WSLA descriptions add SLA capabilities to the Web services. In a formal way, the performance requirements are defined by the WSLA language. This enables suitable monitors to evaluate these definitions and determine whether the current measured values correspond with the specifications (service level targets). To this end, performance guarantees are defined for the Web service operations and business processes via the WSLA. The recording of performance measurement is unambiguous and therefore allows violations of performance guarantees to be established.

Third parties can be incorporated into the evaluation and monitoring process. This allows a supplier of services to use the specification to define SLAs and reach an agreement with the customer. Several performance levels are defined, together with the associated templates. A customer selects the required SLA from this portfolio when concluding a contract. For the supplier, these specifications provide an indication of the resources needed to operate the Web services and the priority of the service for this user. The values are important for the customer for the purpose of setting the measurement and control systems correctly.

Control systems (condition evaluation) establish whether the SLAs are adhered to. In the event that the contractually agreed-upon SLA parameters are violated, warnings are output. With a view to enabling this evaluation, the information relevant for data collection is input to the measurement service. This is done when the contract is activated. An estimate regarding fulfillment of the SLA can then be made using the current measurements.

If the specifications are violated or if an error status exists, the actions of the handling agreement take effect. This may involve an error message, for instance. The control system is made up of the following elements: a data collection system for obtaining measurement data, the measurement service, a measurement component for compiling metrics from the measured values – as specified in the WSLA – and a system for comparing the actual calculated metrics with the specifications. A standardized comparative performance value is assigned to each class of workload using the SLA. This value contains an assessment function that estimates how probable it is that the actual values will exceed or fall below the specified values. For planning purposes, the middleware uses simple procedures for modeling the load and assessing the performance of a Web service using queue systems or something similar.

The Web services are connected, distributed and compiled via the service desk in the Web Service Toolkit. This is done using clusters that connect several services via a shared access point. As a result, an individual cluster is able to determine which service a query starts, trigger appropriate performance measurements for the service processing and control the handling of downtime. The choice of service to be started affects not only availability but also the quality of service specifications in the WSLA and business rules. The decision is made automatically based on a service policy. The service desk permits an abstract view for suppliers and users for the purpose of processing client accesses that are received in parallel in heterogeneous environments, with the underlying implementation being hidden from users.

12.3.5 Use of a Measurement Service

In the following we want to show a possible architecture of a measurement service. This architecture allows the measurement of different attributes (e.g., performance, availability) of several Web services. The Web Services to be measured can be selected freely within the Internet. Furthermore, the functionalities of the measurement service can be used through a Web services-based interface (Fig. 12.5).

The components of the agent perform the following tasks:

- **Measurement probes.** Executes the measurements by the use of one or more methods from the Web service. For the isolation of the processing time of the Web services from the needed time within the network we simply used a "ping" in addition. The "ping" is a simple measurement. This is executed shortly before the actual measurement runs.
- **Configuration of the Web Service access.** Gives the possibilities for the configuration of the measurement agent by the use of an XML file. Adaptation to the particular shaping of the WSDL description from a specific Web Service, selection of the method for measuring, definition of corresponding parameter, establishing of intervals for the measurements.
- **Load driver component.** It allows the simulation of the expected workload. The required performance behavior of the Web Service can be tested on this virtual basis. In detail this component provides the definition of the load mix, definition of response time goals and the necessary substitution of parameters.
- **User configuration and access**. It offers the possibility to administrate users of the measurement service with different access rights. That means rights to read available measurements, rights to configure the measurement of new Web Services.
- **Prediction component**. It is based on existing measurements, forecast models can be developed. These models can be developed by the use of mathematical calculations like the operational analysis.
- **Metrics storage & export component.** For deeper analysis it is necessary to use separate statistical tools like Microsoft Excel or SPSS. The current version offers a comma-separated file, which contains all measurements.

- **WSDL-based access layer.** Provides all functions of the measurement agent as service-oriented interface (this means the agent is even a Web service). On the base of this function the agent can be used to control "service level agreements" for a specific Web service.
- **Web based GUI.** It provides a simple graphical control interface. Provides the configuration of the measurements time interval and measurement goals and generates simple graphical reports too.

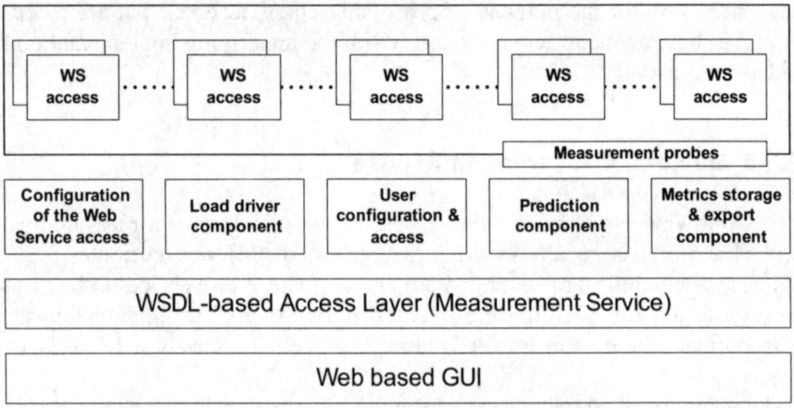

Fig. 12.5. Architecture of a measurement service

A measurement service based on the shown architecture was first implemented under [Schm03b]. It has the possibility to measure the availability, the performance, the functionality and the complexity of a specific Web service from the users (or better integrators) point of view.

12.4 Hints for the Practitioner

An initial implementation (Fig. 12.6, Fig. 12.7) of the proposed concept was realized in cooperation between the T-Systems development center in Berlin and the Software Measurement Laboratory (SMLab) at the University of Magdeburg. For the development of the service we used Java as implementation language and XML for all configuration tasks. The prototype is available for usage under the following URL within the Internet: http://ws-trust.cs.uni-magdeburg.de

This prototype provides the possibility to measure the performance-, stability- and availability-behavior of any Web service provided within the Internet. For a registration of a Web service under the measurement service it is necessary to provide the URL of the corresponding WSDL-file. Based on a dynamic adoption engine, the required application code will be generated dynamically. Therefore, the measurement service is able to adapt on a specific Web Service at runtime (just in time). This function is necessary to provide the functionality of the measurement agent as Web service itself. In the case of a successful code generation, the basic configuration starts. This configuration considers the choice of the methods, the invocation period, aspects of fault tolerance, activities in the case of WSDL changes and the interpretation of possible system errors. Furthermore the type of the result edition will be configured.

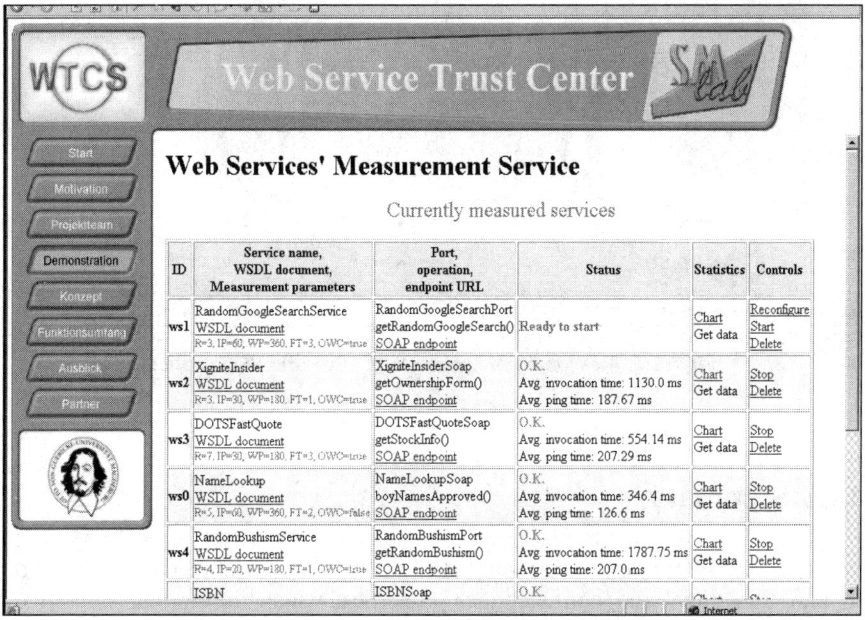

Fig. 12.6. GUI of the implemented measurement service

On this basis, a concrete Web service can be observed regarding his qualitative behavior. The results of this observation can then flow directly in into the selection of a concrete Web service. Furthermore it is possible to estimate the quality behavior of the whole system by the use of the selected Web service. During the selection of a specific Web service the developer should verify the functional behavior and also the nonfunctional behavior.

In the case of the development of a Web service (provided within the Internet or intranet) it is necessary to provide a complete description. This description should explain the whole interface, from a black box standpoint. That means provided functions, possible preconditions, semantic aspects, quality implications, resource requirements and also questions of the maintenance.

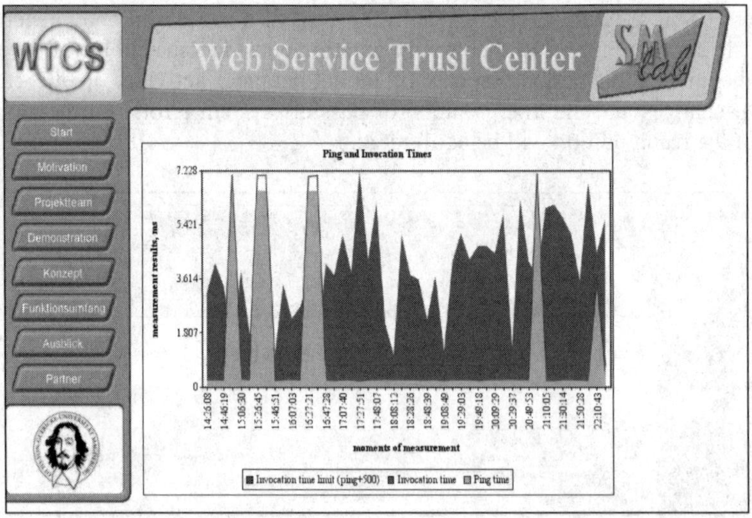

Fig. 12.7. Response time behavior of a specific Web service

12.5 Summary

Web services offered on the Internet usually only have a rudimentary description of their functional and nonfunctional properties, which means that determined properties can usually not be assumed for the Web services offered. Numerous offerings are only available temporarily and do not have a commercial character.

From the viewpoint of the authors, it is vital that the opportunities provided by SLA management in the environment of Web service-based applications are taken into consideration during development. In the process, development should be based not only on the tasks related to process modeling and analysis but also on the actual software development. Web services that take both functional behavior and nonfunctional properties into account and, what is most important, guarantee these during execution need to be positioned successfully on the Internet before commercial solutions can be implemented based on this technology.

The generic WSLA language and the associated architecture offer the opportunity to cover a wide range of negotiating situations between potential contract parties. However, the WSLA approach only addresses selected problems (primarily issues regarding performance) when it comes to guaranteeing a defined service level. The vast majority has to be taken into account during software development.

The task for software development is to create Web services with determined properties. From the viewpoint of the authors, this requires the use of agent technology or, in an initial approach, the instrumentation of technically founded user functions.

13 Case Study: Building an Intranet Measurement Application

Practicing principles matters more than proving them.
—Epictetus

13.1 Applying Measurement Tools

The metrics tool application is one of the main technologies for managing the measurement process in the phases of the measurement itself and during the exploration of the measurement data. However, currently a lot of experience resources in the Web exist for supporting the decision process waiting for migration or adaptation. Fig. 13.1 demonstrates some of the technological aspects included in such support systems [Dumk03a].

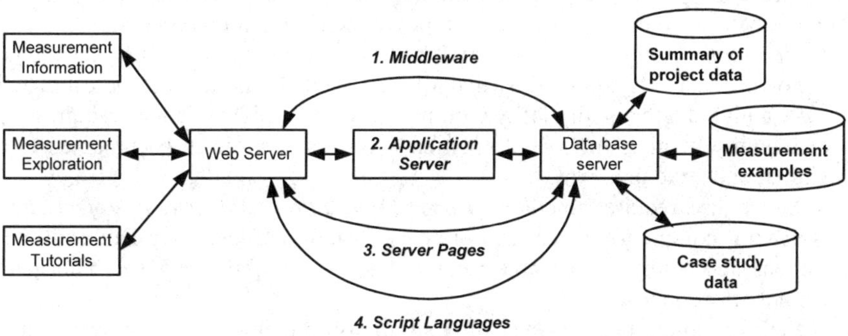

Fig. 13.1. Web-based technologies of measurement experience services

This section describes a Web-based solution based on the International Software Benchmarking Standards Group (ISBSG) *International Repository* including the experience of project estimations (see [Abra03] and [Abra02b]). This approach was designed and implemented in a common initiative of the École de Technologie Supérieur (ETS) in Montreal, Canada, and the SML@b team at the University of Magdeburg, Germany. The solution was realized in two versions, which are described in following. The implemented tool is not generally available, but it demonstrates the possibility of future solutions in this area.

13.2 The White-Box Software Estimation Approach

Reliable software effort estimation is critical for project selection, project planning and project control. Over the past thirty years, various estimation models have been developed to help managers perform estimation tasks, and this has led to a market offering of estimation tools. Some of these tools date from the late 1970s and have been progressively modernized by their vendors. For organizations interested in using such estimation tools, it should be crucial to know about the predictive performance of the estimates such tools produce. In this market segment, however, estimation tool builders have not provided information on the performance of their models, either with respect to their initial data repositories or on their performance when adapted to the evolution of software development technologies. For users, these tools are basically black boxes about which little is known in terms of the reliability of the estimates such black-box tools provide as output.

The construction of an estimation model usually requires a set of completed projects from which a statistical model is derived and which is used thereafter as the basis for the estimation of future projects. However, in most organizations, there is often no structured set of historical data about past projects, which explains their inability to build their own models based on the characteristics of those projects. Traditionally, organizations without such historical data have had four alternatives when they wanted to improve their estimation process:

1. *Collect data from past projects* and *build estimation models* using their own historical data sets – this is particularly useful if the projects to be estimated have a high degree of similarity with past projects. This, of course, requires the availability of high-quality information about those projects documented in a similar and structured way.
2. Take the time required to *collect project information from current projects*, and wait until completion of enough projects to build sufficiently reliable estimation models with a reasonable sample size. Most often, however, managers cannot afford to wait.
3. If their upcoming projects bear little similarity to their own past projects, they may access data repositories containing projects similar to the ones they are embarking on and *derive estimation models* from these. A key difficulty, until fairly recently, has been the lack of market availability of project repositories.
4. *Purchase a commercial estimation tool* from a vendor claiming that the tool basis includes historical projects of the same type as their upcoming projects. This is a quick solution, but often an expensive one.

While alternatives 1 and 2 are under the total control of an organization, alternatives 3 and 4 depend on an outside party. Until fairly recently, for those organizations without their own historical data sets for building estimation models themselves, and who could not afford the long lead time to do so, only alternative 4 was widely available, with the associated constraint of not knowing either the basis of the estimation or the quality of the estimates derived from sources not available for independent scrutiny. In this section, we refer to these commercial tools as black-box estimation tools.

In the mid-1990s, various national software measurement associations got together to address the limitations of alternatives 1 to 4, specifically to overcome the problems of both the availability and the transparency of data for estimation and benchmarking purposes and to offer the software community a more comprehensive alternative in the form of a publicly available multi-organizational data repository. This led to the formation of the ISBSG [ISBS03] whose goal is the development and management of a multi-organizational repository of software project data. The ISBSG organization collects voluntarily provided project data (*functional size, work effort, project elapsed time,* etc.) from the industry, concealing the source and compiling the data into a database. By mid-2003, this repository contained over 2000 projects. It is now available to organizations for a minimal fee, and any organization can use it for estimation purposes. For instance, such a repository can also be used to assess software estimation tools already on the market.

Abran defines the *white-box approach to estimation* as the analysis of a data set for which all the data points are available, and the statistical models of which can be analyzed both graphically and through the results of statistical tests. For a white-box approach, it is necessary to have access to the full data set: access to each of the individual data points allows both visual analysis of the data sets and, for instance, the investigation of obvious outliers to interpret the results in the empirical context of size intervals.

For the prototypes, the *linear regression technique* was selected to build the estimation models over more complex estimation techniques, such as analogy-based and neural network techniques, which have not been shown to better explain the size-effort relationship in software projects on the types of data sets available for such studies, including multiorganizational data sets ([Bria00], [Dola01]). Furthermore, linear regression models are better known by practitioners and simpler to understand and use. Many software engineering data sets are heterogeneous, have wedge-shaped distributions ([Abra96], [Abra02a], [Keme87], [ISBS03], [Kitc84]) and can, of course, have outliers that have an impact on the construction of the models and on their performance.

Therefore, any sample selected needs to be analyzed for the presence of outliers, as well as for visually recognizable point patterns that could provide an indication that a single, simple linear representation would not be a good representation of the data set; for instance, a set of projects within an interval of functional size might demonstrate one behavior with respect to effort, and the same set of projects within another size interval a different one. If such recognizable patterns are identified, then the sample should be subdivided into two smaller samples, if there are enough data points, of course. Both the samples with outliers and those without them should be analyzed.

The visual analysis provides another clue. The following example is provided in [Dumk03b]: A visual analysis of Fig. 13.2 (upper left part) indicates that there are two candidate outliers that might have an undue impact on the regression model. The data point with almost 1,000 *Function Points (FP)* [Albr83] has a corresponding level of effort that is much smaller than that of many projects of much smaller functional size, and a project with 3,700 FP is almost three times as large as the majority of the projects.

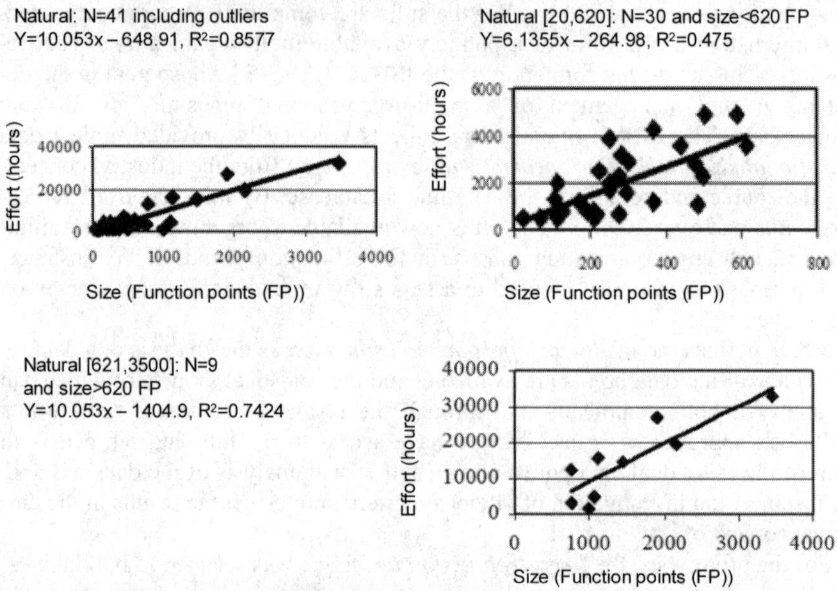

Fig. 13.2. Regression analyses – projects in NATURAL

Two different groups can be identified: one subset of projects between 20 and 620 FP, with a good sample size of 30 observations (Fig. 13.2, upper right part), and the other a more sparsely populated subset of 9 projects between 621 and 3700 FP, a much larger size interval (Fig. 13.2, lower part). It can then be observed visually that in the sample of projects with functional size between 20 FP and 620 FP there is a relationship between the independent and dependent variables: its estimation model (Fig. 13.2, upper right part) is Y=6.135×FP+265 with an $R^2 = 0.475$. In this model, the constant of 265 h could represent the fixed cost of setting up the projects within this size interval, the positive slope then corresponds to the variable cost, which is dependent on the size of the projects. For projects larger that 620 FP in size (Fig. 13.2c), the estimation model is

$$Y = 10.539 \times FP - 1404, \text{ with } R^2 = 0.74$$

But, with only nine data points, caution must be exercised in interpreting the data. For the smaller range, the constant of the regression line is positive; for this larger size interval, the constant of the equation is negative (-1404 h), which is, of course, counter intuitive. This means in particular that there should not be an extrapolation of the model outside the range of values from which it was derived (that is, it is not valid for projects smaller than 621 FP).

This example also highlights the fact that in this ISBSG multiorganizational dataset there is, for each sample and by programming language, a different size-effort relationship, and the strength of this relationship differs. The directly derived models performed as well as models built by other researchers for smaller and older multiorganizational datasets [Dola01] under similar conditions, as well as for more recent software applications: For some programming languages, the relationship of the models is within the range reported in the literature for multi-organizational data sets (that is, R^2 around 0.40) without any indication of their programming languages. Without visualization, the results obtained from estimation tools can be somewhat of a mystery to practitioners and have at times been referred to as "black-box" estimations [Dumk03b]. The "white-box" estimation prototypes we have developed greatly alleviate this problem.

The first generation of prototypes was built as a proof-of-concept for the white-box approach to software estimation. It was based on a business model, which must take into account that, while the ISBSG data can be purchased from ISBSG. A new business model is explored in our second generation of Web-based prototypes: in this new model, the estimation features themselves are marketed through the Web, rather than the data or the software. This means that the pricing policy will be based on the number of requests for estimation, without the obligation of paying for the full dataset or for the software itself. It also means that users do not need to worry about software upgrades or further repository releases.

13.3 First Web-Based Approach

The first Web-based prototype was designed and implemented as an application server model with three tiers. It was programmed as a "Web-based" Java-Applet in a *distributed system using Java (Sun Corporation)* and its *remote method invocation (RMI)* counterpart to the *remote procedure calls (RPC)* [Dumk03a]. Computation results [Weis91] are presented in Fig. 13.3, in both table and scatter-plot format, with Work Effort or Duration displayed (*Y*-axis) depending on the number of Function Points (*X*-axis).

A linear regression line, its equation and R^2 are displayed, using the least squares method of statistics. Depending on the confidence interval selected and the expected size of the project to be estimated, the estimated effort (or duration), its prediction interval and the prediction bounds are plotted. The user can analyze the impact of outliers by using the select/unselect option to delete some data from the sample he is analyzing, and asking the prototype to recompute the estimation results. In the table at the bottom of the display screen, the lower, estimated and upper values for the dependent variables (*project work effort, elapsed time, delivery rate* and *speed of delivery*) are given, together with the number of projects in the sample selected and taken into account in the regression model.

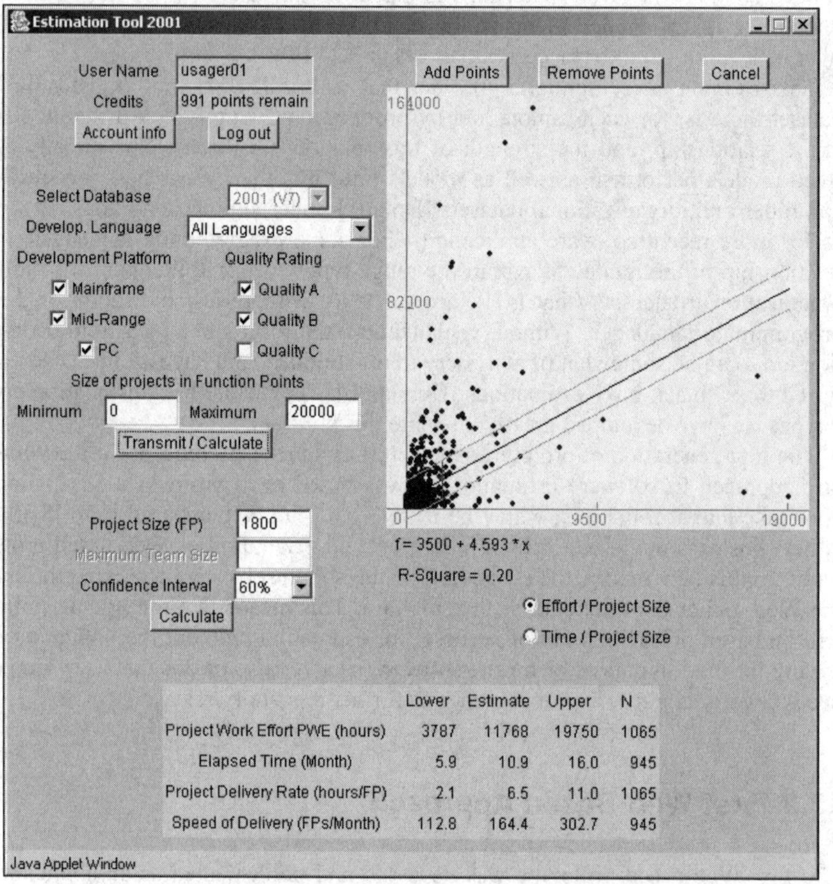

Fig. 13.3. Stand-alone prototype

13.4 Second Web-Based Approach

Of course, as a proof-of-concept, robustness had to be added to the first prototype. Furthermore, the first prototype was built using release 7 of the ISBSG repository. However, not only does ISBSG publish updated versions of its repository at irregular intervals, but it also modifies, for various reasons, the data structures of the dataset made available with each successive release (for instance, new fields for added data variables). In addition to improvements to the management of user accounts, more sophisticated visualization features were recommended to permit the construction of multiple estimation models by selecting ranges of data points from the same sample, as illustrated in Fig. 13.2.

The estimation features were enhanced to provide users with the facility to build multiple estimation models from the same sample, as described in [Dumk03b]. For instance, in this second prototype, a user, after a graphical analysis of the sample she selected, can divide the *X*-axis into ranges of functional sizes (i.e., intervals) to obtain distinct regression models for each size range. Of course, the linear regression curve, associated equation and R^2 are provided for every scatter plot (Fig. 13.4). To improve the management of user accounts, a Java GUI-driven user database handler was implemented to delete a user, add a user or alter the user settings from the GUI instead of direct typewriting at a terminal (Fig. 13.5).

13.5 Hints for the Practitioner

White-box software estimation as shown in this chapter can be a helpful approach for the IT community based on following intentions:

- The construction of an estimation model usually requires a set of completed projects from which a statistical model is derived and that is used thereafter as the basis for the estimation of future projects.
- The white-box approach to estimation consists of the analysis of a dataset for which all the data points are available, and the statistical models of that can be analyzed both graphically and through the results of statistical tests.
- The implemented statistical analysis functions should be easy to understand and really interesting for the user.
- The experience database must be composed of voluntary activities by the IT community.
- In the presented Web-based prototypes, the linear regression technique was selected to build the estimation models over more complex estimation techniques, such as analogy-based and neural network techniques.

13.6 Summary

The construction of an estimation model usually requires a set of completed projects from which a statistical model is derived and which is used thereafter as the basis for the estimation of future projects. Abran defines the white-box approach to estimation as the analysis of a data set for which all the data points are available, and the statistical models of which can be analyzed both graphically and through the results of statistical tests. For a white-box approach, it is necessary to have access to the full data set: access to each of the individual data points allows both visual analysis of the data sets.

The given description of the Web-based project data analysis tool should motivate the IT community for more initiatives using the large facilities in the Web described in Chap. 4 as the future of e-measurement.

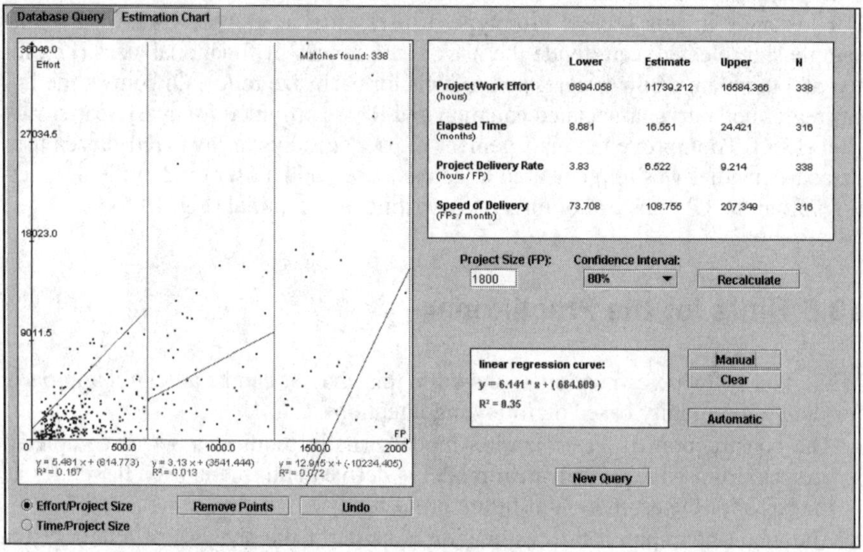

Fig. 13.4. Estimation features – second Web-based prototype

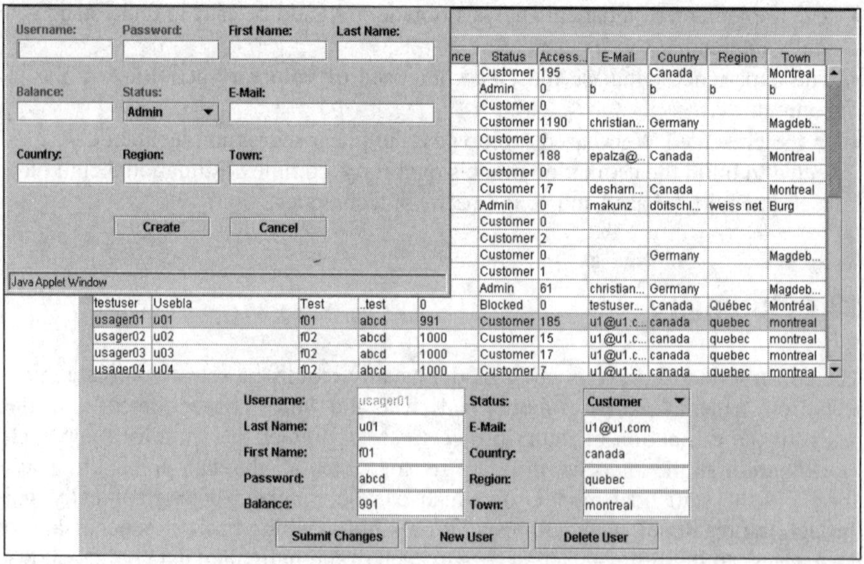

Fig. 13.5. GUI-driven user administration

14 Case Study: Measurements in IT Projects

Project without clear goals will not achieve their goal clearly.
—Tom Gilb

14.1 Estimations: A Start for a Measurement Program

Project estimations are required as early as possible – not only from the contractors but also from every project leader. Because of the importance of early estimation methods Meli and Santillo [Meli99] published a comparative overview of Function Point estimation methods that shows a valuable collection of worldwide efforts in this direction. Since Function Point counts are based on the requirements documentation, so-called Function Point prognoses or approximations proved in practice to be helpful to aid early estimations [Bund98b], [Bund99a].

Our experience shows, that the necessary information for such approximations can be gained very early, at the beginning of a project (or, in stable environments, even before) in discussions with the project leader. In a few cases we used this Function Point Prognosis a year before project start. Of course, we added large percentages for each error, uncertainty, early estimation and risk.

We will in this chapter describe a case study about introducing and increasingly improving an estimation and measurement program inside an IT organization.

About 1995 the IT department of the AXA Service AG in Cologne (the non-insurance part of AXA Germany) started a metrics program with Function Point (FP) metrics, the introduction of a handbook for measurement and estimation, and the evaluation of tools. In the following year the Function Point Workbench and the estimation tool Checkpoint for Windows (CKWIN) were introduced and the base counts of all application systems was started.

In 2001 the IT department completed the total counts of all 78 application systems (excluding Enterprise Resource Planning (ERP) applications, e.g. SAP, Peoplesoft) totaling about 100,000 unadjusted Function Points (FPs). By 2003 the portfolio increased to 98 application systems with about 150,000 unadjusted Function Points. Actually, more than 100 staff members are trained in FP counts and project estimation. In each group of developers there is at least one FP and estimation "expert". The competence center consists of two persons. In 2002 productivity measures were developed, and a baseline for productivity measurement was completed. In 2003 the metrics database was introduced as Version 1.0. Some of the enterprise embedded solutions are presented in this chapter.

14.2 Environment

14.2.1 The IT Organization

The IT department of AXA Service AG includes about 500 IT professionals with approximately 50 project leaders. In addition, there is an outsourced computing center with about 250 staff members. The insurance branches deliver about 160 IT coordinators supporting the IT projects. IT development is mostly host-based with COBOL programming. There exist about 2,700 databases (1,600 CICS, 1,100 IMS), and 2,500 DB2 tables (1,600 production, 900 disposition), and about 7,800,000 transactions per day (5,600,000 CICS and 2,200,000 IMS). PC projects use Optima++, a C++ shell, for programming and Internet programming is done with Java.

FP counts are obligatory in the AXA Service AG, at least at the end of the requirements analysis and at the project post mortem. Function Point Prognosis, – as described here – instead of only FP count is mandatory during the feasibility study and at the start of a project. The counts and their details are documented centrally. Throughout this chapter Function Points mean IFPUG 4.0 unadjusted FPs.

To get access to history data, we use a project register database (Excel), which shows detailed information (extracted from the Function Point Workbench) for each FP count. It contains the quantity as well as the Function Points of EIs (External Inputs), EOs (External Outputs), EQs (External Inquiries), ILFs (Internal Logical Files) and EIFs (External Interface Files) for each of these components and some additional information (platform, VAF (Value Adjustment Factor), adjusted Function Points). When a project was counted repeatedly only the most recent count is shown and older counts are kept in a history table. There are sums of the quantity of EIs and EOs, of ILFs and EIFs, which were needed for our research. IO means throughout this chapter the sum of the number (quantities) of EI and EO.

We started in 1997 with 20 application counts [Bund98a], which increased to 39 counts a year later [Bund99a]. A balanced scorecard was introduced for the department leaders, combining their success in counting all of their application systems with 20% of their financial bonus. This was essential management support for the success of our metrics program.

14.2.2 Function Point Project Baseline

In addition to the investigation of the formulae for prognosis we also investigated the FP proportions and average function complexity of our FP counts and compared it, e.g., with the International Software Benchmarking Standards Group (ISBSG) data. The ISBSG (http://www.isbsg.org) publishes every year a collection of metrics. The actual Release 8 is based on more than 2,040 projects worldwide. Since we did this research several times over the past years, we now have at least three historical annual metrics of our own data for comparison, as can be seen in the following parts of the chapter.

Value adjustment factor. One of the first results of our data collection was the perception that the value adjustment factor (VAF) of our counts is typically in the range of 0.73–1.22, with an average of 0.95 in the 2001 data (0.93 in 1998), and an average of 0.94 for host and 0.96 for PC environment. The average for migrations is 0.73. We have used this metric for quality assurance of our Function Point counts since 1998.

Function component proportions. Table 14.1 shows the historic development of the function component proportions in AXA Service AG. Of course, the first two years are not very representative. The figures from 1998 and 2001 are similar, and the division into Host and PC development shows differences that should be carefully observed in future. The domination of the EIs and EOs (61% together) seems to be the reason for the strong correlation between IOs and the unadjusted FPs – the main result of this research.

It can be seen that EOs dominate in AXA Service AG (39%) compared with the results obtained by Morris and Desharnais [Morr96] (22%–24%), and the quick estimation mode of Checkpoint for Windows (CKWIN), the estimation tool from SPR (Software Productivity Research) in Burlington, MA, (20%), whereas ILFs are of minor importance (16% versus 24% and 43%, respectively). Because of this peculiarity one conclusion was not to use Checkpoint for Windows (EIF + ILF = 46% versus 23% in AXA Service AG) in Quick Estimate mode for the estimation of FPs. The reason for the major importance of EOs may be that AXA Service AG has many centralized management information.

In 2000 we accomplished an error calculation with the 1998 data by using the percentage of each component to calculate 100% from it and compared the result with the actual Function Point count. Errors range from 37% (EOs) to 48% (EQs) [Bund00b. Hence we do use the percentages of the components only as a rule of thumb for the quality assurance of our Function Point counts.

Table 14.1. Function component proportions

2001		Percent of Function Points				
Platform	Number of Application Systems	EI	EO	EQ	ILF	EIF
Total	78	22	39	8	16	14
Host	69	21	40	8	16	15
PC	9	28	31	12	19	10
ISBSG Rel. 6	238 New development projects	33.5	23.5	16	22	5
Metricviews		26–39	22–24	12–14	24	4–12
Checkpoint		20	24	10	43	3
1998 Total	39	25	39	14	17	6
1996/97 Total	20	27	39	11	18	5
1997 Total	12	18	43	12	18	9
1996 Total	8	34	35	11	18	2

Average function complexity. We used the Excel problem solver to calculate from the project register database the average function complexity of the five components, i.e., how many FPs a "typical" EI, EO, EQ, ILF or EIF has in our environment. It is widely agreed that this measure is stable and can be used as a rule of thumb for quick estimation of counts, since the components need not be classified as low, average or high. SPR Function Points, e.g., use the average IFPUG classification for Function Point estimation.

Table 14.2 shows that that the average Function Points increased over time, which may be caused by growing complexity in application development environment. In 1998 we tested the applicability of the typical FPs for estimation purposes by multiplying it with the quantities of the EIs, EOs, EQs, ILFs and EIs, respectively, and compared the results with the unadjusted Function Points of the counts. The error was less than 13%

Table 14.2. Average Function Complexity

2001		Average Function Points				
Platform	Number of application systems	EI	EO	EQ	ILF	EIF
Total	78	4.7	5.9	4.4	8.6	6.5
Host	69	4.7	5.9	4.6	8.7	6.5
PC	9	4.3	5.7	3.8	7.6	6.5
IFPUG		4	5	4	10	7
ISBSG	Release 5	4.3	5.4	3.8	7.4	5.5
	Release 5 Europe	4.2	4.9	3.8	7.2	5.3
1998	Number of application systems	EI	EO	EQ	ILF	EIF
Total	39	4.6	5.7	4.3	8.2	6.1
Host	28	4.8	5.7	4.5	8.5	6.2
PC	11	4.0	5.7	3.9	7.3	5.4
1997	Number of application systems	EI	EO	EQ	ILF	EIF
Total	20	4.6	5.5	4.3	8.1	5.7

Function point ratios. One would expect three inputs (add, change, delete) at least, one output and one EQ for maintenance of a file. The following results show the averages in AXA Service AG (Table 14.3).

Ratios of components. There are remarkable differences between the beforementioned expectations and also some differences between the ratios in our application systems (AS) and the ISBSG findings [ISBS00, ISBS02], as can be seen from Table 14.3.

Ratios of Function Points per component. The ratios of Function Points per ILF, input and output were also calculated (Table 14.4).

Table 14.3. Ratios of components

Application systems	AXA Service AG			ISBSG Rel. 5	
	2001	1998	1997	Europe	Total
Quantity	78	39	20	32	238
EI per ILF	2.6	2.7	2.7	3.8	2.9
EO per ILF	3.6	3.3	3.7	2.6	1.5
EQ per ILF	0.9	1.4	1.2	1.9	1.1
EIF per ILF	0.6	0.5	0.4	-	-
Ratios per input and ratios per output					
78 Application Systems	2001		78 Application systems		2001
EO per EI	1.3		EI per EO		0.7
EQ per EI	0.3		EQ per EO		0.3
ILF per EI	0.4		ILF per EO		0.3
EIF per EI	0.2		EIF per EO		0.2

Table 14.4. Ratios of Functions Points per component

78 AS	2001	78 AS	2001	78 AS	2001
EI FPs per ILF	12.2	EO FPs per EI	8.0	EI FPs per EO	3.4
EO FPs per ILF	21.0	EQ FPs per EI	1.5	EQ FPs per EO	1.1
EQ FPs per ILF	4.0	ILF FPs per EI	3.3	ILF FPs per EO	2.4
EIF FPs per ILF	4.2	EIF FPs per EI	1.6	EIF FPs per EO	1.2

14.3 Function Point Prognosis

Regression analysis on our project register database was used to find correlations between the number of components and the unadjusted Functions Points of the counts [Gaff94]. The result of the research was that the sum of the quantities of EIs and EOs (IOs in our terminology) is correlated with about $R^2 \geq 0.95$ ($R \geq 0.97$) to the total amount of FPs of a count and can thus be used as a Rule of thumb for the prognosis of FPs when the FPs of EQs, ILFs and EIFs are not known.

An interesting result was that the correlation was not as reliable (R^2 mostly less than 0.9) for other components as for data subsets of small, medium and large counts, and it was not better with polynomial regression. Of course, the use of FPs instead of the IOs for the prognosis gives a stronger correlation, but the higher effort for classification of the components instead of only counting the inputs and outputs is not adequate for the higher precision. One should always keep in mind that estimation has to do with uncertainty per se.

The 1998 data were analyzed independently by Noel [Noel98] in a joint research with the Software Engineering Management Research Laboratory, Department Informatique, Universite du Quebec a Montreal (UQAM), Canada, who obtained the same results. He applied the same method to seven projects with COSMIC Full Function Points (FFPs), in order to find a similar correlation for FFPs, but the sample seemed to be too small for reliable results. He reported in his thesis an error margin of 20%. Table 14.5 gives a historical overview of the prognosis formulae. Fig. 14.1 visualizes the regression analysis result for all counts.

Table 14.5. Function Point prognosis formulae

2001	Number of counts	R^2	Error in%	Formula for Prognosis
Total	78	0.9483	13	FP = 7.8 × IO + 43
Host	69	0.9498	12	FP = 7.9 × IO + 40
PC	9	0.9503	21	FP = 6.4 × IO + 172
1998	39	0.9589	20	FP = 7.6 × IO + 50
Host	28	0.9580		FP = 7.9 × IO + 11
PC	11	0.9760		FP = 6.5 × IO + 134
1997	20	0.9525	13 (Median 11)	FP = 7.3 × IO + 56

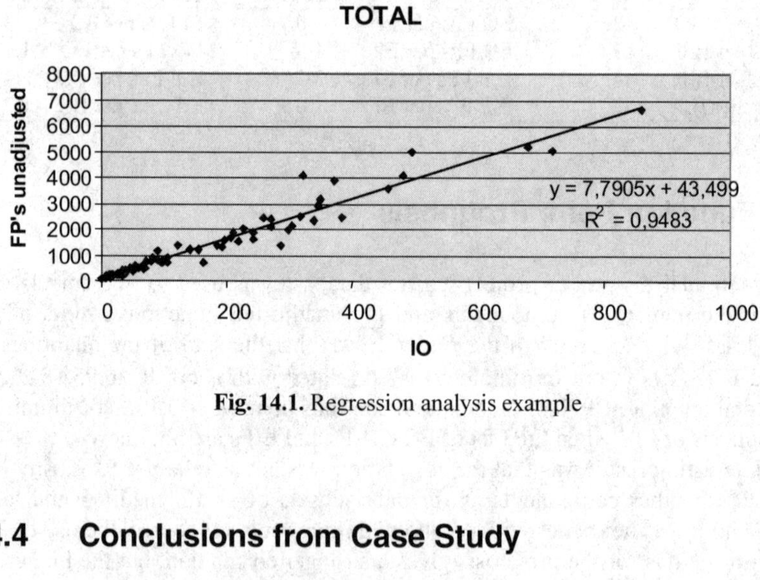

Fig. 14.1. Regression analysis example

14.4 Conclusions from Case Study

14.4.1 Counting and Accounting

A good documentation of counting and estimation data is a treasure for metrics programs. Our investigations show that valuable metrics can be gained from the collected data. A surplus benefit was finding (via regression analysis) a prediction that helped us to estimate FPs very early in the process. Since FPs are an important measure for the estimation of effort we thus gained the synergetic benefit to be able to do reliable estimations very early in the life cycle of our IT projects. Of course, a complete count of FPs at the end of the requirements analysis is obligatory, as well as an improved estimation at this time.

We heard from other organizations that they did similar research. There is strong evidence that different environments will lead to other results, hence each organization should develop its own heuristic solutions. Nevertheless, comparisons with other metrics are valuable for the enterprise.

From the start of the introduction of our metrics program in 1996 it has been a long road to arrive at these results of application counting. The success could only have been achieved with sufficient management support. The year 2002 was devoted to introducing project FP counting and estimation as well as the introduction of productivity metrics.

The quality of a software product is measured by the degree of how well it fits the requirements of the end users. The increasing diffusion of IT in private life leads to increasing requirements and quality of software systems. This consciousness of increased quality made quality one of the most important goals of software development. There exist a lot of relevant and proved measures, methods and techniques for improvement of quality of software and software development.

Quality today is no coincidence, but can and must be exactly planned. For this reason quality assurance in IT projects consists of at least the following functionality:

- quality planning
- quality measures
- quality control
- quality assurance

The first three functions are secured by so-called constructive quality assurance measures, which have to be performed systematically in order to define quality a priori. Constructive quality assurance measures are, e.g., the systematic use of methods, development tools or standardized processes. Quality control is performed by analytical quality assurance measures in order to measure quality or deviations and to correct them.

The focus of these tasks is directed to constructive quality assurance measures, since prevention is better than error correction, or, in a metaphor: fire prevention is better than fire fighting.

This is accompanied by the requirement for the definition of quality goals for the software development process, from which the quality goals of the software can be deducted. Quality is then measured by comparison of the goals and the obtained quality features of the developed software. In IT projects, as part of the requirements, the quality measures are defined at the start of the IT project. This is a direct link to estimation.

14.4.2 ISO 8402 Quality Measures and IFPUG GSCs

The ISO 8402 Quality Measures overlap partially with the 14 general system characteristics (GSC) of the IFPUG Function Point method [IFPU99], which are used to add estimation parameters to the functional size measurement for the calculation of adjusted function points Hence the idea evolved to create an automatic interface to avoid double work for the project leaders. A large organization thus has developed the following Excel chart, which automatically calculates the quality measures from the GSCs and vice versa. The connection between the quality measures and the GSCs was ranked from 1 to 9 by a team, i.e., the sum of each column is 9. Thus, in Fig. 14.2 the quality measure fit is connected with the following IFPUG GSCs (see column 1 in Fig. 14.2 and Table 14.6 for the mapping of the values):

- 1/9 with data communication
- 2/9 with distributed data processing
- 1/9 with online data entry
- 5/9 with facilitate change

Table 14.6. Evaluation of IFPUG GSC and DIN/ISO quality measures

General system characteristics	Mapped to the priority of the quality measure
0	= No priority (0)
1 and 2	= Small priority (1)
3	= Medium priority (2)
4 and 5	= High priority (3)

Value:
High Average Low None
5 4 - 3 2 - 1 0 IFPUG
3 2 1 0 Q-Charact.

Ratings
High Average Low None
9 - 7 6 - 4 3 - 1 0

abs. rating / Value: 45–41 → 3; 40–27 → 2; 26–6 → 1; 5–0 → 0

IFPUG GSC's	Value	Adaptability	Usability	Efficiency	Functionality	Maintainability	Correctness	Portability	Stability	Security	Interoperability	Reusability	Reliability
Quality Characteristic		3	2	2	3	2	2	3	2	3	2	1	2
Data communication	5	1			3			1				1	
Distributed Data Processing	4	2									9		
Performance	4			3		2							
Heavily Used Configuration	5			3						1			
Transaction Rate	0			3		2			1				2
Online Data Entry	5	1	1		3				2				2
End-User Efficiency	4		6										
Online Update	5					5				4			
Complex Processing	4				3		3			1			3
Reusability	2											7	
Installation Ease	4		1				4			2			2
Operational Ease	4						2		6	1			
Multiple Sites	5							8					
Facilitate Change	5	5	1									1	
relative meaning		10,0%	8,9%	6,3%	9,8%	7,7%	8,4%	10,5%	7,9%	9,6%	8,4%	5,6%	7,0%
absolute meaning		43	38	27	42	33	36	45	34	41	36	24	30

Fig. 14.2. Mapping of the DIN/ISO quality measures to the IFPUG GSCs

14.4.3 Distribution of Estimated Effort to Project Phases

With the aid of an Excel chart the distribution of the estimated effort of the project phases can be done with the percentage method. A corporate solution, e.g., would ask for following input:

1. Effort as estimated
2. Effort for interfaces (e.g., computing center, other projects) as individually estimated, or from estimation tool
3. Team size of IT staff for each phase
4. Team size of end-users and specialists for each phase

Fig. 14.3 demonstrates this standard. In the first folder the estimated effort for development and users is divided into the three partial efforts for IT department, user and IT Organization. After input of the effort for interfaces the Project relevant effort will be calculated and the project category is determined (Project Class C in this case). The effort is shown in person hours (PH), person days (PD) person months (PM) .

Effort Distribution						
				Project Class C		
				PH	PD	PM
IT-Department	55,75%	85,98%	51,10%	9.812	1.226,5	61,3
User	29,25%		26,81%	5.148	643,5	32,2
IT-Organization	15,00%		13,75%	2.640	330,0	16,5
Effort 1	100,00%		91,67%	17.600	2.200,0	110,0
Interfaces		14,02%	8,33%	1.600	200,0	10,0
Effort according to Proj.Class		100,00%		11.412	1.426,5	71,3
Effort 2			100,00%	19.200	2.400,0	120,0

Fig. 14.3. Effort distribution

The explanation of terms is as follows:

- **IT-Department.** Effort as estimated with estimation tool. This effort comprises effort for development of the application accomplished by the project team: effort for IT staff, users and specialists, but not the effort for interfaces.
- **User effort** accomplished by users.
- **IT-Organization.** Effort accomplished by other departments, specialists, project management, quality assurance and consultancy.
- **Effort 1**. Effort accomplished by the IT team, comprising all conceptional tasks, programming and test relevant tasks as well as effort for project management and quality assurance.

- **Interfaces**. Effort for interfaces required in other applications or departments that have to change their systems or processes for the integration of the new project.
- **Effort according to Project Class**. Dimension relevant effort is the sum of effort accomplished by the IT team and effort for interfaces. It determines the project category that is used for planning the organizational structure of the project.
- **Effort 2**. This is the sum of Effort 1 and Interface effort.

Fig. 14.4 is used to determine the phase relevant effort for the IT staff and users. The project duration is computed from effort and team size. The percentages shown in both tables were ascertained from the competence center in a large organization, which documented and maintained project data centrally.

	Project		IT-Core Project				User				
Phase	Percent. Phase	Effort (PM)	Percent. Phase	FTE	Effort (PM)	Duration (Month)	Percent. Phase	FTE	Effort (PM)	Duration (Month)	Duration (Month)
Req. Anal.	24,0%	26,4	11,0%	5	12,1	3,23	10,5%	7	11,55	2,2	3,67
Design	21,5%	23,65	15,05%	6	16,56	3,68	3,05%	5	3,36	0,89	3,68
Coding	25,5%	28,05	19,5%	7	21,45	4,09	3,3%	3	3,63	1,61	4,09
Test	14,5%	15,95	6,8%	4	7,48	2,49	5,7%	2	6,27	4,18	4,18
Integr. Test	14,5%	15,95	3,4%	3	3,74	1,66	6,7%	3	7,37	3,28	3,28
Sum	100,0%	110,0	55,75%	25	61,33	15,15	29,25%	20	32,18	12,16	18,89

Fig. 14.4. Phase relevant effort

It is important to mention the work of Jeffrey [Jeff97], which said that the effort in IT projects grows linearly up to a project size of about 10 person years (about 125 to 300 FPs) and exponentially above. The distribution of the estimated effort to the project phases and involved teams is a necessary prerequisite for resource planning. In addition, information about costs, effort, schedule and staff are needed.

14.4.4 Estimation of Maintenance Tasks

Project estimation often does not include the maintenance effort during the lifetime of an application system, but it usually exceeds the other application development costs. Software maintenance is often defined as the modification of a software product after delivery to correct faults, to improve performance or other attributes, or to adapt the product to a changed environment. Practical experience shows that IT systems live longer than expected. It is a common practice that the costs for maintenance are accumulated during the lifetime of a system without controlling the amount and without differentiating between the different kinds of costs.

Like in a supermarket the user is afterwards astonished that the many cheap goods in the basket (i.e., comparably maintenance requirements) accumulate to a large sum at the cash point. It is only a pity that in software maintenance nothing can be removed from the basket afterwards (to stick to the analogy with the supermarket).

Note that the International Function Point User Group (IFPUG) definition [IFPU99] holds that maintenance tasks do not change the functionality of an application system. If it does so, it will be an enhancement instead.

14.4.5 The UKSMA and NESMA Standard

In addition of the ISO 14764 standard "Software Engineering – Software Maintenance", the United Kingdom Software Metrics Association (UKSMA) published together with the International Software Benchmarking Standards Group (ISBSG) published in July 2001 (as part of the UKSMA Quality Measurement Standards) the standard "Measuring Software Maintenance and Support", Version 0.5 Draft [UKSM01], available at: http://www.uksma.co.uk. This standard distinguishes between maintenance, support and operations (Table 14.7).

Table 14.7. The UKSMA activity based model of support and maintenance

Development (1)	Development – defined as in IFPUG 4.1
Enhancement (2)	Enhancement – defined as in IFPUG 4.1 and with ≥ 5 person days effort – changes the functionality
Maintenance (3) and Support (4)	(3) Maintenance Corrective maintenance Perfective maintenance Preventative maintenance Adaptive maintenance (≤ 5 person days effort) – may change the functionality! (4) Ad hoc help desk responses Problem analysis Decommissioning
Operations (5)	(5) System administration Deployment/rollout Database management Information Retrieval Support

The aim of the standard was to define measures from which up to 23 metrics can be derived, such

- **Productivity**. Function Points per person year
- **Departmental proportion minor enhancements**. The proportion of maintenance and support effort devoted to minor enhancements (per department)
- **Proportion minor enhancements**. Departmental effort of minor enhancements divided by the sum of maintenance and support effort devoted to minor enhancements, expressed in percent.

In 2001 the Netherlands Software Metrieken Gebruikers Associatie (NESMA, http://www.nesma.nl/download/FPA) published the Function Point Analysis for Software Enhancement Guidelines Version 1.0 [NESM02], which uses (with special impact factors weighted) so called Test Function Points (TFP) and Enhancement Function Points (EFP) for calculation of the total enhancement effort including testing (E) as:

$$E = (EFP \times \text{hours per EFP}) + (TFP \times \text{hours per TFP})$$

14.4.6 Enhancement Projects

Maintenance is a necessary part of the enhancement of an application system. The ISBSG Data Base from June 2002 [ISBS02] shows 40,7% (322 from 791 projects, see page 23 in [ISBS02]) enhancement projects. On pages 41 and 44 of [ISBS02] the following details of IFPUG 4.0 Function Point counts are published (Table 14.8 and Table 14.9).

Table 14.8. Function Point components percentages in enhancement projects

Functionality	Added	Changed	Deleted	Total
N	408	306	83	454
EI (%)	31.9	37.8	38.0	34.4
EO (%)	31.4	25.9	35.1	29.4
EQ (%)	13.5	16.0	10.7	14.1
ILF (%)	15.6	18.0	11.1	16.5
EIF (%)	7.5	2.3	5.1	5.6
Totals (%)	55.3	42.0	2.7	

Table 14.9. Analyses of changes in enhancement projects

Functionality	N	Percentage
Only added functions	143	31.5
Only changed functions	46	10.1
Added and changed functions	183	40.3
Added and deleted functions	5	1.1
Added, changed and deleted functions	77	17.0
Total	454	100.0

Nevertheless, it should be kept in mind that maintenance does not alter the system size in Function Points due to IFPUG 4.1 rules [IFPU99]. If it does so, it is not maintenance but enhancement instead.

14.4.7 Software Metrics for Maintenance

The analogy with the supermarket directs our attention to metrics for the estimation of maintenance effort. The aim is to develop measures and threshold figures to find out when the service effort will exceed the costs of a new development. Often it is not considered that software – like other products or goods – ages with time and that preventive planning of maintenance or redevelopment is necessary.

Productivity and maintenance effort depend on software size and some other parameters. The COCOMO-M(aintenance) model and SLIM both use only one parameter related to maintenance, while PRICE-S, SEER-SEM and Jones' estimation tool Checkpoint [Jone02] use several such parameters. Parameters related to maintenance may be found in a publication from Abran et al. [Abra02b], e.g.,

- type of application system
- programming language
- age of software
- quality of existing documentation
- necessity of a complete system test
- restrictions in availability of resources
- functional complexity
- technical complexity
- degree of reuse

This field study was done in two organizations concerning 15 maintenance projects with functional changes in one organization, and 19 maintenance projects in the other organization. The result was that there exists a positive but weak relationship between size and effort. The regression analysis gave evidence of other parameters influencing the effort. Introduction of a second free parameter increased the significance ($R^2 = 0.85$ and 0.87, respectively). The average size of the maintenance tasks in the organization with the Web-based environment was four times as large as in the military organization, but the average effort was only two times as much. Thus the average cost per maintenance task in the Web-based environment was only half as much (about 115 person-hours) as in the military environment (221 person-hours).

Zuse [Zuse97] collected the following metrics, which can be used for estimation of maintenance tasks:

- Number of errors occurring after delivery. Often the measurements are performed during six months after delivery.
- Number of changes or change requests.
- Effort for error search and correction.
- Error quote recorded as errors per Function Point.
- Mean time until error occurrence.
- Software Maturity Index (SMI), defined as difference between the number of modules/functions of the actual release (R) minus the number of modules/functions changed, added and deleted in the previous release (P). This difference is divided by the number of modules/functions of the actual release:

$$SMI = (R - P) / R$$

This list can be prolonged by the following metric:

- Effort for maintenance in hours per installed Function Point. If this figure is very high, reengineering or new development should be planned.

Simple counting of maintenance tasks and error reports therefore can hint to error-prone modules and can furthermore deliver information about enhancement of modules/functions. Such metrics and results from collections of the relevant data are beneficial information for know-how collection of organizations and estimation of future maintenance tasks.

Two aspects should be considered:

- estimation of maintenance effort after delivery of the application system
- estimation for (single) maintenance tasks

14.4.8 Estimation of Maintenance Effort After Delivery

Even at the beginning of the 1990s Großjohann [Groß94] from Volkswagen AG (VW) used a VW-specific variant of the Function Point method for estimation of the service effort of IT systems. He calculated the relation between hours per Function Point per year (service factor) and the service year. This so-called bathtub curve (Fig. 14.5, the name is derived from the form of the curve) was calculated by the formula (S = service factor, Y = service year):

$$S(Y) = 1.604 - 0.37268 \times Y + 0.04684 \times Y^2 - 0.00166 \times Y^3$$

The effort for the service of the complete life cycle of an application system (ST) is calculated according to the following formula:

$$ST = FP \times S(Y - 0.5) \times B(Y)$$

In this formula B(Y) are influential factors (skills, number of users, system specific and environment specific parameters) correlating with the year. This total effort is divided into

- maintenance 65%
- user support 25%
- production 10%

If shortages of budgets are decided the maintenance will be reduced and problems may occur since user demand at least correct and complete functionality of the running system, which cannot be guaranteed under this circumstances. Projects for the enhancement of the application system are not included in this formula and have to be added separately.

14.4.9 Estimation for (Single) Maintenance Tasks

Single maintenance tasks are necessary due to legal, technical or organizational requirements as well as for error correction. Often the effort of such tasks is less than 3 person months and therefore the effort for a Function Point count cannot be economically justified.

The estimation Competence Center of the AXA Service AG developed with some project leaders an Excel chart with typical tasks and parameters, which were considered to be influential for maintenance tasks [Bund02b]. Each of these factors was correlated with an estimated effort for estimation, which could be changed by plus/minus 100%. The actual effort was documented, too. During two years five of the application development departments performed more than 220 estimations using these spreadsheets. More than 90 of this estimations contained actual efforts.

The estimations were changed according to the actual averages. In average the reduction of the former estimated efforts was about 44%. Table 14.10 shows the new Excel estimation sheet for host maintenance tasks.

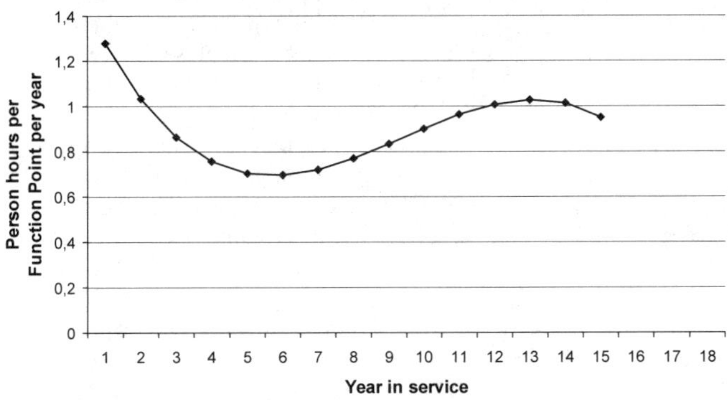

Fig. 14.5. So-called bathtub curve from projects in Volkswagen AG

14.4.10 Simulations for Estimations

One of the most best-known estimation tools is Checkpoint for Windows (CKWIN). The follow-up product is KnowledgePlan. CKWIN is a knowledge-based expert system developed by Software Productivity Research (SPR) from Burlington, MA, USA. It uses about 220 project parameters and a large knowledge base for estimation and planning of IT projects. The database consists of about 6,700 IT projects. The difference between KnowledgePlan and CKWIN can roughly be described as: KnowledgePlan uses fewer parameters than CKWIN, i.e., the estimations can be done quicker. It can be integrated with MS Project, i.e., MS Project plans can be imported into KnowledgePlan, and vice versa. Estimations from KnowledgePlan can be used in MS Project plans as work breakdown structures. A very useful application of Checkpoint/KnowledgePlan (or any other estimation tool that has this feature) is simulations in order to answer questions for process improvement. Questions such as how project durations can be reduced by reduction of requirements creep and project complexity can be investigated.

Table 14.10. The estimation sheet for host maintenance tasks

Parameters:		Effort in person days (PD), 1 PD = 8 person hours
Project Management	Planning, coordination, controlling, management	10% from total effort
Discussions	Number of involved IT persons	0,2 PD
	Number of involved users of insurance branches	0,3 PD
	Number of involved interfaces	0,4 PD
Databases	Number of new tables / databases	3 PD
	Number of concerned tables / databases	2,5 PD
Programs	Number of peanuts program changes	0,1 PD
	Number of small program changes	0,3 PD
	Number of "normal" program changes	3,0 PD
	Number of large program changes	5,0 PD
	Number of all programs to be changed	0,1 PD
Other elements	Number of concerned Program Status Blocks (PSB's)	0,2 PD
	Number of new / to be changed Jobs	0,7 PD
	Number of concerned Formats	0,3 PD
Documentation	Number of concerned pages of system documentation	0,3 PD
	Number of pages of system documentation to be written new	0,3 PD
Test	Number of test cases to be defined new	0,1 PD
	Number of old test cases to be verified	0,05 PD
	IT test effort	0,8 PD
	Number of test cycles for end user test	2,8 PD

Checkpoint/KnowledgePlan (and similar tools, such as SLIM or COCOMO II) support simulations by variation of its input parameters. Hence the concrete goal for the simulations is to find out the most effective parameters affecting project duration using the estimation of a typical IT project. The following steps were chosen in the simulation project.

We started the simulation project with the sensitivity analysis in order to see from Checkpoint/KnowledgePlan the parameters that have the greatest influence on project duration. With the sensitivity analysis Checkpoint/KnowledgePlan shows the 16 strongest parameters for the project goals: duration, effort, productivity and quality. Hence we got a hit list of parameters mostly influencing the matching goal, independent of the actual parameter value. For our investigations only the goal project duration was of relevance.

Next these parameters were improved successively by about one unit at a time, documented in tables and reset afterwards. For the evaluation of the parameters Checkpoint/KnowledgePlan uses a scale off 1 to 5. On this scale a value between 1.00 and 2.99 gives a positive, and between 3.00 and 5.00 a negative influence for the estimation results. The default is N/A (Not Applicable), and the value 3.00 is the industry (database) average. The values can be set in hundreds. But this precision makes no sense since one cannot explain e.g. the difference between 2.75 and 2.76, and the difference in the results would also be marginal. In some cases we used halves, e.g., 3.5 in cases when we could not decide between, e.g., 2.00 and 3.00.

14.4.11 Sensitivity analysis.

When modifying the parameters, according to the hit list of the sensitivity analysis we found that 3 of the 16 parameters could not be used for shorter durations since they had the best values (=1.00) from the start.

The hit list of parameters is sorted in decreasing order. The first parameter has the most effect for shorter duration. The last parameter, delivered a three-day longer duration for some reason. The next step was the summation of the parameters, followed by step-by-step improvement to 1. All simulations were documented in analogous tables, which are not shown here.

Checkpoint/KnowledgePlan shows an alternative for the improvement of an IT project with the report on weaknesses. In this case the weaknesses are the parameters with values between 3.50 and 5.00. Again, these parameters were modified step-by-step and in sum.

The simulations clearly demonstrated that there are a large number of ways to finish projects earlier. But not all parameters can be influenced by senior managers, project mangers or the project team, as e.g., the involvement of the users. Based on the modification of only one parameter, the project duration could improved by 32.60% with equal quality and more staff (138 instead of 86).

The lesson learned is that tools should be used more frequently for simulations. This rule is also valid for project planning tools. We found in daily project life that this rule is almost neglected by project leaders, leaving them without an essential aid for project survival.

14.5 Hints for the Practitioner

There is a business need for early estimations. One of the most influential parameters of estimation is the size, e.g., Function Points. Thus FP prognoses or FP approximations practically proved to be helpful aids for early estimations. Centrally collected information about FP counts allow research that can deliver useful metrics for quality assurance, estimation and benchmarking. Hence the measurement of software size is the most important parameter of estimation. Different environments lead to other results, thus each organization should develop its own heuristic solutions.

Standards for the distribution of the estimated effort to the project phases can be used to develop an organization specific percentage method for estimation. There exist a lot of relevant and proven measures, methods and techniques for improvement of quality of software and software development. The ISO 8402 Quality Measures can be mapped to the 14 general system characteristics (GSC) of the IFPUG Function Point method [IFPU99], which are used to add estimation parameters to the functional size measurement for the calculation of adjusted function points. Simple counting of maintenance tasks and error reports can hint to error-prone modules and can furthermore deliver information about enhancement of modules/functions. Such metrics are beneficial information for estimating future maintenance tasks.

14.6 Summary

This chapter has presented and discussed the experiences in the domain of IT project estimation and measurement within AXA Service AG. One of the major milestones was the development of an early project effort estimation method using approximated FPs, the so-called FP Prognosis. This standard was derived from a central project register database.

A useful aid for the project leaders is an Excel chart mapping the ISO 8402 Quality Measures to the 14 general system characteristics (GSC) of the IFPUG Function Point method [IFPU99]. Additionally, an Excel sheet for the distribution of the estimated effort to the project phases was developed. Software metrics of enhancement projects from the ISBSG database are presented, and a literature overview of software metrics for software maintenance is provided.

Single maintenance tasks are necessary due to legal, technical or organizational requirements as well as for error correction. Often the effort of such tasks is less than 3 person months and therefore the effort for a Function Point count cannot be economically justified. For this reason an Excel estimation sheet for simple maintenance tasks can be developed.

The lesson learned is that tools should be used more frequently for simulations. This rule is also valid for project planning tools. We found in daily project life that this rule is almost neglected by project leaders, leaving them without an essential aid for project survival.

15 Case Study: Metrics in Maintenance

Maintainability is not restricted to code; it describes many software products, including specification, design, and test plan documents. Thus we need maintainability measures for all of the products we hope to maintain.
—Shari Lawrence Pfleeger

15.1 Motivation for a Tool-based Approach

In a time of increasing penetration by software in nearly all areas of our life the software quality is a very important criterion in order to trust in its reliability and functionality. And it is important from a business perspective, e.g., the decision to reuse software or to develop it from scratch. Especially for legacy systems, it is often difficult to get information on software quality, since these systems grow to complex structures over time, and often the documentation is no longer up to date.

Because of the size and complexity of software it is usually impossible to evaluate the software manually; for this reason methods and tools are needed to support this task. This chapter introduces a methodology supporting the tool-based quality evaluation of software systems and demonstrates the application of the methodology for a telecommunication software system (see also Chap. 9). With help of a static software analysis tool the explained theoretical foundations are applied to a large software system, and evaluation examples from the project quality report are presented. The underlying quality model is explained in detail as are the experiences made (e.g., tool handling, surplus value).

Note that there are several tools available for static code analysis with comparable functionality (e.g. Logiscope, Klocwork, LDRA, Splint, QAC). We focus here on Logiscope in this context to provide in-depth examples how such tools are used. Others could have been also used with similar results.

This work presents a methodology for the quality evaluation of large-scale software systems. The evaluations were aimed to accompany the database scheme substitution of a large-scale telecommunication system, in order to provide information about the quality of the software system, its structure and the dependability of the components to each other. The investigations were performed with the Logiscope tool, a CASE tool performing static and dynamic source code analyses.

The advantages of the CASE tool application and the identified problem areas are shown. This chapter is divided into three main parts. After this short introduction, the analyzed software system, a large telecommunication system, is briefly described. The next part introduces the Logiscope tool, which is used for the quality evaluation, and explains its reference quality models. With help of an example calculation the way to obtain a quality statement is illustrated. The knowledge of this information is important to understand and interpret the analysis results. Finally, we present and discuss the reached results for the system under investigation, give a detailed effort consideration and share the gained experiences.

15.2 The Software System under Investigation

The software system under investigation is a large telecommunication system. It supports the realization of administration tasks for digital operator interfaces. The tasks are realized with an OSI-compatible Common Management Information Protocol (CMIP) by a so-called Q3 interface providing the functionality of the operator interface. With the help of Common Management Information Service Element (CMISE) operations it is possible to administrate analog and digital telephone connections.

Because of the OSI-compatible protocol approach, systems of different suppliers (e.g. Siemens, Alcatel) can be administrated inside a single application. Furthermore, the system has a customer relationship management (CRM) system interface for the handling of customer jobs as well as additional interfaces, e.g. for the automatic transmission of e-mails. The system has existed for about ten years and is implemented as object-oriented with C++. The reason for this analysis was the desire to replace the object-oriented database management system in use by a relational database management system. Since the system was developed over such a long time, among other things a general overview of the whole system quality was desired and the critical components were to be identified. We focused on investigating some critical parts of the telecommunication system. For that reason one component out of over 30,000 classes was chosen that is especially involved in the changes caused by the database replacement. Since there was no well-defined persistence layer, the analyzed component realizes parts of such a layer for the reengineered system.

The analysis presented here comprises a prototype of the database access component. Ninety-six files were investigated, some of them in a quite unspecified state. The Logiscope tool could extract 45 classes and 773 functions, but because of the state of the prototype some identified components contained only rough information.

Fig. 15.1 shows the information extracted from the source files by the Rational Rose reengineering component. The extracted structure provides a first insight into the system under investigation. As can be seen later in the quality evaluation (e.g., in the graphical representations of the prototype), the Logiscope tool was able to generate more information about the system under investigation.

15.3 Quality Evaluation with Logiscope

The Logiscope tool can be used for different purposes in the area of software quality management/assurance, such as software quality and structure analyses, tool-based generation of quality reports, and so on [Tele01]. Basically it contains three main components, an Audit component (quality and structure analyses), a RuleChecker component (control of programming rules) and a TestChecker component (test coverage), and among other languages it supports Java, C++, C and ADA.

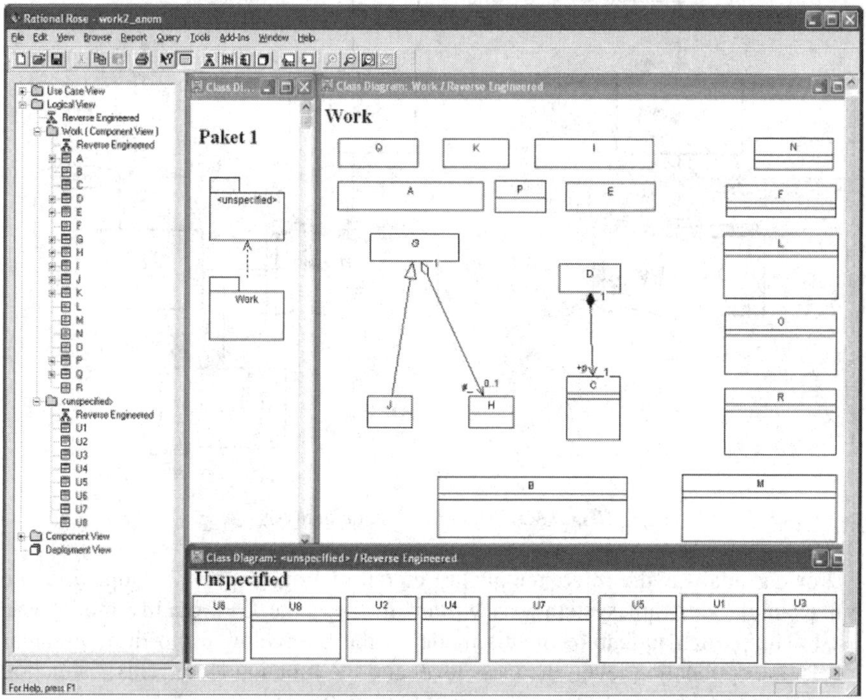

Fig. 15.1. The Rational Rose model of the telecommunication system (made anonymous)

The basic tools within the Logiscope analyses are static analysis (Fig. 15.2; see also Chap. 9 with Fig. 9.3. Criticality prediction for source code based on static code analysis and code history) and dynamic analysis (Fig. 15.3).

The static analysis performs a syntactic and semantic analysis of the source code, is programming language-dependent and delivers the input for complexity measurements, call graphs, control graphs, quality reports, etc. With help of the dynamic analysis, test coverage analysis can be realized. In contrast to the static analysis, the running program is investigated. Before compiling the program the source code is instrumented, and basically the program structure statements are marked. When the program is running after the compilation process it permanently writes information to an execution result file. This file can be used to observe the test coverage, and thus the test case generation is supported as well as a statement about the status of the tests can be derived. In our case only static analyses were used because the software system under investigation is an embedded system on a certain platform and the effort to arrange a running environment seemed to be too demanding.

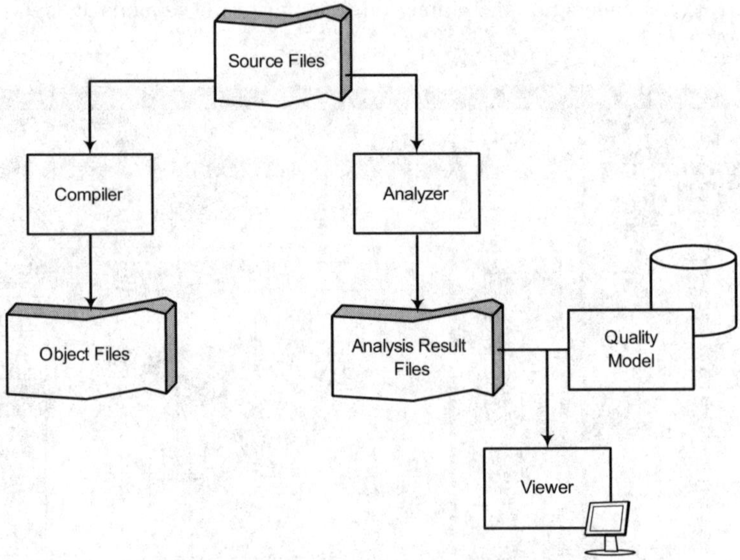

Fig. 15.2. Principle of static analysis

For our analysis the reference quality model of Logiscope was adopted. Since our example software system was written in C++, the C++ quality model was used. The particular feature of this model is the break down into three granular levels, the application level, the class level and the function level. This distinction is dedicated to the object-oriented style of the language C++.

While the analysis on the application level collects metrics and evaluates it according to factors and criteria for the whole program, the class level analysis does the same with respect to the relationships and dependability between the classes. The function level analysis primary focuses on the properties of the functions. For each granularity there are particular results, for instance control and call graphs on function level and inheritance tree graphs on class level.

The quality models are built according to commonly used principles, including the GQM approach (see [VanS00]). First, the model of the application level (Fig. 15.4) will be shown. To clarify: the factor maintainability is defined on the application level.

The maintainability is broken down by analyzability, changeability, stability and testability. The analyzability is derived by the composition of the metrics ap_inhg_levl, ap_mif, ap_aif, ap_cof, AVG_CBO (derived by ap_cbo and ap_clas) and RECU_Ratio (derived by ap_cg_cycle and ap_cg_edge). The other attributes and criteria at the different levels are composed in the same manner. For each metric there is an upper and a lower limit, and during the static analysis it is determined whether the metrics value for the component is within the limits or outside.

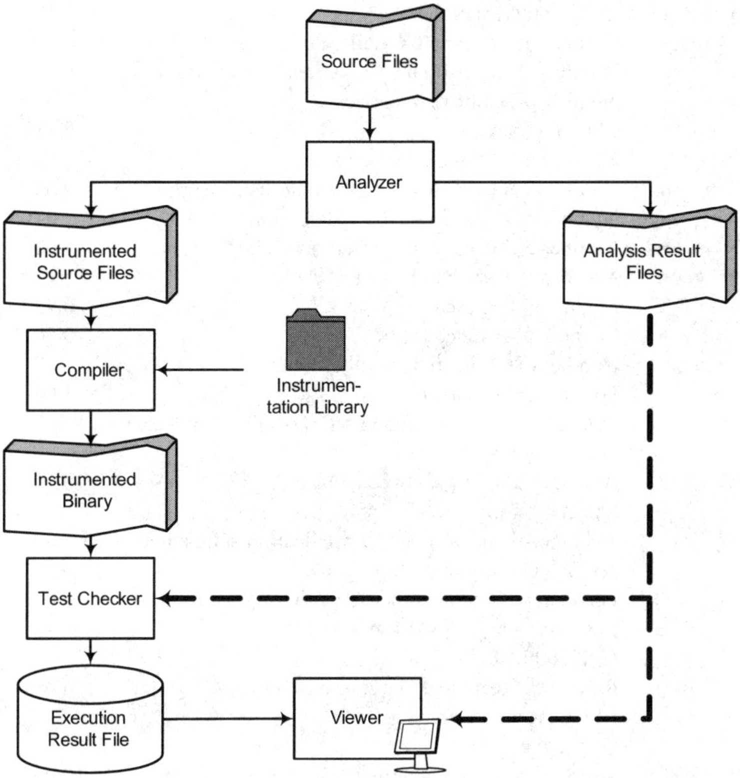

Fig. 15.3. Principle of dynamic analysis

This information is used to derive a statement for the criteria (e.g., analyzability and changeability), and the criteria statements are composed to the factor statements (e.g., for the maintainability). For a more detailed understanding, a rough description of the used metrics is given in the next two sections as well as an example calculation for the application level of our telecommunication software system.

The following tables (Table 15.1, 15.2 and 15.3) show the applied metrics for the different granular levels (application, calls and function levels), including the limits and, if necessary, their composition.

Table 15.1. Metrics and limits overview application level

Short name	Long name	Max	Min
ap_ahf	Attribute hiding factor	1.00	0.70
ap_aif	Attribute inheritance factor	0.60	0.30
ap_cbo	Coupling between objects	+7	0
ap_cg_cycle	Call Graph recursions	+7	0
ap_cg_edge	Number of Edges in the Call Graph	+7	0
ap_cg_levl	Number of Levels in the Call Graph	9.00	2.00
ap_clas	Number of application classes	+7	0
ap_cof	Coupling factor	0.18	0.03
ap_func	Number of application functions	+7	0
ap_inhg_cpx	Hierarchical Complexity of the Inheritance Graph	2.00	1.00
ap_inhg_edge	Number of Edges in the Inheritance Graph	+7	0
ap_inhg_levl	Number of Levels in the Inheritance Graph	4.00	1.00
ap_inhg_uri	Number of Repeated Inheritance	+7	0
ap_mhf	Method hiding factor	0.40	0.10
ap_mif	Method inheritance factor	0.80	0.60
ap_nmm	Number of application member functions	+7	0
ap_pof	Polymorphism factor	1.00	0.30
ap_vg	Sum of cyclomatic numbers (VG) of the application functions	+7	0
AVG_CBO	Average coupling between objects AVG_CBO = (ap_cbo) / (ap_clas)	10.00	0.00
AVG_VG	Average of the VG of the application's functions AVG_VG = (ap_vg) / (ap_func)	5.00	1.00
NMM_Ratio	Percentage of nonmember functions NMM_Ratio = ((ap_func - ap_nmm) / (ap_func)) × (1.000000e+02)	10.00	0.00
RECU_Ratio	Ratio of recursive edges on the call graph RECU_Ratio = ((ap_cg_cycle) × (1.000000e+02)) / (ap_cg_edge)	5.00	0.00
URI_Ratio	Ratio of repeated inheritances in the application URI_Ratio = ((ap_inhg_uri) × (1.000000e+02)) / (ap_inhg_edge)	10.00	0.00

Table 15.2. Metrics and limits overview class level

Short name	Long name	Max	Min
AUTONOM	Rate of class autonomy AUTONOM = ((1.000000e+02) × (cl_func_priv + cl_func_prot + cl_func_publ - cl_dep_meth + cl_data_prot + cl_data_publ + cl_data_priv - cl_data_class)) / (cl_func_priv + cl_func_prot + cl_func_publ + cl_data_priv + cl_data_prot + cl_data_publ)	100.00	30.00
cl_bcob	Number of comments blocks before the class	+7	0
cl_bcom	Number of comments blocks in the class	+7	0
cl_cobc	Coupling between classes	12.00	0.00
cl_data_class	Number of class-type attributes	+7	0
cl_data_priv	Number of private attributes	+7	0
cl_data_prot	Number of protected attributes	+7	0
cl_data_publ	Number of public attributes	+7	0
cl_data_vare	Sum of ic_varpe of class methods	+7	0
cl_data_vari	Sum of ic_varpi of class methods	+7	0
cl_dep_meth	Number of dependent methods	6.00	0.00
cl_fpriv_path	Sum of PATH of private class methods	+7	0
cl_fprot_path	Sum of PATH of protected class methods	+7	0
cl_fpubl_path	Sum of PATH of public class methods	+7	0
cl_func_calle	Sum of dc_callpe of class methods	+7	0
cl_func_priv	Number of private methods	+7	0
cl_func_prot	Number of protected methods	+7	0
cl_func_publ	Number of public methods	+7	0
cl_usedp	Sum of ic_usedp of class methods	+7	0
cl_wmc	Weighted Methods per Class cl_wmc = SUM (ct_vg)	25.00	0.00
COMFclass	Class Comments Frequency COMFclass = (cl_bcom + cl_bcob) / (cl_func_publ + cl_func_prot + cl_data_prot + cl_data_publ)	+7	0.20
cu_cdused	Number of direct used classes	4.00	0.00
cu_cdusers	Number of direct users classes	4.00	0.00
ENCAP	Encapsulation rules ENCAP = cl_data_publ + cl_data_vare	5.00	0.00
FAN_INclass	Fan in of a class FAN_INclass = cl_data_prot + cl_data_publ + cl_usedp + cl_data_vari	15.00	0.00
FAN_OUTclass	Fan out value of a class FAN_OUTclass = cl_data_prot + cl_data_publ + cl_usedp + cl_data_va	20.00	0.00
in_bases	Number of base classes	3.00	0.00
in_noc	Number of children	2.00	0.00
SPECIAL	Specializability SPECIAL = (2.000000e+00) × (cl_data_publ + cl_data_prot) + cl_func_publ + cl_func_prot + (1.000000e+01) × (in_bases)	25.00	0.00
TESTAB	Testability TESTAB = cl_fprot_path + cl_fpriv_path + cl_fpubl_path + cl_data_vare + cl_func_calle	100.00	0.00
USABLE	Usability USABLE = (2.000000e+00) × (cl_data_publ) + cl_func_publ	10.00	0.00

Table 15.3. Metrics and limits overview function level

Short name	Long name	Max	Min
AVGS	Average size of statements AVGS = (N1 + N2) / (lc_stat)	9.00	1.00
cg_hiercpx	Relative call graph Hierarchical complexity	5.00	1.00
cg_levels	Number of relative call graph levels	12.00	1.00
cg_strucpx	Relative call graph Structural complexity	3.00	0.00
cg_testab	Relative call graph System testability	1.00	0.00
COMF	Comments frequency COMF = (lc_bcom + lc_bcob) / (lc_stat)	+7	0.20
ct_bran	Number of destructuring statements	0.00	0.00
ct_exit	Number of out statements	1.00	0.00
ct_nest	Number of nestings	+7	0
ct_path	Number of paths	60.00	1.00
ct_vg	Cyclomatic number	10.00	0.00
dc_calling	Number of callers	7.00	0.00
dc_calls	Number of direct calls	5.00	0.00
dc_lvars	Number of local variables	5.00	0.00
FAN_IN	Fan In FAN_IN = ic_usedp + ic_varpi	4.00	0.00
FAN_OUT	Fan Out FAN_OUT = ic_paradd + ic_varpe	4.00	0.00
ic_paradd	Number of parameters passed by reference	2.00	0.00
ic_param	Number of function parameters	5.00	0.00
ic_parval	Number of parameters passed by value	2.00	0.00
ic_usedp	Number of parameters used	+7	0
ic_varpe	Number of distinct uses of external attributes	2.00	0.00
ic_varpi	Number of distinct uses of internal attributes	+7	0
IND_CALLS	Number of relative call graph callpaths	30.00	1.00
lc_bcob	Number of comments blocks before the function	+7	0
lc_bcom	Number of comments blocks in the function	+7	0
lc_stat	Number of statements	20.00	1.00
LEVL	Number of levels LEVL = ct_nest + 1.000000e+00	4.00	1.00
n1	Number of distinct operators	+7	0
N1	Total number of operators	+7	0
n2	Number of distinct operands	+7	0
N2	Total number of operands	+7	0
VOCF	Vocabulary frequency VOCF = (N1 + N2) / (n1 + n2)	4.00	1.00

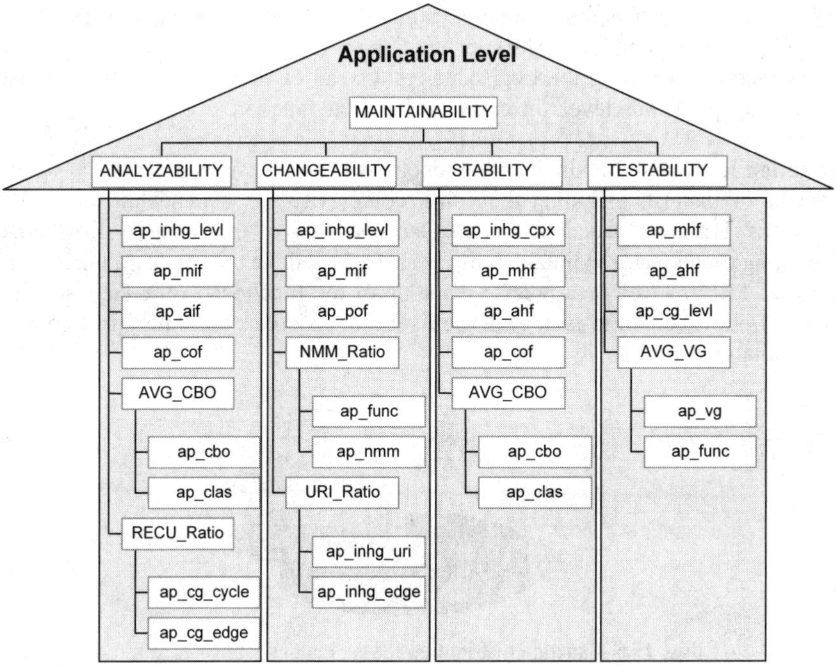

Fig. 15.4. Logiscope quality model application level

15.4 Application of Static Source Code Analysis

In the area of software measurement a number of methods exist to measure and analyze characteristics of software. These methods can be distinguished with the help of different categorizations by their target (software product, process, resources), their assessing manner (counting, measurement, hybrid calculations etc.), their simplicity of application (e.g., experts are needed or not) and their assessing process (e.g., stand-alone assessment, integration in software development process). We will look in this case study into static code analysis. This means analyzing syntactical and semantical attributes of the source code with the goal to identify weaknesses and thus have an indirect quality metric. As an example we use the Logiscope tool. There are other similar tools available, such as Klocwork or McCabe analysis tool suite.

Logiscope is a product measurement tool that can be characterized as a tool for stand-alone source code assessment and evaluation. Therefore, the application of Logiscope in IT software quality assurance requires some investigations for the measurement integration in the software development process (see [Dumk99b] and [Dumk97]). The measurement integration of the Logiscope tool also includes the involvement of a metrics data repository combined with other product or process evaluations such as function point estimation or process level assessments (see [Folt98], [Jacq97] and [Loth02a]).

As mentioned before, the Logiscope results can be divided into three granular levels: the application level, the class level and the function level.

Function level. At function level the functions themselves are considered as components of interest, including their size, complexity and dependability on other functions. Different visualizations give an overview of the function distribution according to the factor maintainability (Fig. 15.5) and the criteria (e.g., analyzability, Fig. 15.6) as well as a precise mapping of the functions to the factor/criteria ranges from excellent to poor (e.g. the listing of functions that rate fair according to the analyzability, Table 15.4).

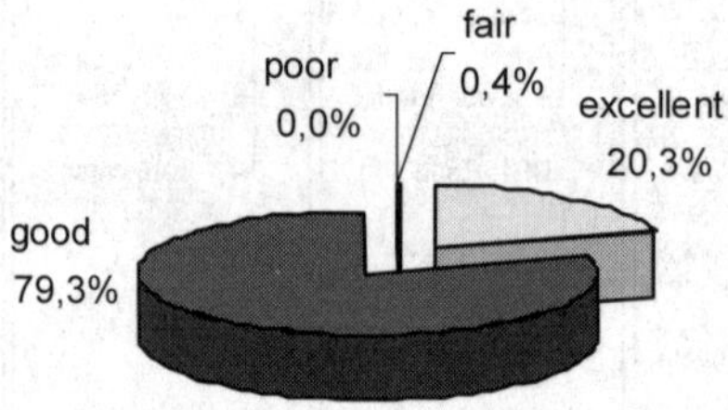

Fig. 15.5. Function distribution for the maintainability factor

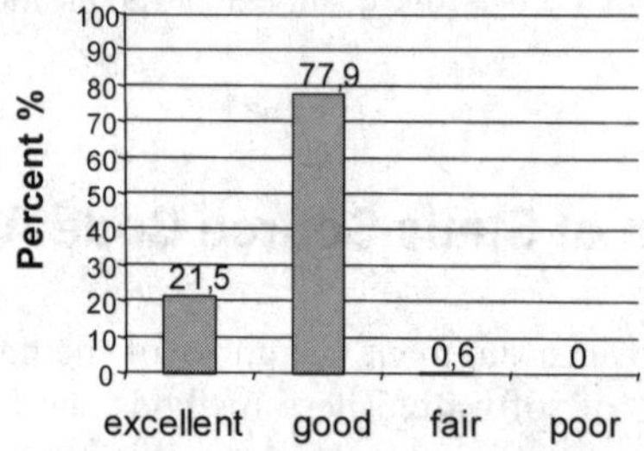

Fig. 15.6. Function distribution for the analyzability criteria

With help of these visualizations a general overview of the functions can be obtained and critical components can be identified (e.g., functions that score fair or worse). Obviously, in our analysis the functions rate quite good for the factor maintainability and the chosen criteria analyzability; there are only a few outliers. Another very powerful view into the functions dependability can be obtained with help of a call graph showing the call relations between the functions.

With help of the different views on the software, basically the source code, the criteria Kiviat diagram (see Fig. 15.7) and the control flow graph (not shown) a good overview of the functions can be obtained, and thus the software decisions (acceptance, redesign etc.) are supported by the tool. With help of the control flow graph program structure statements, conditions and loops can be identified as well as jumps, dead code and exceptions. This graph is a very good view to control, if the function visits the parts as expected.

Table 15.4. Functions scoring FAIR for the analyzability criteria (anonymous)

Criteria: ANALYZABILITY:FAIR
Function Name
Class1::functionA( ) const
Class1::functionB(const Proxy)
Class2::functionC( ) const

The criteria Kiviat diagram (Fig. 15.7) provides the metrics results for the chosen function Object3::functionC mapped to the criteria. Thus problem areas can be identified (e.g., complexity that is too high or a high number of calls), and this knowledge can be included in following recoding or redesign steps. The synthesis gives the overall result for the function.

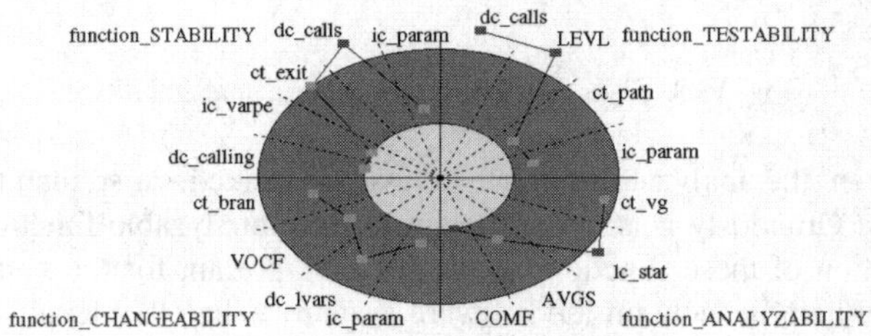

CRITERION	CLASS
function_TESTABILITY	FAIR
function_STABILITY	EXCELLENT
function_CHANGEABILITY	EXCELLENT
function_ANALYZABILITY	FAIR
SYNTHESIS	GOOD

Fig. 15.7. Object3::functionC criteria Kiviat diagram

Class level. At the class level the classes are of major interest, including their size, complexity and dependability on other classes. In the reference quality model the two factors maintainability and reusability are investigated. The results for the example project can be seen in Fig. 15.8.

Fig. 15.9 provides the class distribution for the analyzability in order to enable a comparison between function and class level.

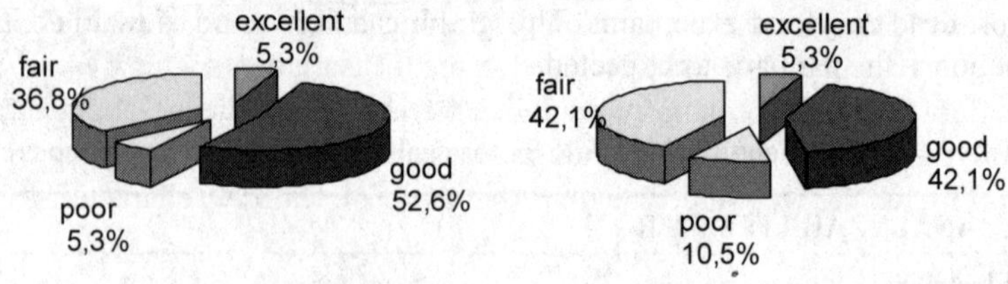

Fig. 15.8. Class level evaluation factors

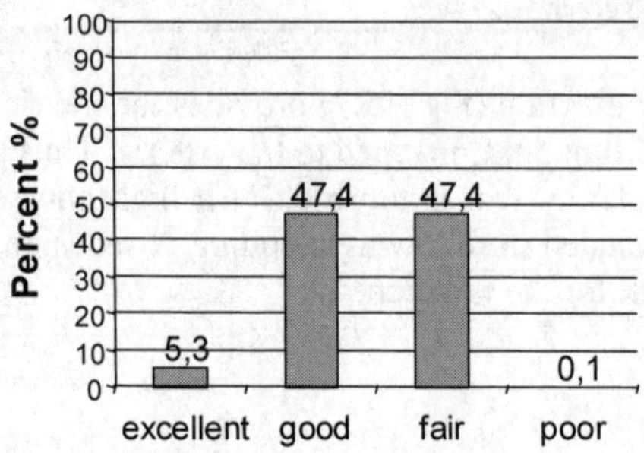

Fig. 15.9. Class distribution for criteria analyzability

As can be seen, the analyzability for the classes is ranked worse than the function analyzability. Obviously it is not sufficient to have analyzable functions but also the composition of these functions to classes is important for the system quality. Another very helpful view on the software system at the class level is the inheritance tree visualizing the static structure of the developed system. With help of the available Logiscope results at class level design decisions are supported as well as the identification of critical classes.

Application level. The application level composes different aspects to a final result for the application under investigation. In our case the system rates at the upper end of the fair range (7 points), as shown in Fig. 15.10.

To sum up, Logiscope provides three granular evaluation levels, the application level, the class level and the function level. The different granularities provide different views on the software, and in our opinion this distinction seems to be very helpful and appropriate.

15.5 Hints for the Practitioner

Usually, measurement tools are applied to selected source code artifacts or components and produce some diagrams for the software evaluation. For large-scale software systems, the following aspects have to be taken into consideration:

- the effort (time) for the preparation (collecting and making available the software elements that have to be included in the measurements or analyses)
- the effort for the information mining (gathering of knowledge about the software system in order to understand the measurement levels and results)
- the effort for the tool understanding (handling of features, characteristics and particularities)
- the effort for the measurement itself.

In our project the *preparation effort* was negligible, because the software under investigation was available as a package. Since this package was a prototype it was known that certain parts of the software were not fully specified or possibly were missing.

Factor Name	Category	Max	Min
MAINTAINABILITY	EXCELLENT	12	12
	GOOD	11	8
	FAIR	7	4
	POOR	3	0

Fig. 15.10. Application level result

The *information mining* was supported by project reports, in particular the so-called cookbook (which contained information about the database substitution) and software models (e.g., Rational Rose models). For the generation of the Logiscope analysis project special emphasis had to be given to the source file suffixes, because they differed from the familiar notation. Diverse ambiguities according to the source file structure and content were abolished in discussions with specialists who were familiar with the code. All in all, a couple of days were required for the information mining, but this effort deeply depends on the familiarity with the software under investigation.

The *tool understanding effort* was quite high. Since it was one of our first large Logiscope projects only some manuals and less experience were available. Several times the tool behaved somehow strangely and in this case even the manuals could not help. Sometimes only the exit and restart of the tool reanimated its functionality. It is not clear if the problems occurred because of the Logiscope tool itself or because of our special software and hardware environment. Especially with respect to the measurement effort (see below), these problems were annoying and a lot of time was lost. In general, the understanding of the granular levels as well as the identification and understanding of the Logiscope quality reference models composite was quite extensive. For the understanding of the quality model a lot of referencing and consulting in manuals was necessary, and not all results were understood. Several Logiscope features are difficult to understand and the manuals did not always help. We absolutely recommend having an expert available who is familiar with Logiscope for all the questions that occur during its application.

The *measurement effort* for the example project took about one week. The project building (the phase where Logiscope generates all its needed information from the source code) took about 20 min, later project reloads (e.g., for new Logiscope sessions after a Logiscope abort) about 5 min and even more calculation-intensive operations within a Logiscope analysis lasted less then 1 min. Most of our time was spent looking at the multifaceted results, for the quality evaluation and for the quality report generation (a customized report was generated manually).

For more complex software systems the measurement effort can increase very quickly, e.g., for a C++ software system with more than 2,000 classes and more than 20,000 functions, the project building phase took about 30 hours, and each project reload lasted at least 40 min. Thus the measurement effort can become a critical cost driver factor. To sum up, the effort considerations show that enough resources have to be budgeted in order to guarantee the success of Logiscope quality analyses. We absolutely recommend the use of the Logiscope tool for continued quality analyses even if some hurdles have to be overcome.

15.6 Summary

The applied methodology shows a practicable way for the quality evaluation of large software systems. With help of the Logiscope tool it was possible to get an overview of the system quality as well as to identify critical components (classes or functions, respectively) and thus to take these components under further investigation. In this way, the software maintenance as well as the software development itself can be supported and test priorities can be placed. For the participated software developer it was the first time to get another system view than source code or Rational Rose models. Therefore the applied methodology was considered to be very helpful for the developer's purposes. Furthermore, it was possible to trace the project progress (important information for the customer) and the training period into the software system was shortened.

An important question for the software developer was whether statements according to the database replacement effort could be derived. Unfortunately, only quality and structure statements could be deduced, because no exact persistence criteria were available, and furthermore, the old and the reengineered components were too different to be comparable. For that reason, no direct statement could be obtained, but at least information about the coupling between classes/functions could be extracted because of the integrated coupling metrics. In spite of this lack of information the developer was satisfied with the results, because a new, very helpful perspective on the software was received.

Altogether the system under investigation rates quite well, even if the application level result is only fair. We found one reason for this result in the unspecified state of some classes. On the other hand one strength of the Logiscope tool is the capability to extract quite a lot information from the source code, even if not all system information is available. The different results for the different granularities (application, class and function level) were interesting. Obviously, it is not enough to program small, high-quality functions but also the composition of these functions to classes and later on to the whole system is very important for the overall quality results.

Even though a couple of hurdles (e.g., tool understanding, measurement effort) have to be overcome, we can strongly recommend the use of a source code analyses tool like Logiscope for quality evaluations of large-scale software systems, because without tool support quality analyses of such systems are nearly impossible. In this context the following statement is very important (from our own experience and as often mentioned in the literature): measurement or metrics programs respectively are basically more (or possibly only) likely to be successful if the measurements can be tool-based and at least semi-automated. Not all desired statements for the developer could be derived (e.g., persistence classifications, impact statements of the data base substitution), but the received information was very helpful for the ongoing decision-making processes.

The applied methodology and tool should be used to continually control the progress of the prototype development (also of the program development), thus enabling the compliance to certain quality goals, rules and restrictions (e.g., design/structure requirements, complexity limits). Only with continued quality control will the quality of the code improve permanently and significantly.

16 Metrics Communities and Resources

Coming together is a beginning, staying together
is progress, and working together is success.
—Unknown

16.1 Benefits of Networking

Software measurement is not easy. Lots of measurement programs fail to deliver actual performance improvements – for numerous reasons, as we showed in this book. To help with introduction, to ensure useful international standards, and to guide with benchmarking and consulting, there exist a lot of software metrics communities across the world.

We provide a selection of those communities with which we have cooperated and thus gained insight in the previous years. The list is far from being complete and we apologize for this obviously subjective selection. All mentioned communities are internationally active and publish their English Internet sites. The authors appreciate update proposals, which we will include in the Web page of this book and also the next edition (see Chap. 1). The selection is sorted alphabetically.

16.2 CMG

The Computer Measurement Group (CMG) is a globally acting non-profit organization of data processing professionals committed to the measurement and management of computer systems (hardware and software). CMG members are concerned with performance evaluation of existing systems to improve performance (e.g., response time, throughput, etc.) and with capacity management. National chapters of the CMG are active in Australia, Austria, Canada, Germany (as CECMG), Italy, South Africa, the United Kingdom (as UKCMG) and the USA. The home page is http://www.cmg.org/.

16.4 COSMIC

The Common Software Measurement International Consortium (COSMIC) was founded in late 1998 by a group of experienced software measurers from industry and science with the aim to design and promote the second generation of software measurement methods. About 40 people from 8 countries combined their efforts voluntarily and proposed some principles for a software functional size measurement method. At the end of 1999, they published the COSMIC Full Function Point (FFP) Version 2.0 Measurement Practices Manual (MPM) [UQAM99], and made it available for free on the Web. A short overview of the COSMIC Full Function Points is documented in the Chap. 7.

The COSMIC-FFP method is based on the strengths of the IFPUG, Mark II [UKSM98] and the NESMA Function Point Method [NESM02]. It uses only four base functional components: Entry, Exit, Read and Write. In developing the method there was a 14-month field trial period starting March 1999 in order to verify in industry the practicability of this new measurement method.

The tests were performed with 18 development projects from 5 organizations (16 new developments and 2 enhancements) on multiple platforms and with 21 maintenance requests of small functional enhancements in a single organization. There was consistent positive feedback about all the test requirements, with the additional benefit of a database of historical data.

The COSMIC-FFP method is the first functional sizing method to be:

- designed by an international group of experts on a sound theoretical basis;
- drawn on the practical experience of all the main existing FP methods;
- designed to conform to ISO 14143 Part 1;
- designed to work across MIS and real-time domains, for software in any layer or peer item;
- widely tested in field trials before being finalized.

The Measurement Manual is available in English, Japanese, French and Spanish. Translation into Italian and German are in progress. Furthermore, the COSMIC-FFP method was approved as an ISO standard in March 2003: ISO 19761. In addition, the COSMIC group has published the COSMIC Guide to the Implementation of ISO 19761. This guide can be downloaded from the Web at no cost at http://www.lrgl.uqam.ca/cosmic-ffp.

The International Software Benchmarking Standards Group (ISBSG) has also approved COSMIC-FFP as a data collection standard. There are several worldwide research activities under way for further improvement and dissemination of the COSMIC-FFP method (ISO 19761).

The COSMIC home page is http://www.cosmicon.com; the standard and publications are hosted at http://www.lrgl.uqam.ca/cosmic-ffp. Publications include case studies as well as a large number of research publications on COSMIC-FFP.

16.6 German GI Interest Group on Software Metrics

The German GI Fachgruppe Software 2.1.10 Software-Messung und -Bewertung. It is concerned with theoretical foundations of software measurement and evaluation as well as with the practical implementation and the problems arising with the integration in the software development process, as e.g., certifications, metrics databases or experience factories. It also fosters and stimulates research programs. Thus there is cooperation with organizations in industry (e.g., the continuing International Workshops on Software Measurement, IWSM) and international cooperation, especially with the École de technologie supérieure, Université du Québec (Montreal, Canada) and the CIM (Center d'Interet sur les Metriques, a Canadian metrics association). The IWSM is organized every year alternately in Montreal, Canada and Magdeburg, Germany. The proceedings of the IWSM are published on the Internet at http://www.lrgl.uqam.ca.

The GI Interest Group on Software Metrics maintains the Software Measurement Laboratory (SML@b) at University of Magdeburg, which is a prototype of a software measurement database in the Internet. It allows Java based interactive entry of measurement data of popular CAME tools such as Logiscope, Datrix or OOM and delivers respective reports.

It hosts one to two meetings per year with an international audience. The home page is http://ivs.cs.uni-magdeburg.de/sw-eng/us/. It presents rich information about software metrics, experiments and literature.

16.7 IFPUG

The International Function Point User Group (IFPUG) in the USA, founded 1984, has developed a standardized Function Point Method Release 4.1.1 [IFPU99] with rules for the counting of Function Points. The measurement of IT projects should be in line with Version 4.1 of the IFPUG Function Point Method in order to be comparable between different organizations.

Furthermore, the IFPUG offers a certification (Certified Function Point Specialist, CFPS), organizes annual conferences for knowledge transfer and has working groups for the further development of the IFPUG method. Thus in 1998, as an enhancement to the existing detailed two case studies, a third one was published, covering Function Point counting in object-oriented projects and environments.

Many people from more than 14 countries are IFPUG members and the number grows every year. The home page of the IFPUG, http://www.ifpug.org, delivers plenty of information about software metrics and estimation as well as links to other IT metrics organizations and IFPUG member services.

In 2001 more than 350 people were Certified Function Point Specialists (CFPS) [IFPU02]. The certification is valid for 3 years, at which time the examination must be repeated. Information about certifications can be found at the IFPUG home page, http://www.ifpug.org.

The book *Measuring the Software Process*, written by David Garmus and David Herron [Garm95], contains an example of a Function Point examination with two sets 45 multiple choice questions (instead of two sets of 50 questions as in the official examination) and a case study that is a little bit smaller than in the official examination. The solutions are documented as well. Preparation for the CFPS examination by practicing this prototype examination five to six times has been proved to be sufficient, since there are typical questions in this example. Candidates who have counted more than 16,000 Function Points during practical work have a fair chance to pass the examination. The examination itself consists of three parts with a total score of 150:

- Part 1 with 50 questions about IFPUG rules (definitions)
- Part 2 with 50 questions concerning the usage of IFPUG rules (implementations), but more complicated than part 1.
- Part 3 with a case study for a complete Function Point count with about 15 transactions and data entities. The case study is formulated verbally and normally follows the transactions and data, with screens and reports to be counted.

For the parts 1 and 2 of the examination one should plan to spend the first two hours (about 1 min. per question) in order to have enough time to understand and count the Function Points of the case study.

At least 90% of the answers must be correct in each of the three parts in order to pass the examination. If only one of the three parts has less than 90% correct answers, the candidate has failed. About 65% of the candidates normally pass the examination.

16.8 ISBSG

The International Software Benchmarking Standards Group (ISBSG) started as a loose cooperation of national metrics organizations. These IT metrics organizations mostly used the IFPUG Function Point method for the sizing of projects. They collected data about software projects with the goal to achieve improvements in software development.

Release 8 of the ISBSG Repository data was published in June 2003 based on 2,048 projects on data disc. The latest report of the ISBSG (The Software Metrics Compendium) [ISBS02] was published in June, 2002 based on 1,238 projects. The indicators in the ISBSG database are closely connected to the Function Point sizing method. It is useful for an organization that wants to participate in an ISBSG benchmark to have historical project data sized using Function Points.

The mission of the ISBSG is the support of international software developers in order to improve global software engineering practices and business management of IT resources through the provision of project data that are standardized, verified, most recent and representative for current technologies.

Some national member organizations/communities of the ISBSG are:

- ASMA (Australian Software Metrics Association)
- IFPUG (International Function Point Users Group) – lead member
- NASSCOM (Indian)
- AEMES (Association Espanola de Metricas del Software)
- DASMA (Deutschsprachige Anwendergruppe for Softwaremetrik and Estimation)
- FiSMA Finland Software Metrics Association
- GUFPI-ISMA (Italian Software Metrics Association – Gruppo Utenti Function Point Italia)
- JFPUG (Japanese Function Point User Group)
- NESMA (Netherlands Software Metrieken Gebruikers Associatie)
- SwiSMA (Swiss Software & Service Metrics Association)
- UKSMA (United Kingdom Software Metrics Association) – associate member

The primary goal of the ISBSG was the development of an international repository of software project data. The collection of the data and the establishment of the ISBSG database in organizations allow software organizations to use a service that is a true alternative to their own analyses. The ISBSG database lets the organization save the effort of developing their own metrics database and additionally allows it to compare its own data with the data of a network that consists of the best performers worldwide. That is benchmarking in its true sense.
Further goals:

- Enable the comparison of software development on an international basis
- Find the world best processes for the improvement and simplification of software development
- Master and improve the global understanding of software engineering techniques
- Enable translation and dissemination of actual techniques for software development
- Extension of available data
- Enhancement of software measurement through the development of a common vocabulary and a unique understanding of technical terminology
- Deliver better information for international business decisions
- Support an international network of practitioners

The ISBSG offers the following services:

- **IT project benchmarking service**. The procedure allows the members of a national metrics organization or ISBSG to deliver their project data free of charge and with a minimal effort to the ISBSG database. The projects are quality approved and compared with similar projects in the database. A report with graphical results will be delivered free of charge.
- **Best practice network**. Everybody who has contributed to the database and who is registered in the ISBSG can participate in the network.

- **"The Benchmark".** A general benchmarking report that is published about every 18 months, containing about 200 analyses and documentation of the collected data. The report has a high benefit for software developers, project leaders, consultants and organizations as well as academics. Organizations that contribute to the ISBSG database can order the report at a reduced charge (Fig. 16.1).
- **Customer-specific analyses and reports**. On special demand of a participating organization the standardized report as well as a customized report according to the organization's data can be delivered. The repository data can also be bought on a disc for own analyses.
- **Research requests**: Interested parties (e.g., academic institutes) can get the repository data for research projects on special application free of charge.
- **The ISBSG repository**: The number of projects in the ISBSG database rises continually. Release 8 [ISBS03] from June 2003 contains 2,048 IT projects (396 in 1997; 451 in 1998; 789 in 1999; 1,238 in 2002) from more than 20 countries from all over the world. Australia delivered the largest portion, followed by the USA. A detailed demographic report of the origin of the projects is published in *The Benchmark*. In mid-2002 more than 200 projects were delivered from Japan with a letter of intent to deliver another 200 projects in 2003. In 1999 and 2001 results of special research of the ISBSG repository was published [ISBS99, ISBS01].

The home page of the ISBSG, http://www.isbsg.org, provides information about its services.

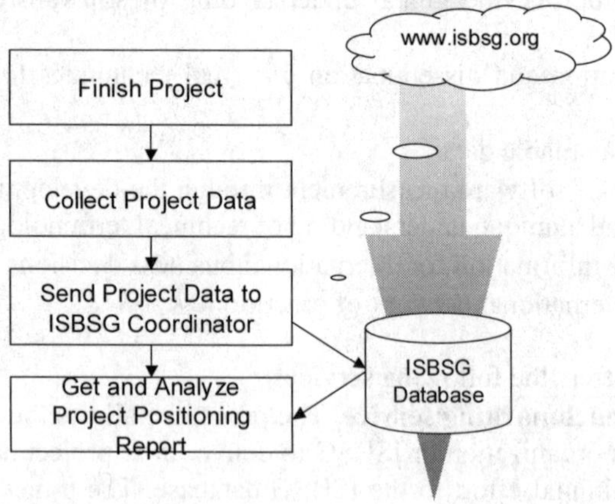

Fig. 16.1. The ISBSG benchmarking database

16.9 ISO

The International Organization for Standardization (ISO) was founded in 1947 and has developed and published more than 11,000 international standards in all economic domains. The Name ISO was chosen from the Greek and means *equal*. The connection of "equal" and "standard" led to the choice of the name ISO. The ISO is independent of any government and does not belong to the United Nations Organization (UNO), although it cooperates closely with many commissions of the UNO. The work of the nearly 30,000 experts from more than 120 countries in the nearly 2.850 working groups of the ISO is voluntary. The groups are managed from the secretary general in Geneva (Switzerland), which also publishes the standards.

In the domain of quality management (including software management) the key standards are ISO 9000 *for quality management and quality assurance* and ISO 14000 *on environmental management*. Fig. 16.2 gives an overview of the ISO framework for measurement. Different types of software measurement related standards, which we refer to in this book, are portrayed in that overview picture, such as ISO 15504 (capability maturity determination and process assessment standard), ISO 9001 (quality management), ISO 14143 (functional size measurements), ISO 15939 (measurement process), ISO 12207 (system life cycle) or ISO 9126 (quality attributes).

Information about the ISO can be found at its home page: http://www.iso.ch/en/ISOOnline.frontpage.

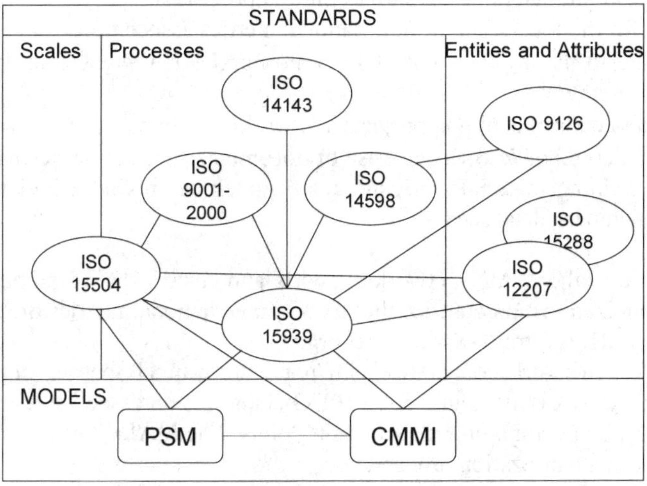

Fig. 16.2. The ISO framework for measurement

16.10 SPEC

The Standard Performance Evaluation Corporation (SPEC) is a nonprofit organization formed to establish, maintain and endorse a standardized set of computer performance benchmarks. SPEC develops suites of benchmarks and also reviews and publishes submitted results from member organizations and other benchmark licensees. The SPEC organization is well known for processor benchmarks, but nowadays provides benchmarks for graphical systems, application servers, Web servers, mail servers or different Java implementations. Information about the SPEC can be found at its home page: http://www.spec.org/

16.11 The MAIN Network

The Metrics Association's International Network (MAIN) was founded 2002 in Brussels, Belgium with the goal to promote, coordinate and exchange experiences among software metrics user groups worldwide. It was decided to exchange information about the activities and results of the national IT metrics organizations and to cooperate with the ISO, ISBSG and other international IT metrics organizations.

MAIN is an international network of autonomous software metrics associations. Its goals are:

- Exchange of experience among associated organizations
- Influence in international standard definition processes
- Support for the foundation of new national metrics associations
- Contribute to the organization of software metrics conferences in cooperation with any other entity
- Initiate and control common projects and working groups
- Develop a common knowledge-base of documents such as metrics papers, case studies, training materials, measurement guidelines, research initiatives database, benchmark database

Furthermore, the MAIN network supports and fosters the development of IT metrics organizations in countries that do not have national metrics organizations. The MAIN URL is http://www.mai-net.org.

The MAIN network cooperates with non-European IT metrics organizations IFPUG and ASMA (Australia). The JFPUG (Japan) is an associate member, as is the COSMIC consortium on Full Function Points. The MAIN Network cooperates with the ISO standardization process.

The following national metrics organizations are (as of 2003) MAIN members:

- AEMES (Association Espanola de Metricas del Software)
- DANMET (Danish Software Metrics Association)
- DASMA (Deutschsprachige Anwendergruppe für Softwaremetrik und Aufwandschätzung)

- FISMA (Finnish Software Metrics Association)
- FPUGA (Function Point User Group Austria)
- GUFPI-ISMA (Gruppo Utenti Funzioni Punti Italiana). Italy is a spearhead for functional size measurements in Europe since legal restrictions for proposals to government bodies demand the declaration of size in Function Points.
- IT/KVIV (Genootschap Software Metrics Belgium)
- NESMA (Netherlands Software Metrieken Gebruikers Associatie)
- SwiSMA (Swiss Software & Service Metrics Association)
- UKSMA (United Kingdom Software Metrics Association)
- JFPUG (Japanese Function Point User Group)
- An interested party is the CIM (Center d'Interet sur les Metriques – Canadian Metrics Association).
- A Russian metrics association is in the starting phase with the support of the FISMA.

16.12 TPC

The Transaction Processing Performance Council (TPC) is a nonprofit organization founded to define transaction processing and database benchmarks and to communicate objective, verifiable TPC performance data to the industry. Information about the TPC can be found at its home page: http://www.tpc.org/. Currently TPC provides benchmarks such as TPC-C to simulate a complete computing environment where a population of users executes transactions against a database or TPC Benchmark W (TPC-W), which is a transactional Web benchmark. The workload is performed in a controlled Internet commerce environment that simulates the activities of a business-oriented transactional Web server.

16.13 Internet URLs of Measurement Communities

Further links are available in the following home pages of metrics organizations:

AEMES, Spanish metrics organization	http://www.aemes.fi.upm.es
ASMA, Australian metrics organization	http://www.asma.org.au
ASQF, Arbeitskreis Software-Qualität Franken, Germany	http://www.asqf.de
BFPUG, Brazilian metrics organization	http://www.bfpug.com.br
CMG, Computer Measurement Group	http://www.cmg.org
COSMIC, The Common Software Metrics International Consortium (Full Function Points)	http://www.cosmicon.com
DASMA, Deutschsprachiger Anwenderverband für Softwaremetriken und Aufwandschätzung e.V., Germany	http://www.dasma.org

ESI, The European Software Institute, Spain	http://www.esi.es
MAIN – Metrics Associations International Network, European metrics organization	http://www.mai-net.org
FISMA, Finnish metrics organization	http://www.sttf.fi
GI Fachgruppe 2.1.10 Software-Measurement und -Bewertung, University Magdeburg	http://ivs.cs.uni-magdeburg.de/sw-eng/us/
GUFPI-ISMA, Italian metrics organization	http://www.gufpi.org
Fraunhofer Institut (IESE) in Kaiserslautern	http://www.iese.fhg.de
IFPUG, International Function Point User Group, USA	http://www.ifpug.org
ISBSG, Australian metrics organization	http://isbsg.org
ISO home page	http://www.iso.ch/en/ISOOnline.frontpage
IT/KVIV, Genootschap Software Metrics - Belgium, Belgian metrics organization	http://www.ti.kviv.be
NASA, National American Space Administration, USA, Parametric Cost Estimation, COCOMO	http://www.jsc.nasa.gov/bu2/
NESMA, Dutch metrics organization	http://www.nesma.nl http://www.nesma.org
PSM, The Practical Software and Systems Measurement Support Center, DoD	http://www.psmsc.com
Research Laboratory of the Université du Québec, Canada	http://www.lrgl.uqam.ca
SEI, Software Engineering Institute, CMM	http://www.sei.cmu.edu
SPEC, Standard Performance Evaluation - Corporation	http://www.spec.org/
SwiSMA, Swiss Software & Service Metrics Association	http://www.swisma.ch
TPC, Transaction Processing Performance Council	http://www.tpc.org
UKSMA, British metrics organization	http://uksma.co.uk

16.14 Hints for the Practitioner and Summary

A lot of metrics communities across the world provide expertise and consultancy for the novice and the practitioner. They are concerned with practical research, building up standards and organization of knowledge transfer, e.g. by organization of congresses. They are fostering benchmarking, networking and awareness for software measurement and metrics. Do not hesitate to contact this experts in case you have any question. All these metrics organizations are networking and linked. This rare species of experts knows each other and will help you in case of need. Naturally they provide a surplus of benefits to their members. The list of Internet URLs is your guide to their know how.

Glossary

The Glossary has been compiled based on entries from various international standards, such as IEEE Std 610 (Standard Glossary of Software Engineering Terminology) [IEEE90], ISO 15504 (Information technology. Software process assessment. Vocabulary) [ISO98], ISO 15939 (Standard for Software Measurement Process) [ISO02], the SWEBOK (Software Engineering Body of Knowledge) [SWEB01], and the PMBOK (Project Management Body of Knowledge) [PMI01]. Entries are adjusted to serve the needs of this particular book. The authors acknowledge the usage of these standards and take all responsibility for deviating adjustments within the text below.

Acceptance criteria. The criteria that a system or component must satisfy in order to be accepted by a user, customer, or other authorized entity.

Acquirer. An organization that acquires or procures a system, software product or software service from a supplier.

Activity. An element of work performed during the course of a project. An activity normally has an expected duration, expected cost, and expected resource requirements. Activities are often subdivided into tasks.

Actual Cost of Work Performed (ACWP). Total costs incurred (direct and indirect) in accomplishing work during a given time period. See also earned value

Allocate. Assign requirements to a project, function, process, behavior, or other logical element of the system.

Application Service Providers (ASP). A company that provides servers and services to host / run applications.

Application software. Software that is specific to the solution of an application problem.

Appraisal. A comparison of an implemented process to a process maturity model Software process assessments and software capability evaluations are examples.

Appraisal cost. A factor of the cost of quality consisting of the defect detection right in the phase where it is introduced. Examples include code reviews or module test.

Architecture. A high level design that provides decisions made about the problem(s) that the product will solve, component descriptions, relationships between components, and dynamic operation description.

Assessment. See: appraisal

Audit. Systematic, independent and documented process for obtaining evidence and evaluating it objectively to determine the extent to which audit criteria are fulfilled

Auditor. Person qualified and competent to conduct audits

Base measure. An attribute and the method for quantifying it. A base measure is functionally independent of other measures

Baseline. A formally approved version of a configuration item, regardless of media, formally designated and fixed at a specific time during the configuration item's life cycle.

Benchmarking. The continuous process of measuring products, services and practices against the toughest competitors or those companies recognized as industry leaders.

Business process. A partially ordered set of enterprise activities that can be executed to realize a given objective of an enterprise or a part of an enterprise to achieve some desired end-result

Business case. Consolidated information summarizing and explaining a business proposal from different perspectives for a decision maker.

Capability. A measure of the system's ability to achieve the mission objectives, given that the system is dependable and suitable.

Capability evaluation. An appraisal made by a trained team of professionals, using an established method (e.g., the SEI software capability evaluation method) to: (1) identify contractors qualified to perform specific task(s), or (2) monitor the state of the process used on an all information pertinent to the systems engineering process.

Capability Maturity Model (CMM). Descriptions of the stages through which organizations evolve as they define, implement, measure, control, and improve their processes. Primarily targeted for software systems.

Capability Maturity Model Integrated (CMMI). A recent release of the CMM that captures also systems or procurement activities. It is fully based on ISO15504.

Cardinality. Describes the constraint on the number of entity instances that are related to the subject entity through a relationship. Cardinality is represented for each entity participating in a relationship by indicating the minimum and maximum number of its instances that may be associated with one particular instance of the related entity.

CASE tool. An engineering tool that is used as an aid to systems or software development.

Causal analysis. The analysis of defects to determine their underlying root cause.

Certification. Acknowledgement based on a formal demonstration that a system or component complies with its specified requirements and is acceptable for operational use.

Change agent. An individual or group that has sponsorship and is responsible for implementing or facilitating change. An example of a change agent is the systems engineering process group. Contrast with change advocate.

Change control. An element of configuration management, consisting of the evaluation, coordination, approval or disapproval, and implementation of changes to work products.

Change Control Board (CCB). A formally constituted group of stakeholders responsible for approving or rejecting changes to the project baselines.

Change request. A formal request to change some aspect of an established baseline.

Collaborative Product Commerce (CPC). CPC is a mode of product and business development in which product value chain partners, motivated by common commercial interests, generate value by sharing product assets, capital and intellectual property. Given the ubiquity of CPC architecture across a broad class of applications, CPC's greatest value is as a business strategy. Used synonymously with product life cycle management.

Commercial Off The Shelf (COTS): Components or tools that are supplied from outside. They are reused as they are (out of the box).

Commitment. A pact that is freely assumed, visible, and expected to be kept by all parties.

Complexity. (1) The degree to which a system or component has a design or implementation that is difficult to understand and verify. (2) Pertaining to any of a set of structure-based metrics that measure the attribute in (1).

Compliance. Meeting the requirements of a standard or meeting specified requirements.

Concurrent Engineering. An approach to project staffing that, in its most general form, calls for implementers to be involved in the design phase. Sometimes confused with fast tracking.

Contingency Planning. The development of a management plan that identifies alternative strategies to be used to ensure project success if specified risk events occur.

Contract. A contract is a mutually binding agreement, which obligates the seller to provide the specified product, and obligates the buyer to pay for it.

Correction. Action taken to eliminate a detected nonconformity

Corrective action. Action taken to eliminate the cause of a detected nonconformity or other undesirable situation

Cost Budgeting. Allocating the cost estimates to individual project components.

Cost Control. Controlling changes to the project budget.

Cost Estimating. Estimating the cost of the resources needed to complete project activities.

Cost of Non-Quality (CNQ). The costs incurred of not having the right level of quality at a given moment. The cost of non-quality includes activities from that moment onwards related to insufficient quality, such as rework, inventory cost, scrap, or quality control.

Cost of Quality. The costs incurred to ensure quality. The cost of quality includes quality planning, quality control, quality assurance, and rework.

Cost Performance Index (CPI). The ratio of budgeted costs to actual costs. CPI is often used to predict the magnitude of a possible cost overrun using the following formula: original cost estimate/CPI = projected cost at completion. See also earned value.

Cost Variance (CV). (1) Any difference between the estimated cost of an activity and the actual cost of that activity. (2) In earned value, BCWP less ACWP.

Critical Path. In a project network diagram, the series of activities which determines the earliest completion of the project. The critical path will generally change from time to time as activities are completed ahead of or behind schedule. Although normally calculated for the entire project, the critical path can also be determined for a milestone or subproject.

Customer. Organization or person receiving a solution, service or product

Customer satisfaction. Customer's opinion of the degree to which a transaction has met the customer's needs and expectations

Defect. Unintended deviation requirement related to an intended or specified use

Defect density. The number of defects identified in a product divided by the size of the product component (expressed in standard measurement terms for that product).

Development. The process of translating a design into hardware and/or software components.

Direct measure. A measure of an attribute that does not depend upon a measure of any other attribute

Earned Value (EV). (1) A method for measuring project performance. It compares the amount of work that was planned with what was actually accomplished to determine if cost and schedule performance is as planned. See also actual cost of work performed, budgeted cost of work scheduled, budgeted cost of work performed, cost variance, cost performance index, schedule variance, and schedule performance index. (2) The budgeted cost of work performed for an activity or group of activities.

Effectiveness. Measure of the extent to which planned activities are realized and planned results achieved

Efficiency. Relationship between the result achieved and the resources used

Effort. The number of labor units required completing an activity or other project element. Usually expressed as person hours, person weeks, or person years. Not to be confused with duration.

Engineering. (1) The application of science and mathematics by which properties of matter and the sources of energy are made useful to people. For the sake of simplicity we typically speak of "engineering" and "projects" in this chapter. (2) In this book, we also call "engineering" any type of organization in the enterprise that is in charge of software projects, applications or products. We consider classic R&D organizations as well as IT departments or outsource development centers.

Engineering process group (EPG). A group of specialists who facilitate the definition, maintenance, and improvement of the engineering process used by the organization. In the key practices, this group is generically referred to as "the group responsible for the organization's engineering process activities."

Estimate. An assessment of the likely quantitative result. Usually applied to project costs and durations and should always include some indication of accuracy (e.g., ± x percent). Usually used with a modifier (e.g., preliminary, conceptual, feasibility). Some application areas have specific modifiers that imply particular accuracy ranges (e.g., order-of-magnitude estimate, budget estimate, and definitive estimate in engineering and construction projects).

Estimate At Completion (EAC). The expected total cost of an activity, a group of activities, or of the project when the defined scope of work has been completed. Most techniques for forecasting EAC include some adjustment of the original cost estimate based on project performance to date. Also shown as "estimated at completion." Often shown as EAC = Actuals-to-date + ETC. See also earned value and estimate to complete.

Estimate To Complete (ETC). The expected additional cost needed to complete an activity, a group of activities, or the project. Most techniques for forecasting ETC include some adjustment to the original estimate based on project performance to date. Also called "estimated to complete." See also earned value and estimate at completion.

Evaluation. A systematic determination of the extent to which an entity meets its specified criteria.

Extensible Markup Language (XML). XML is a standard maintained by the World Wide Web Consortium for creating special-purpose markup languages.

Failure. The termination of the ability of an item to perform a required function or its inability to perform within previously specified limits.

Fault. An incorrect step, process or data definition in a computer program

Functional Size. A size of the software derived by quantifying the Functional User Requirements

Gantt Chart. Gantt chart and bar chart are the same in project management. A graphic display of schedule-related information. In the typical bar chart, activities or other project elements are listed down the left side of the chart, dates are shown across the top, and activity durations are shown as date-placed horizontal bars. Also called a Gantt chart.

Graph. Formally, a graph, G={V,E}, is composed of a set of vertices, V, and edges, E, connecting the vertices.

Indicator. A measure that can be used to estimate or predict another measure

Indirect measurement. A measure of an attribute that cannot be measured directly and thus is derived from one or several other direct measures. Typically used to predict or forecast quality or performance attributes earlier in the life cycle than they are directly measurable.

Information technology (IT). The applications, services and solutions used inside an enterprise to facilitate or automate business processes. We contrast IT with R&D to show the two major instances of software engineering.

Inspection. Conformity evaluation by observation and judgment accompanied as appropriate by measurement, testing or gauging

Institutionalization. The building of infrastructure and corporate culture that support methods, practices, and procedures so that they are the ongoing way of doing business, even after those who originally defined them are gone.

Integration test. The progressive linking and testing of programs or modules in order to ensure their proper functioning in the complete system.

Key Process Area (KPA). A structuring element of the Capability Maturity Model. Each KPA follows the same template, thus facilitating process understanding and change.

Life cycle. The system or product evolution initiated by a user need or by a perceived customer need through the disposal of consumer products and their life cycle process products and by-products.

Life cycle model. A framework containing the processes, activities, and tasks involved in the development, operation, and maintenance of a software product, spanning the life of the system from the definition of its requirements to the termination of its use.

Life cycle cost. The total investment in product development, test, manufacturing, distribution, operation, refining, and disposal. This investment typically is allocated across the anticipated number of units to be produced over the production life cycle, thus providing a per-unit view of life-cycle cost.

Maintenance. The process of modifying a product or component after delivery to correct faults, adapt to a changed environment, improve performance or other attributes, or perform line and depot maintenance of hardware components. That is, it includes maintenance that may be corrective, adaptive, or perfective.

Management system. System to establish policy and objectives and to achieve those objectives

Maturity level. A well-defined evolutionary plateau toward achieving a mature software process. The five maturity levels in the SEI Capability Maturity Model are initial, repeatable, defined, managed, and optimizing.

Maturity model. Models of the stages through which organizations progress as they define, implement, evolve, and improve their processes. It serves as a guide for selecting process improvement strategies by facilitating the determination of current process capabilities and identification of the issues most critical for an organization.

Measure. The number or category assigned to an attribute of an entity by making a measurement

Measurement. The use of a measure or metric to assign a value (which may be a number or category) from a scale to an attribute of an entity

Method. A systematic procedure, technique, or mode of inquiry to create a product or perform a service.

Methodology. A body of methods, rules and postulates employed by a discipline.

Metric. The defined measurement method and the measurement scale. We use metric synonymously to measure and measurement, underlining the need to have a well-defined measurement process and clear mapping to value and scale.

Milestone. A significant event in the project, usually completion of a major deliverable. Used to structure a life cycle.

Mitigation. Taking steps to lessen risk by lowering the probability of a risk event's occurrence or reducing its effect should it occur.

Model. An abstract representation of reality in any form (including mathematical, physical, symbolic, graphical, or descriptive form) to present a certain aspect of that reality for answering the questions studied

Monte Carlo Analysis. A schedule risk assessment technique that performs a project simulation many times in order to calculate a distribution of likely results.

Multi-project management. Optimal allocation of resources to a set of related projects.

Net present value (NPV). See present value

Pareto analysis. The analysis of defects by ranking causes from most significant to least significant. Pareto analysis is based on the principle that most effects come from relatively few causes, i.e., 80% of the effects come from 20% of the possible causes.

Pareto Diagram. A histogram, ordered by frequency of occurrence that shows how many results each generated identified cause.

Peer review. A review of a work product, following defined procedures, by peers of the product's producer for the purpose of identifying defects and improvements.

Percent Complete (PC). An estimate, expressed as a percent, of the amount of work that has been completed on an activity or group of activities.

Performance. A quantitative measure of a product, process, person or project characterizing a physical or functional attribute relating to achieving a target or executing a mission or function. Performance attributes include quantity (how many or how much), quality (how well), coverage (how much area, how far), timeliness (how responsive, how frequent), and readiness (availability, mean time between failures).

Plan. A documented series of tasks required meeting an objective, typically including the associated schedule, budget, resources, organizational description and work breakdown structure.

Policy. Guiding principles designed to influence or to determine decisions or actions. A high-level but concrete commitment that each process has to follow.

Portfolio. All assets and their relationship to the corporate strategy.

Portfolio management. Having the right product mix and performing the right projects to implement a given strategy.

Practice. A technical or management activity that contributes to the creation of the output (work products) of a process or enhances the capability of a process.

Present value: Current value of all future expense and income considering a realistic interest rate with the today's ("present") date as a common reference point.

Prevention cost. A factor of the cost of quality capturing the effort necessary to actively prevent defects. This factor is very difficult to measure since it includes not only dedicated prevention activities, but also analysis of previous defects, etc.

Priority. The level of importance of an event or task

Probability. The likelihood of a specific outcome, measured by the ratio of specific outcomes to the total number of possible outcomes. Probability is expressed as a number between 0 and 1, with 0 indicating an impossible outcome and 1 indicating an outcome is certain.

Process. Set of activities, which uses resources to transform inputs into outputs. A sequence of steps performed for a given purpose, for example, the software development process.

Process Area (PA). A structuring element of the CMMI.

Process improvement. Action taken to change an organization's processes so that they meet the organization's business needs and achieve its business goals more effectively

Process Measurement: The set of definitions, methods, and activities used to perform measurements of a process and its resulting products for the purpose of characterizing and understanding this process.

Process metrics. Quantitative data used for assessing the effectiveness of the process and identifying corrective actions to be taken.

Product. Result of activities or processes.

Product data management (PDM). PDM is a set of applications and capabilities for capturing and maintaining the definition of a product and related data through all phases of a product's life. The four most commonly used PDM applications are library functions (search and file check-in/check-out), management of bills of materials (BOMs), product configuration management (PCM) and engineering change management (ECM).

Product life cycle (PLC). The PLC describes the main activities needed to define, develop, implement, build, operate, service, and phase out a product and all related variants. It is subdivided into phases that are separated by dedicated milestones, so-called decision gates.

Product life cycle management (PLM). PLM is a process for guiding products from idea through retirement to deliver the greatest business value to an enterprise and its trading partners. It comprises all processes to manage and effectively execute the PLC. PLM employs product information and business analysis to support strategy, planning, management and execution through each phase of a product's life cycle. PLM supports an enterprise's ability to monitor activities, analyze challenges and bottlenecks, make decisions and execute decisions.

Product measures. Measurable attributes of a product, such as size or number of defects that generally do not vary over time (i.e., the product measure can be measured at any time).

Program management. Achieving a shared objective with a set of related projects.

Project. A temporary endeavor undertaken to create a unique product or service. In software engineering we distinguish different project types (e.g., product development, IT infrastructure, outsourcing, software maintenance, service creation, etc.). The techniques described here apply to all of them.

Project life cycle. A collection of generally sequential project phases whose name and number are determined by the control needs of the organization or organizations involved in the project. The project life cycle and the product life cycle are orthogonal, i.e., a product life cycle can consist of several projects and a project can comprise several products.

Project management (PM). The application of knowledge, skills, tools, and techniques to project activities in order to meet or exceed stakeholder needs and expectations from a project.

Project management body of knowledge (PMBOK). A repository presenting a baseline of project management knowledge. Serves as a de-facto industry and educational standard and is used for certification.

Project manager. The individual responsible for managing a project. Often technical project manager (TPM) for software projects.

Project plan. A formal, approved document used to guide both project execution and project control. The primary uses of the project plan are to document planning assumptions and decisions, to facilitate communication among stakeholders, and to document approved scope, cost, and schedule baselines.

Quality assurance. Part of quality management, focused on providing confidence that quality requirements are fulfilled

Quality control. Part of quality management, focused on fulfilling quality requirements

Quality goals. Specific objectives, which if met, provide a level of confidence that the quality of a product is satisfactory.

Quality improvement. Part of quality management, focused on increasing effectiveness and efficiency

Quality management. Coordinated activities to direct and control an organization with regard to quality

Quality model. The set of characteristics and the relationships between them, which provide the basis for specifying quality requirements, and evaluating quality

Quality of service (QoS). A metric that describes quality features that are service provides.

Quality plan. Document specifying the quality management system elements and the resources to be applied in a specific case

Quantitative Control: Any quantitative or statistically based technique appropriate to analyze a software process, identify causes of variations in the performance of a software process and bring the performance of the software process within defined limits.

R&D. Research and development. Comprises in this book any engineering activity in the product life cycle.

Reliability. The ability of an item to perform a required function under stated conditions for a stated period of time

Requirement. Need or expectation that is stated, customarily implied or obligatory

Requirements analysis. A systematic investigation of user requirements to arrive at a definition of a system.

Requirements traceability. The evidence of an association between a requirement and its parent requirement or between a requirement and its implementation.

Return on investment (ROI). The tangible outcome or profitability of an investment measured in business metrics (e.g., money). Defined as the ratio of income (result, return) to the directly related effort (investment).

Reuse. The use of an asset in the solution of different problems.

Review. An evaluation of software element(s) or project status to ascertain discrepancies from planned results and to recommend improvement.

Rework. Action taken on a nonconforming product to make it conform to the requirements

Risk. A function of the probability of occurrence of a given threat and the potential adverse consequences of that threat's occurrence.

Risk management. The systematic application of management policies, procedures and practices to the tasks of identifying, analyzing, evaluating, treating and monitoring risk.

Schedule variance (SV). (1) Any difference between the scheduled completion of an activity and the actual completion of that activity. (2) In earned value, BCWP less BCWS.

Service. Intangible product that is the result of at least one activity performed at the interface between the supplier and customer

Service level agreement (SLA). Contracted agreement on a certain service level for services.

Six Sigma. A technique for statistical process control that governs processes with sufficient accuracy and control to stay with its standard deviation of outputs (sigma) within a range allowing that six times that standard deviation just reaches the allowed control interval.

Software Engineering Institute (SEI). An organization at the Carnegie Mellon University in Pittsburgh, USA, established to drive software process improvement. The SEI has created and owns the Capability Maturity Model.

Software process. The process or set of processes used by an organization or project to plan, manage, execute, monitor, control and improve its software related activities

Software tool. A software product providing automatic support for software life cycle tasks.

Software work product. Any artifact created as part of defining, maintaining, or using a software process, including process descriptions, plans, procedures, computer programs, and associated documentation, which may or may not be intended for delivery to a customer or end user. (See software product for contrast.)

Statistics: The science of data. It involves collecting, organizing, analyzing, reporting and interpreting data.

Statistical process control (SPC). A collection of strategies, techniques and actions taken by an organization to ensure they are delivering a product or service within quantitatively defined objectives of quality, cost or time. It measures and identifies out-of-control conditions in a process and takes action to return the process to an in-control state.

Software Engineering Body of Knowledge (SWEBOK). A repository presenting a baseline of software engineering knowledge. Serves as a de-facto industry and educational standard.

Sunk cost. Expenses incurred before the present decision is taken. A paradigm that avoids that decisions get biased by past expenses, which are of no future value.

System. An integrated composite that consists of one or more of the processes, hardware, software, facilities and people, that provides a capability to satisfy a stated need or objective.

Test. An activity in which a system or component is executed under specified conditions, the results are observed or recorded, and an evaluation is made of some aspect of the system or component.

Test coverage. The extent to which the test cases test the requirements for the system or software product.

Traceability. The ability to trace the history, application or location of an item or activity, or similar items or activities, by means of recorded identification

Unit test. A test of individual programs or modules in order to ensure that there are no analysis or programming errors.

User. An individual or organization that uses the operational system to perform a specific function.

Validation. Confirmation by examination and provision of objective evidence that the particular requirements for a specific intended use are fulfilled.

Verification. Confirmation by examination and provision of objective evidence that specified requirements have been fulfilled.

Work product. An artifact associated with the execution of a process

Literature

[Abra01a] Abran, A.: COSMIC – Deployment of the second generation of FSM methods. Presentation at JFPUG 2001. http://www.lrgl. uqam.ca (2001). Cited 15 Dec 2003

[Abra01b] Abran, A., Desharnais, J., Oligny, S., Symons, C.: COSMIC FFP Measurement Manual Version 2.1. Common Software Measurement International Consortium, 2001. http://www.lrgl.uqam.ca (2001). Cited 15 Dec 2003

[Abra02a] Abran, A., Silva, I., Primera, L.: Field studies using functional size measurement in building estimation models for software maintenance. Journal of Software Maintenance: Research and Practice. 14: 31–64 (2002)

[Abra02b] Abran, A., Dumke, R., Desharnais, J., Ndyaje, I., Kolbe, C.: A strategy for a credible & auditable estimation process using the ISBSG International Data Repository. In: IWSM'02: Software Measurement and Estimation. Dumke, R., Abran, A., Bundschuh, M., Symons, C., 12th International Workshop on Software Measurement, Magdeburg, October 2002, Shaker, Aachen (2002) pp. 246–258

[Abra03] Abran, A., Braungarten, R., Dumke, R.: The second generation of the ISBSG Effort Estimation Prototype. In: Dumke R., Abran A., (eds) IWSM'03: Investigations in Software Measurement, 13th International Workshop on Software Measurement, Montreal, September 2003. Shaker Aachen (2003) pp. 218–231

[Abra96] Abran, A., Robillard, P. N.: Function Points analysis: an empirical study of its measurement processes. IEEE Transactions on Software Engineering, 22: pp. 895–909 (1996)

[Aher03] Ahern, D. M., Clouse, A., Turner, R.: CMMI Distilled – A Practical Introduction to Integrated Process Improvement. 2nd edn. Addison-Wesley, Boston (2003)

[Albr83] Albrecht, A. J., Gaffney, J. E.: Software function, source lines of code and development effort prediction: a software science validation. IEEE Transactions on Software Engineering, 9: pp. 639–647 (1983)

[Alon04] Alonso, G.; Casati, F.; Kuno, H.; Machiraju, V.: Web Services – Concepts, Architectures and Applications, Springer Berlin Heidelberg, (2004)

[Auru03] Aurum, A. et al. (eds.): Managing Software Engineering Knowledge. Springer, Berlin Heidelberg New York, ISBN: 3-540-00370-3 (2003)

[Benk03] Benko, C.A., McFarlan, W.: Connecting the Dots. Aligning Your Project Portfolio With Corporate Objectives. McGraw-Hill, New York (2003)

[Binn95] Binney, G. and C.Williams: Leaning into the Future. Nicholas Brealey Publishing, London (1995)

[Boeh00] Boehm, B. W.: Software Cost Estimation with COCOMO II. Prentice Hall Inc. (2000)

[Boeh88] Boehm, B.: A Spiral Model of Software Development and Enhancement, IEEE Computer, 21: 61–72, (1988)

[Bowe95] Bower, J.L. and C.M.Christensen: Disruption Technologies – Catching the Wave. Harvard Business Review, Jan-Feb (1995)

[Bria00] Briand, L. C., Langley, T., Wieczorek, I.: A Replicated Assessment of Common Software Cost Estimation Techniques. International Conference on Software Engineering – ICSE, Limerick, (2000), pp. 377—386

[Bund00a] Bundschuh, M., Fabry, A.: Aufwandschätzung von IT-Projekten. MITP Bonn (2000) p. 331

[Bund00b] Bundschuh, M.: Function Point Approximation with the five Logical Components, FESMA 00, Madrid, Spain, October 18—20, (2000)

[Bund02b] Bundschuh, M., Estimation of Maintenance Tasks, in: Dumke, R. et al. (eds.) Software Measurement and Estimation – Proceedings of the 12th International Workshop on Software Measurement, 2002, Shaker Aachen (2002) ISBN 3-8322-0765-1, pp. 125—136

[Bund04] Bundschuh, M., Fabry, A.: Aufwandschätzung von IT-Projekten, MITP Bonn (2004) ISBN 3-8266-0864-X (2nd edition)

[Bund98a] Bundschuh, M.: Function Point Prognosis, FESMA 98 "Business Improvement through Software Measurement", Antwerp, Belgium, May 6—8, (1998), pp. 463–472

[Bund98b] Bundschuh, M.: Function Point Prognosis. In: Metrics News, Vol. 3, No. 2, December 1998

[Bund99a] Bundschuh, M.: Function Point Prognosis Revisited, FESMA 99, Amsterdam, Netherlands, October 4—7, 1999, pp. 287—297 [Bund04] Bundschuh, M., Fabry, A.: Aufwandschätzung von IT-Projekten, MITP Bonn (2000) ISBN 3-8266-0534-9 (2nd edition to appear in 2004)

[Büre99] Büren, G., Kroll, I.: First Experiences with the Introduction of an Effort Estimation Process. In: CONQUEST'99: Quality Engineering in Software Technology, Conference on Quality Engineering in Software Technology. Nuremberg (1999), pp. 132—144

[Buzz87] Buzzel, R.D. and B.T. Gale: The PIMS Principles – Linking Strategy to Performance. The Free Press, New York (1987)

[Cai98] Cai, K.: On Estimating the Number of Defects Remaining in Software. The Journal of Systems and Software. Vol. 40, No. 2, pp. 93—114 (1998)

[Carl92] Carleton, A.D. et al.: Software Measurement for DoD Systems: Recommendations for Initial Core Measures. Technical Report CMU/SEI-92-TR-19. (1992), Pittsburgh, USA.

[Chri03] Chrissis, M.B., M.Konrad and S.Shrum: CMMI. Guidelines for Process Integration and Product Improvement. Addison-Wesley, Boston (2003).

[CIO03] The CIO newsletter: http://www.cio.com http://www.cio.com/research/itvalue/cases.html. Cited 15 Dec 2003.

[COSM03] COSMIC: COSMIC FFP Measurement Manual, Version 2.2. 2003. http://www.lrgl.uqam.ca. Cited 15. Dec 2003.

[Czac01] Czachorowski P.: Demonstrating a Scalable STP Solution, CSC's Consulting Group – Systems Performance Center, (2001)

[Debu03] Debusmann, M.; Keller, A.: SLA-driven Management of Distributed Systems using the Common Information Model. In: IFIP/IEEE International Symposium on Integrated Management (IM2003), Colorado Springs, USA, 24.-28.3.2003. IEEE Computer Society Press, Los Alamitos, USA (2003)

[Dekl97] Dekleva, S. and D.Drehmer: Measuring Software Engineering Evolution: A Rasch Calibration. Information Systems Research. Vol. 8, No. 1, pp. 95—105 (1997)

[DeMa82].DeMarco, Tom: Controlling Software Projects. Yourdon Press, New York, NY, USA (1982).

[Deva02] Devaraj, S. and R.Kohli: The IT Payoff. Financial Times/Prentice Hall, Englewood Cliffs, USA (2002).

[Dola01] Dolado, J. J.: On the Problem of the Software Cost Function. Information and Software Technology. Vol. 43, No. 1, pp. 61—72 (2001)

[Dumk00a] Dumke, R., Wille, C.: A New Metric-Based Approach for the Evaluation of Customer Satisfaction. In: IWSM'00: New Approaches in Software Measurement, ed by Dumke, R., Abran, A., 12th International Workshop on Software Measurement, Berlin, September 2000. Springer, Berlin Heidelberg New York (2000) pp 183—195

[Dumk00b] Dumke, R., Abran, A. (eds.): New Approaches in Software Measurement. Proc. of the 10th IWSM'00. Lecture Notes on Computer Science. LNCS 2006, Springer, Berlin Heidelberg New York (2001) p. 245

[Dumk01] Dumke, R., Abran, A. (eds.): Current Trends in Software Measurement. Proc. of the 11th IWSM'01, Shaker, Aachen (2001) p. 325

[Dumk02a] Dumke, R., Rombach, D. (eds): Software-Messung und –Bewertung. Deutscher Universitätsverlag, Wiesbaden (2002) p. 254

[Dumk02b] Dumke, R., Abran, A., Bundschuh, M., Symons, C. (eds.): Software Measurement and Estimation. Proc. of the 12th IWSM'02, Shaker, Aachen (2002) p. 315

[Dumk03a] Dumke, R., Lother, M., Wille, C., Zbrog, F.: Web Engineering (Pearson Education, Boca Raton (2003) p. 465

[Dumk03b] Dumke, R., Abran, A. (eds): Investigations in Software Measurement. Proc. of the 13th IWSM'03. Shaker, Aachen (2003) p. 326

[Dumk96a] Dumke, R., Foltin, E., Koeppe, R., Winkler, A.: Softwarequalität durch Meßtools – Assessment, Messung und instrumentierte ISO 9000. Vieweg Braunschweig Wiesbaden (1996) p. 223

[Dumk96b] Dumke, R., Winkler, A.: Object-Oriented Software Measurement in an OOSE Paradigm. Proc. of the Spring IFPUG'96, February 7—9, Rome, Italy (1996)

[Dumk96c] Dumke, R.: CAME Tools – Lessons Learned. Proc. of the Fourth International Symposium on Assessment of Software Tools, May 22—24, Toronto (1996) pp. 113—114

[Dumk97] R. Dumke, H. Grigoleit, Efficiency of CAME Tools in Software Quality Assurance. Software Quality Journal, 6: pp. 157—169 (1997)

[Dumk99a] Dumke, R., Foltin, E.: An Object-Oriented Software Measurement and Evaluation Framework. Proc. of the FESMA, October 4—8, 1999, Amsterdam, (1999) pp. 59—68

[Dumk99b] Dumke, R., Abran, A. (eds): Software Measurement – Current Trends in Research and Practice Proc. of the 9th IWSM'99. Deutscher Universitätsverlag Wiesbaden (1999) p. 269

[Dunc01] Duncan, H.: The Computing Utility: Real-Time Capacity on Demand, CMG Conference, Anaheim, USA (2001)

[Dunn00] Dunn, T.; Jones, D.: MQSeries Integrator for AIX V2. Performance Report, IBM, (2000). http://www-306.ibm.com/software/integration/support/supportpacs/individual/ip63.html. Cited 14. June 2004.

[Eber01] Ebert, C. and P.DeNeve: Surviving Global Software Development, IEEE Software, Vol. 18, No. 2 (2001) pp. 62—69.

[Eber03a] Ebert, C. and M.Smouts: Tricks and Traps of Initiating a Product Line Concept in Existing Products. Proc. Int. Conference on Software Engineering (ICSE 2003), IEEE Comp. Soc. Press, pp. 520–527, Los Alamitos, USA (2003).

[Eber03b] Ebert, C., J.DeMan and F.Schelenz: e-R&D: Effectively Managing and Using R&D Knowledge. In: Managing Sofware Engineering Knowledge. Ed.: A. Aurum et al., pp. 339–359, Springer, Berlin (2003)

[Eber96] Ebert, C., Dumke, R.: Software-Metriken in der Praxis, Springer, Berlin, (1996), ISBN 3-540-60372-7

[Eber97a] Ebert, C.: Experiences with Criticality Predictions in Software Development. In: Proc. Europ. Software Eng. Conf. ESEC / FSE '97, Eds. M. Jazayeri and H.Schauer, pp. 278–293, Springer, Berlin Heidelberg New York (1997)

[Eber97b] Ebert, C.: Dealing with Nonfunctional Requirements in Large Software Systems. N.R.Mead, ed.: Annals of Software Engineering, 3: pp. 367–395, (1997)

[Eber99] Ebert, C., T.Liedtke, E.Baisch: Improving Reliability of Large Software Systems. In: A.L.Goel, ed.: Annals of Software Engineering. 8: pp. 3–51 (1999)

[Econ03] Economic Data Web Site. http://www.economy.com/ (2003). Cited 15 Dec 2003.

[Eick03] Eickelmann, N.: An Insider's View of CMM Level 5. IEEE Software, Vol. 20, No. 4, pg.79–81 (2003)

[Eman98] Eman, K. E., Drouin, J., Melo, W.: SPICE The Theory and Practice of Software Process Improvement and Capability Determination. IEEE, Los Altimos (1998) p. 486

[Emea03] e-Measurement Pearson Web Site: http://www.pearsonedmeasurement.com/emeasurement/ (2003). Cited 15 Dec 2003

[Endr03] Endres, A., Rombach, D.: A Handbook of Software and Systems Engineering – Empirical Observation, Laws and Theories. (Addison-Wesley, Boca Raton (2003) p. 327

[Erdo02] Erdogmus, H., Tanir, O.: Advances in Software Engineering – Comprehension, Evaluation, and Evolution. Springer, Berlin Heidelberg New York (2002) p. 467

[Evan94a] Evanco W.M., Lacovara R.: A model-based framework for the integration of software metrics. Journal of Systems and Software 26, 77–86 (1994)

[Evan94b] Evanco, W.M. and W.W, Agresti: A composite complexity approach for software defect modeling. Software Quality Journal, 3: pp. 27–44 (1994)

[Fent97] Fenton, N. E., Pfleeger, S. L.: Software Metrics – A Rigorous & Practical Approach. Thomson, London (1997) p. 236

[Fetc00] Fetcke, T.: Two Properties of Function Points Analysis. In: Dumke, R., Lehner, F. (eds.). Software Metriken – Entwicklungen, Werkzeuge und Anwendungsverfahren. Deutscher Universitätsverlag, Wiesbaden (2000) pp. 17–34

[Fetc99] Fetcke, T.: A Generalized Structure for Function Point Analysis. Proceedings of the International Workshop on Software Measurement, Lac Superieur, Mon Tremblant, Canada (1999) pp 1–25

[Folt00] E. Foltin, R. Dumke, A. Schmietendorf: Entwurf einer industriell nutzbaren Metriken-Datenbank. In: Dumke R., Lehner F. (eds.): Software-Metriken. Deutscher Universitäts Verlag, Wiesbaden (2000) p. 95

[Folt01] Foltin, E.; Schmietendorf, A.: Estimating the cost of carrying out tasks relating to performance engineering, In: Dumke, R.; Abran, A.: New Approaches Software Measurement, Lecture Notes on Computer Science LNCS 2006, Springer-Verlag Berlin Heidelberg (2001)

[Folt98] Foltin, E., Dumke, R. R.: Aspects of Software Metrics Database Design. Software Process – Improvement and Practice, 4: pp. 33—42 (1998)

[Gaff94] Gaffney, J. E. Jr.: A Simplified Function Point Measure. In the Proceedings of the IFPUG 1994 Fall Conference, Oct. 19—21, 1994, Salt Lake City, Utah

[Garm95] Garmus, D., Herron, D.: Measuring the Software Process, Yourdon Press Computing Series, Prentice Hall PTR, Englewood Cliffs, New Jersey (1995)

[Gart02] Gartner Research Notes #TU-11-0029 (A Project Checklist) and #SPA-13-5755 (IT Portfolio Management and Survey Results). Similar survey results in: Vanderwicken Financial Digest, Standish Group, http://www.iqpc.com. Cited 15 Dec 2003.

[Glas98] Glass, R.: Software Runaways. Lessons learned from Massive Software Project Failures. Prentice Hall PTR, NJ (1998)

[Grad92] Grady, R.B.: Practical Software Metrics for Project Management and Process Improvement. Prentice Hall, Englewood Cliffs, NJ (1992)

[Groß94] Großjohann, R., Über die Bedeutung des Function-Point-Verfahrens in rezessiven Zeiten. In: Dumke, R., Zuse, H. (eds.), Theorie und Praxis der Softwaremessung, pp. 20–34, Deutscher Universitäts Verlag, Wiesbaden (1994)

[Hall01] Hall, T., Baddoo, N., Wilson, D.: Measurement in Software Process Improvement Programmes: An Empirical Study, in: Reiner Dumke, Alain Abran (eds.) New Approaches in Software Measurement, Proceedings of the 10th International Workshop, IWSM 2000, Berlin, October 2000, Springer, Berlin Heidelberg New York (2001) pp.73–82, ISBN 3-540-41727-3

[Harv93] Harvey-Jones, J.: Managing to Survive. Heinemann, London (1993)

[Hein02] Heinrich, L. J.: Informationsmanagement – 7th edition, R. Oldenbourg, Munich (2002)

[Hitt95] Hitt, L. and E.Brynjolfsson: Productivity, Business Profitability, and Consumer Surplus: Three Different Measures of Information Technology Value. MIS Quarterly, 20: pp. 121—142 (1995)

[Hump89] Humphrey, W.S.: Managing the Software Process. Addison-Wesley, Reading, USA (1989)

[Hump97] Humphrey, W.S.: Introduction to the Personal Software Process. Addison-Wesley, Reading, USA (1997)

[Idea00] IDEAS International, Übersicht zu ausgewählten Benchmarkergebnissen (TPC, SPEC, SAP, BAPCo, AIM), http://www.ideasinternational.com/benchmark/bench.html. Cited 15 Dec 2003.

[IEEE90] IEEE Standard 610.12-1990. IEEE Standard Glossary of Software Engineering Terminology. IEEE, New York, NY, USA. ISBN 1-55937-067-X (1990).

[IFPU02] IFPUG, IT Measurement – Practical Advice from the Experts, Addison-Wesley Indianapolis (2002) ISBN 9-780201-741582

[IFPU99] IFPUG, Counting Practices Manual, Release 4.1, IFPUG, Westerville, OH, 1999

[IQPC03] The International Quality & Productivity Center: http://www.iqpc.com/. Cited 15 Dec 2003.

[ISBS00] ISBSG, The Benchmark, Release 6, ISBSG, Warrandyte, Victoria (2000) ISBN 0 9577201 6 5

[ISBS01] ISBSG, Practical Project Estimation, ISBSG, Warrandyte, Victoria (2001) ISBN 0 9577201 1 4

[ISBS02] ISBSG, The Software Metrics Compendium (The Benchmark, Release 7), ISBSG, Warrandyte, Victoria (2002) ISBN 0 9577201 2 2

[ISBS03] ISBSG, Estimating, Benchmarking and Research Suite (Release 8). International Software Benchmarking Standards Group, Warrandyte, Victoria. http://www.isbsg.org/. (2003) Cited 15 Dec 2003

[ISBS98] ISBSG, The Benchmark, Release 5, ISBSG, Warrandyte, Victoria (1998)

[ISBS99] ISBSG, Software Project Estimation – A Workbook for Macro-Estimation of Software Development Effort and Duration, ISBSG, Melbourne, Victoria, 1999, ISBN 0-9577201-0-6

[ISO00] ISO/IEC JTC1/SC7 Software Engineering, CD 15939: Software Engineering - Software Measurement Process Framework, Version: V10, (2000)

[ISO02] ISO/IEC/IEEE Standard for Software Measurement Process. IEEE Std 15939:2002, IEEE, Piscataway, USA (2002)

[ISO97a] ISO/IEC/IEEE Standard for Developing Software Life Cycle Processes. IEEE Std 1074:1997, IEEE, Piscataway, USA (1997)

[ISO97b] ISO/IEC/IEEE Standard for Software Life Cycle Processes. IEEE Std 12207:1997, IEEE, Piscataway, USA (1997)

[ISO97c] ISO 14756: Measurement and rating of performance of computer-based software systems. ISO/IEC JTC1/SC7 Secretariat, Canada (1997)

[ISO98] ISO/IEC TR 15504-9:1998. Information technology. Software process assessment. Vocabulary. ISO/IEC JTC1/SC7 Secretariat, CANADA (1998)

[Jacq97] Jacquet, J. P., Abran, A.: From Software Metrics to Software Measurement Methods: A Process Model, Third International Symposium and Forum on Software Engineering Standards, Walnut Creek, Canada (1997)

[Jeff97] Jeffery, R., Software Models, Metrics, and Improvement. In: Proceedings of the 8th ESCOM Conference, Berlin (1997) pp. 6—11

[Jone01] Jones, C.: Software assessments, Benchmarks, and Best Practices. Addison-Wesley, Reading, USA (2001)

[Jone02] Jones, C.: How Software Estimation Tools Work. Technical Report, Software Productivity Research Inc., Burlington, MA (2002)

[Jone95] Jones, T. C.: Return on Investment in Software Measurement. In: Proc. 6. Int. Conf. Applications of Software Measurement. Orlando, FL, USA, (1995).

[Jone96] Jones, C., Applied Software Measurement, McGraw-Hill, New York, (1996), ISBN 0-07-032826-9

[Jone97] Jones, C., Software Quality, International Thomson Computer Press, Boston, MA, (1997), ISBN 1-85032-867-6

[Jone98] Jones, C.: Estimating Software Costs. McGraw-Hill, New York, (1998)

[Juri01a] Juristo, N., Moreno, A. M.: Basics of Software Engineering Experimentation Kluwer Academic, Boston (2001) p. 395

[Juri01b] Juric, M. B., Basha, S. J., Leander, R., Nagappan, R.: Professional J2EE EAI. Wrox-Press, (2001)

[Kapl92] Kaplan, R., Norton, D.: The Balanced Scorecard - Measures that Drive Performance. Harvard Business Review, (Jan. 1992)

[Kapl93] Kaplan, R., Norton, D.: Putting the Balanced Scorecard to Work. Harvard Business Review.(Sept/Oct 1993)

[Kell03] Keller, A., Ludwig, H.: Journal of Network and Systems Management, Special Issue on E-Business Management, Volume 11, Number 1, Plenum Publishing Corporation, March (2003).

[Keme87] Kemerer, C. F.: An Empirical Validation of Software Cost Estimation Models. Comm. ACM 30(5), 416—442 (1987)

[Kene99] Kenett, R. S., Baker, E. R.: Software Process Quality – Management and Control. Marcel Dekker, New York Basel (1999) p. 241

[Khos96] Khoshgoftaar, T.M. et al: Early Quality Prediction: A Case Study in Telecommunications. IEEE Software, 13: 65—71 (1996)

[Kitc84] Kitchenham, B. A., Taylor, N. R.: Software Cost Models. ICL Technical Journal, 4: 73—102 (1984)

[Kitc95] Kitchenham, B. A., Pfleeger, S. L., Fenton, N.: Towards a Framework for Software Measurement Validation. IEEE Transactions on Software Engineering, 21(12), 929—944 (1995)

[Kitc96] Kitchenham, B.: Software Metrics – Measurement for Software Process Improvement. NCC Blackwell, London (1996) p. 241

[Krai00] Kraiß, A.; Weikum, G.: Zielorientiertes Performance-Engineering auf Basis von Message-orientierter Middleware. In: Tagungsband zum 1. Workshop Performance Engineering in der Softwareentwicklung, Darmstadt, (2000)

[Kütz03] Kütz, M. et al: Kennzahlen in der IT. Dpunkt-verlag, heidelberg, Germany, (2003).

[Lind00] Lindvall, M., Rus, I.: Process Diversity in Software Development. Guest Editor's Introduction to Special Volume on Process Diversity. IEEE Software, Vol. 17, No.4, pp. 14—18, (2000)

[Loth01] Lother, M., Dumke, R.: Points Metrics – Comparison and Analysis. In: Dumke, R., Abran, A. (eds.) IWSM'01: Current Trends in Software Measurement, 11th International Workshop on Software Measurement, Montreal 2001. Shaker, Aachen, (2001) pp. 228—267

[Loth02a] Lother, M., Dumke, R.: Efficiency and Maturity of Functional Size Measurement Programs. In: Dumke et al. (eds.) Software-Messung und -Bewertung. Proceedings of the Workshop GI-Fachgruppe 2.1.10, Kaiserslautern 2001, Deutscher Universitätsverlag, (2002) pp. 94—135

[Loth02b] Lother, M., Dumke, R.: Application of eMeasurement in Software Development. Proc. of the IFPUG Annual Conference, San Antonio, Texas, (2002), chap. 5

[Loth03a] Lother, M., Dumke, R., Böhm, T., Herweg, H., Reiss, W.: Applicability of COSMIC Full Function Points for BOSCH specifications. In: IWSM'03: Investigations in Software Measurement, ed by Dumke, R., Abran, A., 13th International Workshop on Software Measurement, Montreal, September 2003, Shaker, Aachen (2003) pp. 204—217

[Loth03b] Lother, M.: Functional Size eMeasurement Portal. http://fsmportal.cs.uni-magdeburg.de/FSMPortal_Start_d.htm (2003). Cited 15 Dec 2003

[Lyu95] Lyu, M.R.: Handbook of Software Reliability Engineering. McGraw-Hill, New York, (1995)

[Macd94] MacDonnell, S. G.: Comparative Review of functional complexity assessment methods for effort estimation. Software Engineering Journal 8(5), 107—116 (1994)

[McCo98] McConnell, S.: Software Project Survival Guide. Microsoft Press. Redmond, USA, (1998)

[McCo03] McConnell, S.: Professional Software Development. Addison-Wesley, Boston, USA, (2003)

[McGa01] McGarry, J. et al: Practical Software Measurement. Addison-Wesley Longman, , Reading, USA, (2001)

[McGi96] McGibbon, T.: A Business Case for Software Process Improvement. DACS State-of-the-Art Report. Rome Laboratory, http://www.dacs.com/techs/roi.soar/soar.html#research, (1996). Cited 14. Apr. 1999.

[Meli99] Meli, R., Santillo, L.: Function Point Estimation Methods: A Comparative Overview. In: Proceedings of the FESMA Conference 1999, Amsterdam, (1999) pp. 271–286

[Mend02] Mendes, E., Mosley, N., Counsell, S.: Web Metrics – Estimating Design and Authoring Effort. http://www.cs.auckland.ac.nz/ ~emilia/Assignments/ (2002). Cited 15 Dec 2003

[Meta02] Meta Group: The Business of IT Portfolio-Management: Balancing Risk, Innovation and ROI. White Paper. (2002). Available at: www.metagroup.com or whitepapers.silicon.com. Cited 17. Juni 2004.

[Mill02] Miller, A., Ebert, C.: Software Engineering as a Business. Guest Editor Introduction for Special Issue. IEEE Software, Vol. 19, No.6, pp.18–20, (Nov. 2002)

[Mill72] Mills, H.D.: On the Statistical Validation of Computer Programs. Technical Report FSC-72-6015, Gaithersburg, MD : IBM Federal Systems Division (1972).

[Morr02] Morris, P.: Total Metrics Resource, Discussion Paper: Evaluation of functional size measurements for real-time embedded and control systems. http://www.totalmetrics.com/ (2000). Cited 15 Dec 2003

[Morr96] Morris, M., Desharnais, J. M.: Validation of the Function Point Counts. In: Metricviews, summer 1996, (1996), p. 30

[Muru01] Murugesan, S., Deshpande, Y.: Web Engineering. Lecture Notes on Computer Science 2016, Springer, Berlin Heidelberg New York (2001) p. 355

[Musa87] Musa, J.D., Iannino, A., Okumoto, K.: Software Reliability – Measurement, Prediction, Application. McGraw-Hill, New York, (1987)

[Musa91] Musa, J.D., Iannino, A.: Estimating the Total Number of Software Failures Using an Exponential Model. Software Engineering Notes, Vol. 16, No. 3, pp. 1–10, July 1991 (1991).

[Muta03] Mutafelija, B., Stromberg, H.: Systematic Process Improvement Using ISO 9001:2000 and CMMI (Artech House, Boston (2003) p. 300

[NASA95] NASA: Software Measurement Guidebook. Technical Report SEL-94-102. University of Maryland, Maryland, (1995) p 134

[NESM02] NESMA, Function Point Analysis for Software Enhancement, Guidelines Version 1.0, 2002, http://www.nesma.org. (2002) Cited 15 Dec 2003.

[NIST03] NIST Web Site: see http://www.cstl.nist.gov/ (2003). Cited 15 Dec 2003

[Noel98] Noel, Damien: Analyse statistique pour un design plus simple de la methode de measure de taille fonctionelle du logiciel dans des contextes homogenes. Doctoral dissertation, UQUAM, Montreal, Cananda, 2.8.1998 (1998)

[Nort00] Norton, T. R.: A Practical Approach to Capacity Modeling. Tutorials WOSP 2000, Ottawa, Canada, Sept 17–20, 2000, (2000)

[Numb97] NumberSIX, MetricsONE User's Guide Version 1.0, Washington 1997, URL: http://www.numbersix.com. Cited 05. May 1999 (1999).

[Oman97] Oman, P., Pfleeger, S. L.: Applying Software Metrics. IEEE Computer Society Press, Los Altimos (1997) p 321

[OMG01] OMG Object Management Group: Software Process Engineering Metamodel Specification, (2001)

[Paul95] Paulk, M.C. et al (eds): The Capability Maturity Model: Guidelines for Improving the Software Process. Addison-Wesley, Reading, (1995)

[Pete88] Peters, T.: Thriving on Chaos. Macmillan, London, (1988)

[Pfle97] Pfleeger, S.L. et al: Status Report on Software Measurement. IEEE Software, Vol. 14, No. 2, pp. 33—43, Mrc. 1997 (1997)

[PMI01] A Guide to the Project Management Body of Knowledge. PMI (Project Management Institute). ISBN: 1880410230, January (2001). See also at: http://www.pmi.org, http://www.pmi.org/prod/groups/public/documents/info/pp_pmbokguide2000excerpts.pdf. Cited 15 Dec 2003.

[Putn03] Putnam, L. H., Myers, W.: Five Core Metrics – The Intelligence Behind Successful Software Management. Dorset House Publisching, New York (2003)

[Reif02] Reifer, D.J.: Making the Software Business Case. Addison-Wesley Longman, Reading, USA, (2002)

[Reit01] Reitz, D.: Konzeption und Implementation von palmbasierten Werkzeugen zur Unterstützung des Softwareentwicklungsprozesses. Thesis, University of Magdeburg, (2001)

[Reme00] Remenyi, D. et al.: The Effective Measurement and Management of IT Costs and Benefits (2nd eds.). Butterworth Heinemann, London, (2000)

[Royc98] Royce, W.: Software Project Management. Addison-Wesley. Reading, USA, (1998)

[RSM98] Ressource Standard Metrics Version 4.0 for Windows NT, M Squared Technologies, URL: http://www.tqnet.com/m2tech/rsm.htm. (1998) Cited 03. Feb. 2000.

[Scha98] Scharnbacher, K., Kiefer, G.: Kundenzufriedenheit: Analyse, Messbarkeit und Zertifizierung. Oldenbourg, Munich (1998)

[Schm00a] A. Schmietendorf, A. Scholz: Performance Engineering - Ein Überblick zu den Aufgaben und Inhalten. HMD 213, dpunkt, Heidelberg, (2000)

[Schm00b] Schmietendorf, A., Scholz, A., Rautenstrauch, C. (2000): Evaluating the Performance Engineering Process. In: ACM (Eds.): Proceedings of the Second International Workshop on Software and Performance. WOSP2000. Ottawa, ON, (2000) pp. 89—95.

[Schm01a] A. Schmietendorf: Prozess-Konzepte zur Gewährleistung des Software-Performance-Engineering in großen IT-Organisationen, in Schriften zum Empirischen Software Engineering, Shaker-Verlag, Aachen November 2001 (2001)

[Schm01b] Schmietendorf, A., Dumke, R.: Empirical Analysis of the Performance-Related Risks. In Proc. of the International Workshop on Software Measurement IWSM'01, Montreal, Quebec, Canada, August, 2001 (2001)

[Schm03a] Schmietendorf, A., Lezius, J., Dimitrov, E., Reitz, D.: Web-Service-basierte EAI-Lösungen, in Knuth (eds.), M.: Web Services, Software & Support Verlag, Frankfurt/Germany, (2003)

[Schm03b] Schmietendorf, A., Dumke, R.: Empirical analysis of availabe Web Services, in Dumke, R.; Abran, A. (eds.): Investigations in Software Measurement. pp. 51—69, Shaker Aachen, September 2003 (2003)

[Scho99] Scholz, A., Schmietendorf, A.: A risk-driven performance engineering process approach and its evaluation with a performance engineering maturity model. In: Proceedings of the 15th Annual UK Performance Engineering Workshop. Bristol, UK, (1999).

[Schw00] Schweikl, U., Weber, S., Foltin, E., Dumke, R.: Applicability of Full Function Points at Siemens AT. In: Dumke, R., Lehner, F. (eds.): Software Metriken – Entwicklungen, Werkzeuge und Anwendungsverfahren. Deutscher Universitätsverlag, Wiesbaden, (2000) pp. 171—182

[Simo98] Simon, H., Homburg, C.: Kundenzufriedenheit Konzepte Methoden Erfahrungen, Gabler, Wiesbaden (1998)

[Sing99] Singpurwalla, N. D., Wilson, S. P.: Statistical Methods in Software Engineering – Reliability and Risk. Springer, Berlin Heidelberg New York (1999) p. 295

[Smit90] Smith, C.: Performance Engineering of Software Systems. Software Engineering Institute. Addison-Wesley, (1990)

[Smit94] Smith, C.: Performance Engineering. In: Maciniak, J.J. (eds.): Encyclopedia of Software Engineering. Vol. 2, John Wiley & Sons, (1994), pp. 794–810

[Smit98] Smith, C. U.; Williams, L. G.: Performance Evaluation of Software Architectures. In: Proc. of First International Workshop on Software and Performance – WOSP 98, Santa Fe/NM, October 1998 (1998)

[Smit99] Smith, C., Williams, L.G.: A Performance Model Interchange Format. Journal of Systems and Software, 49 (1999) 1

[Smla03] SML@b Web Site: see http://ivs.cs.uni-magdeburg.de/sw-eng/us/ (2003). Cited 15 Dec 2003

[Snee96] Sneed, H. M.: Schätzung der Entwicklungskosten von objektorientierter Software. Informatik Spektrum, Springer Berlin Heidelberg New York, (1996) 19: pp. 133–140

[SPEE98] SPE∘ED Quick Start 2. Performance Engineering Services Division, L&S Computer Technology Inc., Austin, TX, (1998)

[Stan02] Standish Group, Chaos Reports: http://www.standishgroup.com/. Cited 11. Dec 2002 (2002).

[Star94] Stark, G., Durst, R. C., Vowell, C. W.: Using Metrics in Management Decision Making. IEEE Computer, Vol. 27, No. 9, pp. 42–48, (1994).

[SWEB01] Guide to the Software Engineering Body of Knowledge (SWEBOK). Prospective Standard ISO TR 19759. (2001) See also at http://www.swebok.org. 18.April 2001

[Symo01] Symons, C.: Come Back Function Point Analysis (Modernized) - All is forgiven. In: Proceedings of FESMA-DASMA 2001, Heidelberg, (2001)

[Tele01] Telelogic Tau Logiscope 5.0, Diverse Manuals, http://www.telelogic.com, (2001). Cited 15 Dec 2003.

[Thur02] Thuraisingham, B.: XML Databases and the Semantic Web. CRC Press, Boca Raton (2002) p. 306

[Turo02] Turowski, K.: Vereinheitlichte Spezifikation von Fachkomponenten, Memorandum des GI-AK 5.10.3, February 2002 (2002)

[UKSM01] UKSMA, Measuring Software Maintenance and Support, Version 0.5, Draft, July 1st, 2001, http://www.uksma.co.uk. Cited 07. Dec. 2001 (2001).

[UKSM98] UKSMA, MK II Function Point Analysis Counting Practices Manual, Version 1.3.1, http://www.uksma.co.uk, (1998). Cited 04. Jun. 1999.

[UQAM99] UQAM, Full Function Points Measurement Manual, Version 2.0, Accessible at: http://www.lrgl.uqam.ca/cosmic-ffp/manual.jsp (1999). Cited 17. June 2004.

[VanS00] Van Solingen, R., Berghout, E.: The Goal/Question/Metric Method: A Practical Guide for Quality Improvement of Software Development. McGraw-Hill, London, (2000)

[Wads90] Wadsworth, H. M. (Ed.): Handbook of statistical methods for engineers and scientists. McGraw-Hill, New York, (1990)

[Wall02] Wallin, C. et al.: Integrating Business and Software Development Models. IEEE Software vol. 19, No. 6, pg. 18–33, November/December (2002)

[Wang00] Wang, Y., King, G.: Software Engineering Processes – Principles and Applications. CRC Press, Boca Raton New York London (2000) p. 708

[Warb94] Warboys, B.C. (eds): Software Process Technology. Proc. of the EWSPT'94, Lecture Notes on Computer Sience, vol 772, Springer, Berlin Heidelberg New York, (1994)

[Wayn93] Wayne, M. Z., Zage, D. M.: Evaluating Design Metrics on Large-Scale Software. IEEE Software, Vol. 10, No. 7, pp. 75 -81, Jul. 1993 (1993)

[Webm03a] WebME Web site. http://sel.gsfc.nasa.gov/website/documents/ (2003). Cited 15 Dec 2003

[Webm03b] Web Measurement Standards. http://www.ifabc.org/web/ (2003). Cited 15 Dec 2003

[Weis91] Weiss, N. A., Hasset, M. J.: Introductory Statistics (3rd edn). Addison-Wesley, Boca Raton New York London, (1991) pp 600—651

[Wigl97] Wigle, G.B.: Practices of a Successful SEPG. European SEPG Conference 1997. Amsterdam, 1997. More in-depth coverage of most of the Boeing results. In: Schulmeyer G. G., McManus, J. I. (eds.): Handbook of Software Quality Assurance, (3rd edn), Int. Thomsom Computer Press, (1997)

[Wink03] Winkler, D.: Situation des eMeasurement im WWW. Research Report, University of Magdeburg, March 2003 (2003)

[Wohl00] Wohlin, C., Runeson, P., Höst, M., Ohlson, M., Regnell, B., Wesslen, A.: Experimentation in Software Engineering: An Introduction. Kluwer Academic, Boston (2000) p. 204

[Wohl95] Wohlwend, H., Rosenbaum, S.: Schlumberger's Software Improvement Program. IEEE Trans. Software Engineering. Vol. 20, No. 11, pp. 833—839, Nov.1994

[WSTK02] IBM Web Service Toolkit, (2002), URL: http://www.alphaworks.ibm.com/tech/webservicetoolkit. Cited 15 Dec 2003.

[Zuse97] Zuse, H., A Framework for Software Measurement. DeGruyter, Berlin, (1997), ISBN 3-11-015587-7

Index

Printing: Strauss GmbH, Mörlenbach
Binding: Schäffer, Grünstadt